Argumentation

Keeping Faith with Reason

D0209551

EDWARD **SCHIAPPA**

Massachusetts Institute of Technology

JOHN **P. NORDIN**

University of Minnesota

Boston   Columbus   Indianapolis   New York   San Francisco   Upper Saddle River
Amsterdam   Cape Town   Dubai   London   Madrid   Milan Munich   Paris   Montréal   Toronto
Delhi   Mexico City   São Paulo   Sydney   Hong Kong   Seoul   Singapore   Taipei   Tokyo

The authors dedicate this book to their first teachers of argument and debate, Duane Douglas Daily and Roger Brannan.

Editor in Chief: Ashley Dodge
Senior Acquisitions Editor: Melissa Mashburn
Editorial Assistant: Megan Hermida
Director of Marketing: Brandy Dawson
Executive Marketing Manager: Kelly May
Marketing Coordinator: Theresa Rotondo
Managing Editor: Denise Forlow
Program Manager: Maggie Brobeck
Senior Operations Supervisor: Mary Fischer
Operations Specialist: Mary Ann Gloriande

Manager, Central Design: Jayne Conte
Cover Designer: Karen Salzbach
Cover Image: intheskies/Fotolia
Director of Digital Media: Brian Hyland
Digital Media Project Manager: Tina Gagliostro
Full-Service Project Management and Composition: Saraswathi Muralidhar/PreMediaGlobal
Printer/Binder: Courier
Cover Printer: Courier
Text Font: 10/12 Sabon

Credits and acknowledgments borrowed from other sources and reproduced, with permission, in this textbook appear on appropriate page within text and page 390.

Library of Congress Cataloging-in-Publication Data

Schiappa, Edward
  Argumentation: keeping faith with reason / Edward Schiappa, Massachusetts Institute of Technology;
John P. Nordin, University of Minnesota.
    pages cm
  Includes index.
  ISBN-13: 978-0-205-32744-7
  ISBN-10: 0-205-32744-3
  1. Persuasion (Rhetoric) 2. Reasoning. I. Nordin, John P. II. Title.
  P301.5.P47S33 2013
  808.53—dc23

                                                                        2013012806

10 9 8 7 6 5 4 3 2 1

ISBN-10:   0-205-32744-3
ISBN-13: 978-0-205-32744-7

CONTENTS

PART IV   Supporting and Defending Your Argument

CHAPTER 12

Finding Evidence   198

CHAPTER 13

Evidence and Your Argument   219

CHAPTER 17
Argument by Example   281

Introduction   281

PREFACE

The authors began their joint exploration of argumentation in the fall of 1968. We were partners on the Manhattan Kansas Junior High School debate team that fall and later would be part of Manhattan High School's first state championship in debate. We have been keeping faith with reason ever since.

As teachers of argumentation, we both were unsatisfied by current textbooks available on the subject, so we decided to do something about it and write one ourselves. The book you now hold is the result. We believe it has several features that make it distinctive:

We describe a **conceptual framework** involving three types of claims (fact, value, policy) that are advanced by forms of reasoning (definition, example, cause, sign, and so forth). This framework allows us to describe a wider variety of arguments and provide a degree of intellectual consistency compared to other argumentation textbooks.

A systematic discussion and use of the Toulmin model: Many books refer to Stephen Toulmin's helpful model, but then don't really use it to help diagram arguments. We use Toulmin's model systematically throughout the book to surface issues and clarify concepts. We also develop an extension of Toulmin to cover networks of arguments that make the model more useful for examining real-world arguments.

A more thorough discussion of value claims: Chapter 7: "Analyzing Value Claims" examines value claims in detail. We explain why this common type of claim is typically done poorly and provide examples of how to do them better.

A thorough discussion of credibility: Most argumentation texts will say credibility, or Ethos, is important, advise you to attend to it, but hardly delve into it at all. We have an extensive chapter on it.

Focusing on Kairos: Adding Kairos to the traditional forms of proof of Logos, Pathos, and Ethos allows us to describe communication events in a manner that does not assume argument is isolated from larger contextual factors. In particular, a focus on Kairos allows traditional analysis to include contemporary concerns with crosscultural communication.

We also discuss the practical issues of writing a student paper—or any form of written argument. We provide practical examples to help students write clearly. We discuss **models of argument presentation** and describe various ways to order and structure an argument. Our approach also provides an opening for instructors to consider cultural issues in how arguments are made. And we provide practical advice on how rebuttal arguments should be structured.

Last, we make a considerable effort to use both simple examples as well as real-world issues of some interest and controversy.

TO THE INSTRUCTOR: GOALS OF THE TEXT

This text is designed to introduce students to basic concepts in argumentation theory, criticism, and practice. Ideally, argumentation classes involve both the *production* and the *critical analysis* of arguments. We live in a world saturated with arguments, and to be a competent communicator requires one to be able to make a reasoned case for one's beliefs, just as it requires one to be able to judge the case set forth by others. Accordingly, we have provided students with the vocabulary and conceptual apparatus to *make* good arguments as well as to *evaluate* the arguments they encounter.

This book is designed to be of use in the several types of classes taught involving argumentation, including those that emphasize theory and those that emphasize practice, including composition classes, oral communication classes, and introductory classes concerned with debate. The book is not organized as an introduction to competitive debate; however, given the background in debate of both authors, the book contains all of the basic principles of argumentation that a competitive debater should know.

Above all, we believe that students learn the most about argumentation by actually arguing and evaluating arguments, which is why the book is heavily populated by examples and suggested exercises. Acquiring *and using* a vocabulary with which to describe, understand, and evaluate arguments is, we are convinced, the best way to enhance the critical thinking, speaking, and writing skills of our students.

TO THE STUDENT

Everyone argues, but not everyone argues *well*. It is likely that you have seen a commercial, read an OpEd piece, or heard a friend trying to persuade another about some belief or action, and had a feeling that there was something especially compelling—or especially wrongheaded—about the argument you encountered. A primary objective of this book is to give you the tools you need to understand why some arguments are better than others. Our hope is to turn you into *argument critics*. By "critics" we do not mean that you will find a flaw in every argument you see. A film critic gives a thumbs up to some films and not others. What we value is that critic's ability to describe and explain a judgment about the film. Similarly, our goal is to enhance your ability to judge the quality of arguments that you encounter.

In addition to *judging* arguments, this book is also designed to help you *make* better arguments. By understanding the interrelationships between your claim, evidence, form of reasoning, and your audience, we sincerely believe that you will be a better arguer and advocate for your beliefs.

PLAN OF THE TEXT

Part 1 provides an introductory framework from which we will draw throughout the book. We begin in Chapter 1 by explaining *why* we keep faith with reasoned argument as a way of making decisions and why it is fundamental for a democracy. Chapter 2 stipulates a definition of argument that distinguishes it from other activities. Chapter 3 describes forms of proof that date back about 2,400 years and that we still find useful today—*Ethos, Logos, Pathos,* and *Kairos.* Chapter 4 explains our version of what is known as the Toulmin model of argument—a deceptively simple tool with which to diagram arguments that we believe has enormous value in analyzing arguments.

Part 2 contains Chapters 5 to 8, which provide an introduction to three basic categories of claims—Fact, Value, and Policy. Understanding the kind of claim that an advocate is making is indispensable to evaluating the argument of which that claim is a part. Part 3 focuses specifically on you, as an advocate, and how you can enhance the quality and effectiveness of your own arguments. The concepts we discuss include audience analysis and Kairos (Chapter 9), developing your credibility (Chapter 10), and how to organize your argument most effectively (Chapter 11).

Part 4 is about supporting and defending your argument. By learning about how to best support your argument, you also will have a better understanding of how to evaluate the support offered for others' arguments. Chapter 12 is devoted to finding evidence, Chapter 13 to how to choose the best evidence to use and cite it properly, and Chapter 14 offers a framework for how to go about responding or rebutting arguments with which you disagree.

Part 5 provides an in-depth introduction to the basic forms of reasoning employed in arguments. We believe that argument—*no matter what the context is*—relies on a core group of *kinds* of reasons. After introducing this idea in Chapter 15, we provide a series of seven chapters that explain forms of reasoning: Definitional arguments (Chapter 16), argument by example (Chapter 17), argument by analogy and parallel case (Chapter 18), causal argument (Chapter 19), argument from sign (Chapter 20), argument by dilemma (Chapter 21), and argument from authority (Chapter 22). We believe Part 5 is the most important part of the book, which is why it requires the reader to acquire a fair amount of knowledge of arguments and their construction before we get to the subject of forms of reasoning. One particular strength to learning about forms of reasoning the way we have introduced them is that the often tiresome topic of "logical fallacies" is explained as, if you will, forms of reasoning gone bad. Hence the objective is to understand better and worse use of forms of reasoning rather than to memorize a standard list of fallacy names.

Finally, Part 6 concludes the book with what we believe are five things all students should remember throughout their lives as you make and evaluate arguments.

INSTRUCTOR AND STUDENT RESOURCES

Nordin prepared the Instructor's Manual (ISBN 0205943837) that accompanies *Argumentation: Keeping Faith with Reason.* The instructor's manual includes the following resources for each chapter: Chapter Summary, Additional Examples,

Class Exercises and Resources, and Study and Test Aids. These supplements are available at www.pearsonhighered.com/irc (access code required).

For a complete listing of the instructor and student resources available with this text, please search for *Argumentation: Keeping Faith with Reason* at www.pearson.highered.com/.

This text is available in a variety of formats—digital and print. To learn more about our programs, pricing options, and customization, visit www.pearsonhighered.com.

ACKNOWLEDGMENTS

The authors are grateful to Karon Bowers for her patience and support during the long gestation of this book. While they are grateful for many who have supported this project, they wish to express a special appreciation and thanks to all the students who have taken classes in argumentation with the authors over the years. The book is better than it would have been otherwise, also, thanks to the feedback of the various reviewers of this project, including Travis Cram, University of Wyoming; Jeffery Gentry, Rogers State University; Randall Iden, Lake Forest College; Charles E. Lester, Palm Beach Atlantic University; Aimee Richards, Fairmont State University; and Ken Sherwood, Los Angeles City College.

Schiappa wishes to acknowledge a profound debt to Professor David Zarefsky. The approach to argumentation acquired in Z's classes three decades ago had a profound and lasting impact that infuses the theory of practical argumentation found in this book.

Nordin wishes to thank the many colleagues at the University of Minnesota with whom he has had innumerable conversations about argumentation. At the head of the list would go office mates Dr. Jeremy Rose and Dr. Tim Behme, colleagues Nan Larsen and Diane Odash, and the numerous teachers of the Analysis of Argument class. A lively and congenial bunch, they regularly share examples of arguments both good and bad and have "test driven" earlier drafts of this text. Nordin was gifted with educated parents who gently inculcated an interest in finding things out and an appreciation for multiple points of view. He only wishes they could have lived to see this book. Thanks go also to his aunt Dr. Marian O'Connor for providing a wonderful setting for a writing retreat. It is common to end with a word of thanks to a long-suffering spouse, but in the case of Debra, that is particularly true; she has given up much.

Why Study Argument?

THE ALTERNATIVES TO ARGUMENTATION

The most obvious question you might have in an argumentation class is: Why are you here? That is, why should you devote a whole college course to the study of argument?

We titled this book *"Argumentation: Keeping Faith with Reason"* because the basic premise for this book and the class for which you are reading it involves a leap of faith. Specifically, we have faith that argumentation is a superior means of making decisions compared to the alternatives.

What are those alternatives? Let us say that you need to make a decision about buying a used car. One way to make such a decision is through "random chance": You could simply put up today's newspaper ads for used cars, throw a dart, and buy whatever car the dart lands on. For some decisions, flipping a coin, pulling a name out of a hat, or tossing a dart may be the easiest and quickest way to make a decision. There are now computer programs that allow you to set parameters for what sort of restaurant you want to eat at and then the program randomly generates a choice based on those parameters. However, most of us would agree that we would not be comfortable making important decisions randomly. Imagine a nation deciding whether to go to war, or the Supreme Court making a decision about the constitutionality of a law, based on a coin toss.

A second way to make decisions that has a long history in human culture is by "divine guidance." If one believes that one's rulers or priests know the will of God (or Gods, in some cultures), then it is sensible that one would trust those rulers or priests to make important decisions. If, on the other hand, one has doubts either about the existence of God(s) or about the ability of humans to know God's will perfectly, then one might not be willing to put all of one's faith in divine guidance for all important decision making. Moreover, reliance on divine guidance breaks down if there is a conflict between two or more interpretations of divine guidance: How does one decide between competing visions of divine will?

A third way to make decisions is through the exercise of "force." Whatever the disagreement, whoever is more physically powerful, or controls weapons or an army or the police, would simply make a decision and compel others to follow. Even as children, we probably resisted such decision making as "not fair" and wanted a better explanation for decisions than "because I said so." By definition, a democratic form of governance (which, admittedly, may not apply to many families!) is based on faith in the superiority of group decisions over individual decisions enforced through brute power.

> "... instead of looking on discussion as a stumbling-block in the way of action, we think it an indispensable preliminary to any wise action at all."
>
> Pericles in Thucydides, The Peloponnesian War
>
> "... since the general or prevailing opinion on any object is rarely or never the whole truth, it is only by the collision of adverse opinions that the remainder of the truth has any chance of being supplied."
>
> John Stuart Mill, "On Liberty"
>
> "Congress shall make no law respecting an establishment of religion, or prohibiting the free exercise thereof; or abridging the freedom of speech, or of the press; or the right of the people peaceably to assemble, and to petition the Government for a redress of grievances."
>
> First Amendment to the United States Constitution
>
> "Come now, let us argue it out, says the Lord."
>
> Isaiah 1:18
>
> "Is not inquiry the cure of ignorance?"
>
> Mohammad, reported in Sunan Abu Dawud 337
>
> "Use soft words and hard arguments."
>
> English proverb
>
> "People generally quarrel because they cannot argue."
>
> Gilbert K. Chesterton

Notice that some of these ways of making decisions may be acceptable on an *individual* basis. We will not try to argue in this book that all decisions can and should be made "rationally." If one has a choice of a used car down to two final choices and is having difficulty deciding, it is not necessarily a bad idea to flip a coin. And we would not try to persuade students that their personal religious faith should not inform their beliefs and actions. However, when it comes to group decisions, especially matters of public policy, we have the most faith in argumentation as the best means of making such decisions.

In fact, one way to understand the U.S. Constitution is as a form of government based on faith in reason. Our laws are enacted through a process of argument and deliberation, and conflicts between parties are sometimes resolved in courts, which are based on a model of argument. Our Constitution was conceived and written in a time known as the Age of Enlightenment, which was defined by its faith in reason.

In short, we study argumentation because we have faith in reason and prefer to make decisions involving other people through rational argument rather than chance, divine guidance, or brute force.

Furthermore, we believe there is value to studying argument for students both as "producers" of arguments and as "consumers" of arguments. The study of argument can be dated back to the fifth century BCE when Greeks began to teach young adults how to present compelling arguments in such places as the law courts and the legislative assembly. It was understood from the beginning that some people are better arguers than others and that one's argumentative skills could be enhanced through study and practice. We live in an argument-rich environment, one in which we are constantly bombarded with attempts to persuade us to buy this product or to vote for that candidate. In turn, almost all of us will find ourselves in professional or public settings in which we are expected to argue for a particular choice or course of action. This book will help you learn how to *make* better arguments as well as how to *evaluate* the quality of arguments made to try to persuade you.

ARGUMENTATION IS A REQUIREMENT FOR DEMOCRACY

The benefits of argumentation as a means of deciding issues are not only for personal or practical situations. Argumentation as a means of deciding what to do is an essential requirement for a free, democratic society.

Many would argue that free elections with secret ballots is the defining mark of democracy. While not diminishing the importance of elections, we contend that open deliberation among citizens is every bit as essential. And to have good deliberation, the society needs to have the skills of argumentation.

One of the most striking features of the first sustained democratic society—classical Athens—is that they did not have a large number of elected offices. They chose many of their leaders by lottery instead. What they did have was an assembly where all citizens (albeit limited to adult males who were not slaves) could attend, listen, speak, talk among themselves, and then vote. Before the term democracy was in common use, Greeks used the term *isegoria*—which means that "everyone could have a say." The marketplace (of ideas) was open and all should be able to participate on an even basis. And as imperfectly as they implemented that, it was still true that here was a city where decisions were not made by a small group deciding in secret, or by a hereditary king or a military ruler, but out in the open in front of everyone.

Turning to contemporary nations that are representative democracies, such as the United States, we see a contrast. Many are concerned that while we still have elections, the quality of our public deliberation is not what it should be. Surveying the evening news, the talk shows, the radio commentators, magazines, and the newspapers does not reveal a strong belief in the qualities of reasoned discourse that we will discuss in this book. Features such as the use of evidence, a commitment to admit and correct one's errors, listening to different views with respect, an understanding of what sort of reasons prove a claim—these are hardly in abundance.

Regardless of how you assess contemporary society, deliberation is a crucial feature of maintaining a free society. One sign of this is that tyrannies almost always attempt to limit debate. People wanting to seize power will proclaim that some urgent crisis means that debate has to be restricted. National security requires secrecy. A threat requires the suspension of rights and even elections. If not legally restricting speech and debate, intimidation will be used, such as labeling opponents as traitors or racists or some other term designed to diminish their viewpoints and prevent them from participating.

Nor are such tactics limited to governments. One way of viewing the Protestant Reformation is as a revolt against a demand for unquestioned belief in the pronouncements of the church hierarchy. Many of the reformers wanted to democratize the process of reading and interpreting the sacred texts—letting everyone study and debate for themselves. That would force the church to be more democratic.

Nor can it be said that a defense of deliberation is only a left-wing attack directed against right-wing tyranny. Extreme leftist movements have also sought to undermine faith in the possibility of arriving at truth by debate by engaging in censorship. A certain type of radical postmodernism denies that reasoned debate is ever anything but a cover for self-interest. All of these views reveal a lack of faith in the value of open, unfettered debate.

If a group has little political or financial power, one of the things it can do is reveal the truth of its situation. It can point out to the larger society how it is being treated. It can call on the society to live up to its ideals. It can make arguments that appeal to principles of fairness and justice. When it cannot do that openly, it often does it clandestinely, such as in the *samizdat* writings that Soviet dissidents circulated. When a group has no political power, all it may have is its ability to persuade others.

AN ASSET FOR LIFE

The value of argumentation goes far beyond politics. We will argue in the next chapter that reasoned debate is a key component of many aspects of professional and personal life. You need to study argumentation because you cannot reliably learn these skills from the culture in general.

As with politics, so with consumer products, sports, business, and other aspects of life: One does not always see people making the best arguments. Maybe you don't typically see that. What gets picked up by the media, what attracts notoriety, is not generally the best, the most careful, the most nuanced.

So you need to study argumentation to defend yourself against this and to acquire the skills to make better arguments.

HOW TO USE THIS BOOK
A Note to Students

If you are having trouble deciding on a topic for your papers, here are a couple of ideas. Look at the examples we use, both the big examples we describe in detail and those we just briefly mention. Maybe one of them will be interesting to you to explore in more depth. Some chapters have lists of famous examples or current case studies that you can explore.

Secondly, what if you discover you don't like one of our examples or think we've got it wrong? Argumentation applies, as you'll learn in the next chapter, to every single issue humans are involved with. We're unlikely to be infallible experts on every one. And while we've been careful and held ourselves to the same standards we are trying to teach in this book, the odds are that there is likely some example where we should have studied it further or time has brought new insight that we haven't included. We'll fix those problems when we discover them, but it is also an inherent part of argument that you are always learning, your conclusions are always subject to revision, and tomorrow will likely bring new information. So, go ahead, write a paper attacking one of our examples. If you follow the principles we set forth here, we'll be happy.

A Note to Instructors

We have provided several features to assist teaching. Some chapters contain either a detailed case study or shorter lists of areas where the specific argumentation concepts are used. You may wish to expand on one of those or substitute other examples for your teaching. Chapters have summary information in a box that can provide students with study guide material.

But Isn't It More Complicated?

Yes. Argumentation in real life is generally more complicated than we describe here. But what we do here is common to beginning texts in any subject. We break the topic down into separate concepts, we use examples that illustrate those examples, and we try to teach skills one at a time. Integration of skills comes after you have the skills and practice, practice, practice.

What Is an Argument?

INTRODUCTION

In general usage, the word *argument* can refer to a fight or conflict—a verbally violent exchange full of angry words, hurt feelings, cutting accusations, and more accusations in return. In the study of argumentation, however, the term has a different and very specific meaning. We define argument as a claim, supported by reasons, and intended to persuade. This brief definition has wide-ranging consequences and forms the foundation of what we present in this book.

In this chapter we start learning about argumentation by considering that definition from several angles. We'll look at what an argument is and what it is not. We'll consider various aspects of how arguments are used as well as seeing what we can learn from some situations where arguments break down.

THE DEFINITION OF AN ARGUMENT

An Argument Is a Claim Supported by Reasons

It is common to define an argument by using two terms and the relationship between them. The two terms are: a *claim* (singular) and *reasons* (typically plural). To capture the two terms and their relationship, some authors use phrases like "a claim with reasons" or "reasons offered to prove a claim," or "words intended to persuade." We'll use the phrase "a claim supported by reasons."

> M: I came here for a good argument!
>
> O: Ah, no you didn't, you came here for an *argument*!
>
> M: An argument isn't just contradiction.
>
> O: Well! It CAN be!
>
> M: No it can't! An argument is a connected series of statements intended to establish a proposition.
>
> O: No it isn't!
>
> M: Yes it is! 'Tisn't just contradiction.

O: Look, if I *argue* with you, I must take up a contrary position!

M: Yes but it isn't just saying "no it isn't."

O: Yes it is!

M: No it isn't!

O: Yes it is!

M: No it ISN'T! Argument is an intellectual process. Contradiction is just the automatic gainsaying of anything the other person says.

O: It is NOT!

Monty Python, "The Argument Sketch," 1972

Let's start by looking at the term "claim." This can also be called a thesis. In order to have an argument you must be asserting something: some point, some idea, some proposition. You must be making a claim. Argument typically involves multiple claims but our unit of analysis in this text will be one statement—one claim. And, we will expect that a claim can be given in one sentence. If you cannot write out your claim in just one sentence, it often means you are not clear about what you are intending to argue.

This observation hardly seems revolutionary. But claims will prove the center of considerable analysis. Later on we will divide claims into three types (fact, value, and policy), we'll help sharpen up claims by properly qualifying them, we'll use claims as one component of the Toulmin six-part model of argument, and we'll discuss how networks of claims connect together.

But a claim by itself isn't an argument, it's just an assertion. To make it an argument, you must offer some other statements that will persuade someone to accept your claim. These are your reasons (also called grounds). There has to be at least one reason to support your claim, but often there are more.

When a parent says to a child, "You should go to bed now," that is a claim, an assertion of parental authority. But the moment a reason is given, "Tomorrow is a school day," something more than a command is being offered; now there is an attempt to persuade and obtain agreement—now there is an argument. Of course, the parent has authority over the child and can order the child to go to bed.

Reasons can be evidence or inferences, employing logic, data, or referencing sources. Reasons may turn out to be subsidiary claims that have to be proved with more reasons. Reasons can also involve the stature or credibility of the person making the claim. A parent has authority, but (hopefully) children look up to their parents as wise guides to the world and are willingly persuaded by them.

When you watch a public debate, notice how often claims are advanced without any reasons, any reasons at all, good or bad. Notice how rarely people are asked to substantiate their claims, how seldom they get asked "What's your evidence for that?" or "Why do you think that is true?" Indeed it often happens that should someone attempt to go into the background to support their claim, they are cut off by the moderator lest they allow any boring facts to interrupt a chain of colorful accusations.

So, we have claims, and we need reasons. But, they have to connect. The reasons can't just be anything; they must validly support the claim. We'll spend much of this book discussing "forms of reasoning"—assessing which reasons actually support a claim. Many argument fallacies involve sorting out situations where reasons appear to support claims or are assumed to support them but actually do not.

If you have studied logic or argumentation in other settings, you may have encountered a definition for an argument like the following: "A set of premises from which you can logically infer a conclusion." This is quite a similar notion to what we are working with here. The premises are our grounds; you must engage in valid inferences (so there will be support for your argument); and you are trying to get to a conclusion (our claim).

An Argument Is Intended to Persuade

From what we've discussed, you can anticipate what makes an argument different than a fight. First, let's consider the attributes of fights. A clash of opinions ("yes it is," "no it isn't") is not an argument. It is more likely to be about who can yell the loudest or threaten the most. The winner will achieve victory by intimidation or the threat of force. If a reason is given, it may be only "because I said so" or "because I'll kill you (or leave you or fire you) if you don't see things my way."

And even if reasons are shouted at each other in the middle of a fight, if the ultimate decision is about power and not persuasion, then this isn't an argument, even if it appears that everyone agreed to the outcome. Fundamentally, arguments are about freely given assent to claims—and that assent comes through persuasion because they find the reasons to be compelling—compelling by reason, not by force.

In between freely given assent and force lies manipulation, otherwise known as spin, guilt-tripping, brainwashing, snow jobs, emotional abuse, propaganda, peer pressure, and other terms. These activities can take the superficial form of an argument with claims and reasons but there is something false about them. Part of the task of someone versed in argumentation is to penetrate and expose manipulation. Part of why universities want you to study argumentation (and part of what we hope this textbook can help with) is so you can be equipped to resist manipulation.

So, we are talking about persuasion leading to freely given assent. Now it is true that conversations that start out as conflicts may wind up with some persuasion resulting in freely given assent. But when we use the word "argument" we are talking about the claims and reasons that prove persuasive to someone.

An Argument Takes Place in a Context

If arguments are to persuade, then they must be persuading someone. And so now we have to grasp that arguments are not simply some claims and reasons floating in a pure vacuum. They are offered *by* someone (we'll call this person the *advocate*) and offered *to* one or more people (termed the *audience*). They are presented in some medium, be it written or oral, using some technology for transmission (audio, video, multimedia, website, podcast, etc.) or face-to-face. And arguments take place in a specific situation, a specific time and place where there have been all manner of events, arguments, and life experiences going on before and during the communication.

An awareness of the context is important because all these factors influence how the audience comprehends the message. What might be well received in one situation will not be well received in another. Changing the media changes the communication. What you might need to say to one sort of audience could be very different than what you need to say to a different audience—even if you are advocating the exact same claim to both audiences. And *who* makes the argument also impacts how it is received.

Issues of context are obvious to see when communication goes across genders, national boundaries, cultures, or ethnic groups. However, more subtle issues of context affect almost all of our communication efforts. Various chapters of this book will be devoted to explaining how presenting an argument must take account of these factors.

This simple diagram attempts to summarize these factors of context. An advocate (left-hand figure) makes a communication (the arrow) to an audience (on the right) amid a certain context (the enclosing circle). While simple, a large number of factors have to be considered to analyze properly all the components listed in this diagram.

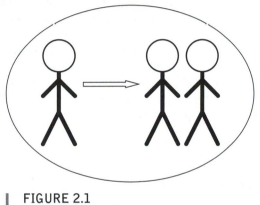

FIGURE 2.1
Communication as Contextual.

In subsequent chapters on Ethos and Kairos, we will delve into these aspects in more detail.

"Argument" Means Both the Product (the Claim and Reasons) and the Process (the Exchange of Claims and Reasons)

Despite our attempt to be precise about the meaning of the word "argument," there is one possibility of confusion. The term "argument" is used both to mean "My argument is this claim and these reasons," and also to mean "Our ongoing exchange of claims and reasons over time is an argument." In practice, this dual use does not normally cause confusion.

THE BOUNDARIES OF ARGUMENT

Not everything should be considered an argument. But more things are arguments than you might think, and some things commonly thought not to be arguments actually are. So it is useful to look at some categories of human interaction and assess if they are or are not arguments.

Insults Are Not (in and of Themselves) Arguments

We live in a culture that often assumes that insults settle an argument. Coming up with the perfect one-liner, some great putdown, can cause those around you to laugh and the person on the receiving end to feel defensive.

However, it is worth explaining just what is different between an insult and an argument. The front page of the satirical paper *The Onion* once showed a picture of President George W. Bush with an odd expression on his face under the headline, "Bush asks country to be quiet for a minute so he can think." Some of you reading this laughed, some were upset. But what is going on here? That picture and headline are an indirect way of claiming: "George Bush is not very smart." We can recognize that as a claim—but as we know, a claim isn't an argument until we supply some reasons. *The Onion* didn't give any reasons. And here is the point: Insults usually present a claim but seldom provide any reasons in support of the claim.

It would be very different if you set out to prove that the president was not very smart. You could do that by starting with a discussion of how you measured intelligence and then by giving a series of examples and reasons that you would contend supported this claim about the president. If you did that you would be making an argument—an argument that defenders of President Bush could reply to with evidence and reasons of their own.

Insults shouldn't be persuasive, not until someone offers reasons in support of the underlying claim. In the chapter on Ethos, we will discuss the *ad hominem* attack, a form of insulting people. We'll discuss under what conditions it can be a valid argument—but the conditions always involve giving reasons.

Descriptions and Explanations Are Arguments

In another class you may have been asked to give a persuasive speech and then an informative speech. Speech contests sometimes have similar divisions. There seems to be something different between advocating a position and just telling you about something.

However, while there is a difference, both are arguments and both involve persuasion as we are using the terms here. A persuasive speech may ask you to change your opinion from one side to the other. An informative speech is attempting to persuade you that the information is accurate, relevant, and important. Such a speech may take you from "I didn't know that" to "This is how that works." And while many informative and descriptive communications are not controversial or do not encounter much resistance from the audience, such disputes are always lurking below the surface. Consider this paragraph.

> Although the world has just discovered it, India's economic success is far from new. After three post independence decades of meager progress, the country's economy grew at 6 percent a year from 1980 to 2002 and at 7.5 percent a year from 2002 to 2006—making it one of the world's best-performing economies for a quarter century. (Das, 2006)

Perhaps no one would argue with this. India's rapid economic growth is pretty widely known. However, this paragraph makes a number of claims and offers data to support them. Someone might dispute how the numbers are measured. Someone might dispute the relevance of those particular numbers or argue that it doesn't capture what is going on in a country with such contrasts of rich and poor. We can go farther. Are those particular bits of data the best way to explain India's growth? Maybe you have better, more current or compelling facts. So now we could argue over which would be the best paragraph to write. And of course, someone might step back from this focus on economic growth to question what real growth would be. Gandhi, for example, might have thought this was going down the wrong path.

Also, consider how the audience affects the reception of this paragraph. If you were discussing India with someone who had only some decades-old prejudices about India being a basket case, you would indeed be persuading them, and you might need more than this paragraph to do it.

So yes, many informational presentations are not controversial, but they can quickly become controversial. To be sure, that last example was political and open to controversy. What about a set of instructions, like how to use a table saw to build something? What persuasion is involved there? The instructions are attempting to persuade you that this is the way to do it. And suppose you have five different descriptions—five different sets of instructions—to perform some task. Do they disagree? Do they have the steps in different order? Do they include different safety instructions? Do they make different assumptions about what expertise the audience has? Now we can see we have arguments.

Even in literature there are attempts to persuade. This is the introductory paragraph to Willa Cather's 1918 novel *My Antonia*. It is a well-known passage.

> Last summer, in a season of intense heat, Jim Burden and I happened to be crossing Iowa on the same train. He and I are old friends, we grew up together in the same Nebraska town, and we had a great deal to say to each other. While the train flashed through never-ending miles of ripe wheat, by country towns and bright-flowered pastures and oak groves wilting in the sun, we sat in the observation car, where the woodwork was hot to the touch and red dust lay deep over everything. The dust and heat, the burning wind, reminded us of many things. We were talking about what it is like to spend one's childhood in little towns like these, buried in wheat and corn, under stimulating extremes of climate: burning summers when the world lies green and billowy beneath a brilliant sky, when one is fairly stifled in vegetation, in the colour and smell of strong weeds and heavy harvests; blustery winters with little snow, when the whole country is stripped bare and grey as sheet-iron. We agreed that no one who had not grown up in a little prairie town could know anything about it. It was a kind of freemasonry, we said. (p. 9)

To be sure, it doesn't sound like an argument. But the author is trying to persuade us of something. It would seem that she wants us to feel something of the rural Midwest, to think sympathetically about the bracing sensory pleasures of that life. This description is generally regarded by critics to succeed at its task. She could have written something different. A writer that wanted to persuade you that rural life is full of backward people and sensory deprivation would have written something different. In her choice of descriptions, she aims to convince you, and, in doing so, is offering an argument.

But, you may still wonder, how can such explanations or descriptions be arguments if no one is disagreeing—if there is nothing in dispute? This is to still cling to the idea that what defines an argument is conflict. We're suggesting that a better definition of argument is persuasion—persuasion mediated via making a claim with reasons. Some communication is persuasive enough not to produce any disagreement. But that is a situation that can change when new information appears.

Opinions Are Arguments

Many contrast facts and opinions as if they were polar opposites. "You can't argue with the facts." On the other hand, "It's just my opinion," or "I'm entitled to my opinion." "No one can tell me what to think." "It's just a question of taste."

Many think there are two categories: something is either a fact or it is an opinion. Sorry, but this doesn't work. It turns out that you can argue about the facts, and you can also argue about opinions.

First of all, our accepted stock of facts is constantly changing. How does that come about? How do we decide that something is a fact when we didn't think it was one previously? The answer is: We had an argument, and we reached consensus that this was a fact or that this had to be removed from the list of facts. The notion that continents could move was once thought to be akin to believing in UFOs, but research and study continued and now this is accepted as a fact. A thousand other examples could be given of our evolving knowledge of the universe.

Thousands, perhaps millions, of individual facts that we now accept were unknown a century ago. They became established as facts to us because somebody made a reasoned argument that was generally accepted.

Certainly, there are many facts that no one will want to argue about. That only means that the argument took place already and we've all (or almost all of us) been persuaded. But each fact now accepted had to be proven at some point—and could need to be proven again.

When someone says "That's a fact!" what they are really trying to assert is that there is a strong consensus of opinion.

But what about those views commonly called opinions—about what food you like, or where you want to go on vacation, or if a movie is good? When we turn to opinions, we also discover that we can, and do, argue about them all the time. There are several things to sort out here. When someone asserts that they have a right to an opinion, they are asserting their rights as an autonomous human being. They are defending themselves against coercion and social pressure. And they are right to do so.

But that doesn't mean that two or more people can't willingly engage in discussions about subjects that we'd call matters of opinion. People debate the merits of a movie, their judgments on Angelina Jolie's relationships, their view of Shakespeare, or Green Day. People present reasons and make claims and the other side responds to them.

Film critics argue if a movie is "good." They offer data, analogies, accuse each other of inconsistency, and debate the standards for evaluating movies. In other words, they do a lot more than just make assertions.

The same standards apply for opinions: You have to offer a claim and reasons. If you just give your judgment and refuse to say why you think so, then that is just a claim. And, unless you will also claim that you are an expert (and give evidence to substantiate that second claim), then no one has to be convinced by your opinions. But, we do often give reasons for our opinions. And now we're in an argument.

Consider this evaluation of a wine:

> 93 Points. This is succulent and fruity, with concentrated flavors of dark plum, blackberry, and chocolate mousse that are backed by good grip. The snappy finish features hints of licorice. Drink now through 2025. (Staff, *Wine Spectator*, 2012, p. 91)

To someone like the authors, who are not wine experts, this may appear to be gibberish or an exercise in self-delusion. But we feel confident that wine experts could argue about this opinion. "The finish is not that good" or "There is no pear flavor here." Reference could be made to other wines of similar or different backgrounds. Is this description consistent with other descriptions of similar wines? Is the opinion unbiased or slanted because of the power of the winery or the person doing the evaluation? Debate could be had about if this wine is getting better or worse as it ages.

What about more personal opinions? "I like blue clothes." Well, if someone says they like blue clothes because they look good in them, you can discuss if that is an opinion shared by all. You can give reasons for why blue might or might not go with someone's hair, skin color, or personality. Even the pure opinion, "I like blue clothes," leads a friend to naturally ask "Why?" or to observe that there are other blue things you like or don't like. If you say you like blue clothes but don't own any, a friend may point that out, and you will likely feel obligated to explain. This too is an argument.

So, the popular division of opinion from fact is often quite misleading. Not every fact is cut and dried. There are things we think are facts or some think are facts; there are things we suspect might be proven to be facts after some more research and things that are thought to be facts but we dispute them. In other words, it is common to have opinions about facts. It is common to argue about your opinions about the facts.

We have opinions about which things are facts. It would be better to think that facts are things upon which, after a period of discussion, we've reached consensus. When someone asserts that something is a fact, what they mean is that there is no credible evidence to dispute the opinion that this is true.

Emotions Are Reasons (or Reasonable)

Since we are promoting reasons, and debate and being rational, some may be tempted to see this as a rejection of emotion: a claim that the head should always rule the heart. This is absolutely not the case. In the next chapter we'll include emotion, under the term *Pathos*, as one of the ways we persuade each other. Being reasonable and truthful (or being manipulative or false) are properties applicable to logic and emotion both.

Arguments Typically Have More than Two Sides

Time and again in this book, argumentation will be presented in terms of being for or against a claim. We will talk about defending or rebutting an argument. So, it is worth being clear from the beginning that most arguments have more than two sides. Thinking in oppositional terms can often blind you to the possibility of a third (or fourth or fifth) position.

When we discuss argumentation in terms of two sides, we are doing so to simplify the context so that basic principles can be illustrated. Falsely contending that a situation only has two sides is common and can be an example of a fallacious application of argument by dilemma (discussed in a later chapter).

IMPLICATIONS OF OUR DEFINITION

Arguments Are Used in Many Types of Communication

Now that you know more of what an argument is, where do you find arguments? You can guess that the answer is "almost everywhere," but it's worth exploring.

Sometimes people approach an argumentation course assuming that all that will be discussed are public policy issues, such as the Iraq war, abortion, or taxes. But, in fact, as you could infer from what we've said above, almost any conversation can be taken to be about persuasion and thus it will be useful to look at different types of persuasive conversations.

In academia, you often have to offer convincing reasons for something. An article in a scholarly journal is a classic presentation of an argument. When you teach, or listen to teaching, you are involved in various forms of persuasive conversations.

Business locations are places where the ability to "make your case" is important. You want money for a project. You want to launch a new product or ask for a raise. And, the higher you rise in management, the more this becomes important as more and more of your job is to persuade other managers. It is a mistake to think that being a manager means mostly that you issue orders to people who follow them. Managers are constantly attempting to persuade workers to work more effectively, to believe in a corporate vision, or to change a behavior. A wise manager is open to persuasion from workers with good claims and reasons.

If you go to court or become involved in the legal process, you will spend time learning the specialized forms of argumentation of the law. You will write and respond to briefs—arguments. You may have to persuade a jury that your arguments are better than those offered by the other lawyer. To avoid going to court, you may have had to rebut the claim of a police officer about your behavior.

In sports, your coach will attempt to motivate or move you to perform better and provide reasons for why certain forms of exercise are better than others. And as a fan, you will argue about which team is better than others.

All sorts of small groups from jury rooms to committees in volunteer organizations involve the skills of separating out types of claims and evaluating the reasons supporting them.

Even between friends or lovers there is a place for thinking about argumentation. Many personal relationships run aground due to communication problems. And while many issues are involved in that, the inability to state clearly what you want and to offer reasons that support it make those conversations more difficult. To give one example, we'll discuss later on the concept of "qualifying a claim." How many times has one person said to another "You always do this ..." when they should have said, "You sometimes do this ...." Getting your claim right matters.

"New coach Tim Brewster has a lot of work to do, including replacing starting QB Bryan Cupito. He will have an impressive group of running backs, led by Alex Daniels. An easy early schedule will help QB Tony Mortensen get the handle on the offense, but the young Gophers will likely wilt under the pressure once the Big Ten schedule gets under way. A bowl game is possible again, but this is not an upper-division team."

CBS Sportline College Football 2007 Season preview, p. 39

How many different claims are made in this prediction? Notice that reasons are offered for the claims. They are opinions ("impressive group of running backs") but, if asked, the author could explain why he thinks they are impressive. Even if we don't have a precise definition of what is or is not "impressive," reasonable people could probably agree in general on how impressive (or not) this group was. That is an argument.

If you are studying communication, you will likely take classes in the special forms of communication involved in small groups, in companies, between cultures, or between people. We certainly are not claiming that those subjects only involve the principles of argumentation that we are laying out in this textbook; that would be both absurd and arrogant. However, we do suggest that aspects of communication in those settings can be illuminated by understanding the issues we will discuss here. In other words, argumentation is (almost) everywhere.

Looked at from another perspective, we can see that arguments are used for a variety of purposes and not simply to fight about politics. Arguments are used as part of the process of finding the truth, to persuade, to negotiate, to teach, to assist in motivating others to follow a decision.

An Argument May Be Implicit

In 1964, a commercial now known as the "Daisy Ad" aired during the presidential campaign between Lyndon Johnson and Barry Goldwater. The ad featured a young girl in a field, pulling the petals off of a flower and counting in an adorably childish manner. The camera slowly zooms into the child's eye, where the image is transformed to an atomic bomb exploding, complete with a huge mushroom cloud. We hear a voiceover of President Johnson speaking of the importance of peace, and the announcer states, "Vote for President Johnson on November 3. The stakes are too high for you to stay home" (Daisy, 2012).

The ad was tremendously controversial. Critics charged that the ad claimed that Goldwater would start a nuclear war. *But the ad never even mentions Goldwater's name.* The message of the ad with respect to Goldwater depended entirely on the audience's knowledge that he was considered a pro-war "hawk" and hence the audience, rather than the ad itself, would make the inference that his election would be dangerous. But such a claim is never made explicitly in the ad.

The argument, in other words, is implicit. The claim is never explicitly mentioned. Much advertising fits in this category. A car sweeps across the screen, a happy woman looks admiringly at the man driving. It is a little too simple to suggest that the claim is "Guys, buy this car and you will get a wife like this"; perhaps the claim is just "Buy this car and you will be happy."

But implicit claims are not limited to advertising. Consider the claim "Support the troops" that we see on the backs of many cars. What does that mean exactly? Some see that and think it means "Support the policy of the president about the war" or even "If you don't support the war, you are a traitor." Others think it doesn't mean that at all and just means "Let's not do to soldiers now what we did to them after Vietnam."

(Practical) Argumentation Is Not the Same as Formal Logic

Formal logic is concerned with formal proofs and often writes formulas in the form "If P then Q" and undertakes precisely defined operations to manipulate such statements into other statements. There is also a tradition of considering proofs in the form of syllogisms and defining reasoning as either inductive or deductive.

While this tradition is drawn on for use in the discussion of argumentation, it does not provide an adequate basis for evaluating arguments as conducted in the real world. What we are discussing is sometimes called practical argumentation to distinguish it clearly from formal logic.

ARGUMENTATION REQUIRES SHARING ASSUMPTIONS

As we've mentioned, argumentation takes place in a context where there is someone to be persuaded. Grounding that exchange of views is a set of assumptions and criteria of what counts as "proof" that are shared by all participates in the discussion. And if you turn out to have disagreements about some of those assumptions, you have to have some way of conducting an argument to resolve your disagreements.

One way of illustrating how essential these shared assumptions are is to consider three cases where arguments break down—where failure to agree on assumptions leads to problems.

Case 1: Conspiracy Theories (Violations of Logos)

It's fun to list conspiracy theories. The government caused 9/11 or allowed it to happen. The CIA assassinated President Kennedy. A missile from a U.S. navy ship shot down TWA 800 in 1996. AIDS came from a government lab. Marilyn Monroe was murdered. Kurt Cobain was murdered. Princess Diana was murdered. The government killed John Lennon. The moon landing was a fake. The government knows about visits from UFOs. Area 51 is where they keep the aliens from the UFOs. Bill Clinton had a number of people murdered while he was governor of Arkansas. The Obama administration, headed by a Kenya-born Muslim, is preparing plans to confiscate all the guns in America and round up conservatives to place them in camps. There is a huge group of satanic followers who have killed thousands of children. The Trilateral commission runs everything. The Federal Reserve runs everything. The Jews run everything. The Freemasons run everything, perhaps in collaboration with the Bavarian Illuminati. The United Nations will run everything if we're not careful.

In Minnesota in 2007, a bridge across the Mississippi River collapsed, just a few hundred yards from where the authors work. Within a short time, several conspiracy theories were floating about including that it was a deliberate demolition, that the state government knew the bridge was about to collapse, that the debris was not recovered promptly to hide a large number of dead Somali citizens and (our favorite) that the collapse was associated with a burst of low-frequency radiation from nearby Augsburg College.

We will leave an analysis of why such theories are so compelling to experts from a different field. But we will suggest that belief in conspiracy theories requires a suspension or outright overturning of a number of assumptions that are critical to making argumentation work. They are characteristic fallacies.

These characteristic fallacies often include:

- Heavy reliance on arguments from silence. An "argument from silence" is when you use the absence of evidence against your position as proof for your position. For example, suppose no one has ever confessed to being part of the conspiracy. Advocates of the conspiracy theory will take that as proof that the conspiracy is very effective.
- The use of negative evidence as positive evidence. For example, suppose that the group you think are terrorists has issued a statement denouncing terrorism. You cite that as evidence they are deceptive.
- Disregarding the uncertainty, accidents, and coincidences of ordinary life. In real life, people are slow to respond, do contradictory things, don't figure things out. In a conspiracy, that is all taken as intentional obstruction.
- Violation of what is most probable or likely.
- Assume great precision and coordination from people who are also said to be stupid and incompetent.

If you have ever argued with someone who believes one or more of these theories, you probably did not convince them. You were perhaps argued into silence but you left the argument feeling that your defeat was not really valid in some way—and you were likely correct. The advocates of these conspiracy theories do not share our assumptions about logic, about probability, about human behavior, and so they cannot be argued with effectively. It is as if you are playing basketball with people following the rules of football. And, it is certainly clear that people of all political orientations can succumb to the lure of such theories.

Case 2: Cult of Personality (Violations of Ethos)

Some people we respect and view as authorities. They have standing or credibility with us. In a subsequent chapter we'll use the term *Ethos* to describe how much credibility we give someone. Anyone who is a leader of a group or a company or a nation will be given respect because of their office.

However, when credibility earned from actions and character start increasing beyond limits, a cult of personality can develop. These invest a particular leader with godlike infallibility. A cult of personality gives infinite credibility to a person and so the leader speaks, and that defines reality. Nothing needs to be investigated, thought about, or debated. Truth consists in obedience to the leader.

There have been many examples of this. Chairman Mao and his little red book come to mind. Idi Amin from Uganda and Hastings Banda of Malawi are examples. David Koresh or Jim Jones would be examples from religious cults. There are smaller examples from every walk of life—a leader who dominates some group, a teacher whose every pronouncement produces gasps of awe and so on.

If conspiracy theories are a failure of the advocate, cults of personality are failures of the audience, which has surrendered its duty to think and reason and be persuaded in favor of simply obeying. This is not the same as simply admiring someone or respecting a leader. It passes into cult territory when the thought process in the audience stops and mere pronouncements of the leader are unquestionably obeyed.

> "When the president does it, that means it is not illegal."
>
> former President Richard Nixon, to David Frost, May 1977

Case 3: Fundamentalism: There Is Nothing to Argue About

A different kind of violation of shared assumptions involves fundamentalist conviction. There is fundamentalist Islam and fundamentalist Christianity and even fundamentalist atheism. There was once a fundamentalist Stalinism, but there are also people with extreme convictions about abortion, Nazism, and a variety of other topics.

Fundamentalists behave as if truth does not need to be discovered or debated: It already exists and all one must do is look up the answer and apply it (Altemeyer and Hunsberger, 2005).

Note that this is not a critique of religion. Religious traditions, including Christianity, Judaism, and Islam, have long traditions of reasoning about various questions, with perspectives of distrusting any particular leader and emphasizing the fallibility and contingent nature of all human knowledge. Their traditions often include an awareness of the always imperfect understanding of their sacred texts. They also have a tradition of limiting the power to coerce others as a safeguard on those who would take drastic actions based on their convictions.

Fundamentalism, as we understand it, labels a set of views as absolute, not subject to improvement or being misunderstood. Truth is not something to quest for, it's not hard to find, there are no dilemmas, tradeoffs, or contradictions. Everything is clear, obvious, and without difficulty. There is no progress either; everything is known and the only issue is the degree of fidelity to the rules.

And—crucially—when you have made this move, then you are truth itself. Then you no longer need to persuade others—now you can coerce them. And that marks the breakdown of argument. When this point has been reached, other people become instruments that can be manipulated. And it becomes natural to view outsiders as not as pure as those in the group. From fundamentalism comes fanaticism.

Argumentation as a Shared Process Requiring Shared Assumptions

What each of these three cases illustrates is that for argumentation to work, it needs those involved to possess shared assumptions about how arguments will be resolved and even to agree that one should enter into argument.

It takes a certain amount of cooperation in order to disagree with someone. In order to have a fruitful disagreement, that is. In order to have arguments, in the sense we mean for this book, the people involved must share some assumptions and attitudes.

- They must have a willingness to be persuaded. No matter how convinced you are that you are right, you have to agree that there is something the other side could say that would cause you to abandon your position and adopt a different position that you now understand to be superior to the one you started out with.
- There is an external world that would exist even if we did not. It may be next to impossible to find out what is going on or what is true or not, but an advocate will approach any argument agreeing that there is something beyond them that they will have to accept as real.
- There are shared rules about what counts as evidence. This is implied by the last point. All participants agree on how we will decide that something is true—or agree on how to decide the criteria. We'll discuss this more in the evidence chapter.
- There are shared criteria for what will persuade. Our study of claims and forms of reasoning will flesh out these criteria.
- The decision will be based on persuasion not power. These shared assumptions will be how we decide the question.

ARGUMENTATION IS A COMMUNAL PROCESS FOR REACHING CONSENSUS

Of course, we learn to argue so we can win arguments. But, if advocates follow what we have described in this chapter, the result will be a search for truth in which bad ideas will slowly be replaced with less-bad ideas.

People will disagree. And as they disagree, they disagree by exchanging ideas about what is the truth or what is closer to the truth. They are committed to be open to new ideas, to trying to use the same or similar criteria as their opponents are using. They will concede when they are convinced that others have better ideas. And thus, positions will converge.

Of course this is an ideal, seldom achieved. Of course it sounds naive about how people really are and the complexity and indeterminacy of profound questions. Nonetheless, in many communities, one can see this process happening, perhaps only on some issues and only some of the time.

Even if formal consensus is not reached on questions, there can be a consensus on how to approach some of life's problems.

Make no mistake; argumentation is not just about trumping your neighbor. It is about promoting a marketplace of ideas in which we will all benefit.

Locating Practical Arguments

Conversations don't always start, or remain, as the sort of pure reasonable arguments we are discussing. Of course, a real discussion will veer off into unsupported claims, to random accusations or insults and include irrelevant material.

Sometimes people start arguing, then discover they really agree with each other or have no need to convert each other.

> "Blessed is he who learn show to engage in inquiry, with no impulse to harm his countrymen or to pursue wrongful actions, but perceives the order of immortal and ageless nature, how it is structured."
>
> Euripides, fragment from unknown play, quoted in *The Closing of the Western Mind*, p. i

Something might present itself as an insult or as an uncontroversial description, but, when probed, turn out to have something interesting to argue about.

CONCLUSION

By this route something of the rhetorical motive comes to lurk in every "meaning," however purely "scientific" its pretensions. Wherever there is persuasion, there is rhetoric. And whenever there is "meaning" there is "persuasion." (Burke, 1969, pp. 172–3)

Sometimes words like "argument," "rhetoric," or "persuasion" are interpreted to include only a small subset of all communication. Sometimes people can think that the subject of argumentation only refers to formal debate between two people or only to issues of public policy.

We've staked out a much broader position. To a lesser or greater extent, each time we open our mouths or use some medium to communicate we do so for a purpose that involves affecting the world. We are always making arguments: some explicit, some implicit, some controversial, some to reinforce views already accepted. We're not trying to persuade you that argumentation is the only thing— just that it is a crucial thing.

SUMMARY OF WHAT IS AN ARGUMENT?

Definition

An argument is a claim, supported by reasons, intended to persuade.

Issues and Aspects

Explanations are arguments; insults are not.

We have opinions about what is or is not a fact.

Arguments are found in almost all areas and types of rhetoric, not just political debates.

Study Questions

- What is the one-sentence definition of an argument?
- How are we using the term "argument" in this class?
- What separates an argument from insults and from formal logic?
- What shared assumptions are needed for an argument to work?

Forms of Proof

INTRODUCTION

We defined an argument as a claim supported by reasons. But don't confuse "reason" with "purely rational." Reasoned argument is more than pure logic, as we will see.

Arguments do involve not only the meanings of logical propositions but also our emotions, who is making and receiving arguments, and the context around the communication. A way of making sense of this complicated communication process is to assess arguments along four dimensions: Logos, Pathos, Ethos, and Kairos. These are important aspects of how persuasion is accomplished; they are forms of proof and key diagnostics to use for understanding why arguments do or don't work.

The first three of these terms were described in the writings of Aristotle. He lived from 384 to 322 BCE, after the high point of the classical period of ancient Athens but before Alexander the Great's conquests (Aristotle was Alexander's tutor when the latter was a child). In a work entitled *On Rhetoric* (which is still studied by scholars of communication today), Aristotle proposed that there are three different ways of effecting persuasion:

> Of the pisteis [belief] provided through the speech there are three species: for some are in the character [ethos] of the speaker, and some in disposing the listener in some way [pathos], and some in the argument [logos] itself, by showing or seeming to show something. (Aristotle, 2006, p. 37)

In modern times, a fourth Greek word, *Kairos*, has been revived to capture how persuasion is affected by the circumstances surrounding the presentation of the argument. We'll discuss each of these four in turn and then apply them to helping us understand a number of arguments.

THE FOUR FORMS OF PROOF

Before we begin, it is important to understand that there is no preference among these four; all can be valid ways of proving an argument. Additionally each of them can be done well or badly, be effective or ineffective, be appropriate or inappropriate. Each can be used to support arguments for the best of purposes or the worst of them.

Logos: Proof by Reason, Logic

Logos is a Greek word that had a wide range of meanings in ancient culture. When used in argumentation, it means the logic of your case. Do your premises support your claim? Are your premises true? Think of the processes of the classic scientific method or the step-by-step proof of a theorem in math.

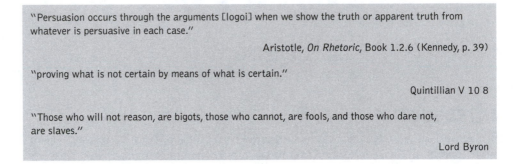

"Persuasion occurs through the arguments [logoi] when we show the truth or apparent truth from whatever is persuasive in each case."

Aristotle, *On Rhetoric*, Book 1.2.6 (Kennedy, p. 39)

"proving what is not certain by means of what is certain."

Quintillian V 10 8

"Those who will not reason, are bigots, those who cannot, are fools, and those who dare not, are slaves."

Lord Byron

The perfect example of a Logos-based appeal is the scientific research paper. There is nothing here likely to invoke strong emotions, no personal attacks. Even joy in discovery or the exhaustion of a long bit of work is excluded. Everything is transparent and in the open. The procedure used in the experiment is laid out step-by-step in detail. The objective is to describe your results in such a clear way that anyone else could duplicate them. That "others could duplicate" your results implies that a logical argument is somehow independent of who is making it or when it is being made.

In assessing a logical appeal, we would decide if the propositions were coherent, if they justified the specific conclusion being made, or if anything unnecessary had been added to the argument.

Consider the following paragraph:

Where the Social Democratic or Communist tradition was strong, unionization high, and labor-movement culture active and well supported, the cohesive power of the socialist milieu generally proved resistant to the Nazis' appeal.... Social and cultural factors accounted for their appeal, rather than economic ones; for the unemployed voted Communist, not Nazi. (Evans, 2005, p. 263)

The Nazis. Few, if any topics, could generate more emotion. But there is little or no overt emotion in this paragraph. The author is breaking down who voted for the Nazis and who did not. Behind those sentences is a numerical analysis of voting patterns. This is very different than someone writing about the moral horror of this regime.

How persuasive is logic? Humans are not always very logical. Logic can be a cover for self-interest. But, as with each of the four types of proof, we will have to decide if a Logos appeal is being done well or badly, if the logic is sound or not.

We can't quite make up our minds about Logos. One strand of our culture sees it as the only real way of proving anything; another sees it as always a projection of self-interest. Logical arguments can be assumed to just be a cover for deeper unexpressed motivations. Logic can be regarded as cold and unfeeling, and it can also be viewed as the engine that fuels our progress.

While logic applies to any argument, consider it as one form of proof among others that people do find persuasive when done well and used appropriately. We will discuss some of the issues around logical appeals in the chapters on fact claims and causal arguments.

Pathos: Proof by Emotion, Appealing to the Sympathies of Your Audience

> [There is persuasion] through the hearers when they are led to feel emotion [pathos] by the speech; for we do not give the same judgment when grieved and rejoicing or when being friendly and hostile. (Aristotle, 2006, p. 39)

No, we do not give the same judgment when we are grieved as when we rejoice. If we are debating a question of justice, it might help if we felt the injustice. If we are debating a question of economics, it might help if we could feel what facing bankruptcy or homelessness felt like. Failing to feel the pain may make us insensitive and affect our judgment. On the other hand, an emotional appeal can be stripped of context and mislead us as well.

As with Logos, in our culture we have a certain ambivalence about feelings. We can despise them as illogical but can also use a feeling to trump all the data. We are frustrated by people who get emotional but we also are concerned about people who are unfeeling.

There are many ways to analyze Pathos claims. Let's consider three of them:

- Is the appeal **effective**? Did it work? Just saying "I was really hurt" conveys no emotion if said in a flat voice with a neutral facial expression. A statistic about deaths probably is less effective than a story of one single death.
- Is the appeal **authentic**? Is the appeal sincere or truthful? A saying is that "Sincerity is everything, because once you can fake that, you've got it made." Emotional appeals can be inauthentic if they are based on stories that are fake, phony representations of what people feel, or omit important data that would change our emotional reactions. Our emotions can be manipulated by people who are insincere. We can't just blindly accept whatever emotion an advocate wishes us to feel.
- Is the appeal **moral**? Which emotion does the appeal target? They are not all equally noble. While emotional appeals can stir us to anger, play on our prejudices, or induce us to violence, emotional appeals can also inspire us, encourage us to persist in time of trouble, revive us, or motivate us. Martin Luther King Jr.'s "I have a dream" speech stands in our culture as one of the most powerful speeches ever, and its appeal is primarily by Pathos. Likewise, in a quieter mode, Abraham Lincoln's Gettysburg Address speech also appeals to our imaginative sympathies. At the other end of the spectrum, television advertisements and political speeches use Pathos as well, but do so in ways that often leave us feeling degraded or patronized.

An appeal to emotion can involve stories or lengthy presentations, but it can also be done in a single word or a phrase. Imagine a group of people who remain after some event has caused the majority to move on. This group could be termed a "remnant," the "leftovers," "the faithful," or "the bitter-enders." There is a wide range of emotions represented in that choice of a single word.

Advertising uses a particularly rich form of rhetorical choices to induce emotion. Products are "new," "improved." They use pictures of appealing animals or attractive humans to induce warm feelings. Autos are sold to us as exciting or daring choices. It's implied that products for our appearance will remove our negative feelings of unattractiveness or failure.

Likewise, our political decisions are often influenced by emotional appeals that try to cause us to be afraid, or resent what others are getting, or to have us associate patriotism and love of country with one candidate or another.

Being unaware of the emotional weight certain words hold can confuse an argument. If you watch a movie on an iPad, do you pay less attention to it than if you see the movie in a theater? A classroom discussion on distractions got a bit confused on this subject. Some seemed to resent even talking about this or were feeling that iPads were a good thing, so why were they being attacked? Clarity was reached when it was pointed out that "distraction" has a negative emotional connotation. "Multitasking" describes the same thing, but in a more neutral term. Now it was easier to discuss the effects of watching a movie on different media. Get the facts established first and then have a second discussion about the desirability of those effects.

Notice that emotions can be analyzed, perhaps even logically. Again, do not assume that a class on reasoned argument is denigrating emotions. Also note the discussion of emotions, and further examples, in chapter 11 on the "pathos-centric" model of presenting an argument.

Ethos: Proof by the Credibility of the Advocate

> [There is persuasion] through character whenever the speech is spoken in such a way as to make the speaker worthy of credence; for we believe fair-minded people to a greater extent and more quickly [than we do others] on all subjects in general and completely so in cases where there is not exact knowledge but room for doubt. (Aristotle, 2006, p. 38)

Under this topic we are concerned with the credibility of the person making the argument and also how the argument is made—the credibility the advocate *brings* to the argument and the credibility the advocate *demonstrates* in the argument.

People with reputations like Nelson Mandela, Abraham Lincoln, or Gandhi carry a lot of credibility, which means that many would be inclined to accept their words because of who they are. Most of the rest of us, without that level of credibility, need to study how we can enhance the weight our words are given. This is the subject of the chapter on Ethos later in this book.

Kairos: Context Affects the Persuasiveness of Our Argument

Kairos refers to the idea of using the right word and the opportune time. What is going on around the argument can also contribute to its persuasiveness, as much as the words themselves. We identify four components of the concept of Kairos.

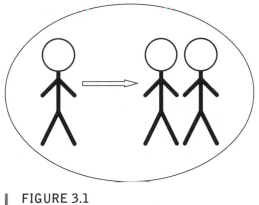

FIGURE 3.1
Communication as Contextual

The **audience** has to be assessed by advocates before they decide how to proceed. The audience may be favorable or unfavorable, knowledgeable or uninformed, open to listening or bored. How you speak to a group of children is not how you address senior citizens. How you speak to people from your own group would be different than how you address an audience of a different culture.

The **medium** refers to how your message will be communicated. Will you write, speak, prepare a website or use audio? Words by themselves have a different impact than words with music. Still photos with captions are not like video. Reading is not the same as hearing.

The **history** of previous communications can support or impede a current communication.

The **occasion** is the events and setting around your presentation. What happened yesterday? What will likely happen tomorrow? Where is the communication taking place? A message that is welcome at one moment or in one time and place, may be offensive at another.

In June of 1963, President Kennedy stood at the wall that divided Berlin and spoke these words:

> There are many people in the world who really don't understand, or say they don't, what is the great issue between the free world and the Communist world. Let them come to Berlin. There are some who say that communism is the wave of the future. Let them come to Berlin. And there are some who say in Europe and elsewhere we can work with the Communists. Let them come to Berlin. And there are even a few who say that it is true that communism is an evil system, but it permits us to make economic progress. Let them come to Berlin.

Consider how that speech gained its power from being spoken at that particular place and how he used the circumstances to make his point. It would still have been an effective speech if spoken at an upscale club in some U.S. city, but much would have been lost.

It is possible to misread and misuse the occasion as well. Fred Phelps is a pastor of a small independent Baptist church who believes that many disasters and terrorist attacks on the United States are the result of our society tolerating homosexuals. So he and his followers attend the funerals of soldiers killed in action and hold up signs such as "Thank God for Dead Soldiers," arguing that the soldier was fighting to defend a country that accepts homosexuals, and thus God exacted retribution by the death of the soldier.

It seems hard to imagine a more inappropriate use of the occasion than this. Even a person with extreme antiwar views would be very unlikely to seek to disturb a family during such an intense moment of personal grief. Even a very peaceful person might be enraged by this sort of protest. And most people who themselves oppose acceptance of homosexuals would recognize that this protest at this time will only bring discredit on a view they support.

ASSESSING ARGUMENTS

We have to sort out some concepts. While we refer to a particular argument as "a Logos appeal" or an "Ethos appeal," any argument can be examined using all four of these terms. That is, we can always ask "What is the role of Pathos in this argument?" The answer in some cases may well be "Not much." When we say that argument was "a Logos appeal," what we mean is that Logos was the primary or most obvious way the argument was being made. But you should always be asking how all four are at work in an argument.

The president of the United States is making a speech. He stares firmly into the camera, he is sitting at his desk in the Oval Office. He argues for his position. Words like "hope," "the future," "our children," are used. He cites the budget and various figures of multiple billions of dollars.

Now let's look at this event using each of the forms of proof. There is Logos: the budget, the numbers, the logical propositions that if this law is not changed, there will be bad effects. There is Ethos: the stature of the office, the credibility and charisma of this particular individual and how they are regarded by citizens. There is Pathos: the appeal to a better tomorrow, to help for our troubles. And there is Kairos: the setting with all the years of history and various momentous decisions that have taken place in that room. And there is the Kairos of the public moment that produced the speech: the crisis that is at hand, the political positions being taken, the mood in the country.

Often in one particular speech, the appeals to emotion are more prominent, and in other, the appeals to logic. Sometimes the events outside dominate the actual speech, sometimes not.

Examples: What type of appeal is it? Let's work through some examples. Keep in mind that any argument can be assessed along all of these forms of proof, yet most arguments emphasize one or perhaps two of the four forms of proof.

Example 1

Clinical trials clearly establish that timely replacement of estrogen conserves bone mass and protects against osteoporotic fracture. (Greenspan and Gardner, 2001, p. 315)

This is primarily a Logos appeal. Reference is made to scientific studies, the conclusion would follow logically from the application of estrogen. Yet, Ethos is also involved, in a sort of "behind the scenes way" in that to be persuaded, you must believe that the authors are reporting this accurately (since they don't give a citation to a source of the study).

Example 2

Table 18—FERGUS FALLS BRANCH.

3- 111	Ms	February 28, 1954.	112 -2
P M	...	(Central time.)	P M
‡ 9 30	...	lve . . . . + St. Paul ⓣ🚗 . . . . arr.	11 00
‡ 10 15	...	lv . . . . + Minneapolis ⓣ🚗 . . . . ar.	10 27
† 6 00	...	lve . . . . + Staples ⓣ . . . . arr.	5 55
6 35	0	+. . . . . Wadena ⓣ	5 23
6 58	10	+. . . . . .Dear Creek	5 01
6 13	18	+. . . . . Henning.	4 45
7 26	24	. . . . Vining.	4 32
7 36	29	. . . . Clitheral	4 21

A timetable doesn't look like an argument; it seems to be just explaining something. Yet, we learned in a previous chapter that explanations are attempting to be persuasive. In this case, they want to persuade you that the bus or train is, in fact, leaving at the time they claim it is. This, then, is a pure appeal to Ethos. You either trust the source or you don't.

Example 3

Last year, a blowout almost took down America's financial system. ... Allstate believes that a modern regulatory system for property and casualty insurance would greatly benefit American consumers. ... One of the reasons America got into this mess is because there was no national oversight of the entire system. (Atlantic, 2010, p. 100)

This appeal feeds off of Kairos. It uses the context of the Great Recession to convince you of the urgency of change and to imply that this could have been avoided if their proposals had been in place. The advertisement will go on to offer other kinds of proof, but notice how it launches itself from the context of events.

Example 4

After the space shuttle Challenger exploded in 1986, President Reagan offered a eulogy, saying in part:

> Your loved ones were daring and brave, and they had that special grace, that special spirit that says, "Give me a challenge, and I'll meet it with joy." They had a hunger to explore the universe and discover its truths. They wished to serve, and they did. They served all of us. We don't hide our space program. We don't keep secrets and cover things up. We do it all up front and in public. That's the way freedom is, and we wouldn't change it for a minute. We'll continue our quest in space.

This is an appeal to Pathos. Notice how he uses simple words and sentences effectively to communicate his sincerity. He attempts to reframe the grief and dismay of his audience into pride and determination to persevere. It is generally regarded as one of his most effective speeches.

Example 5

> During the July 4 holiday weekend, the latest in a series of cyberattacks was launched against popular government Web sites in the United States and South Korea, effectively shutting them down for several hours. It is unlikely that the real culprits will ever be identified or caught. Most disturbing, their limited success may embolden future hackers to attack critical infrastructure, such as power generators or air-traffic-control systems, with devastating consequences for the U. S. economy and national security. (Clark and Levin, 2009, p. 2)

While the tone is sober and professional, there is a strong element of Pathos here: Look out! We're under attack! The authors are going to argue that you should be worried about this threat and what it could do to the United States. Because the first author, General Clark, is a retired four-star general who also ran for president briefly, it gains credibility from his ethos as a national leader with experience in assessing threats. Further, there is Kairos to consider: The article appears not in a general circulation magazine, but in perhaps the leading U.S. journal on foreign affairs—a journal read by decision makers and often featuring articles by national officials and officeholders. The medium this appears in also contributes to its appeal.

CHOOSING WHAT FORM OF PROOF TO USE

Now, we have to turn and look at these four concepts from another perspective. For any given argument that we are trying to make, we can choose from a number of ways to make it. And our choices can emphasize one or more forms of proof. Let's suppose you are attempting to convince your boss to give you money to launch a new product. How could you make an appeal using each of the four types of proof?

TABLE 3.1		
	Nature of the Appeal	Comment
Proof by Logos	Cost-benefit analysis.	You would prepare budgets, estimate costs, and generate models of future cash flow to show that this would be profitable.
Proof by Pathos	Tearful moms who need our product.	You might also inspire by reference to the excitement of being first, of making money, or of the joy of winning.
Proof by Ethos	"Warren Buffet and Jack Welch and the Wall Street Journal advocate this."	You invoke the views of experts, using their ethos to persuade that this is a good idea.
Exploiting Kairos to be persuasive	"Our competitor just released a new version."	Also relevant here would be your analysis of what exactly your boss finds persuasive and how to present your case in a way that communicates authority.

But certainly, one can make a choice of appeals for less serious matters as well. Consider various strategies for inducing someone to go out on a date with you. We'll leave you to supply the commentary.

TABLE 3.2	
	Getting a Date
Proof by Logos	"You care about security. I have great prospects for making a lot of money."
Proof by Pathos	"I'll be sad and lost without you, a lonely person slowly dying." (Add a hang-dog expression and sad eyes.)
Proof by Ethos	"I'm on the football team."
Exploiting Kairos to be persuasive	"I just rescued you from a shark, so date me."

EXERCISES

The following may be useful ways of practicing your ability to detect and use forms of proof. Find an example of an argument and:

- Decide which forms of proof it emphasizes.
- Describe how you would make the same argument emphasizing a different form of proof.
- Describe how you would change some aspect of Kairos to substantially change the persuasiveness of the argument?

SUMMARY

The following table may be useful for a quick comparison of the dimensions.

TABLE 3.3

	Logos	Ethos	Pathos	Kairos
Function	Making your claim	Finding your voice	Moving the audience	Knowing when to speak
Purpose	Make your argument sound	Increase your credibility as an advocate	Put the audience in a certain frame of mind	Matching the previous three dimensions to the situation
Related Terms	Logic, inference, reason The scientific method	Credibility Impression management	Emotion The heart Psychology	Situational awareness Audience analysis Carpe Diem
Best	Star Trek's Mr. Spock The calm explanation of a confusing situation	The prophet The leader who inspires	Inspiring us Overcoming our prejudices	The insightful and patient counselor
Inept	Microscopically detailed proof of something that doesn't affect the overall argument	Claiming to be something you obviously aren't	Crying at a presentation in a corporate boardroom	Asking someone for a date at a funeral
Worst	The bad lawyer The conspiracy theorist	The con man Cults of personality	The guilt-tripper The manipulator Stirring us to hate	The insensitive
Common Confusions	That Logos is the only "real" part of an argument That Logos is a "Western" horrible denial of all that being human means	That an "ethical" appeal is only about personal ethics	That a "pathetic" appeal is "painfully inferior or inadequate" That appeals to Pathos are always invalid That appeals to Pathos are always more real than Logos-based appeals	That this is about saying one thing to one person and something contradictory to someone else

Modeling Argument (The Toulmin Model)

INTRODUCTION

In this chapter we introduce a simple, but widely applicable, model for diagramming arguments. Despite its apparent simplicity, it also is one of the more theoretically challenging chapters of this book. We suspect the challenging nature of this model has to do with the unfamiliarity of the concepts it explicates. By contrast, many of the concepts you are learning from this textbook put a more formal, or more carefully thought out, framework around ideas you already "sort of" know. You know you need evidence to support an argument, but we will push you to support it better (in the evidence chapter). You know that some people are more persuasive than others because of who they are. Chapter 10 of this book delves into that topic more deeply.

The Toulmin model is rather unlikely to be something you've encountered before. But, make no mistake, this is a very important model to conceptualize what makes arguments valid. And this model will be used again and again in the rest of the book.

THE MODEL

Background

In 1958, the philosopher Stephen Toulmin presented his model of the "layout of arguments" in his book, *The Uses of Argument*. He was motivated by a conviction that the rules of formal logic could not describe what actually occurred when people conversed with each other. Formal logic, or mathematical logic in his view, was valid, but it was not adequate to help people understand arguments or help them form arguments.

Toulmin's model is both widely accepted and widely criticized. It has a significant status within the communication studies field among those who focus on informal logic or practical argumentation, but it has encountered more resistance among philosophers.

The Toulmin model focuses on the Logos dimension of an argument. It is a heuristic tool to help unpack the logic of claims and the support offered for them. As a heuristic tool it gives us a way of "disassembling" an argument, but it does not provide us with a tool that can mechanically decide for us if an argument is valid.

Heuristic

A heuristic is a "rule of thumb" or a "rough guide" to something. It is in contrast to a law, which is something that is always true. Heuristics are useful in many situations, but you have to decide if they apply in a given circumstance.

Overview of the Six Parts

We will quickly describe the six parts of the model, and the following sections will explore each part in more detail.

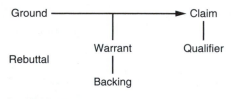

FIGURE 4.1
Toulmin Model.

Claim—This concept we've already discussed. Toulmin, in a later book written with Reike and Janik, describes a *claim* as "assertion put forward publicly for general acceptance" (1979, p. 29). This highlights that a claim is an assertion (which has to be supported), you want it to be accepted by some audience, and therefore, you have to make it public. Note that this still is a good definition even when you are arguing with yourself because a key part of debating with yourself is to clarify for yourself what you are thinking and what you want.

Ground—This was called "reasons" in an earlier chapter; we'll generally use "ground" from now on. Toulmin sometimes called this "data," a term we find misleading, since grounds can not only be datum (facts, numbers) but also reasoning as in logic or quotes.

Warrant—As the drawing above shows, this is what connects grounds to a claim; the statement (it will be a sentence) that justifies that the claim is in fact supported by the ground. We will spend much of the rest of the chapter talking about warrants.

Backing—The support for the warrant. It provides support for a warrant like the ground supports a claim.

Qualifier—This refers to how claims are limited or made specific.

Rebuttal—This floats free in the diagram above because, when you attack an argument, you can go after any of the other five components. We have a chapter on rebuttal later in the book.

CLAIMS

Finding the Claim

Remember at the beginning when we said claims can be implicit? The Toulmin model, to work, requires us to think out what our claim actually is. If the claim is unstated, we have to look for it, to ask what is really being argued in a given situation.

We will insist that any argument starts with a *one-sentence claim*, not a paragraph of points. The exercise of working out our claim into one simple sentence is a useful one to promote clear writing. Remember that we are not telling you how to compose poetry or a novel. The genre of persuasive writing emphasizes clarity and transparency of thought. And we see no surplus of that in our culture. Hence, we're not going to back down or cut you slack because of your tortured, complex soul: Make your claim in one simple sentence. (We can't help but mention the student who submitted an 81-word sentence as her claim. It was a grammatically correct sentence, so we had to admire her effort. But don't copy her.)

But what if you find it hard to get your claim into a simple sentence? You have too much to say or too many points to make. A couple of things may be going on here. Is what you're writing like this?

"We should do X because … and because … despite …"

What is happening here is that those "because" clauses introduce grounds to support your claim. The "despite" clause might be a rebuttal to some argument you anticipate. In the Toulmin model, all these are needed but they are written as separate sentences.

Consider some specific situations where the claim needs some work.

- "The common view of X is incorrect in many ways." There are two directions you could be going in. Do you really want to focus on a group with incorrect views and explain why they are wrong? Or, was this just a sort of introduction and your real aim is to tell your audience what is the correct view about subject X? If it is the latter, then your paper could start by describing the common view of X but you would spend most of your time on the correct views.
- "Y is actually far more interesting than you think." This needs some focus. Can you say in what specific way Y is interesting? Are there reasons why the audience should care? Do you want to persuade them that Y is interesting, or do you really want to persuade them to take some action about Y?
- "I found out all sorts of things about Z." Well, good for you. But, this is not a very useful claim for a paper. Why would you tell us these things? Do you want to make the claim that Z is, contrary to popular opinion, actually quite fascinating? Or that people should pay attention to Z? Perhaps some of the interesting things you found out will be useful to support a specific claim about Z.

We'll come back to this subject in the "qualifying claims" section below.

Grounds

Various chapters of this book deal with what is and is not a valid ground for supporting an argument. But we should just briefly note here that grounds for a claim can include a number of different types of information. It can be quotes, data provided by a source, or something you create. Grounds can be numbers, or conceptual information, or even visual evidence.

Grounds can, in fact, also be claims: subsidiary or secondary claims that are used to build up a larger argument. After we present the full Toulmin model, we will discuss more complex argument networks near the end of this chapter.

Grounds have to match your claims. One crucial way for grounds to be mismatched to claims is when you haven't properly qualified your claim.

Qualifying Claims

Failure to properly qualify claims, to claim too much, or to mismatch claims and grounds, dooms many otherwise promising arguments. Let's consider a number of common cases.

Good vs. Best

C1: "Hillary Clinton would make an excellent president."

C2: "Hillary Clinton is the best person running for president in 2008."

While those two claims sound fairly similar and people would typically slide from one to the other, they are, in fact, not the same and require very different sorts of evidence to prove. If you are arguing C1, you can discuss then-Senator Clinton in relation to the demands of being president, but you really do not have to consider anyone else. If you are arguing C2, then you must explicitly compare Clinton to all the other candidates. C1 might be true, but there might be other candidates who are even more excellent.

Nor is that a problem affecting politics alone. The authors regularly receive papers arguing, for example, that "The Minnesota Vikings will win the Super Bowl next year" (it's always next year). These papers typically talk about how Minnesota improved this or that aspect of its team—but do not compare the Vikings to any other team. Perhaps Minnesota did get better—but so did other teams.

All vs. Many

C1: "All X do Y."

C2: "Most X do Y."

C1 is a claim that requires only a single counterexample to refute it. C2 is a much easier claim to make and is harder to refute. This problem regularly surfaces in interpersonal communication when one member of a loving couple asserts "You always do ..." when what they have evidence to support is "You've done that twice in the last six months."

Comparisons and Superlatives

C1: "X is better than Y."

C2: "X is good."

C3: "X is perfect."

What are you asserting? That this car is better than your old one? That your car is "good" in some sense? Or that it is the best of all possible cars? In each case, what you are comparing "X" to is different.

This distinction is regularly used in advertisements to confuse you:

C4: "None better."

C5: "This product is better than the rest."

Marketers regularly put C4 or some equivalent on their products or advertisements. Many read that as if it was C5. But they are different. The first just argues that among the products that are the best is this one, the second asserts their product is actually superior to the first—a harder claim to prove and one that might involve them in legal action if they could not support it.

Essential vs. Helpful

C1: "X is essential."

C2: "X is helpful."

A student was writing a paper on the need for using animals to test medical products for humans. She provided a number of examples of how animal testing speeded up the testing process, saved money, and was more convenient than the alternatives. This evidence proves that testing is helpful, or saves money, or saves time. It does not prove that all that product development would stop if animal testing were to stop.

Increasing vs. Serious

C1: "This is a big problem!"

C2: "This problem is getting worse!"

C2 sounds more serious than C1. But to prove C2 you have to supply data about a trend. For C1 you just have to supply current data on how bad things are.

Proved vs. Not Proved

C1: "You haven't proved X."

C2: "I have disproved X."

This is a confusion of qualifications that often occurs in rebuttal. Person A claims that X is true. Person B disputes this. But what exactly did B set out to do? Show that person A failed to offer enough evidence for their claim (C1) or to actively attempt to disprove the claim (C2)? What often happens here is that person A misreads C1 as asserting C2 or even a C3:

C3: "I am opposed to X."

Consider the dynamic that occurred in the run-up to the Iraq war when administration officials were asserting a claim like: "Saddam Hussein is a bad person (because he is a tyrant and has weapons of mass destruction). Opponents offered a C1-type response: "You haven't proved he has weapons of mass destruction," which was (perhaps intentionally) misheard as a C3 claim: "You love Saddam Hussein!"

Instructors have the same problems with student papers. The student offers a loveable claim but gives weak evidence for it, say "Kittens are wonderful," and the instructor responds by observing (C1 style) "You've not given any reason why kittens are wonderful." The student is mystified as to how someone could be so cruel as to dislike kittens.

Because we want to support your instructor (and help you understand their feedback), let's look at this in another way:

C4: "You are wrong."
C5: "You are not persuasive."

It is easy to hear C5 as C4. It's easy to say one when you mean the other. But they are very different. C5 means your case needs to be stronger. C4 means the person disagrees with your case. C5 might be said by someone who agrees with you.

Proving vs. Not Proving There are a number of qualification problems surrounding claims of truth. Here is another one:

C1: "You can't rule X out."
C2: "X is true."
C3: "X is false."

C1 does not assert that X is true or that it is false. It asserts that, so far, insufficient evidence has been put forward to prove that X is false. There still is a chance that X is true.

Overqualifying Claims

However much precision of language is valuable, it is possible to go too far. Sometimes qualification is implicit, a sort of shorthand that most understand. Someone might say "All Republicans think ... " when what "all" is understood to mean here is "public leaders of the party, such as well-known senators, representatives, popular talk-show hosts, and speakers often asked to present their opinions at national gatherings of the party." Some qualification of the claim is still a good idea, but an insistence on total definition in casual speech would slow everything down. Some allowance can be made for conventions of language.

It is possible to overqualify a claim into meaninglessness. The authors grew up near a large dam. It was billed as "the sixth largest earthen-filled dam in North America." Even as teenagers, the authors wondered just how many significant "earthen-filled dams" there were in North America—eight? Companies that bill themselves as "the largest bookstore in the northwest suburbs" or "the finest university in the county" may be claiming a lot less than it looks.

You have seen the claim made that some product is "best in its class." Just how wide is the class? How many are in it?

WARRANTS

With the concept warrant, we now come to the core of what is new and different in the Toulmin model or at least most likely new to you. *Warrants* have a deceptively simple definition: They are what connect the ground to the claim. We (sort of) introduced that concept in the "qualifying claims" section when we discussed how claims and grounds could be mismatched. Now we will get more systematic.

Let's consider a simple example and then look more carefully at the properties of warrants.

We make the claim:

C1: "There is a fire."

And the ground we offer for support of that claim is:

G1: "I see smoke."

If we ask ourselves, "How does seeing smoke justify a claim that there is a fire?" you are likely to reply with a sentence that will be a warrant:

W1: "Where there is smoke, there is fire."

The warrant provides a justification for thinking that the ground does support the claim. Consider some twists on this example.

C1: "There is a fire."
G1: "I see smoke."
W2: "New homes cost more than older ones."

Instinctively you know that this warrant has nothing to do with the claim and grounds; it is "detached" from them. And thus, this argument is invalid. Likewise, if the following were offered:

C1: "There is a fire."
G2: "This house is the wrong color."
W1: "Where there is smoke, there is fire."

You would also instinctively know that this didn't work. The warrant is a valid statement, in and of itself, but the ground is unrelated. They don't connect. A more common problem in your writing is likely to be something like this:

C1: "There is a fire."

G2: "This house is unsafe."

W1: "Where there is smoke, there is fire."

What's wrong here? Isn't a fire a very, very good example of why the house is unsafe? What's wrong here is that a step, connecting fire to lack of safety, has been left out. When we look at networks near the end of the chapter, we can reformulate this to make a valid argument.

So now, before we give some more complicated examples, let's lay out some heuristics about warrants.

- Warrants explain how the ground **supports** the claim (restating what we said above). If a warrant does not connect the two, our argument has a problem.
- Warrants are a **rule of inference**. They describe some aspect of how we view the world, how we think about the world. This observation leads to two more.
- Warrants are **not always controversial** or difficult. They may be difficult to identify or difficult to start thinking about, but don't let that mislead you into thinking that warrants are always some complicated rule. As in our fire example, warrants can be commonplace ideas or maxims.
- Warrants have a **scope beyond the current argument** (unlike the claim and grounds). Notice that our claim was about a fire (in a particular place and time) and our ground was evidence that a particular person was seeing smoke at a particular place and time, but the warrant was more general and had validity beyond the current set of circumstances. This is to be expected. The warrant is what makes our argument (about some new data and circumstances) intelligible to people, but it is based on rules they already know (or we hope they know).
- Warrants are **typically not stated explicitly**. In most communication situations, people do not name their warrants or even refer to them. This can be true even when the actual argument is a dispute about warrants, as we will see below.
- Warrants are **not universal truths**; they can be unknown, known only by a particular group, or disputed. One problem occurs when you use a warrant that your audience is unaware of or even disputes. This will be highlighted below in the section "fields of argument."

Between these last two points ("not stated" and "not agreed"), there is ample room for communication to misfire. A common scene in households with young children is that mom or dad is on the phone and the child comes into the room talking. Eventually the parent screams "I'm on the phone," and the child may or may not stop talking. What has happened? The parent is really offering the following argument:

C1: "Do not interrupt me."

G1: "I am on the phone."

W1: "When you are talking to a person (even on the phone) you should not be interrupted."

The child does not have that warrant, or they argue that the scope of the warrant only applies to direct conversation or, perhaps, they are offering another argument:

C2: "Stop what you are doing and pay attention to me."

G2: "My conversation is important to me."

W2: "I am the center of the universe (so what is important to me must be important to everyone)."

In other words, the dispute is about warrants, but the parent simply offers the grounds on the (perhaps mistaken) assumption that the child is actually unaware that the parent is engaged in conversation.

Some time ago, busses around the University of Minnesota campus contained the slogan: "Cigarette smoke has the same ingredients as rat poison." This was really an argument of this form:

C1: "Stop smoking cigarettes."

G1: "Cigarette smoke has the same ingredients as rat poison."

W1: "People should not ingest poison."

In this argument, not only the warrant but also the claim was left unsaid on the (reasonable) presumption that the audience shared enough information to fill in the claim and warrant on their own.

We'll have more examples of warrants below.

Having trouble figuring out what is what? Try this:

What's your point?

The claim

Why do you say that?

The grounds

How is that connected?

The warrant

BACKING

What happened to "backing"? Backing for warrants is precisely analogous to grounds supporting claims. Therefore, we think it simpler to focus your attention on the triad of terms claim, ground, and warrant. This will allow us to extend the Toulmin model to argument networks in the final section of this chapter.

How can you tell if a statement is a ground or a warrant or a claim? You can't—at least not just by looking at the sentence in isolation. The role of any particular statement in an argument is *context dependent*. You have to examine the role it plays in a particular argument. A statement that is a claim in one context can be a ground or a warrant in another context. We'll see that in the section below on argument networks.

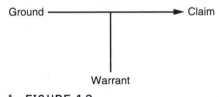

FIGURE 4.2
Simplified Toulmin Model.

FIELDS OF ARGUMENT

Toulmin wrote about "fields" of argument. While that term became controversial and is defined in different ways in the profession, we use it here to raise awareness that one group of people may have a number of rules of inference in common, and that set is different in a different group.

Civil engineers hold a number of rules of inference in common about structures, materials, loads, stresses, project management, and many other things. Lawyers hold a number of rules of inference in common about precedents, settled principles of law, rules of evidence, rules of procedure, and many other things. There is some overlap, but an argument that would be understood immediately by one group might be incomprehensible to another.

It is worth thinking more carefully about what makes arguments different in different communities.

- Not just different subject matter. Different communities argue about different subjects to be sure. Rules for "stop and frisk" are probably not a hot topic among civil engineers, just as lawyers are probably not often discussing maintenance issues for bridge decks. On the other hand, what makes arguments different in different communities and cultures is more than differences of subject matter.
- Not different rules of logic. It is not that 2 plus 2 is 4 for some people or 5 for another or that logic works differently for different cultures.

- The accepted set of rules of inference will be different. This is what we were referring to above with the examples of lawyers and civil engineers. Lawyers need rules about precedents. Civil engineers use precedents also, but will need more rules about how to evaluate materials and the safety of construction.
- Accepted modes of arguing may be different. We'll see later on that argument by parallel case is commonly used in the legal field. Lawyers in particular have developed this extensively. Engineers can use this also but are more likely to use other forms of argument.

Don't make the mistake of thinking of communities as sealed off from each other with nothing in common. And, don't think of a community as uniform with an identical set of rules that everyone in it agrees with. Nonetheless it is useful to think about the person you are trying to persuade and what they will know. This will be discussed in the audience analysis chapters.

WORKING WITH THE MODEL

Let's work through some examples and see how Toulmin helps us spot problems.

Diagramming Arguments

Example 1

The following claim has been made:

C1: "It will rain tomorrow."

G1: "The weather forecast predicts rain."

What is the warrant? You will probably think of something like this:

W1: "The official weather forecast is our best information about the upcoming weather."

But what if this is the argument:

C1: "It will rain tomorrow."

G2: "My elbow hurts."

Some thought may be needed to figure out that the following warrant is implied:

W2: "Weather changes in advance of rain can often cause joints to experience pain."

Both arguments are potentially valid and are consistent, but the warrants are not interchangeable. As we've said, they have to connect the claim and the grounds.

Example 2

Let's consider fixing an invalid example. A student argued as follows:

C1: "The U of Minnesota does not help with the cost of student living expenses."

G1: "The U of Minnesota does not offer an adequate amount of housing."

W1: "Seven dorms scattered throughout a very large university can hold only a fraction of U students."

If you apply the rules we offered above, you can figure out why this doesn't work. First, the warrant is not more general than the claim and the ground; in fact, it seems like it is more evidence for the claim or maybe a second argument. There is also a gap between the claim of "living expenses" and the ground concerning "amount of housing." Of course, the cost of housing is a big part of living expenses, but our goal here is to make these connections explicit and not rely on assumptions. Depending on what argument you want to make, there are at least two ways of fixing this:

C1: "The U of Minnesota does not help with the cost of student living expenses."

G2: "The U of Minnesota does not offer an adequate amount of low-cost housing."

W2: "Housing costs are a significant fraction of living expenses."

Now we've focused on the cost of housing, and we're giving a warrant that is a general rule that many would agree with—it's not specific to the University of Minnesota. But we could fix this in a different way.

C1: "The U of Minnesota does not help with the cost of student living expenses."

G3: "Seven dorms scattered throughout a very large university can hold only a fraction of U students."

W3: "A university should house its students."

In some ways, this is a better reformulation because it exposes the hidden assumption that was behind the previous examples—the assumption that a university has some obligation to house its students or provide some low-cost options for them. Maybe it does, maybe it doesn't—but that issue has to be addressed if you want to make this argument.

By working out this example with the Toulmin model, it helps get us to a more direct, more logically persuasive argument.

Example 3

Let's consider another campus example, this one from a school with an internal bus system run by the university.

C1: "The campus bus system is not efficient."

G1: "The bus does not come on schedule."

W1: "Many students are late for class because of the bus system."

As with the previous example, the warrant doesn't seem general—it seems like evidence supporting the claim. We can fix the argument this way:

C1: "The campus bus system is not efficient."

G1: "The bus does not come on schedule."

W2: "Observing schedules is a mark of an efficiently run system."

Now we've got an argument that is more persuasive. But we wonder, is it the argument you want to make? And we've lost the point about getting to class on time. Let's back up and properly qualify our claim to make sure we are really arguing what we intend to. Which claim are we making?

C1: "The campus bus system is not efficient."

C2: "The campus bus system is not very good."

C3: "The campus bus system is not well run."

C4: "The campus bus system should better serve students."

We suspect most actual complaints about a campus bus system might first be articulated by C2 (rather than C1). But what exactly do we mean by "not very good"? Do we mean a specific critique, which could be that it isn't using resources well (C1), doesn't serve the audience we think it should (C4), or suffers from bad management (C3). Once we've sorted that out, we're in a better position to develop an argument.

C1: "The campus bus system is not efficient."

G2: "They use older, low-mpg busses."

W3: "Fuel-efficiency is a significant aspect of efficiency."

C3: "The campus bus system is not well run."

G3: "They paid too much for the busses."

W3: "Well-run enterprises manage money efficiently."

Note that there are several potentially valid arguments to make here. Which one you want to make would depend on several factors. But again, Toulmin can help you sort out what your goal is.

Example 4

Toulmin is useful for detecting more subtle mismatches in claims and grounds.

C1: "Filtered coffee has health benefits."

G1: "Studies have shown no increase of risk of cardiovascular disease from drinking filtered coffee."

Doesn't this work? Aren't both claim and grounds about health? Yes, but the claim is that there are affirmative benefits to drinking coffee, and the ground is that it doesn't harm your health. "Makes you better," and "doesn't harm you" are not the same claim. You need different evidence for each.

Assessing Arguments

We can use the notion of warrants and the framework of the Toulmin model more generally, not just by diagramming arguments as we have above. We can use the concept of warrants linking claims and grounds to help us see what people are talking about.

Example 1: Conflicting Warrants

Certain public policy disputes in the United States seem to be disputes about which warrant applies. Should we have a national system of health insurance? That debate turns on many issues, but in part it is that one side believes in the value (the warrant) that "you are responsible for your own life" and the other side thinks the warrant that "we should share the risks of being human" applies.

These are values and involve all the issues of value claims we will discuss later, but they also are unstated warrants.

Those favoring universal health insurance, thinking about "sharing the risks of being human," will present evidence that those risks are unequal or that insurance companies forced some to arbitrarily pay unfair amounts. They will tell stories about people abandoned by the current system.

On the other hand, people opposed to a universal insurance system may point to people abusing insurance or emergency rooms or demanding excessive amounts of health services and use their unstated warrant of "individual responsibility" to argue that such incidents justify not having a national system.

The problem isn't choosing the correct warrant; both of them are valid in many circumstances. The real issue is finding the right balance between them and deciding which applies to health care.

Example 2: Arguing the Warrant

Toulmin can help us recognize a kind of "bait and switch" argument where the author appears to be supporting their case but really isn't. This quote appeared in an online discussion:

> To my surprise, I found tons of articles online concerning this diabolical movement. I say "diabolical" because feminists are actually trying to redefine God by perverting the Scriptures. God is NOT made of clay, friend, you can't just shape Him into whatever type of god you want. God is the Potter, and we are the clay. Isaiah 64:8, "But now, O LORD, thou art our father; we are the clay, and thou our potter; and we all are the work of thy hand." We were created in God's image; we CANNOT create God in ours. Tragically, the feminists have recreated their own false god that allows women to rule over men, and a woman to disobey her husband. This wicked twisting of the Bible is known as "feminist theology" and it's straight from Hell. —Stewart (n.d.)

In Toulmin terms:

C: "Feminist theology is bad."

G: "Feminist theology reinvents God."

W: "Reinventing God is bad."

That's a nice, tight, internally consistent argument. However, the author hasn't given us (very much) evidence that feminist theology reinvents God; he's given us evidence that reinventing God is bad. His evidence supports his warrant, not his grounds. So it appears like he's proven his case, but he hasn't.

Example 3: Disputed and Unstated Warrants

Warrants can be the point in dispute, but still not be expressed. Consider this quotation from a piece written during the 2008 presidential campaign.

> ... the campaigns have to contend with an American public fixated on a paradox: About 70% of polled people say the country is on the "wrong track," notwithstanding that the scenery along the track includes some three years of strong-to-moderate economic growth, 4% unemployment and a stock market that's been on an upward march for three years. So what's the problem?
>
> ...
>
> The generalization that emerges from the Post survey's data is that independent voters ... have deep concerns about ... everything. Combining those who say an issue is "extremely important" to them or "very important" puts the totals well above 50% for health care, the economy, terrorism, immigration, taxes, corruption and of course, "the situation" in Iraq. ... This is the Worry Wart vote, a condition brought on by spending too much time with politics. (Henniger, 2007, p. a14)

There are actually three arguments made here: (1) what he believes, (2) what voters believe, and (3) his view of voters. Let's diagram each of them in turn.

What he believes:

C1: "The United States is on the right track."

G1: "(various positive economic indicators)"

W1: "The state of the economy is the best indicator of the state of the country."

First, in fairness to Mr. Henniger, this was written prior to the start of the 2008 Great Recession. To show America is doing well, he cites economic data; his unstated warrant is that economic data is what you should look at to evaluate how things are going in the United States.

What the voters believe:

C2: "The United States is on the wrong track."

G2: "(negative indicators: health care, immigration, war policy, standing in the world)"

W2: "Economic, social, and political issues are all important indicators of the state of the country."

Let's put to one side whether or not he has fairly characterized voters and just accept this as valid for the purposes of this analysis (and we have no reason to disagree with his view on this). Clearly voters have formed a different opinion, and they've done so not because they *disputed* the economic data, but rather because they were looking at other data and valued other measures of how the country was doing. The conflict between him and the voters is not about what facts are true, but what weight to place on different facts.

When he calls this issue the "worry wart" vote and writes that people are "spending too much time on politics," he is disputing the warrant voters hold.

His view of voters:

C3: "Voters are worrying about things they shouldn't."

G3: "Voters are worrying about health, immigration, taxes, corruption, and Iraq."

W3a: "Social and political problems are not things to worry about."

Perhaps the warrant should be posed as:

W3b: "Economic well-being is more important than social and cultural status."

Once we could surface this disagreement, then we might be able to move the conversation forward. We could ask Mr. Henniger if he really thinks that those other factors are unimportant. The conversation could move to discussing the real issue.

Argumentation Theory and the Toulmin Model

Not all argumentation scholars applaud the Toulmin model. Those who approach argumentation from a philosophical orientation were not happy with the heuristic quality of the model. Toulmin has also changed his use of the term "field" and has at times used inconsistent terminology to describe parts of his model. We think our use of the model here avoids those problems.

Toulmin is not the only way of looking at an argument. One thing it does not do is give you tools for assessing how an argument evolves over time. The Toulmin model is a static snapshot of an argument. Using Toulmin may well suggest how you need to evolve your argument, but it has nothing to say about the dynamics of a back-and-forth conversation.

Does the Toulmin model allow us to prove that an argument is sound or not? Not exactly. It is not a "turn-the-crank" model that can produce an answer. Rather, as we started out by saying, it is a heuristic, a tool, that allows us to assess if the grounds connect to the claim and thereby test the internal consistency of an argument. It is only one tool, a tool that focuses on internal validity. It can't tell us if our grounds are false, for example.

> … Toulmin's argumentation model can be useful in three ways when analyzing public debates. Firstly, incomplete or flawed claims can be defeated by exposing missing or mismatching argumentation elements. … Secondly, weaknesses in argumentation can be identified by making explicit warrants and backing. … Thirdly, analyzing the type of backing used, allows inferences about the persuasion approach taken. (Ladikas and Schoeder, 2005, p. 216)

USING MULTIPLE GROUNDS

All our examples have been simple, three-statement arguments. Now it is time to expand beyond this. We'll do that in two ways: first, looking at examples of how multiple grounds can support one claim and then looking at more complex networks.

Multiple Grounds with Multiple Warrants

Suppose we have more than one reason to be upset at our hypothetical campus bus system. It doesn't keep to the schedule, and the schedule is wrong.

> C1: "The campus bus system is not well run."
> G1a: "The bus does not come on schedule."
> W1a: "Well-run bus systems operate on time."
> G1b: "Many students miss class due to schedule problems with the bus."
> W1b: "A well-run student bus system would minimize disruption to students."

We have two grounds supporting our claim. Each has its own warrant. This is an internally consistent argument. Both grounds are connected to a single claim. Each warrant is a general statement that most people would agree with. Obviously we can go on from here to have three and more grounds.

> C1: "The campus bus system is not well run."
>
>   ...
>
> G1c: "The busses are not energy-efficient."
> W1c: "Energy efficiency is a mark of a well-run organization today."
> G1d: "The vehicles are often too big for the demand."
> W1d: "Too much unused capacity is a mark of a poorly run organization."

Notice that every ground and warrant connects back to the original claim. You could write or diagram each C/G/W set independently with them all using the same claim.

Multiple Grounds with a Single Warrant

If we don't think smoke is enough to conclude that a fire is happening, maybe we need this:

> C1: "There is a fire."
> G1a: "I see smoke."
> G1b: "I feel heat."
> G1c: "I heard sirens."
> W1: "Fires are accompanied by signs including smoke, heat, and the arrival of the fire department."

This could be written with a separate warrant for each ground, but the form above works fine.

The grounds in the previous example were fairly independent of each other. And the claim could be justified with two of them or even any one of them. But sometimes multiple grounds really are needed.

C1: "We should do X."

G1a: "We are not doing X now."

G1b: "X is good."

W1: "Implementing something good is a good thing."

In this case, to make your argument you have to explain both that something is desirable and that we are not doing it now. Each ground alone would not prove the claim. The warrant is an example of an *obvious* or *uncontroversial* warrant.

Here is another example that comes up in almost every season for almost every team.

C1: "Our team will lose to University X."

G1a: "Our team lost to University Y."

G1b: "University X is better than University Y."

W1: "You are likely to lose to teams better than teams you already have lost to."

ARGUMENT NETWORKS

Where arguments really take off is when we can chain together a series of propositions.

We'll start with a simple example to illustrate what we mean.

Consider our first example above.

C1: "There is a fire."

G1: "I see smoke."

W1: "Where there is smoke, there is fire."

Now suppose someone wishes to dispute the warrant. They simply start, in some good Socratic fashion, by asking you for proof that your warrant is true. For the moment, you shelve the main argument to focus on defending your warrant. This would be asking for "backing" in the original Toulmin model, but we think it makes more sense to see that we've now got a second argument:

C2: "Where there is smoke, there is fire."

G2: "Most combustion causes the emission of smoke."

W2: "If it is true that A is the primary cause of B, then it can be true that B is a sign of A."

The ground sounds like the claim, but notice that the direction of action is reversed. When we talk about arguments by sign later in the book, you'll discover why this reversal is fraught with problems, but nonetheless, it is often true that you can reason backward (note the careful qualification of W2).

You will notice that the same sentence appears in both triads of statements, but the first time it appears as a warrant and the second time as a claim. Remember, we said that the function of a sentence is context dependent.

Now our full argument looks like this:

C1: "There is a fire."

G1: "I see smoke."

W1/C2: "Where there is smoke, there is fire."

C2: "Where there is smoke, there is fire."

G2: "Most combustion causes the emission of smoke."

W2: "If it is true that A is the primary cause of B, then it is often true that B is a sign of A."

This is what we mean by an *argument network*. We still have triads of C/G/W, but we now have two of them. Notice that it is still true that every sentence is connected and that you could lay these out in a diagram where everything started from C1. Also notice the duel nomenclature of "W1/C2," which alerts us that this sentence will appear again.

We can also develop networks through a ground.

C1: "There is a fire."

G1/C2: "I see smoke."

W1: "Where there is smoke, there is fire."

C2: "I see smoke."

G2: "I see a cloud-like structure that is dark and billowing upward."

W2: "Smoke is a collection of very small, dark particles that can rise on hot air currents."

Modeling encourages us to unpack our arguments by compelling us to go step-by-step. Consider this example.

C1: "The campus bus system needs to be improved."

G1/C2: "It does not serve students well."

W1: "Serving students is an important standard for a campus bus system."

C2: "It does not serve students well."

G2a: "Busses do not run on time."

G2b: "The schedule is not aligned with class times."

(And so forth...)

We've left off the warrants for G2a and b for clarity.

Laying out this network alerts us to there being a sort of two-step argument that we need to make. If we launch immediately into complaining about the schedule and on-time performance, we might be vulnerable to someone asking us to stop and identify what the goals of the system are or to explain why it matters that a bus system just shows up randomly at the bus stops.

Laying out these networks does require a bit of mental gymnastics. Perhaps the following checklist can help.

- Make sure that all sentences in your network are connected to each other.
- Make sure that all sentences lead back to your "C1"—your primary claim.
- The order of sentences in the network is not necessarily the order you would use to write out a full argument.
- Sometimes it is easier to build your network from the bottom up rather than starting from the top and breaking it apart.

As hard as this can be, it is very valuable to force you into thinking clearly about exactly what you are trying to prove.

AN EXERCISE

Procedure

You wouldn't write a paper using sentences labeled C/G/W, but as an exercise you can write a paper using a form of this. Imagine this as the outline of your paper:

I claim that …

There are [two/three/four] reasons why this claim is true.

The first reason is …

This reason supports the claim because …

The second reason is …

And so forth …

The first sentence is your claim (C1). The second sentence is a forecast of what you are going to provide. The sentence "The first reason …" would be your G1a. The sentences that start "This reason supports the claim because …" are your warrants.

How would you do a network? Like this:

The first reason is …

The first reason is true because …

Example

Here is a concrete example of writing this way:

I claim that the University of Minnesota is a very large university.

There are two reasons why this claim is true.

The first reason is that the U of M has one of the largest student enrollments of universities in the United States. This reason supports the claim because the number of students is an accepted measure of the size of a university.

My first reason is true because the U of M has one of the ten largest student enrollments in the United States. This supports my first reason because being in the top ten is an accepted measure of being one of the largest.

The second reason is that the U of M has a budget larger than almost all other universities. This reason supports the claim because the size of a budget is an accepted measure of size for universities.

*

Note that the next to last paragraph implements a network. The first ground (many students) was turned into a claim and supported by the ground "top ten."

Yes, this is a little stilted. But it would be a very good drill to go through. By laying out your structure so clearly, you communicate in a powerful way that you know what you're talking about.

If you try this out, you may want to "cheat" a bit and provide the Cs, Gs, and Ws along the left-hand side for even more clarity.

But there certainly are occasions where making a case this specifically, and even mechanically, would be advantageous.

CONCLUSION

Have you ever seen a protest sign or heard someone make a claim that just brought you up short? You couldn't figure out what they meant, but they seemed to think they were saying something clear and powerful. Rather than yelling at them or dismissing them as a fool, see if Toulmin would help. Identify the claim, find out what reason or reasons are being offered in support of the claim, and identify what warrants are being assumed. If you did that, you might not agree with them, but you'd understand what they meant—and they might well start to reflect on what they were saying.

If this level of detail seems like a lot of work, remember, what you will get out of it is a very clear, transparent outline for making your case. And remember, the genre of persuasive writing requires that. You can vastly increase the power of your case by being this specific.

The Toulmin model is one of our major tools for finding what is left out of the publically expressed part of an argument. We will use it repeatedly throughout the rest of this book.

SUMMARY OF THE TOULMIN MODEL

Aspects

- The Toulmin model was invented in 1958 by Stephen Toulmin and is an important part of the theory of informal logic.
- It is composed of six main parts: claims, grounds, warrants, backing, qualifier, and rebuttal.
- Three parts are the most used: claims, grounds, and warrants.

- Warrants connect the grounds and the claim.
- Warrants are seldom openly discussed in actual arguments, but the failure to have an agreed warrant dooms many arguments to failure.
- The designation of a statement as a claim, ground, or warrant is context-dependent and can be different in different situations.
- Real arguments typically involve networks of claims and grounds.

Study Questions

- Have you made your claim in one simple sentence?
- What does qualifying your claim mean?
- What are the common attributes of warrants?
- Can you read an argument and unpack it into claims, grounds, and warrants?

Introduction to Claim Types

INTRODUCTION

This part of the book is about claims. We'll divide claims into three types, learn how to tell them apart, and then discuss the particular problems with making successful arguments with each of the types.

Why is it useful to divide claims into types? There are several reasons:

- Each type of claim is proved in a different way.
- Each type has certain unique issues that you have to address as you build an argument.
- Confusion about claim type leads to arguments that never make progress.

We'll also discuss claims that appear to be one type but are really another type. Being confused like this is a fine way to talk past each other and not understand what point the other person is making.

THREE TYPES OF CLAIMS: FACT CLAIMS, VALUE CLAIMS, AND POLICY CLAIMS

Many in the discipline of argumentation agree to divide up claims this way. Some use other names, and some divide claims differently. However, we think this tripartite division has great merit and can describe almost any claim a person makes.

In this chapter, our goal is for you to be able to examine a claim and decide what type it is.

Fact Claims

Fact claims assert that something is true or false, was true or false, or will be true or false. Fact claims often assume forms like the following: "X has occurred," "X is occurring," "X does occur," "X will occur," "X is true," "X is false, "X is true at a 90 percent confidence interval," "We can't rule out X being true," "We don't know if X is true."

The following are examples of fact claims:

- "The number of abortions is increasing."
- "Fashion models are thinner than they were ten years ago."
- "Pepsi is regarded by the 18- to 24-year-old group as the best tasting soda."
- "There is a civil war going on in Iraq."
- "Our product sales increased 20 percent last quarter."

Remember, what we are talking about are *factual claims* not "things everyone accepts as a fact." There are certainly disputes about what is or is not a fact. For example:

- "Al Gore received more votes in Florida in 2000 than George Bush" is a factual claim that is disputed. It may never be possible to prove to a high degree of certainty what actually occurred.
- "Continents move" is a factual claim that used to be viewed as false, even ridiculous. However, more research was conducted and gradually, sometime in the late 1950s or 1960s, this became an accepted scientific fact.

But, also remember that having an active, ongoing dispute is not necessary to make something a factual claim. "Two plus two is four" is a factual claim. No adult disputes this, but you might have to prove it to a three-year-old.

Fact claims are proved by offering evidence or logic about the way the world is. Reasoning about facts draws on the shared inheritance of the Enlightenment and often requires us to rely on the methods of science.

Value Claims

A value claim asserts the worth of something (e.g., an idea, a behavior, a thing). They often have one of the following forms: "X is right," "X is good (in a moral, aesthetic, or ethical sense)," or "X is valuable." Some call these "evaluation claims." The person making a claim is evaluating something.

The following are examples of value claims (using the same topics as we did for fact claims):

- "Abortion is (morally) wrong."
- "Very thin models have a bad influence on young girls."
- "Pepsi is part of your exciting life."
- "Our invasion of Iraq was immoral."
- "Our product is elegant and beautiful."

Calling something a "value" is sometimes used as a way of saying "it's just my opinion" or "no one can prove it," but this is erroneous. A value claim is not a dispute over facts. And a value claim is not a dispute over your right to be an autonomous person, either. It is a dispute about things such as esthetics, justice, meaning, or purpose.

It is indeed possible to offer grounds and evidence in support of value claims. If your claim is that some movie is good (or bad), you can discuss if the characters are well formed, the plot is plausible, the degree to which the movie engages your imagination, how it is photographed, or any number of other issues. If your claim is that some action violates human rights, you can point to declarations of universal rights, ask people how they would like to be treated, or use other evidence of how people are valued.

Policy Claims

A policy claim is a claim that advocates a *course of action*—that this action be done or not done. Policy claims often have the form of "We should (should not) do X." You can have policy claims about national political issues as well as what you personally intend to do.

The following are examples of policy claims (using the same topics we did for fact and value claims):

- "Abortion should be made illegal."
- "Models appearing in mass media should have a BMI above 18."
- "You should buy Pepsi."
- "Our troops should be withdrawn from Iraq within a year."
- "We should open more sales offices in Asia."

Policy claims are not quite a third distinct type. Rather, supporting a policy claim will always involve you in making subclaims of fact and value. Policy claims are always built "on top" of fact and value claims. They are distinct from fact and value claims in that supporting a policy claim requires dealing with issues of practicality, such as how much something costs or who will benefit by it.

WHAT TYPE IS IT REALLY?

Confusing Fact and Value Claims

Consider this claim:

C1: "I believe the government is less efficient than private business."

Is this a fact or a value claim? It's in the form of a fact claim. Efficiency is something that can be measured. We could compare dozens of federal programs with similar ones run by the private sector and assess which did better. But there is that word "believe" in the claim. For some people, the view of the superiority of the private sector does not, in fact, rest on facts. They hold a value that it is better to have decisions decentralized and not associated with the coercive power of the government. That value can be defended *even if* the private sector would be less efficient. We suspect that many who make this (apparent) factual claim are really asserting a value claim.

However, it can often be dangerous to have your view of the "facts" be determined by your values. What if we do show that, for example, Medicare (a government program) is more efficient than private insurance companies? Will people holding a belief in the superiority of the private sector change their views? It's not likely, because their view comes from their values and therefore involves more than factual questions of efficiency.

On the other hand, there are situations where viewing the facts through a set of values can be beneficial. Consider this claim:

C2: "If you dare to dream, and believe in your dreams, you can accomplish anything."

There is no conceivable way that you can "do anything you dream." Most of us could never play basketball in the NBA or be a Navy SEAL or a rock star or write an award-winning novel. And even if we are one of those who could, accidents, twists of circumstances, or economic or political upheaval might still stop us.

What that statement is really arguing is that "it is better to try and fail than not to try." And it is arguing that those who act like they can accomplish their dreams live a better life than those who are always talking about how they are a victim. So, this is most productively understood as a value claim, once you get beneath the surface.

Confusing Value and Policy Claims

As you could mix fact and value claims, so also you can confuse value and policy claims. For example, debates about what should be illegal (a policy decision) are often made in terms of what is immoral (a value decision). The abortion debate comes to mind. It is perfectly legitimate to have values inform what public policy you argue for. The problem occurs specifically when you ignore the practical issues by focusing entirely on the value argument. The United States and many other countries do not have a law against adultery, despite its understood immorality, because enforcing such a law would likely be very impractical and could well cause more harm than it solves. In some places adultery is illegal, and we generally don't like the sort of societies that try to criminalize it.

Confusing Fact, Value, and Policy Claims

"Minority group X scores lower on intelligence test W than do white people."

Taken literally, this is only a fact claim. We administered test W, at time G, to a statistically significant group of people of the same age, and here are the results we got. Yet, that isn't all that is going on. Hearing that claim, in the context of a society with a tangled history of maltreatment of various groups, we may fear that this statement will be heard as a lot more than a neutral statement of fact.

Some would hear that fact claim as a value claim: "Group X is stupid!" Some would hear it as a policy claim of "Group X can be made fun of," or "Group X should be discriminated against" or worse.

Some would worry that this fact claim would trump other values we have. Maybe we have a value that how we treat individuals should have nothing to do with assumptions about the group they are from. But we also know that many do not have that value and that it is very difficult to separate our view of a group from how we treat the next individual from that group. And maybe we might have a value that facts of test scores are irrelevant or even dangerous.

Even as a pure fact claim, we can quickly slide into other issues. Why did that group score the way they did? Is the test culturally biased? Is it a reflection of poverty and lack of resources in the home? Does that culture have problems that don't support the value of doing well in school? Our values, and our fears or hopes for public policy, will quickly influence what conclusion we look for, accept, or dispute.

Separating out our claims is very valuable. But we do that separation to help us argue better the larger issue which almost always will involve claims of fact, value, and policy. And any policy issue inherently involves fact and value claims.

So How Can We Tell?

What if we can't tell or are not sure what type of claim it is? Ask yourself two questions. First, is there more than one issue here? Try separating them out. Then, if you really can't tell what type one specific claim is, ask yourself how you would prove it.

- Fact claims will rely upon empirical evidence, scientific methods, experiments, or theories about how the physical world works.
- Value claims will discuss a system of values.
- Policy claims will have implications for various practical issues of cost and enforcement and will involve subclaims of fact or values or both.

Test Cases

A couple of examples may help us work through the issues.

> C1: "High-fashion models are so thin they are unattractive."
>
> C2: "High-fashion models are unattractive to 65 percent of men aged 18 to 24."

(And we just made up the numbers in C2.) The first statement is a value claim, an evaluation. The second claim is a fact claim. It is asserting that a survey was conducted and these were the results of the survey. What people's evaluations are is a fact; their evaluations are values.

> C3: "The U.S. Supreme Court is usually right."
>
> C4: "I agree with the Supreme Court most of the time."

This case illustrates how our use of language can be misleading. Most of us think we're right most of the time, so anyone who agrees with us must be right. And we'd likely assign a high value to anyone who does agree with us.

However, C3, as stated, is a value claim. C4 is, as it is written, a fact claim. Here are my views, here are the court's, and they overlap. We suspect, however, that someone who says C4 is likely getting ready to make a positive evaluation of the court.

CONCLUSION

While we've used simple, one-sentence examples to show these three types of claims, things are often more confused in the real world. Sometimes you have to examine how the claim is actually developed in practice in order to determine if the argument is really about facts, values, or policy.

Moreover, any significant issue is almost always going to involve multiple claims and claims of all the various types. Policy issues will have to involve arguments about facts and values, and value claims often involve subissues of facts.

The value for your writing is that thinking through what type of claim you are making can help you organize your thoughts. You can separate out the issues and then write about each in turn.

The following chart may help you sort out the claim types.

TABLE 5.1

	Fact	Value	Policy
Description	Assert something is true or false.	Assert the worth of something.	Advocate a course of action.
Typical explicit form of the claim	"X is true." "X is false." "X has occurred, X is occurring, X does occur, X will occur." "X has (good/bad) (physically verifiable) effects."	"X is right." "X is good" (in a moral, aesthetic, religious, or ethical sense).	"We (should/should not) do X."
Means of evaluating validity of claim	Invoke shared empirical processes (e.g., scientific method) Use evidence Use logic	Refer to a value system. Argue how value system mandates the claim. Deal with alternative value systems that are proposed.	Evaluate current policy in terms of harms. Offer a plan that can solve or reduce harm. Defend your plan in terms of costs, benefits, practicality. Has subclaims of facts and values.
Undisputed example	Two plus two is four.	My life is important.	We must resolve our foreign wars as fast as practically possible.
Disputed example	Gore got more votes than Bush in Florida in the 2000 election.	You are responsible for what happens to you.	We should send more troops to our foreign military conflicts.
False example	The moon is made of green cheese.	It would be best if I ruled the world.	We should have presidential elections every two months.
Common misunderstandings	That they involve only "facts" and therefore there is nothing in dispute.	That they are "personal" and not subject to discussion. That they are "just your opinion" and so nothing can be decided. That the underlying value system is obvious to all.	That they can be proven by arguing the issue as a value claim. That values have no place here.
Shared problems	Cross-type contamination. Ambiguous claims (not qualified).		
Shared contribution	Many actual arguments involve claim types from all three of the types.		

Analyzing Fact Claims

INTRODUCTION

It's often said that "You can't argue with the facts." But what if we disagree about which things are facts? Actually, we have and will disagree about what is and is not a fact. Hence, we have fact claims. A fact claim asserts that something is true or that it is false.

In the chapters ahead, as we describe various types of arguments, we will use the terms "explicit form(s)" and "implicit form(s)." By *explicit form* we mean a way of describing a claim that openly and clearly shows what is going on. *Implicit forms* are examples of how that argument may be clothed in language that, while perfectly acceptable, does not clearly and concisely reveal the type of argument being made.

For fact claims:

Explicit forms: "X is true," "X was true," "X will be true."

Implicit forms: Can include statements such as: "X has occurred," "X is occurring in this location," "X is true sometimes," "X is clearly the case," "We can't rule out X being true." "We don't know if X is true." "X is true at a 90 percent confidence interval."

The scope of fact claims is vast, as you would suspect. Every field of human knowledge is full of them. Even fields that one might think would be about value claims primarily (say art) also have many factual issues (Is this painting authentic? What techniques and materials were used?).

Fact claims involve some significant issues. We have to sort out (again) just what we mean by "opinions" as they relate to facts; we have to talk about theories as ways of organizing sets of facts. But first of all we have to consider if it is possible to know what is and is not a fact.

CAN WE KNOW WHAT TRUTH IS?

> "Everyone is entitled to their own opinion, but not their own facts."
>
> Sen. Daniel Patrick Moynihan (quoted in Sobel, 1996)

Behind this quote lies an interesting problem that starts to raise some of the issues we have to deal with. This quotation is widely attributed to Senator Moynihan and is not attributed to anyone else. Yet, no one seems to be able to pinpoint reliably the source of the quotation: no speech, writing, essay, or book by the senator contains it. So, did he say it? Is it a true quotation or a false one? What if it "sounds like" something the senator would have said? What should we do now?

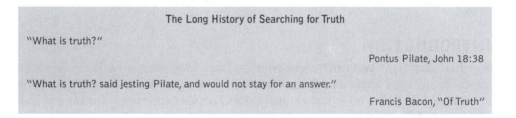

> **The Long History of Searching for Truth**
>
> "What is truth?"
>
> Pontus Pilate, John 18:38
>
> "What is truth? said jesting Pilate, and would not stay for an answer."
>
> Francis Bacon, "Of Truth"

We could hide that uncertainty and just use the saying, since it so readily fits as a starting point for this chapter. That would be to perpetuate a problem and not be very honest. We could refuse to use the saying because we can't document it. But that is to ignore the common view that it is something he said and would deprive us of the value of the insight—an insight we are eventually going to have to revise a bit. So we do what we are doing—use the quote, but call attention to the fact of the uncertainty about this fact.

Just What Are We Uncertain About?

Consider the ways you could be uncertain:

- We don't know if a fact is a fact. It's a new area for us, we haven't looked it up, we don't know if something is considered a fact or not. In this case we need to figure out how we can reliably (and efficiently) find out if something is or is not thought to be a fact.
- No one knows if it is a fact. A factual issue is undecided at this point. It's something no one can offer a good argument for one way or the other. So we know that we don't know.
- Some fact is only known approximately or tentatively at this point. We've got an idea, but not an exact number or don't know for sure.
- We hold a view of something being a fact but we don't know what everyone else thinks about it.

Notice how we are looking not just at "Is this true?" but also "What does the majority think is true?" This comes into play in many issues. Compare these two claims:

C1: "The theory of global warming is losing support among scientists every day."

C2: "While widely accepted, the theory of global warming has problems."

C1 and C2 both express opposition to the theory of a changing climate. The difference between them is in the claim made about what most people believe. Regardless of if the theory is true or not, it is certainly widely accepted among scientists. C1 reveals that in addition to holding a minority view, you are also in error about what others think. C2 shows that you do know what the majority believes, but you disagree with it.

Truth. Views high ...

"Truths everywhere are compatible; no truth clashes with any other truth. They are all the inhabitants of the same mansion and the stars of the same constellation. One truth in one corner of the world has to be harmonious and compatible with all truths elsewhere, or else it is not a truth."

Abdolrakim Soroush, *Reason, Freedom, and Democracy in Islam*, p. 21,
quoted in Peter D. Schmid, "Expect the Unexpected: A Religious Democracy in Iran,"
The Brown Journal of World Affairs, IX:2, p.181

... and low.

"As scarce as truth is, the supply has always been in excess of the demand."

Josh Billings, 1869, quoted in Robert Byrne,
The Third 637 Best Things Anybody Ever Said

"Whoever tells the truth is chased out of nine villages."

Attributed as a Turkish Proverb in George Seldes,, ed.,
The Great Quotations, Pocket Books, 1967, p. 917.,

You can't handle the truth.

A Few Good Men, 2005.

Do We Encounter the Truth on a Regular Basis?

Most of us get a good chunk of our information about the world from the mass media, directly or indirectly, and we make decisions about what is true based on that evidence. In the evidence chapter we discuss in more detail the faults of the media. But the bottom line is that their objective is to sell things, not to conduct research in a dispassionate search for truth. And thus, media representatives are not experts in separating fact from fiction.

On the one hand, we do understand this at a subconscious level, but, on the other hand, we don't tend to take that knowledge into account when we use the mass media to form our views on a subject.

Students can mistake this analysis of the media for a purely left-wing critique, understandably so, since so much of mass media is owned by very large companies that (quite often) seem to be promoting monopoly capitalism and prioritizing the needs of the rich. But this is to shrink the point we are trying to make. Our argument is not just that mass media is full of nonsense; it is that by being in that environment day after day we become influenced by it. And this means that most of us are not very good at separating fact from fiction since we haven't seen it done very well or very often.

In other words, being able to tell truth from fiction is not just about "saying what you feel"; it is a discipline, a skill, something you have to study and work at exactly like learning to play the piano or being a carpenter or running the offense on a basketball court. Intuition isn't enough, consulting a friend isn't enough. You can get fooled.

But there is an even bigger challenge here. Maybe we no longer believe in an objective, "out there" truth that can be reliably determined.

POSTMODERNISM OR SOPHISTICATED MODERNISM?

Many in our culture do not agree that there is an objective truth that can be found and validated. There are a number of factors at work here.

- **Academic postmodernism.** This view argues that there can be no direct path to a single true account of things; instead, there is a multiplicity of meanings inherent in any attempt to interpret the world. It suggests that judgments about truth have more to do with who holds power than about a dispassionate search to be objective. And therefore, a claim of objectivity is an illusion and a cover for oppression.
- The association of the concept of *objective truth* with **one privileged group**—white, heterosexual males of European descent—and the struggle of everyone else to achieve opportunities to join in the process, has, in some minds, tainted the concept of objective truth. Instead of seeing the pursuit of truth as a universal good, it seems to be associated with one particular group. So, an argument is made that there must be other ways of finding truth than the methods of rational argument.
- In popular culture there is a belief that things can be "**true for me**" and that my judgments about truth are mine to make and are not subject to critique by others.

This is a very complex subject, worthy of your serious thought. But for the purposes of this book, we have to cut to the chase. We support a philosophical viewpoint best described as *sophisticated modernism* that concedes that "absolute" or "timeless" truths are not humanly possible, but insists that such a conclusion does not render the idea of facts useless. Let's make a few observations.

- There is a difference between claiming that there is truth and claiming we can be sure we have found it. At the minimum, our faith in the value of reason is also combined with an awareness that all of our stock of facts is always up for review. Something we've thought of as fact might, after more study, turn out not to be a fact.
- Our social location, our position in society, does affect our view of things. People's judgments are indeed influenced by their gender, economic class,

race, culture of origin, native language, religion, sexual orientation, family background, and many other factors. But we would argue that this is true for everyone; there is no privileged group, no matter how powerful or how oppressed, that can simply make assertions about themselves and the world and have those assertions be exempt from the process of finding the truth.

- Truth is a process, not a destination. Remember our discussion of fundamentalism in chapter two? The view that truth was already known? Again we reject that stance. We are describing methods for discerning fact from fiction, but not laying out what the end of the trip looks like.
- The trip is worth it. Pursuing this process does indeed get somewhere; we can advance and not simply replace one idea with another.

Out of these ideas comes a certain perspective on the process of arguing factual claims.

- It would be better to abandon a binary notion of things being either true or not true and accept a probabilistic concept. That is, instead of insisting that things are either true or not, we would explicitly include with our facts an assessment of just how certain we are about that. We might be pretty sure of one group of facts, really sure of a second group, and only kind of certain about a third set. This involves keeping track of just what sort of evidence we have to support our fact claims.
- While we can defend the facts we have with the concepts we have, we also know that time will advance and some of the things we firmly believe (with good reason) now will have to be abandoned in the future.
- The goal should be, in philosopher Richard Rorty's words, solidarity rather than objectivity (1989). The best way to produce claims that can stand the test of time as factual are those we *argue* about and win the assent of other reasonable people.

WELCOME TO THE COMMUNITY OF TRUTH SEEKERS

Facts are something that do not belong to us as individuals. Precisely because we don't fully trust ourselves, we allow the community to help decide with us what is true.

- We accept that there is a "marketplace of ideas." Factual claims are debated in public and others get to comment and critique our factual opinions.
- To make that marketplace of ideas work, there have to be shared criteria for what is considered to be true. Remember the discussion in the second chapter about how arguments will break down when there is an absence of shared processes for deciding.

As a result of this, we probably need to revise the quote attributed to the senator. Let's try this:

Everyone is entitled to their own opinions (but I can argue with you about them), but not their own facts (when the relevant community has, through rational argument, reached a near-consensus on a fact being true—but you can always offer counter-evidence as long as it follows the conventions for determination of validity).

That doesn't really fit on a bumper sticker nor can we shout it at someone in an argument. But it is a little closer to what can work.

THAT'S JUST A THEORY

There has been an ongoing battle in the United States over the teaching of the theory of evolution in schools. Why that issue is such concern to some is beyond the scope of our book. Part of the debate has concerned how theories should be regarded. The statement "That's just a theory" is used to imply that this is only speculation or without foundation. The attack is based on a very fundamental misunderstanding about theories and their relationship to the community who formulates and evaluates them.

Theories are ways of organizing information into patterns. Theories do change over time, are sometimes overturned, but the larger the theory—the more it explains, the more it has been tested—the less likely it is to be overturned. And even when a theory is proven wrong, it often is simply absorbed into a broader theory or is shown to be a special case of a bigger generalization. Theories are not guesses or hunches. They are not unconnected to data.

There are various lists of criteria used to judge theories; one set might include the following:

- Agreement with data. The theory has been tested and tested by more than one person.
- Coherence. The theory is internally consistent.
- Scope. The more a theory explains, the more valuable it is.
- Fertility. The theory suggests new ideas to test or research.
- Simplicity. A simple theory is preferred to a complex one, other things being equal.
- Predictions. A theory predicts how things will behave; it can be used to anticipate how things will turn out.

There are also things that do not fatally undermine a theory, even though some use them to attack a theory:

- Unexplained data. Data that a theory can't explain is not the same as data that directly contradicts a theory.
- Data that contradicts other data.

In other words, all theories have "loose ends." We don't have a theory of everything and likely never will do so. But the existence of some anomalies does not disprove a theory that has met the criteria we gave to judge theories.

We can perhaps explain this better by considering an example. There is a theory that Hitler killed about six million Jews and members of other groups he called defective and did so at various camps in Eastern Europe. That theory has been attacked by people called "Holocaust deniers."

What evidence do they offer? They point to some eyewitness testimony that has been contradicted by physical evidence. They point out that there has never been a document produced that is an order from Hitler to kill all those people. There are some missing records, and there isn't a specific count of missing individuals that number six million.

And? On the other hand, there is ample testimony about a system of intentional killing from people in the camps, guards, German officials, and Allied troops who invaded Germany. Hitler had orated about the evil of the Jews for years and repeatedly called for them to be removed from Germany. And there is other affirmative evidence (such as forensic evidence and photographs) as well.

In short, there are thousands of pieces of evidence to support the theory. Additionally, the theory is in agreement with our other theories about Hitler and the leaders around him and the views of the German people at that time.

All the alternative theories advanced to explain all those missing people—privation of war, emigration, etc.—have far worse problems with data, more loose ends, and more contradictions to overcome.

If there was no Holocaust, then many other theories would have to be overturned. And the few anomalies in the data for the existence of the Holocaust are no different than the residual problems and inconsistencies that affect any attempt at historical reconstruction. So, believe that the Holocaust happened.

THAT'S JUST YOUR OPINION

Now we need to take another look at the (false) division of facts from opinions. Consider this claim:

> "Two plus two equals four."

That's about as solid a fact as you could get. But, as mentioned before, have you ever tried to teach it to a two year old? Well, what about:

> "Climate change is happening, and it is due to human action."

Even people who think that is true might be caught using the term "opinion" to describe it, but in what way is it different than the first claim? The world is either getting hotter or not, temperature is a real thing, human action either contributed to it or not. It's not that the first claim is simple and the second is complex—proving the first, really proving it, not just asserting it, requires some actual thinking.

The second claim is different in that we may be uncertain about it. We could be uncertain about if climate change is occurring or we could know it is happening but be uncertain about how much and how fast the world is warming up. It is also different in that some disagree with it, while it is hard to think of any adults who disagree with the first claim. But most people with professional expertise in the relevant science are quite certain about the second claim.

So what does it mean when someone who disagrees with the second claim announces that "it's just your opinion" that the claim is true? This is an attempt to reduce the judgment of the first person to a personal preference, a whim. It shouldn't be persuasive. The opinion in this case is not a personal whim, or arbitrary preference; it is the result of judgment, based on a range of data, by a person involved with others who are also expressing their judgment.

But, the majority isn't always right. Should we allow the majority to silence minority views? We maintain a careful balance. People are autonomous, and we don't have thought police who monitor what judgments people have. You can hold whatever view you like without fear of being put in prison.

But there are consequences (in intellectual terms) of holding a variant view. If you can't defend your view, then people are entitled to lower their opinion of you. If you can defend it, then people may not agree with you, but they should at least respect you and listen to you.

In terms of the global warming debate, there is a difference about ways that those in the minority reject the claim. Someone who says something like "Oh, those scientists, they're always coming up with something about how everything is our fault" deserves not to be taken seriously. Their view is unconnected with anything else and is generally given without any data to support it.

Someone else who takes issue with a particular temperature reading, raises specific questions about data, disputes a specific causal mechanism—those people cannot be dismissed. Both of these have opinions: one is part of the normal process of give and take, the other is not.

So, to summarize about opinions:

- Opinions are judgments about the truth or falsehood of a fact. They can be evaluated by others.

DO WE VOTE ON TRUTH?

We've been discussing the notion of "consensus" about something being a fact. However, even if we limit ourselves to a community of experts and the consensus views they hold, we can easily find examples where the majority turned out to be wrong. This is true not just in humanities, social sciences, and related fields, but also in the so-called "hard" sciences as well. The majority is not always right.

But the majority should get some consideration. Behind that majority view, in any field of endeavor, is a community that has deliberated, discussed, and argued an issue before coming to a consensus. It is that process and the steps along the way that privilege the consensus view and give it a status to be respected.

So now someone comes along who wants to question the consensus view. Sometimes we dismiss those people out of hand, and sometimes we give them an almost romantic status as outlaws or renegades and think they must be on to something just because they espouse a minority view. Neither is a very good idea.

Some better things to take into account would be the following:

- Are they part of the community, participating in the arguments, or have they rejected the entire ongoing community of discourse in their subject? In other words, do they take the elements, the pieces that went into a consensus view, and rearrange them, challenge a few of them, propose new ones, or are they totally outside the methodology of how the community operates?
- Have they rejected the methodology and the assumptions of the community but retain the larger principles about finding truth?
- Do they use the very same methods for determining truth, or are they even rejecting the ways truth is found?

The first of these examples is how communities progress. What that person is doing is challenging a blind spot of the community. They accept the rules for finding truth but argue that the community isn't consistently applying them. But, in the second and third examples, they are rejecting more and more of the tradition and therefore they need to have more and more evidence and proof for their view.

So now we can posit some rules for challenging the consensus:
You are entitled

- to make a case for what you think is true;
- to disagree with the consensus opinion, even an overwhelming consensus;
- to remind the majority that truth is not determined by voting but by deliberation leading to consensus.

But you are not entitled

- to make assertions without evidence;
- to assert your own rules of finding the truth—but you can argue that you have found a new one and present evidence for it;
- to pretend there is no consensus of opinion or that consensus is automatically wrong.

BUT WHAT ABOUT A HERO?

We've all read stories about people who had an idea that no one else believed. They labored alone, without friends, overcame roadblocks, suffered public ostracism for years, until finally one day, they were vindicated as being right.

"They laughed at Einstein, they laughed at Newton," so don't we find out things by brave people who ignore what the world says? Doesn't it seem like the world has to be dragged forward by visionaries? How many movies and television shows do we see where everyone knows what has happened but one person "has a hunch" and is always proven to be right?

Well, for every Einstein, there are a score of other people who have an idea, labor alone, are convinced they are right, and know the rest of the world believes an illusion—and are total crackpots or just misguided people. And the world laughs at them too.

Do you think we'd be better off if we just accepted uncritically everyone who had a passionate belief in their own correctness? Would that really give us better results? Or would we be better off if we just quit trying, just said it was all politics and spin and power and there was no way we could ever actually improve our understanding of what is and what is not true?

Again, the process of finding out the truth is not simple or perfect, but we don't seem to know of any better way.

Does that seem too simple? You might be thinking of instances where the majority was blind to the facts of the suffering of an oppressed group, had developed a "scientific" theory to justify racism, held that women's brains couldn't do what men's could, or anyone of dozens of other examples. Or, maybe you're in some community where you're tired of the consensus being thought a "fact" that women are nicer than men, or you wonder at the "science" that proves that religions have caused all the evil in the world. The majority can be wrong and can and does inflict a lot of pain on minorities of all type.

But again, what other procedure would be better *for all situations*? And remember, that part of this process is always to maintain a degree of tentativeness and openness to being wrong. The holder of a minority view can certainly remind the majority of that.

MEANWHILE, BACK IN YOUR WORLD

From all we've written in this chapter up to now, it might appear that the issue of fact claims only apply to serious issues in science or the scholarly community in general. Few of you, in the next few weeks, will be arguing about the exact chronology of the battle of Marathon or attempting to pin down how many dimensions are needed for string theory (we won't be either). What about the ordinary, day-to-day, decisions of fact we all (including scholars) make? What if our claims are about if busses run on Sunday or who left the window open last night and let the bugs in?

What happens in this case is the same process, but vastly scaled down. Let's consider a factual claim:

C: "Course X is required for graduating in major Y."

You think it is, your neighbor down the hall is certain it isn't. So we're back to being uncertain about a fact and uncertain about how widely this fact is believed. So what do you do? You likely check, don't you? You gather more data. You decide to ask the advisors and to check the departmental website for graduation requirements.

When you (wisely) pick those two sources, you might say that these are authoritative sources (consult the chapter on argument from authority), but we'd draw your attention to how each of these two sources are deeply embedded in the relevant community of experts. The website is looked at by the community (the department)—if anything is on there and wrong, many people will see it fairly soon. The advisors are talking to many students and talking to other advisors and to their supervisors. If they give out wrong advice, they should hear about it soon.

But wait, you say, "I heard a story about some advisor who was clueless, and the departmental website is old and out of date." Remember, we told you there was no guarantee, and no one (or no document) gets a pass for being assumed to be perfect. If you pick up a hint that something is amiss, what will you do? You'll go to some authority in the department and, in effect, argue that "I think there is a mistake here, and here is my evidence for that."

But wait, you say (again), "I remember how last year some student had to take weeks to prove to the dean of undergraduate studies that they'd set up two contradictory requirements. She almost didn't graduate." Well, remember (again) that we told you the majority can be wrong? But to prove they are wrong that student needed to use forms of truth-finding that she and the department agreed upon. They didn't take her word for it, and they shouldn't have taken her word. She had to assemble documents and organize a logical argument to make her case.

But wait, you say (yet again), you did all this, got confirmation from everyone about what the requirements are, got it in writing on your graduation plan, and that guy down the hall just said to you, "Well, that's your opinion" and still thinks he's right. Now, you are permitted and advised to, on this particular subject and without being mean, ignore him. Tell him we said so.

Sorry, but that is life. That's either bad news (because there is no utter, total, absolute certainty) or good news (because we're all on a great adventure together to figure out the universe).

DEVELOPING A FACT CLAIM

You want to write a paper advancing and defending a fact claim. How do you do it? The ideal would be that your evidence for your claim would meet all of the following criteria.

- **Multiple sources**. You have more than one piece of data, more than one source that supports your idea.
- **Reproducible** results. Whatever data you are relying on has been verified by others. Your claim does not rest on the laws of physics being different for you.
- **Tested** conclusions. You can show that if your factual claim is true, it would lead to certain predictions or expectations about behavior, and you can further show that these predictions are accurate.
- **Traceable** data. You are not relying on any secret or hidden data. Everything is out in the open.
- **Consistent** with other generally accepted facts. Your fact claim fits into the world of fact claims. Your claim being true would not require other known facts to be overturned. Or, if you are proposing a change in what is known, you at least can indicate what other facts should be challenged and perhaps even show how our erroneous view occurred.

CONCLUSION

Proving that something is true is perhaps a bit harder than you expected. But knowing that, you can understand why those who do go through the effort to prove their claims in the marketplace of ideas inhabited by other experts are resistant to unsupported ideas claimed by those who are not in dialog with other experts.

Finding the truth is hard, we are often fooled, perhaps we will never shed all of our illusions—but it is a worthy goal. We can recognize the difficulties without yielding to nihilism.

SUMMARY FOR FACT CLAIMS

Description
A fact claim asserts that something is true or false.

Explicit form
"X is true."

Implicit forms can include statements like:

"X is true at a 90 percent confidence interval." "X has occurred," "X is occurring," "X does occur," "X will occur." "We can't rule out X being true." "We don't know if X is true."

Examples of statements that would typically be developed as fact claims

"The number of abortions is rising."
"Fashion models are thinner than they were ten years ago."
"Pepsi is regarded as the best tasting soda."
"There is a civil war going on in Iraq."
"Our product sales increased 20 percent last quarter."

Issues and Aspects

- Fact claims can be false.
- Even noncontroversial statements are fact claims.
- We have opinions about facts.
- The concept of "theory" is widely misunderstood as meaning a speculative opinion.

Study Questions

- What does "supported by an accepted theory" mean?
- What should you do if you think the majority is wrong about something?
- Why is the division of "facts" vs. "opinions" very misleading?

Analyzing Value Claims

INTRODUCTION

> If there is magic on this planet, it is contained in water. Its least stir even, as now in a rain pond on a flat roof opposite my office, is enough to bring me searching to the window. A wind ripple may be translating itself into life. I have a constant feeling that some time I may witness that momentous miracle on a city roof, see life veritably and suddenly boiling out of a heap of rusted pipes and old television aerials. (Eiseley, 1959, p. 15)

What sort of claim, what sort of argument is being made here? The author certainly does not intend to make a factual claim that a pile of rusted pipes will, under laboratory conditions, generate a flock of birds or an elephant. He is using language in a poetic style to evoke (and defend) a way of looking at the world. He argues that it is better to see the world full of possibilities, tending toward life. And that is a value claim.

Value claims will often involve factual issues (as we will see), but value claims are about something else. They are about meaning, purpose, what is good, virtuous, or moral. They are sometimes called *evaluation arguments* because they ask for a judgment on something: Is this a good movie? Is that the proper behavior? So value claims certainly are about ethics and morals but they include more than that.

The simplest form of a value claim would be:

C: "X is good." (in a moral or ethical sense)

The Scope of Value Claims

Value claims form a part of many hotly debated topics. Value claims encompass a very wide range of issues, including:

- "Big issues" of life and society like religion, moral dilemmas, and how we live in society together. Is it right for the state to employ capital punishment for murderers? Is abortion wrong? Do we have a right to torture people if we think they might have information on terrorism?

- Important personal issues about the direction of our lives. Am I wrong to party so much and so hard? Should our child be able to see R-rated movies? Is it wrong that we've not gone to church this year? How should I treat my neighbor who is different from me? Should I tell jokes that are racist?
- "Everyday issues" like what are the best clothes to wear, if that is a good hotel, or what your preferences are in weather or food.
- Esthetic issues concerning art, movies, or literature.

Even harder is trying to figure out how to make and defend value arguments.

WHY VALUE ARGUMENTS ARE DIFFICULT

With value claims, we now enter a very different world from fact claims. While we all sort of understand what values are, and we all have values and we defend our values, it will turn out that getting a firm handle on how to develop, present, and rebut value arguments will be quite difficult. In general, people have no clear idea how to structure an argument based on values.

What Is a Value Argument About?

We should begin by thinking about the term "values." A useful definition is provided by Rokeach:

> A *value* is an enduring belief that a specific mode of conduct or end-state of existence is personally or socially preferable to an opposite or converse mode of conduct or end-state of existence. A *value system* is an enduring organization of beliefs concerning preferable modes of conduct or end-states of existence along a continuum of relative importance. (Rokeach, 1973 p. 5) **[Emphasis in Original]**

Note how values are placed within a larger construct called a *value system*. These are ways of organizing our approach to the world. Values describe what we think is important about how we should behave. When we argue about values, we're arguing not about what is or is not "out there in the world." We're arguing about what is the right way to behave.

But, right away, it gets complicated.

There is No Single, Universally Accepted Set of Criteria for Evaluating Value Questions

There isn't just one value system that everyone agrees to. In fact, there are many sources of values that people use to organize their approach to life. It is worth listing some.

- Religion (Christianity, Judaism, Islam, Eastern religions, Native religions, New Age religions, Wicca, Gaia, civil religion, universal religious values)
- Secular religions (Scientism, Social Darwinism, Communism, Stalinism, Nazism, the Market)

- Nature/Ecology that includes views about the spiritual value of wilderness, the rights of animals, and the rights of nature
- Cultural norms that include such concepts as dignity, honor, hospitality, being a good neighbor, eating rituals, proper roles for men and women, customs for bribery, haggling, gift giving, the status of elders (and others), the view of the family or clan and tribe
- Folk beliefs and maxims such as "what you put into life is what you get out of it" or the evil eye
- Personal growth (self-actualization, self-help, the personal journey)
- National (patriotism, loyalty to nation, following the American Dream)
- Democratic (liberty, justice, freedom, separation of powers, majority rule, minority rights, freedom of speech, freedom of religion)
- Values specific to the culture of the United States that might include concepts such as: being on time, winning, individualism, consumerism, big-time sports, innovation, moral exceptionalism, rejection of learning other languages, anti-intellectualism
- Utility (maximize benefit, minimize harm, greatest happiness for the greatest number)
- Feminist or Womanist
- Systems based around long cultural traditions such as Africa or Asia
- Esthetic (art, music, literature, film), placing worth on concepts such as innovation, creativity, and challenging accepted views
- Business/Competition, with values thought essential for life in a capitalist society such as competition being virtuous, self-reliance, teamwork, negotiations, sportsmanship, financial rewards as virtuous
- The warrior, as for example in Homer, promoting values of honor, duty, a noble death, battle prowess as a requirement for leadership, "smack talk" as a virtue
- Science, with values like rationality, objectivity, dispassion, testable hypotheses, disclosure, transparency, the pursuit of knowledge
- Engineering, with values such as elegance, simplicity, or "form follows function"

This is quite a list, and the authors have no confidence that the list is complete. And we certainly are not claiming that the way this list is framed and sorted is the best, the only, or even a consistent way of doing it. We are merely trying to point out that "values" is a category with a very diverse set of concepts in it.

Why are there so many value systems? Why do they continue to persist? That question takes us beyond the scope of this book, but it is something we, as advocates, have to deal with. Perhaps, in part, this diversity is because each system is incomplete in some way and does not provide an answer to all human situations. Because there are many value systems, arguments about values will often involve disputes between value systems or even involve arguments about which value system applies in a particular case. We will discuss this later in the chapter.

Some of the attempts to gain consensus on certain aspects of shared values are reflected in documents such as the U.S. Declaration of Independence, the Universal Declaration of Human Rights, the U.S. Bill of Rights, and other constitutional declarations.

The Consequences and Opportunities Created by the Existence of Multiple Value Systems

That more than one value system exists is not simply a philosophical problem. Each of us hold values from several different systems, and most of us really haven't worked out all the boundaries and contradictions between the systems for ourselves. On a day-to-day basis we instinctively choose what values to invoke and seldom consciously debate how to reconcile our views.

> Each group to which a person belongs inculcates that person with its values and their ranking of importance. Individuals do not unquestioningly absorb all the values of the groups to which they belong; they accept some and reject others. Most individuals belong to more than one social group. The values of each group are often in conflict: religious values may conflict with generational values or gender values with organizational practices. (U.S., *Counterinsurgency* [Army Field Manual], 2006, p. 3)

Note the source. The general given charge of U.S. forces in Iraq in 2007, David Petraeus, was often referred to as the one who "wrote the book on counterinsurgency." Well, this quote is from that book. The book was generated during a recent example of the consequences of failing to understand the values of others we deal with and failing to understand how to work with the multiple value systems of others. This problem has generated much trouble in many situations and not just for American foreign policy.

We can explore this further. To take an example from the issues addressed by the Field Manual, many in the United States wonder why many Arabs can contend that they are peaceful and yet express an admiration for Bin Laden or for Saddam Hussein. Doesn't this contradict a value system of justice and peace? But there is also the value system that values self-respect and reacts negatively to humiliation. In that frame of reference, those two, otherwise despicable, people are seen as people who stood up to those who humiliated the Arabs. We are not entirely different. We have the expression, "He's a jerk, but he's our jerk." It describes a common situation where on the one hand you don't value how someone is behaving, but you also do not value others criticizing someone who is part of your group. You may utterly despise your parents, but woe to anyone outside the family who criticizes them.

So people navigate among their value systems, choosing what to emphasize and what to downplay. On a more personal level, one of the authors knew a woman in college who was studying to be an electrical engineer in the days when few women went into engineering. Her conservative father was not too happy about this; he held the value that a woman's place was in the home. However, he loved his daughter and couldn't deny her ambition, so he invoked a different value system and chose to see her career ambition through the lens of family pride and looking out for one's own, his expressed value being that "No one is going to tell my daughter what she can't do." This distinction—choosing which values system to frame an issue rather than rejecting a previously held value—will reappear below when we discuss how to construct a defense for our value claims.

People Do Not Change Their Values Easily

Values are not just a casual opinion that we have nothing much invested in; they are often part and parcel of our very definition of our selves.

Values are tied up with our view of the world and our place in it. We all die, but how should we live? Party like there is no tomorrow? Work hard and be respectable? Try to give your children something better? These are value questions tied very closely to ultimate questions.

We also take values from what group we belong to and our pride at being part of a heritage and a way of life. Values are often affected by our gender, ethnic group, age, sexual orientation, religion, citizenship, financial status, and other factors. Values are how we were raised, what we have felt "in our bones" is right since we could think about such things. Thus people closely identify with them, and changing a value is not something done lightly.

Don't expect that in a brief argument that you can change someone's values. And because of what we have just said, challenging a person's values is often taken personally in a way challenging a factual opinion is not.

However, values do change over time. In the last fifty years in the United States, there have been major shifts of values concerning civil rights, protection of the environment, the role of women in the workforce and the legal rights they are entitled to. We've become far more informal in our dress, profanity has become acceptable in more situations, and the depiction of violence in the media has increased. There has also been a major shift in the acceptability of divorce, sex outside of marriage, and of homosexuality. Of course, none of these shifts is complete or undisputed, but it is undeniable that the United States today has very different values on these issues than fifty years ago.

But, the difficulty of these changes underscores the tenacity with which values are held. None of those changes occurred without strife. In some cases the strife was all between individuals or within families, but in the case of the civil rights movement, for example, the debate over values led to violence and murder.

Can You Even Argue Values?

With all these diverse values, it might be odd to realize that some seem to believe that values cannot be argued at all. Values are thought to be "personal" or "my opinion." People will say that "I just believe that" or "I don't care what you say, I was taught this." It is often said that values are "just a personal opinion," and how can you argue a personal view?

We think there are two issues here that are being mixed together. Most of us hold a value that says that adults are autonomous and can, to a greater or lesser extent, run their own lives. Not every culture puts such a high value on individual autonomy as does the United States, but most have some notion of a freedom of opinion. In this view, it is not right to force someone to believe something. Despite all the coercion done in the world, the belief systems of cultures, nations, and religions generally agree on people being free in their personal views.

But, this freedom from coercion does not mean that people do not debate values. In recent years in the United States many debates have occurred on various social issues. These public debates have had value disagreements at their core. What is the value of refraining from torture of suspected terrorists? What is the value of wilderness? Is the increasing violence in the media affecting us? Abortion, the size of government, homosexuality—it's one thing to have your personal opinion about those issues (and others) but we have to decide on laws, and so there is no choice but to try to debate and persuade others.

Debates over values also occupy us in our personal relationships. A couple debates what values will govern how they choose to spend money, raise children, relate to others, and so on. We teach values to our children or try to. We debate moral choices with ourselves. The college years are often a time when young people have many debates about how to sort out the basic approaches to living life.

So, values are in fact disputed and discussed. But there are reasons why those discussions do not proceed well, and we have to examine those. Perhaps some of the reason for thinking that values are "just my view" of the world is that we are not very good at articulating why we hold those values and not very good at debating others who aren't very good at articulating why they hold their values.

It's Hard to Argue About Something That You've Always Assumed Is Right

Perhaps you've gotten into an argument about some issue of behavior, only to have the other person just say forcefully, "It's just wrong!" perhaps with some fist-pounding to go along with it. Maybe you've done that yourself. And when the person who says "It's just wrong" is questioned, the answer is often, "Because it just is!" By now you should recognize that this is an assertion, not an argument.

"Everyone has a right to …. How can you deny anyone their rights?"

In this example it appears that an argument is being made. The writer is asserting that people who wish to deny a right need to make a case for their view. But this is actually yet another assertion. Why does "everyone have a right to" the specific topic we are discussing? If asked, this right may be linked to "freedom" or "not to be discriminated against" but it's seldom defined or explained how it is applied to the current situation.

Here is a somewhat longer example of the same thing from a student paper:

"I would like to state that I am personally against physician-assisted suicide because I believe it to be wrong for someone to be given the option to end their life early by a single lethal injection. It is not right for people to be given the option to die sooner than they have to even if there is intense pain or suffering involved. Yes, I feel sorry for these people that have to suffer but I still believe it to be wrong, especially in our culture, with all of our new medical advances and improvements. To me, I simply see this as being an easier form of suicide and I don't believe in this at all."

While this might seem like an extended defense of his position, read carefully and you can see that it is simply a chain of assertions that boil down to the statement "This is wrong." This is an example of the fallacy of "assuming the conclusion." Instead of providing an argument to prove that assisted suicide is wrong, he asserts it.

This is not a problem of students only:

> "I know what I believe. I will continue to articulate what I believe and what I believe—I believe what I believe is right."
>
> George W. Bush, said during an informal meeting with journalists in Rome, Italy, July 22, 2001

It sounds like a forthright and noble declaration of commitment—but there is no content here.

If you've come this far in this book, you know that an unsupported assertion is not an argument and shouldn't be very persuasive with people. We'll have to do more.

The Implications for Your Arguments

What we have presented so far leads to two implications for how you develop value arguments. First, you will need to work at how to articulate your case in terms of a value system. We'll have a lot to say about that in the rest of the chapter. But you should be on the alert that this is harder than you might think it might be.

Second, any given value argument probably involves multiple value systems and an audience who holds values from those various systems. Thus, to make your case, you have to not only sort out what values and value systems apply but also what value systems (warrants) your audience is using. This sorting is hard, but is also an opportunity to the advocate to reframe a debate into a different value system. We'll show you some examples of that later in the chapter.

FACTS AND VALUES

As we start to move in the direction of formulating a defense for value claims, there are a number of concepts that are useful to sort out. The first of these is to examine the complicated set of connections between fact statements and value statements.

Value claims can be presented as fact claims. When we first discussed the three types of claims, we stressed the ability to look at a one-sentence claim and tell what type it was. But we hedged our bets by pointing out that often people don't frame their claim in a way that accurately points you to how they intend to develop it. So, we need to consider some situations where the claim superficially looks like one type of claim but is better understood as a different type of claim.

Example 1

C1: "There is always an alternative to getting an abortion."

This looks like a factual claim, but it's probably not. Let's rephrase this in two possible ways to show the difference.

C2: "Whatever the circumstances, it is physically possible for a pregnant woman not to have an abortion."

C3: "Abortion is so wrong that you should spend a great deal of effort to try to find an alternative to having one."

C2 is a fact claim. But most likely the person making the claim meant C3, which is a value claim. The advocate thinks that abortion has such moral consequences that it is worth spending significant time and money to avoid one. This example is interesting, because even a person who meant C3 might well choose to develop their argument using statements that sound like support for a fact claim.

Example 2

Connections between facts and values can be more complicated. Consider the following statement (and feel free to substitute your university in the claim):

C: "The University of Minnesota is the best school for Communication Studies in the Big Ten."

That sounds like it is a factual claim. But it's not that simple. The person arguing for this could mean one of three (or more) rather different things. We can expose this by thinking about what sort of grounds would be offered in support of the claim. Consider this:

G1: "Here are several objective and accepted criteria of quality in an academic institution that put the University of Minnesota at the top."

In that case, it is possible that this argument will be a factual claim. The argument would be about if the school did or did not meet the criteria. But wait, what is the definition of "quality" that would be hiding in a warrant?

W1: "The best academic institutions prepare their students to be successful in their careers."

W2: "The best academic institutions train their students to search for knowledge and the truth, wherever it leads them."

Choosing between those warrants is a value question, not a factual issue. But, let's look at a different type of ground that could be offered for the claim:

G2: "It's a great and fun place to be, and my fellow students are cool."

In this case, we have a value claim. Criteria about being fun or fashionable are not really factual issues. You could be debating if you are having fun or if students here are more enjoyable than other schools—and that would be factual, but by and large we're moving away from factual issues. But here is a third set of grounds:

G3: "The instructors are all progressive."

This is clearly now a value argument. The warrant that being progressive is a good thing for instructors at a university is a value judgment, not a factual claim. Thus, that is an argument over values.

Example 3

One of the most common value claims presented as a fact claim is this one that we briefly looked at before.

C1: "If you try hard enough, you can do anything."

This has many variations involving believing in your dreams, never giving up, and so on. If it really was a factual claim, it is totally absurd. Most of us, no matter how hard we work, cannot play in the National Basketball Association, write a great novel, ride in the Tour de France, become an astronaut, or any one of many other hard things. And if "anything" is meant literally, then it seems odd that no one has solved cancer, walked on water, cured the common cold, or provided adequate parking at your university. The claim must mean something else. Here are some things that claim might mean.

C2: "You can do more than you think you can."
C3: "You are more often defeated by your own acceptance of limitations than you are by external circumstances."

These could be factual claims. Now that they are limited and specific, they might form the basis for an interesting discussion. However, most likely, people mean something like these claims:

C4: "It's better to try and fail than not to try."
C5: "Go for it."
C6: "It is better to live optimistically than to live afraid."

Those are value claims. There are many examples like this from the self-help industry. Claims such as C1 are aimed at situations where believing that you can do something is a perquisite for motivating yourself to do it. There's nothing wrong with this, but this is clearly about values, not facts.

Our values can drive our decisions about facts. A different type of fact-value confusion is when we let values drive our perspective on the facts. Here, our views of what we want to be true affect our judgments of what is true. An example of this is the last several years of the debate about global warming.

Why has this debate generated so much anger from some? Isn't the question of "Is climate change occurring due to human action?" a purely scientific question of fact? Why do some seem eager to believe it, while others so passionately reject the data? This has become clearer in recent years when the data for the existence of climate change has become more persuasive.

Each side has certain values—and each side assumes the other side has certain values—values they disagree with.

Let's start with two quotes from global warming "deniers":

The primary advocates of global warming remain the environmentalists. They propose a drastic solution to a non-existent problem—a solution which is, amazingly, the same political policy they have unsuccessfully sought to impose for decades. Many of their leaders oppose free markets and seek to limit human development, and global warming is currently the best means to these ends. If people are hurt in the process, so be it. (Johnston, 2001, p. A10)

In fact, this false religion was founded upon the most base materialistic motivations. It's not about saving the planet. It's not about God and spiritual matters. It's not even about doing good. Instead, it's about money and power. It's just the latest and most sophisticated effort by elitists to empower themselves at the expense of the people and the rule of law by redistributing wealth as they see fit. (Farah, 2008)

Both quotations attribute certain values to those who think global warming is real and should be dealt with. The authors of these quotations (who do not believe in global warming) suspect that proponents (who do believe in it) are opposed to the free market or are elitists who want to redistribute money from those who have it to those who don't. By inference then, we can understand the values of these authors (and others like them) who find these values alarming: They value the free operation of economic entities and oppose regulations for social purposes. They would likely value maximum personal freedom and see policy changes to deal with global warming as restricting their choices.

From this perspective, their opposition becomes more understandable. From a different perspective, significant climate change would likely mean new opportunities for business to produce more energy-efficient products. Shifting populations and crops will create business opportunities and carbon-offsets, and other new economic developments will need to be financed. It would seem that the opportunities to develop wealth from climate change might excite those who identify with unfettered capitalism.

But opponents see climate change as empowering a group who they view as hating capitalism. Then their opposition, their angry opposition, can be understood: If climate change is real, then people with values they object to will gain power.

This dynamic also can affect those who quickly adopted the view that climate change was real and adopted it without careful review of the science. Among those who quickly adopted the view that climate change was real would certainly include those who saw it as one more example of why large concentrations of economic power should be broken up or further proof that wilderness was valuable, or why living simply was a moral imperative. In other words, whatever the intense scientific debate that has occurred, many people decided on their view of the facts based on which facts would be the most consistent with their values.

We are not accusing either side of being conniving or questioning their motives. If you view the world a certain way, you tend to notice things that confirm your view of the world.

The lesson for us as advocates is this: If you encounter a debate that, on the surface, seems to be just about a factual dispute, but is generating a large amount of passion among the participants, it might be useful to ask yourself what values are involved on both sides.

But it's a fact! Be careful when someone (or you) tries to argue that values are actually facts. "It's just a fact that a kid needs two parents—a mom and a dad." We will discuss in the next section some situations that do link factual debates to value claims, but we think something else is going on here. We give weight to facts; they seem to be trump cards in our debates. They are unanswerable (or so we suppose). So, we can hope to gain persuasiveness for our value arguments if we can claim they are factual arguments. But values, at the core, are not just about facts. They are about judgments of worth and how we sort through our choices in life.

Racist views can be supported by factual claims about the inferiority of certain groups. Attacks on the conservative movement can be buttressed by claims about the factual ignorance of right-wing people or by claims that their only motivation is racism.

Additionally, there are also much more serious efforts to argue that all value arguments can be reduced to discussions about maximizing happiness or about promoting the survival of the species or that values can be found in studies of the brain. Often all these claims do is to assume that one particular value (like maximizing happiness) are "obviously" true.

We'd encourage you not to devalue value claims or to try to convert them into fact claims. There should be *more* discussion about how we should view life and decide how to make our choices. This is something quintessentially human. It has occupied philosophers, theologians, and artists for centuries and motivated the production of many of our most valued cultural artifacts.

CLARIFYING TYPES OF VALUES

Some of our difficulty about arguing values is because we have different types of values. These different types each seem good and right, but there are some inherent conflicts between them. If we can become aware of the conflicts, we can improve our arguments. In this section we describe three sets of contrasting types.

Instrumental Values vs. Terminal Values

Terminal values are about ultimate goals or desires. Instrumental values are about how one may permissibly go about achieving terminal values. Terminal values are about end states, such as a desire for a comfortable or exciting life. Instrumental values are about behaviors such as ambition, courage, or persistence.

This distinction affects public policy debates. Should we judge a proposal on the means it uses or the ends it achieves? We want justice, for example, but do we judge the *process* or the *result*?

This choice was one of the issues reflected in two famous books attempting to define what principles would govern a just society. John Rawls fired the first shot in his 1971 book, *A Theory of Justice*. He came down on the side of a just result. Robert Nozick replied in 1974 in *Anarchy, State and Utopia,* arguing for a just process. These books were about much else, of course, but did reflect this choice.

These two perspectives illustrate one aspect of the debate in the United States over affirmative action in its various forms. If, for example, blacks are 12 percent of the population but only 2 percent of some job category (such as enrollment at elite law schools) then is that in and of itself proof of injustice? If you value a just result, then you are inclined to say that this disparity is, in and of itself, proof of injustice and discrimination. A just result would be for each group to be represented proportionately in various jobs.

On the other hand, if you value a just process, you may object that any process that gives priority to people on the basis of skin color is inherently unjust. You will focus on the individual who loses a place to someone else on criteria other than pure performance.

One example that came up in these books concerned the salaries of wealthy celebrities and athletes. Is it right that a Kobe Bryant or any other mega-star make so much and school teachers (and college professors!) make so little? That doesn't seem like a just result. But suppose that inequality can be shown to come about as the result of a just process. Specifically, that millions of people freely choose to pay some money to see Bryant play or go to a movie to see a particular actor who got paid millions for performing. That seems like a fair, just process. We let people decide how to spend their own money. Who could object? But this just process does not lead to a just result. So which is right?

The same dynamic can be seen in views about Title IX, which provides a number of tests for universities to prove they are offering women equal opportunity to men in athletics. (Note: contrary to popular belief, the law does not mandate a 50–50 distribution of places on sports teams; it is more complicated than that.) Suppose it really is the case that a smaller percentage of women want to play sports than men. Is that the result of a patriarchal system that has convinced women to oppress themselves, or is that just the result of free choices? Your view of that might depend on if you prefer a just process or a just result.

We bring up these examples to illustrate the issue of instrumental and terminal values. Of course, actual policy choices in these areas involve many other issues and considerations. Certainly concerns about justice mask baser motives in some cases. But the conflict is real.

"The ends don't justify the means." Well, the ends must justify some means or we'd never do anything. Which ends justify which means?

Example

Each of the examples we gave could be probed further. For example, in the Title IX case, suppose we don't find enough women to fill spots on teams but we are turning away men who want to play. Should we devote more efforts to find more women? Should we say the men are just out of luck, too bad, but it was your way for years? Can we argue that the expressed preferences of women are not their real preferences—that they are afraid to try out for sports due to social pressure or have been denied opportunities and role models? Or does that sound like forcing people to do things they don't want to do?

There are other examples of this collision of perspectives.

Consider the typical job interview. You know you can do the job (or you are confident you can "fake it till you make it"), you like the job, but you don't have the qualifications to be considered. Can you exaggerate on your resume just a bit (unjust process) to get a job you are truly suited for and would do well at (just ends)?

Principles vs. Consequences

Is something wrong because it leads to bad things (pain, loss, grief), or is it bad because it violates some rule or principle? Is morality based on consequences or principles? This is a far harder question to sort out than you might suppose. Why is adultery wrong? Is it wrong because it leads to anger, breakdown of families, pain to those cheated on, and divorce? Or is it wrong because it violates a consistently held rule of religious and social systems?

But, that neat distinction starts to break down when we ask further questions. Consider the list of bad consequences to adultery that we listed. Now, ask yourself, why is inflicting pain wrong? Why is breaking up of a family wrong—perhaps people grow from painful experiences. Why has someone the right to feel cheated, and why do you feel bad for making others feel bad? You could reply that it is a principle that people have value. Now we've found that the consequences are bad because they violate principles.

You can go around this circle the other way also. Many religions prohibit adultery and often indicate that this prohibition is a command from God, a fundamental principle of how humans were designed to be. However, religions also commonly claim that God's rules are designed for our welfare, that is, bad consequences will happen to you if you disobey these commands. Now it appears that the principles are rooted in consequences.

Both options have worth. But we want you to be aware, however, of these two choices of reasons for values when you construct your arguments. You should think about why and how you want to argue a value. If you are building an argument based on principles in and of themselves, then you must make sure your audience accepts the validity of the source of those principles.

Immanuel Kant, whose "categorical imperative" is a key example of principle based on moral reasoning, gave an example that showed the difference between principles and consequences. Imagine a child goes into a shop with money from her or his allowance and asks the price of some item. The store owner can easily lie to the child, and the child can't prove the owner wrong. The child has no power over the owner. There will be no consequences to the owner for giving the child the wrong price.

In some situations there might be consequences. The owner is found out, customers abandon him in disgust. But this is one transaction involving one child. The child isn't running an errand for the parents, so the parents won't check up. No one will find out.

But you say, "Lying is wrong!" As you explore why, resist the temptation to say "But there could be consequences." That's not the point here. There are no consequences.

We should beware of reducing all morality issues to questions of consequence. When one of the authors was a teenager he was subject to a series of stories in church intended to teach proper behavior. This was the era of "relevance" when "blind obedience to the rules" was no longer in vogue. So the stories all had a similar form. Some kids go out to the store. Some of the kids decide it would be "cool" to shoplift. One kid refuses. The rest laugh at him for being "square" or a "loser." The kids steal something and nearly get out of the store before the store owner catches them. Now the kid who didn't steal is proved to be right.

What does this story teach? That morality is prudent, the careful thing to do. Like that you should wear a helmet when you ride a bike so you don't get a head injury. While the need to teach this way to children may be necessary, there is something wrong about this type of focus on consequence to the exclusion of principle. Much better to write a story where the kids do get away with stealing and the one kid who doesn't steal only has the satisfaction of having done the right thing and having a clear conscience. At the risk of turning a short story for juveniles into a full-blown Russian novel, it might be better to show impacts on character of petty stealing and lying in contrast to a life of more upright character. Otherwise the story is vulnerable to the argument that things are only wrong if you get caught. And that risks teaching that if you are going to be a criminal, you should be careful.

Further Examples

That this distinction of consequences and principles is not simply some sort of illusion can be shown by examining cases where the issue of consequences and principles point in different directions.

Can you tell a "white lie" to spare someone's feelings? Or to get out of an embarrassing situation? Would it be a better principle that you should never lie and get a reputation for never lying? Or can you justify lying when the consequences of telling the truth would be bad?

Is democracy the best form of government? Why is it good? Because it promotes other values like freedom or liberty? Or because the consequence of democracy is richer lives for more people. Would democracy really be better if its consequences were shown to be chaos?

Why is it wrong to get hooked on painkillers? You might reply that you could go to jail, you could suffer medical problems, you could lose your job, you could fail to function properly. These are all consequences, and so your argument seems very practical. You could make a different argument based on how addiction leads to the degeneration of your character by seeking to find a solution to your problems in a pill. The question of whether this will lead to the degeneration of your character is a factual issue; the value placed on your duty to make the most of your life and character is a principle-based value argument.

However, imagine a relative trying to convince you not to take on a risky job. You have ambitions to be the person who jumps out of a Coast Guard helicopter into the freezing cold ocean to rescue people off sinking boats. It would be easy to imagine this relative giving you a list of consequences that was at least equal in severity (but not identical) to the consequences of addiction to painkillers: injury, persistent medical problems, risk of death. But now, however, the purpose for assuming the risk is totally different: the addiction seems self-indulgent, the job of rescuing people noble. The principles behind the choice of behaviors overrule, in our minds, the level of consequences. We admire people who risk their lives for others.

Short-term vs. Long-term Values

A large class of decisions in both personal as well as social policy seem to turn on a trade-off between what is desirable in the short run and with our judgment about long-term benefits. Questions about eating and exercise would be a clear example here. Are you willing and able to suffer the pain of controlling your desires for food and accepting the pain of exercising for the benefits that will occur months or even years later? Perhaps the same conflict arises in the trade-off about options for Friday night: study or go out with friends.

One way these trade-offs get dealt with is to find some benefit in the short-term activity like finding an exercise program that will be desirable. Or some people seem to find self-denial a positive value.

Further Examples

Investments of all types—personal and financial—seem to pose trade-offs like this. Spend money now (and receive a benefit now) or delay spending and hopefully receive a bigger benefit later.

Companies have similar issues. Maximizing profits in the next quarter may actively conflict with maximizing them over the long haul. Paying large bonuses now may impact motivation to perform in the future.

Which is the best way to live? "You only live once, so enjoy the moment" or "Sacrifice to achieve your real goals"?

Class Exercise: Why Is Cheating Wrong?

Work through these various arguments in terms of the various categories we have been discussing. You are trying to make an argument to a friend that they should not cheat on their girlfriend/boyfriend with whom they are in a serious relationship.

C: Cheating on your girlfriend/boyfriend with that person is wrong.

1. G1: The Bible says adultery is wrong (regardless if you get caught or not).
   W1: The Bible is the appropriate source of rules for behavior.
   Comment: The value system assumed is "Christian values."

2. G2: You will get caught. (Assuming: There will be consequences if you are caught.)

   W2: People break relationships if they are two-timed.

   G2b: Getting caught is bad because they will break up with you, you will get a bad reputation, you will have problems finding a new relationship.

   Rebuttal: I won't get caught, I'm being careful.

   Comment: Notice that by using a consequence-based reason in a value argument, you become vulnerable to a consequence-based response. In this case, you'll likely wind up arguing about the probability of being caught, which isn't really what you wanted to argue.

3. G3: You're in a committed relationship (you made a promise).

   G3b: This will break your promise.

   W3: Breaking promises is wrong, especially important promises.

   But why is breaking promises wrong?

   B3a: Getting a reputation for breaking promises will harm your life.

   B3b: Breaking promises leads to other morally degenerate behavior.

   B3c: God has told you not to break promises.

   B3d: The proper functioning of society (personal relationships) depends on trust.

   Comment: Since keeping promises is a fairly universally held value, no one is likely to attempt to prove it is okay to break them. Instead, their reply will likely introduce new issues, "No one will know," "I love this (other) person," and so on.

ARGUING VALUES

Now it is time, having discussed all manner of difficulties with value claims, to try to show you some constructive ideas for how to prepare your arguments.

First, we will discuss how to do this in general, and then we'll discuss some of the variations that occur in practice. We will propose that there are three different scenarios depending on exactly where the dispute is located: Value arguments can be about (a) what maximizes a value, (b) values vs. values, and (c) value system vs. value system.

As we often say, real arguments are seldom this neat and are likely to roam among the three options. Sometimes you adopt one of the three for tactical reasons when your real view is different. But it is still useful to work out how arguments behave in these three cases. We will develop three different value arguments and work them through the three cases.

But first, let's look at the basics of developing a value argument.

Supporting a Value Claim

The basic framework you will have to develop is this:

- State a claim that something is good or bad.
- Identify the warrant that is likely the relevant aspect(s) of the value system shared between advocate and audience.

- Grounds are what you offer as evidence that your claim is good or bad in the value system.

In other words you need to explicitly put forward some criteria that allow you to judge if your claim is consistent with the value system.

We're going to work through some examples. We'll show three different cases and three different arguments.

Case 1: What maximizes our agreed value? A value argument with no dispute over values? Yes, this is paradoxical. But this case is still a value argument because the ultimate objective is to make a value claim. It just happens in this case that there is no real dispute between the advocates as to what values apply and what they mean. What is at stake is this question: What maximizes the value?

Let's examine three cases.

C: "Homosexuality is wrong."	C: "We have a right to use Alaska's oil."	C: "We should expand into new products."
G1: "The Bible and Christianity prohibit homosexuality."	G1: "It's the best way to lower the cost of gas."	G1: "If you're not growing, you're dying."
G2: "The Bible is where Christian values are defined."	G2: "We need to keep gas prices low."	G2: "Maximizing profits is the objective for a business in a capitalist system."
W: "The Christian value system is normative."	W: "Earth's resources are for human benefit." or "Human economic welfare is the value system to use to judge resource decisions."	W: "Capitalism is how a business should be run."
Rebuttal: "Accept Christian values as found in the Bible. However, careful examination of the Bible shows that it doesn't really prohibit homosexuality."	Rebuttal: "Accept that we need to lower gas prices, but drilling in Alaska is not the best way to do it. It would be cheaper to improve energy efficiency of cars."	Rebuttal: "Accept that we should maximize our profits, but a better way to do that is to focus on our core competencies."
W2: "Can use modern methods of interpretation to understand the text."	W2: "Efficiency is a key economic value."	W2: "Companies without focus cannot compete in a capitalist economy."
Debate is within the value system of Christianity. Argument is over how to read the texts. What approach best uses (maximizes) the Bible?	Note the role of factual issues in support of a value claim. The question is: What will maximize our enjoyment of life?	Note that profit maximization is the shared value.

In each case here there is a dispute, but the dispute is not about the choice of values to use to govern the issue. The dispute is about what action will really be faithful to the values in a particular case. The two sides agree, but it probably won't feel that way. In practice, this will probably feel like a value dispute, and one side is quite likely to mistakenly attack the other for rejecting its values.

However, sometimes fights over values would benefit if the parties realized that both sides actually accept the same values and are really arguing about how best to implement their values. The war on terror and its debates come to mind. Advocates of a tough military response to terrorism are quite willing to attack all their opponents as being "un-American," "advocating surrender," and the like—thinking there is a dispute over values. However, a good chunk of the opposition to bombing our way to peace is based on practical objections— that the value of defending this nation will not be advanced by an exclusively military policy.

Naturally, it is easier to deal with your opponents if they are "traitors" or "weaklings" then it is to have a tactical debate over the proper methods of dealing with an asymmetrical threat. Hopefully, studying the particular dynamic here will assist in creating better arguments on this subject.

However, we should also remind you that there are real, complex, and difficult issues about defining the proper criteria for value arguments. For example, even within the Christian value system, there has been a centuries-long argument about where is the ultimate authority for interpreting the faith. Is it (a) the authority of the church (the traditional Catholic view), (b) the tradition as exemplified by the early Christian authors (advocated by the Orthodox), (c) the text of the Bible (Protestant), or (d) God speaking to you directly (Charismatic)?

Case 2: Value vs. value In this scenario, we are debating which value should apply, but the values are both within a single value system that all sides to the discussion accept. What is being argued is that certain values can be "traded off" or analyzed relative to each other. So, we might have the following issues:

- One value **maximizes another value.** For example, it can be argued that "Economic justice facilitates peace." In order to achieve your value of peace, you should adopt a plan to eliminate poverty.
- One value is **broader** than another. For example, "Abortion rights are a subset of liberty." You can make your argument for abortion rights more appealing to more people by reframing it in a "larger" or more general value such as liberty.
- One value has **more desirable consequences** than another. For example, "Gains from drug testing of athletes outweigh the damage to privacy." That is, while drug testing does involve a reduction in people's privacy, there are greater gains to our value of fair competition.
- One value is a **prerequisite** or necessary condition to another value. For example, "Without life, freedom is meaningless." So it is pointless to worry about the details of how much freedom some people have if their very life is being threatened.

Let's consider our three arguments again. The affirmative case stays the same, but the rebuttal arguments now propose a different reason for rejecting the argument.

C: "Homosexuality is wrong." G: "The Bible and Christianity prohibit homosexuality." G2: "The Bible is where Christian values are defined." W: "Christian value system is normative."	C: "We have a right to use Alaska's oil." G1: "It's the best way to lower the cost of gas." G2: "We need to keep gas prices low." W: "Earth's resources are for human benefit." or "Human economic welfare is the value system to use to judge resource decisions."	C: "We should expand into new products." G1: "If you're not growing, you're dying." G2: "Maximizing profits is the objective for a business in a capitalist system." W: "Capitalism is how a business should be run."
Rebuttal: "Accept Christian values as found in the Bible. However, the Christian value system has a definition of sin. Homosexuality doesn't meet that definition; thus it is not a sin." W2: "Sin is a key concept in Christianity for deciding if behavior is right or wrong."	Rebuttal: "Accept that we need to consider economics, but we have to plan for the long term when oil runs out. W2: "Planning for a long-term economic future is an important value."	Rebuttal: "Accept that we're in a capitalist society, but running an ongoing enterprise requires balancing multiple values such as employee retention, the legal environment, and other items. W2: "Must take a broader view of capitalist values."
Debate is within the value system of Christianity. But now the debate has widened to include an examination of just how the entire value system establishes right and wrong behavior.	Debate is within the economic value system, but arguing about the proper balance of short-term and long-term objectives.	Argument takes place entirely within the frame of a capitalist system. Can I maximize the value of capitalism by only considering profit? Or is capitalism also a way to advance other objectives such as choice?

The frame has widened out beyond the specific issue at stake. Now the argument becomes one about how the value system should be sorted out.

This dispute will feel like a much more fundamental dispute than the previous one. The two sides will likely feel they are in total, fundamental disagreement, but they actually share a broad commitment to see issues in the same larger frame of values.

Case 3: Value system vs. value system Now, we consider the most conflicted situation. The two advocates do not agree on anything, it appears—the very choice of value system is up for grabs. Not surprisingly, this can lead to very heated arguments—particularly if either or both advocates do not realize that the dispute is about value systems.

In most cases, it will be very difficult to find outside criteria for deciding which value systems apply. Most value systems have an internal rule that their system is the only or best way of dealing with issues. When one side invokes those rules, the

C: "Homosexuality is wrong."

G: "The Bible and Christianity prohibit homosexuality."

G2: "The Bible is where Christian values are defined."

W: "Christian value system is normative."

C: "You have no right to intrude in the lives of homosexuals."

G1: "Two consenting adults should be able to do what they like."

G2: "The United States should be governed by a value of freedom and not a Christian value."

W2: "Liberty is the most important value."

Try to show which value system applies "Christianity is not the value system that should govern our secular society."

C: "We have a right to use Alaska's oil."

G1: "It's the best way to lower the cost of gas."

G2: "We need to keep gas prices low."

W: "Earth's resources are for human benefit." or "Human economic welfare is the value system to use to judge resource decisions."

C: "We have an obligation to preserve the earth and live simply on it."

G: "Drilling in Alaska will damage the environment."

W2: "Ecology and spirituality are more important than consumer lifestyles."

Try to show which value system is most affected by this issue:
"For a tiny improvement to your lifestyle, you will destroy a major ecosystem."

C: "We should expand into new products."

G1: "If you're not growing, you're dying."

G2: "Maximizing profits is the objective for a business in a capitalist system."

W: "Capitalism is how a business should be run."

C: "These new products are wrong."

G: "The products are useless to society and exploit foreign workers."

W2: "We should not make worthless things nor exploit poor people."

Issue could be framed within the profit maximization value system ("People will boycott our products if we do this."), but that might be a mask for the real value.

FIGURE 7.1
Value Claims.

other side is generally not persuaded—and the original advocate is deeply offended at the rejection. That's not just the case in religious arguments, but can be an equally verbally violent situation in other cases.

What to do? You have a number of options:

- Propose that a different value system should apply. The first case below, on homosexuality, will illustrate this. You don't have to reject the value system of your opponent; instead you shift the ground and claim that the value system shouldn't apply to the current issue.
- The argument might be at the periphery of the first value system but at the center of the second. In this case you are appealing to some sort of common ground—hoping that both sides actually hold both of the value systems in play. You make the argument that what is a tiny "badness" in one system achieves a major "goodness" in the other system.
- People may be more easily persuaded to shift *which* values they see govern a particular issue as opposed to getting them to overturn a value they hold. Think of the case of the author's engineering friend above. No values were rejected; instead, the person reframed the dispute into another value system.

As before, the affirmative case stays the same, but the response changes.

Advocates often make a tactical choice to suppress their real rejection of their opponent's value systems (case 3) and instead position their argument within the value system of their opponent (case 2). This can show respect for an opponent, but if it is suspected that such tactical framing is insincere, it can rebound against the advocate.

AESTHETIC ARGUMENTS

The evaluation of artistic productions generates many value claims. Advocates will seek to argue about what is "beautiful," "in good taste," and can also be in defense of what is "challenging" or what "pushes people to see things in a new way," among many other criteria. These arguments would be about a movie, art, play, literary work, or other cultural artifact. This is a very large area, and we will only make a few selected observations about this sort of argument.

Clarifying Claims

> C1: "I didn't like that movie."
> C2: "That was a bad movie."

The first asserts your personal view. Others may disagree with you or think less or more of you because of it, but in the end, all you are claiming is that you are accurately expressing your view about the movie. C2 asserts something more—that others should agree with you and that you are hoping to persuade others to adopt your view.

Clarifying Criteria

What criteria are being put forward as normative in these sorts of debates? Is the argument about the item in isolation, or are you discussing its impact on those who view it?

Does watching films of people doing horrible things to each other promote violence or bad behavior in people? Values are at stake in these arguments, and they typically turn on the "consequences" type of value argument. In other words, there are claims made that watching certain types of productions will produce bad behavior. This argument in turn relies on a causal argument: "Watching X causes Y". We'll discuss causal arguments that involve influence in a later chapter.

However, arguments about the negative impacts of movies can also be made using the "principle" type of values. Here, you are not claiming that watching *Saw IV* turns you into a serial killer; you're arguing that it is degrading to you as a person and that you don't want to spend your time on such things.

Advocating an Aesthetic Value

Why would listening to music promote desirable values?

> "The skills one brings to listening to music—imagination, abstract non-linear thinking, instinctive reaction, and trusting those instincts—must be consistently renewed and cultivated if they are to stay with us, alive and strong. Music, as a universal, nonverbal language, allows us to tap into the social, cultural, and aesthetic traditions of different times and different places; and in doing so we become more aware of our shared humanity and the wisdom and vision of others."
>
> Robert Greenberg, quoted in *The Teaching Company 2010 Catalog*

Notice how he supports the value argument. He does not just assert that listening to music is good. He provides specific reasons. Those reasons are that music will promote a series of other values—values that he is assuming most people think are important. If you value learning about other cultures, if you view all humans as sharing something important, he contends, then listen to music.

This is different than an argument that is asserting that music is fun or that partying to a good dance track helps you let go of stress.

What Is the "Top 10" List Measuring?

Who is the best contemporary writer? The best musical act? The top 100 operas?

Again, starting by clarifying the values you want to use to judge would be useful. Are you actually using popularity among all people or popularity among specialists as your criteria? Or are you using other criteria of merit?

Are you establishing who is "the best" or who has been the "most influential"?

EXAMPLES OF VALUE DISPUTES

In this section, we will just briefly put forward some areas where values are being argued. You may consider developing these in a class discussion or a paper. Note that many of these are phrased in ways that look like policy arguments. You'll learn in the next chapter that values are often a key aspect of many public policy decisions. For now we focus in on the values behind these questions.

We divide the examples into those that focus on subject areas and those that bring to the fore issues of conflicting values.

Subjects with Value Disputes

What is just? Let's suppose that your claim is that some action is just. You are appealing to a value system that says we should be just or fair to people. Well, fine, few would dispute that, but what is the definition of justice? You need some criteria or standard for deciding if an action is just. There are a variety of rules you could suggest:

- "Give to each person what they deserve."
- "Give to each person their basic needs."
- "Treat each person the same."
- "Allow each person to grow and develop."
- "Apply the law equally to each person."

And there could well be more choices. But notice that these do not all have the same implications. Applying the law equally can be thought to be unfair if people are in different situations. Giving each what they need might be acceptable in a communist framework and rejected in a capitalist one. But the point is that unless you explain what your criteria of justice are, we have no way of knowing if your claim is really just or not.

Is a war "just"? Here is one place where there is a widely accepted set of criteria, called "just war theory." The precise formulation varies a bit, but here is one way of setting out the criteria. For a war to be justified, the following criteria have to be met:

- The damage inflicted by the aggressor (your opponent) on the nation or community of nations must be lasting, grave, and certain.
- All other means of putting an end to it must have been shown to be impractical or ineffective.
- There must be serious prospects of success (that is, the war could solve the problem).
- The use of arms must not produce evils and disorders graver than the evil to be eliminated. The power of modern means of destruction weighs very heavily in evaluating this condition.[1]

If you wanted to argue that a war is justified, you would invoke these principles and then show that each one applied to the particular war you were contemplating.

We offer this example mostly because of its rarity. Most of the time you will not find near-universal agreement on the criteria to use to assess value claims. You will have to propose and defend your criteria.

So, you want to argue that some action is "discrimination" or "unjust"—think about giving some explanation of what the term means.

---

[1]The Catechism of the Catholic Church, en.wikipedia.org/wiki/Just_war

What rights do animals have? Is making animals fight each other for our sport wrong? If so, why exactly? Animals do fight each other, but, if we make them fight for our entertainment, that seems different. Are there ethical considerations about using animals for medical research? Is some research wrong, but some acceptable?

Is the issue actually the violation of the rights of animals or is it the violation of moral behavior by the person? As an example to separate out those points, if you found a person really cursing out a piece of furniture, you don't say the furniture had its rights violated. You think the person was being immature. So a person who mistreats a horse? You can frame that as a person failing to be a responsible steward of something entrusted to him, or you can see it as a violation of the dignity of the horse.

Can we have objections to activities that provide pleasure to others? If someone else is doing something that they enjoy and that does not directly harm another person, are there situations where we could legitimately object to their behavior? We tend to say no in the abstract, but some cases are more difficult. Can a church ring its bells on Sunday morning and force non-Christians to listen to them? Does a Jew have to accept a neo-Nazi group meeting next door? If you are an atheist and your neighbors all put up crosses on their lawns, have you been oppressed?

More complex would be cases where the behavior you object to is done out of sight. Can I object if my neighbor engages in sexual practices in private that I find repugnant? Or reads pornography?

Does the value of "tolerance" have limits? And are we consistent in applying that tolerance?

Could we make a distinction between what the society can't prohibit (because the prohibition itself would cause problems) and what I might advise or entreat a neighbor or friend to stop doing?

Do campus groups receiving university funding have a right to restrict their membership? Can a conservative Christian group refuse to admit homosexuals? Can the campus Republican group refuse admittance to Democrats? Does "openness" and "nondiscrimination" require that no qualifications for membership be allowed? Can a male-only group get funding?

And, are there student groups that shouldn't be allowed to receive funding because of their beliefs? What about a group for students who are into S&M? Or a white-supremacist group?

Does a view that a campus should be a "safe" place where no one is "intimidated" require restricting the public nature of some activities? And if so, do we have to take the word of someone who says they were offended, or can their views be rejected in some cases?

Did Pete Rose's betting on baseball games mean he does not deserve to be in the Baseball Hall of Fame? This question can be applied to any similar conflict between on-field and off-field activities. If the only criterion for entry to the Hall of Fame is on-field performance, then Pete Rose more than qualifies. But can off-field activities be so heinous that they trump that? Does it matter if the activities damaged the integrity of the game (such as Rose's betting) or were unrelated (such as belonging to a disreputable group, holding a repugnant view, or being convicted of a crime—none of which apply in the Rose situation)?

Should people be protected from their weaknesses? Most agree it is good if a bar refuses to serve people who are drunk. How aggressive can you be at stopping a person who wants to drive home from your party when they are drunk? What if someone has a weakness for buying things they see advertised they can't afford? Or eat too much? Or get pulled into a cult-like group? Or is consistently emotionally vulnerable to people who take advantage of them?

Does your answer depend on the relationship you have with this person, and why would it? Is there a duty you owe to any human being? Or do people need to fail so they will learn?

Do instructors have an obligation to reach out to failing students? Should teachers email students who don't turn in papers? Should teachers try to "intervene" with students who they know are in academic trouble? Or is that an invasion of privacy? Is the best value to teach that everyone is responsible for their own actions so that letting a student fail actually would help them in the long run?

Are there occasions where profit is not the best economic value to pursue? What exactly is wrong with WalMart (or other such stores) if all they do is provide goods cheaper than everyone else? Does a corporation have any responsibility to do something other than pursue profit?

Sometimes it is said, "If you don't like what the company does, don't shop there" or "Don't work there." Do people always have a choice? And if I do not shop or work there, do I still get a voice in how my community is shaped, especially if a store like WalMart will cause other stores I do shop at to go out of business? Should I restrict my investments to companies that have certain moral and ethical values?

Are child beauty pageants wrong? Those pageants that feature very young children, mostly girls, all dressed up in adult costumes and making moves usually associated with adult sexuality—are they repulsive, "kiddy porn," or are they the beginning of a young person's acquisition of poise and self-confidence?

There is such a thing as child pornography—and it isn't exactly like these pageants, but is it close enough to carry some degree of moral condemnation?

Do we have any actual evidence of the impact (the consequences) on children of being in these pageants, or are one or both sides speculating?

VALUE CONFLICTS

In this section, we change the focus and zero in on the conflict of values, looking at examples of situations where these conflicts might appear.

Justice vs. Mercy

The student has finally admitted it. He was BS'ing about just needing one more day to get the paper in. Or she admits she forged that doctor's note. Or he admits he copied his paper from a printed source. Justice demands punishment, doesn't it—a drop of grade, a fail, a formal note on the transcript? And if you fail to punish, aren't you letting them get away with it? And you will put the honest students at a disadvantage.

On the other hand, they are sorry. They are humiliated. They had to confess to you. They had to expose their private issues to a near stranger. Wouldn't it be better to extend some mercy, let them do something to make up for it, and trust that they learned their lesson? No sense ruining someone for one mistake.

This comes up in regard to first-time offenders of the law, even in regard to repentant people who have committed very harsh crimes. After twenty years in jail for a murder, if the person has turned their life around, the full sentence may be justified, but would mercy be better?

Honesty vs. Kindness

"Honey, do these pants make me look fat?" That's the cultural cliché of the impossible dilemma for a spouse or partner. Other stereotypes are typically at work when a partner is expected to extend admiration of heroic proportions for their mate cutting the lawn or cleaning a toilet.

Our romantic connections are not so bound to clichés any more, which is a good thing, but many day-to-day situations present this trade-off. The person who says something gauche at a party, who forgets some social obligation, says something inadvertently offensive to us, or who is not doing a very good job—we don't have the heart to shatter their dreams so we say nothing.

Some degree of kindness and restraint seems almost a requirement to keep social interactions from spinning out of control. But some subgroups (and some partners) seem to make things work with brutal honesty going in both directions, confident in the ties that keep the group together.

Turning a Profit vs. Social Responsibility

It is asserted that the only duty of a corporation is to make money for its stockholders. But is that the only duty of the people who work and make decisions in a corporation?

Companies seem to have a duty not to kill their customers, not to lie to them, not to expose their workers to danger—all things that lower profits. Does the duty go farther, into a company's duty to the community or nation it is part of?

If outsourcing production would increase economic efficiency and profits, are there any circumstances where that should be put aside to preserve a community or specific jobs in the community?

Are Taxes Theft or a Duty?

"Why should anyone think the government can spend my money better than I can?" "All taxes are theft. I worked for that money and the government just comes along and takes it. If someone takes my wallet, that is theft."

On the other hand:

"Taxes aren't theft; they're the means by which we pool our resources, fairly and with order, to underwrite this common life."

Bishop Peter Rogness, *Minneapolis StarTribune*, Feb. 6th, 2011.

If you benefit from the roads, water, sewer, schools, police, fire, ambulance, electric power, and the administrative mechanisms that set standards and review the actions of people who sell you food, clothing, cars, and everything else, does that mean you incur an obligation to pay for the cost? What if you have profound and deep objections to some ways that tax is spent, such as on foreign wars?

Individual Freedom vs. Social Responsibility

"People should be able to do what they want in their private lives." That is a value statement that many would agree with. But some private decisions can have consequences beyond private lives. Consider the question of "helmet laws" that require motorcyclists to wear helmets. If someone refuses to wear a helmet and says, "I understand the risk, but that risk is on me," shouldn't we let people choose to do that? While the primary risk is to the person riding the motorcycle, there are also consequences to the society: More accidents and more severe accidents mean higher medical costs to be born by insurance. A severely disabling injury imposes costs on family members also. Do these effects give society a right to regulate risky behavior, even if the main risk is to the person choosing to do the behavior?

Is the Morality of Public Officials Private or Public?

Was President Clinton's sexual activity inappropriate for a public official, or was it properly considered private? What about Newt Gingrich committing adultery twice? Or New York governor Eliot Spitzer using prostitutes? In 2011, the wife of the Speaker of the House of Commons in Great Britain posed in front of the parliament building wearing nothing but a sheet—should that diminish the respect her husband has?

If a public official has made pronouncements about what is proper morality or has claimed that he obeys a certain standard and then is proved to have violated that, we seem to agree that is therefore a proper public concern: They are a liar or a hypocrite, and we can rebuke them for it. If they've used their official power to pressure someone into sex, we agree that is abuse, and we can prosecute them.

But what if there is no direct connection between private and public actions. We used to regard divorce as something that would disqualify someone from a number of public offices; do we think adultery still does?

Does it matter what position the person has? Should ministers and clergy be held to higher standards? Should pop culture figures be held to lower ones?

And what about nonsexual issues such as how they treat their staff, how they respond to strangers, their use of aggressive tax avoidance strategies, or how lavishly they spend money?

Are other cultures always to be respected, or can we object to their practices? Can native peoples be allowed to hunt some species of animal even if that animal is endangered or if their hunting practices are less than the most humane? Does it make a difference if the culture in question is at the margins or poorer than the culture that wants to limit them or (like Japan) is a fully developed one?

Can we object to cultural practices that violate our ethical norms such as female genital mutilation, honor killing, or eating domestic pets?

If a local, likely poor, community invites economic development in a way that is likely to cause ecological damage or produce a rampant consumerism that could well destroy the indigenous culture—do richer outsiders have a right to try to stop it? What if the alternative is a lack of development and the community continues to fall behind?

And if there is to be intervention, what are the parameters for it? Should we think of deciding this one way or the other, or would it be best to enter a process of dialog with the locals, sharing our concerns and listening to theirs?

CONCLUSION

Value arguments are difficult, but inevitable and essential. Values are part of what define us as humans, a key attribute of our identity and purpose. The men and women we admire the most are often people who have faithfully lived out a value we admire. We should try to be clear about what our values are and be able to defend them in conversations with others.

Don't fall into the trap of just asserting your claim, but try to think through how you can support your position.

There are many interesting books that explore aspects of value conflicts. One recent example is the 2010 book *Justice: What's the Right Thing to Do?* by Michel Sandel. He explores issues of what justice is and offers many interesting test cases.

SUMMARY OF VALUE CLAIMS

Description:

Value arguments are about what is good, right, moral, ethical, virtuous, proper, or fitting. They are also about what is beautiful or if an artistic production (such as a movie or painting) is "good" or "bad." A value claim asserts the worth (or lack of worth) of something. And while issues of fact can often be involved, value claims require a judgment about something other than facts.

Explicit forms for a value claim:

"X is right/wrong," "X is good/bad" (in a moral, aesthetic, religious, or ethical sense).

Implicit forms for a value claim:

"That's impressive."
"The best in the industry."

Examples of claims that would typically be developed
as value arguments:

- "*Darjeeling Limited* is a charming and insightful movie."
- "Using painkillers to get high is (morally) wrong."
- "Topeka is a boring town."
- "People who commit adultery demonstrate their bad character."
- "The desert is beautiful."

Argumentation Strategy

- Appeal to a value system you share with the audience.
- Determine what is authoritative in the value system.
- Provide reasons why the value judgment is mandated by what is authoritative in the particular value system.

Issues and Aspects

There is no single value system that all accept for all situations. People tend to have a strong identification with their values.

Study Questions

- Name and explain the three pairs of value types.
- Name and describe the three cases for what can be in dispute in a value claim.
- How many different value systems can you identify that you accept?

Analyzing Policy Claims

INTRODUCTION

The papers report that new laws are being considered to restrict sex offenders. There is concern that kids out trick-or-treating on Halloween might knock on the door of a registered sex offender. The kids could get lured in and possibly abused. So laws are proposed that prohibit sex offenders from leaving their homes on Halloween night, prohibit them from answering the door, and require them to have their porch lights turned off. Some proposed laws require that offenders post a sign stating that they are a registered sex offender.

But, it is widely suspected that such people do not always obey the rules, so how will we be sure that the rules are followed? Therefore, it is reported that we will require law enforcement officers to knock on the doors of registered sex offenders on Halloween night to check for observance of the rules. But—if the law says that offenders can't answer the door, then will the occupants be arrested for answering the door, or should they be arrested for failing to answer it and thereby raising suspicion that they've left the house? So the law needs an exception.

And what about posting that sign? Isn't that an invitation to be abused or harassed? And while we have no sympathy for sex offenders, we don't want to encourage vigilante justice or people taking revenge into their own hands. And if sex offenders cannot go out of their houses on Halloween, does that mean they cannot do any activities with their own families or children? Even if other adults are there to supervise?

Well, you might say, so what if the risk to kids is small and we have to go to some hassle to protect them on Halloween, isn't that a good idea? "You can't be too careful," we'd say, "especially where it concerns the safety of our children." But, Halloween is one night—and kids might knock on a door of a sex offender to collect money for the paper, to sell things, or for other reasons. Why focus on Halloween? Maybe the risk is larger at Halloween.

If law enforcement officers are out on patrol checking the homes of sex offenders, then they are taken away from whatever else they might have been doing that night, including, possibly, working safety at places where children are gathering for group Halloween activities. If we put extra police on duty that night, then that is an additional expense to the taxpayers. But, if it protects children, aren't we in favor of it?

We might ask how many children have been abducted on Halloween night. The answer quite possibly is zero. And for that matter, apparently no child on Halloween has ever received an apple with a razor blade in it either.

So, the risk is near zero, it costs money, and it probably doesn't save any children. Does that mean we'll decide it isn't worth the effort and we'll put our resources into situations where the risk to children is greater? Probably not. Anyone who opposed these proposed laws about sex offenders would likely encounter strong opposition and accusations that they supported sex offenders.

So what is going on here? The situation we just described raises a number of the issues that pertain to policy claims, issues that we will explore in this chapter.

A *policy claim* advocates a course of action. We can advocate a change, or we can advocate maintaining our current actions. And by "action" we mean a very wide variety of things. The list certainly includes issues of public policy such as health care, foreign policy, what would be good for the economy or the environment. It also includes policy issues closer to home such as funding the university, tuition policies, requirements for graduation, what should be researched, or who should win awards. And policy claims also concern our personal decisions about choosing an apartment, who to date, what clothes to purchase, or what car to drive.

Policy claims are different from fact claims in that we are not only trying to decide what is true, but we are also deciding what to do. Policy claims are different from value claims in that we are not only trying to decide what is right or best, but also how to implement it.

We have contended from the beginning of this book that it is important for the citizens of a democracy to understand how to argue well. When we consider policy claims, it becomes very obvious why that is necessary. Policy claims are about who we invade, how much risk we put on our armed forces, how much money we pay in taxes, how much freedom we have, how our children are taught, how our infrastructure is maintained, and how we are allowed to live in community, among other things.

ASPECTS OF POLICY CLAIMS

Before we delve into some of the aspects of policy claims, let's make sure we understand what they are.

Policy Claims Advocate a Course of Action

So, "If we don't change the packaging on our product, sales will fall" is a fact claim. "We should change the packaging on our product because that will increase sales" is a policy claim. The first makes a claim about a fact that will come true in the future, but doesn't ask us to do anything. The second advocates that we do something. Of course, as always, people may imply one thing and say another. Someone who wants us to change our product packaging may start off by saying sales will fall, assuming that no one wants that, and so the need for action will be obvious. But that just means their real claim has not been stated as yet.

While policy claims often advocate a *change* in a course of action, they can certainly advocate for *maintaining* a current course of action. "We should not change our product packaging but keep it the way it is" is also a policy claim.

And while the word "should" is often a sign that a claim is of the policy type, that word does not have to appear in our claim. "Let's do this!" or "This is the house we want to buy" or "I don't want to do this" are policy claims.

Policy Claims Also Include "Personal Policy" Arguments

The word policy in some contexts means specifically "public policy" (that is, political decisions) but the scope of policy claims is much broader than that. Any course of action, be it in society, in a business, concerning a group of friends or even a personal resolve for yourself is subject to policy claims. "Will you marry me?" is a policy claim phrased as a question. "I should study tonight" is also. The key is "advocating a course of action."

Policy Claims Are Also Evaluated on the Plans and Projects Needed to Implement Them

Advocating something good is wonderful. And we can have interesting debates about just whether or not a policy should be enacted. But, and this is the beginning of a set of problems about how we decide policy questions, part of deciding if something is a good idea is deciding how to do it. When President John Kennedy said in May of 1961 that "I believe that this nation should commit itself to achieving the goal, before this decade is out, of landing a man on the moon and returning him safely to the earth," he was advancing a bold policy claim. NASA, however, had to come up with thousands upon thousands of pages of plans for turning that goal into a reality. And those plans had to be implemented in numerous separate projects to develop technologies, build rockets, factories, computing centers, ground stations, facilities, hire and train staff, and many other things to implement the project.

One way that policy claims go wrong is failing to turn the goal of a policy claim ("We should abolish cancer") into a plan ("We will double funding for basic medical research") or having a plan, but a plan that cannot be implemented. There is a difference, in other words, between a policy claim that is really only a wish ("We should double our sales in three years") and a policy that could actually happen ("We will expand our sales force to reach more prospects").

This issue will reoccur in several aspects of our discussion in this chapter.

Policy Claims Tend to Be about the Future (but You Can Do "Thought Experiments" about the Past)

As a practical matter, most policy claims, we suspect, are about the future. We want to propose a change to what we are doing now to be implemented in the future, or we want the future to be like the present. But it is certainly possible to conduct "thought experiments" about the past. These can be of interest to a few, or occasionally they attract widespread interest. Debates about if the United States should have dropped a nuclear bomb on Hiroshima still generate interest and passion over 60 years later.

Just because the course has already been chosen (since the United States has already dropped that bomb) does not mean you cannot debate if that course of action was wise or not and debate what would have happened if another course had been chosen.

Policy Claims Always Involve Sub-Arguments of Facts and Values

While fact and value claims have a number of complicated connections, they are, in the end, separate types of claims. However, policy claims are not quite like that. Policy claims cannot be made without developing other claims of fact and value. If you are advocating banning smoking in public places, you will most likely have to prove the factual claim of the danger of secondhand smoke and discuss value claims about personal liberty versus the right to be free from injury.

Policy claims are not a third type parallel to the other two, but a sort of special application of claims. So why are they analyzed separately? Doesn't our discussion of fact and value claims include all we need to know? First, policy claims are quite common in practice and cover a wide variety of issues. But more importantly, these arguments have a series of common mistakes or fallacies with them that lead to massive amounts of financial and physical harm. So there is good reason to isolate them as a type and analyze how to develop better arguments for them.

To see this, imagine a policy argument with the following general argument in Toulmin form:

C: "We should do X."

G1: "X will make life better."

G2: "X will cost less than the benefits it provides."

W: "Projects that have larger benefits than costs should generally be done."

The bulk of your case would be proving that G1 and G2 are accurate. Those are fact claims, and so you now have two fact claims to prove. But the warrant is not a fact claim, but a statement about values. Someone might oppose that with another warrant: "Live simply and stop building things, which reflects different values.

This aspect of policy claims being built on top of fact and value claims can prove confusing to students. You notice one of the contested fact or value issues, or most of what you hear about an issue, is debating a particular fact or value, and so you think the entire claim must be of that type. But the key is that the real claim, the actual point being argued, is advocating a course of action. That makes it a policy claim.

We think that all policy claims involve both fact and value claims. It may be that in a given situation everyone agrees on the values at stake and so they're not being debated. Or, alternatively, the value issues loom so large that no one is looking at the fact issues. But dig deep enough, and you'll find both.

WHAT IS UNIQUE ABOUT POLICY CLAIMS?

Policy claims have a number of special aspects to them. Not every policy claim has all of these aspects, but each aspect is relevant to many policy claims.

Policy Claims Typically Involve Collective or Complicated Decision-making Processes

The issue Who makes the decision? Who has the authority to decide? In many countries, the legislature passes laws and the executive signs laws into force, but the courts will also be involved as will regulatory agencies. Beyond that formal process, there will likely be a host of other actors that have significant influence such as lobbyists, professional organizations, unions, corporations, regional groups, and the media.

In a business context, there may be one or a very few executives with the formal authority to decide, but there will be many other stakeholders who have influence over the decision or can affect how it is implemented. In a family or among a group of friends, authority may be very complicated to figure out. For some decisions, there may be covert sources of authority, such as criminal organizations, or those created by corrupt processes or even secret ones.

In short, the decision for or against a proposed policy may involve people with different sorts of decision-making power or influence.

Implications for your arguments The point is that for some policy questions it may not be so obvious who makes the decision. That has implications for you as an advocate. Who do you make your case to? Who is your audience? Who do you need to persuade?

A different aspect of this occurs when there are multiple decision makers and therefore multiple arguments to make. They may be different arguments as different people need convincing about different aspects of the problem. Further, if you only focus on those with formal authority and ignore those with informal authority, it can cause problems getting your policy adopted. The wise advocate will give thought to how to communicate to all the different audiences involved with the policy.

Implementing a Policy Claim Typically Will Create a Complex Mix of "Winners" and "Losers" Who Are Unequally Affected by the Policy Change

The issue It's been proposed to build a new highway through an urban area. Some people will have their homes taken from them by the use of eminent domain. Others will have the view from their homes changed and experience more noise after the road is built. Businesses will be affected by construction and by changed traffic patterns afterward. Some contractors will be chosen to build the road, some will be passed by, thus some workers will get jobs and some will not. Financial agencies will compete to offer loans and will have to strive to get the work. Government agencies will have work to manage the project, prepare reports, and defend the plan in court. Citizens may organize through environmental groups, business groups, or neighborhood associations and spend years of their lives supporting or opposing the project.

After the project is built, some drivers will have faster and more convenient commutes to work or travel to errands. Others may actually have their drives disrupted. Some workers will be needed to maintain the highway, and money will have to be allocated to pay for maintenance. The bonds issued to pay for the construction may take thirty years to pay off.

How do you add this up? Is the road a benefit or a loss to society? If 10,000 people save five minutes off their drive to work five days a week, that works out to nearly twenty-five years of saved time each year the road is in existence. Does that compensate for twenty families having to lose their homes? Is the amount of pollution put into the air now less (because of saved time and less idling in traffic) and thus fewer birds killed and fewer people experiencing respiratory problems? And we haven't considered nonquantitative gains and losses such as quality of life, the beauty of the urban area, or opening up people to experience new parts of the urban area. Nor have we assessed this road compared to the equally complex gains and losses of building mass transit, bike paths, telecommuting, or simply doing nothing.

But the point we want to make here is not so much the issue of whether the total impact is positive or negative, but to notice that different people had different impacts. Some gained, some lost. Some were impacted marginally, some significantly, and some in life-altering ways. Even policies with massive gains to most of society tend to make somebody worse off.

Implications for your arguments The risk is that in constructing your policy claim you may omit some group that would be significantly impacted by the project. You may just discuss one group that will gain and leave yourself vulnerable to a rebuttal from someone who points out who you missed. In addition to the logical problems this can bring to your case, there are strong emotions that can be stirred up if you fail to consider impacts on some group, especially groups such as the poor, the elderly, minorities, women, disabled, or others traditionally disadvantaged in society.

You may also run into people who insist that no policy can be implemented if it has any negative impact on any person or group. That might sound noble, but it basically prevents almost all policies from being implemented.

Again, this highlights that there are multiple audiences for policy claims.

Constraints of Time, Money, and Other Resources Force Choices among Policies

The issue When debating fact claims, we can pretend we can be on an endless and unlimited search for truth. When discussing value claims, we can parse them as deeply as we like in a search for moral correctness. When deciding what to do, we have serious limitations on our ability to act. In particular, policy arguments live in a world where time, money, technology, and other resources are limited.

Most of our policy proposals will require tax money, or corporate money, or our own money to implement. We'd be happier if we owned a fabulous car, lived by the beach, or bought whatever we wanted—or at least we think we'd be happier. But we have a budget. We'd like to have twice as many police, enough courts so there is no waiting, brand-new schools for our children, great parks. But raising taxes is never popular.

Time is similarly limited. We have more projects to do than we have time, so we have to choose. Business situations also are driven by time constraints—a new product needs to be out by fall, or before the competition, or before the annual sales meeting. That means that not every feature can be added to it.

Resources are also limited. In the example that opened this chapter, we had to realize that the police can't be everywhere at once. If we have them focus on sex offenders on Halloween, then they are not available to do something else, like checking for drunk drivers.

In the world of project management, it is common to discuss these limitations in terms of a triangle of time, money, and requirements for the project. Project managers tell their supervisors that those ordering the project can set two, but not three of the sides of the triangle. If the company dictates to the project manager the time and the budget, then the project manager will tell the company what requirements can be met. If the company insists on certain requirements in a certain period of time, then the project manager will submit the bill for how much money is needed to achieve that.

However, it is also quite common that those ordering projects are at war with project managers over this very fact. If asked which of the three dimensions the company would like to specify, the usual answer is "all of them," and project managers have to constantly fight to convince people of the reality of limited resources forcing decisions.

Versions of this battle play out all the time. We don't like prioritizing, and we don't like hearing that we can't do everything. We tend to evaluate a policy against the alternative of not doing it—rather than against the alternative of doing something else.

Arguments We Don't Ever Want to Hear Again:
"You Can't be too Careful."

Yes, you can be too careful—when being careful in one area affects some other area negatively. If you have a limited amount of time, resources, and money, then you cannot do everything. Being very careful about one issue means you have to be less careful about some other issue.

The phrase "you can't be too careful" may sound wise, but it is a claim that there are no constraints, no trade-offs, and that is never true.

What the advocate may have meant to say is that "On this issue, it is worth being very careful." That's different. Now we are comparing impacts and making a case for the priority of one particular project.

The concept of "opportunity costs" is another way of looking at trade-offs. It might cost you $50 to get your car fixed but only $10 if you do it yourself. So it looks like you could save $40 by doing it yourself. However, if you do it yourself, you will spend an entire day on it. But suppose you could instead spend that day working and earn $100. So, by working on the car yourself, you lose the opportunity to earn $100. When you consider opportunity costs, you actually lost money by doing the repairs yourself. Similar examples occur in business all the time.

It is true that over time, technological and social developments can change what we can get for how much money and in what amount of time—but we have to take some of our resources and invest in the work to improve technology, so that also limits what we can do now.

Implications for your arguments In considering your policy claims, are you realistic about what constraints exist? You cannot just wave your hands and insist that something can be done. But people do that. A common dynamic in policy arguments is for one person to propose something noble and wise, but be vague on how it will be paid for, what would have to be sacrificed to accomplish it, or assume some unrealistic things will occur to pay for it or make it happen. Then, somebody criticizes the plan pointing out that lack of realism. Whereupon, the original proposer of the plan gazes into the distance with a firm expression and talks about dreams, hopes, believing in the possibility of the future, and that s/he prefers to be an optimist.

Well, that's nice, and sometimes you can do more than you think you can, but if a policy requires money we don't have or would mean abandoning other needed policies, it is valid to critique the plan on that basis. Policies require choices: Doing one thing means not doing other things.

But, you practical types, be aware that in the culture of the United States and some other countries, that being optimistic is considered wiser than being skeptical. You can win the argument on Logos and lose it on Pathos by being too negative—especially if the policy being proposed has much emotional appeal.

You should be aware of a particular dynamic that works against those discussing limits of options. If one person, for example, advocates a policy on the basis that it will save the lives of some children and you point out that in order to adopt this policy we would have to take money away from other policies that save even more children—it seems almost inevitable that your position is heard as saying "I want to kill children."

So, however logical this discussion of trade-offs sounds, the advocate must be aware of the massive emotional energy around certain policy questions. Normally, people isolate a particular decision from its wider implications. So, the question is not seen as "save one life here vs. five lives there," but rather just "save one life here." Thus, you, if you try to speak of these trade-offs, will sound pretty cold—as if you enjoy killing off small children.

What you should do is to bring the emotional implications of these trade-offs into the discussion. Show people the emotional implications of failing to consider all people by failing to consider the trade-offs.

Policies Have Multiple Goals That Force Trade-offs

The issue There is another form of limits that also has to be considered. If the previous point was about the external context of our policies, it is also true that there are trade-offs among the objectives *within* our plans—our various goals are in conflict. Consider the engines on our commercial aircraft. In January of 2009 a US Airways flight taking off from New York flew into a flock of Canadian geese. These damaged the engines causing them to stop working. The successful landing in the Hudson River and the rescue of all the passengers was widely hailed as a remarkable achievement.

Aircraft engines are designed and tested to withstand strikes from small birds in flocks and single hits from larger birds. But the birds that hit the engines on the flight in question were larger than the design standards for aircraft. So, should those standards be made tougher? Should a screen be put over the front of the engine? Any change would likely make the engine heavier or lower the fuel efficiency of the engine. That would increase the cost of flights and likely increase the amount of pollution emitted.

And there are more trade-offs. Modern jet engines have several series of blades (or "fans") on a common shaft. Expanding gases from combustion cause one of these fans to spin. The fan at the front of the engine (the one you can see) is driven by the shaft, forcing air backward and driving the airplane forward. Some experts believe that if these fans could spin at different speeds, the engine could be made both more efficient and quieter, certainly desirable objectives. But in order to make the fans spin at different speeds, some sort of gearbox or transmission would have to be added to the engine. That would likely make the engine heavier (meaning more dead weight to lift into the air) or would add more moving parts that could break and need maintenance. And the reliability of jet engines is an extremely desirable objective—since lives may depend on a single engine functioning reliably for hours if a two-engine aircraft has an engine failure over the middle of an ocean.

Almost every single policy claim, not just those involving engineering issues, involves striking the right balance among multiple objectives that are in conflict. Such objectives as safety, efficiency, low noise, less pollution, low operating cost, low maintenance cost, and low weight, among others. The nature of the universe seems to be that these objectives are usually in conflict. Safety adds cost. Efficiency increases complexity. Low cost adds noise, and on and on. The nature of these trade-offs shifts over time, and new ideas can often allow us to achieve gains that rewrite where the trade-offs occur—but they will still exist.

Another painful trade-off occurred in the United States during 2011 when flooding threatened to cause rivers to overflow dikes and flood urban areas. By deliberately opening holes in the dikes in rural areas and flooding farmland, the cities could be saved. The idea was that the damage to farmland could be repaired cheaper than the damage to houses and urban infrastructure. But suppose it was your farm scheduled to be flooded? It would be a good case study to follow up on these decisions and see what happened: Who had the authority to decide and what was the reaction after the decision got made?

A number of thought experiments along these lines illustrate how painful these decisions can be. Google the "trolley problem" for a series of interesting cases.

Arguments We Don't Ever Want to Hear Again:
"You Can't Put a Price on Human Life."

A series of very painful trade-offs for policy arguments revolve around the question of "putting a value on human life." That sounds like something we shouldn't do. Human life is "priceless," we think, nothing is more important. But, in fact, we actually do put a price on human life, and, in fact, it is impossible to avoid doing so. If we spend a million dollars on making jet aircraft engines safer to reduce the risk of people being killed in accidents, then we don't have that million to spend on making cars safer. If we fix dangerous parts of highways, then we have less money for separate bike paths. If we invest in one lifesaving measure, we don't invest in another. And we are monumentally inconsistent about our choices. We avoid flying because we think it is risky and then drive—and incur much higher risks. We've heavily invested as a society in the safety of people who fly, but not so much in the safety of people in cars or on bikes. Since we cannot spend an infinite amount of money that would be needed to make these modes of transportation perfectly safe, we have, in effect, put a price on human life.

How much medical care should people receive when the chances of them living is very slight? During the debates in 2009 over changes in health-care policy in the United States, there was a brief flurry of panic over nonexistent proposals for "death panels" who would decide if someone was too old or too sick to receive care. Horrors, we don't want that! However, societies have always made such choices. Often the choice is made on financial grounds—an elderly person cannot afford drugs or surgery so they don't receive it. The society at large decides how much to invest in research on lifesaving medical drugs and procedures (to say nothing of preventive care), and if the amount is less than infinite, then we're making choices about how much we think a life is worth.

Those decisions may be faced at the beginning of life. It seemed shocking and cruel to hear some leaders of the Church of England argue in 2006 (*The Observer*, November 11, 2006) that some newborn infants with severe medical problems, who were very unlikely to live, should have treatment withheld from them, knowing that they will die sooner as a result. But if the millions spent to save a very few severely sick newborns could instead save more people who had decent changes to live—shouldn't we do that instead? Often we find those decisions so painful we deny that we actually make them, we in effect hide the decisions from ourselves.

Implications for your arguments Conflicts among goals within a policy (as opposed to the issue about conflicts between policies in the previous point) highlight the multiple audiences that policies have to deal with. This is where the multiple decision makers (and multiple stakeholders and multiple groups) affected by the policy have their impact. It seems safe to say that, as in the previous point, most people resist the reality of conflicting goals. They want your policy to achieve everything and are unabashed about insisting that their particular issue is the crucial one. If you continue to insist that not everything can be included, you will likely be accused of not caring. If you ask people to explain how everything can be done, they can again reply that optimism and unwavering belief in plucky courage and working hard will let you achieve everything at once. But this isn't enough.

So, again, you have to attend to the multiple audiences of your claim. You can, of course, appeal to a common good—and shouldn't hesitate to do so.

Policy Claims Typically Involve Making Predictions about Imperfectly Understood, Complex Causal Processes

The issue As if the previous issues weren't enough to contend with, we also have to consider the problems posed by imperfect knowledge. Many policy arguments involve dealing with some very complex process such as the national economy, the biology of the human organism, an ecosystem, a city, to say nothing of the dynamics going on in your frat or sorority. In the chapter on causal arguments, we'll discuss the *fallacy of oversimplified cause*, so we will not spend a lot of time on it here. The lesson here is that we will not know exactly how some social, biological, or economic system will react when we change it. Things happen that are not expected, leading to a category of events sometimes termed *unintended consequences*. The plant Kudzu was introduced in the American southeast to strengthen earthworks; it wound up taking over and driving other plants out. Rabbits were introduced into Australia for sport; now they are a major pest. Laws increasing the penalties for drunk driving may have increased the number of hit-and-run accidents. Rent control can lead to housing shortages and a decline in the quality of housing stock.

When unintended consequences happen in foreign policy or covert operations, it is sometimes called "blowback"—such as how funding the Afghan Mujahideen to fight the Russians may have been a contributing factor to the rise of Al-Qaeda, how funding Saddam Hussein to fight the Iranians may have contributed to his persistence in office, or how smashing the Taliban in Afghanistan after 9/11 may have contributed to increasing the opium production in that country. And there are older examples. After World War I, the punitive Treaty of Versailles that was imposed on Germany contributed to the dynamic that led to the rise of the Nazis.

Perhaps one of the most spectacular instances of unintended consequences involves the events leading to the fall of the Soviet Union and the breakdown of the division between Eastern Europe and Western Europe in 1989. Soviet leader Gorbachev, most seem to think, only intended to reform the communist system, not abolish it. But events quickly spun out of his control.

Because all these systems are complex, you will note that we only claim that these unintended consequences *may* have occurred and may have *contributed*, not forced, the resulting problems. Even after the fact, such consequences are hard to sort out. And yes, there are unintended consequences that are beneficial, sometimes.

Implications for your argument A list of unintended consequences can seem like an argument for doing nothing or that all decision making is doomed to failure. That is an excessive conclusion. Sometimes the unintended consequences are smaller than the benefit of the policy change. But, more than that, you cannot assume that doing nothing has no cost. There are unintended consequences of failing to act as well.

Moreover, there is no escape from what is called "decision making under uncertainty." You cannot propose to study a problem until we know with certainty exactly what will happen. That would take forever or be impossible to fully achieve. And the underlying system would likely evolve while you were studying it—so now you're trying to hit a moving target.

The key is judgment and balance among various issues. Some study is worthwhile, some risks can be anticipated, and previous experience can help us make better decisions next time. At some point you have to act.

Policies Exist in the Cold, Cruel, "Real World" of Imperfect Human Beings

The issue By now you may have become convinced that policy claims are hopeless. Well, don't worry, we've saved the biggest problem for last: Policy claims involve people. And nothing can confuse and complicate an issue like involving people! The motivations of people are not fully logical and not consistent emotionally either. We all have mutually contradictory desires. We are vulnerable to certain scams. We are all a mixture of selfish and altruistic, of wise and foolish.

Human behavior and habits can play out in policy issues in several ways. We want government to be tough on crime, and then we oppose building jails in our neighborhood. We want better schools and vote down the bond issues to build them. There is the "free rider" problem—everyone can watch PBS whether or not they buy a membership.

And just as our motivations seem rational to us, we can dismiss the motives of others. Our concerns seem totally justified, but everyone else's seem silly. We can excuse our failures, while demanding perfection from others. In other words we apply different standards to ourselves than we do to others. We're more concerned about harms to ourselves and people we know than we are to harms to strangers. We're also not always that open to new information. We have values that affect what facts we are inclined to believe.

Perhaps one of the more remarkable instances of this problem occurs in the United States where many (or maybe even a majority) of voters are firmly convinced that the amount of taxes they pay has no connection with the amount of services provided by the government and that it is perfectly possible to expect significantly lower taxes and increased services at the same time.

All of these factors play into why the lawmaking process is so ugly to observe.

Implications for your argument You cannot just add up mathematically the gains and losses of your proposal and advocate it on that basis; you have to anticipate how people will react to your proposal. As mentioned earlier, you will have to consider multiple audiences for your argument and may have to make different arguments to different segments of the audience. You have to attend to the emotions and blind spots people have and adjust your approach to deal honestly and respectfully with them.

In constructing a policy argument, you need to think about what background information you will have to educate people about and what factual opinions of your audience you will need to rebut. The chapter on models of argument presentation is particularly relevant to this topic.

BUILDING YOUR POLICY CLAIM

How do you build an argument for a policy claim? We will walk you through a series of questions to ask yourself as you form an argument and give you a suggested outline for writing your policy argument.

Issues You Must Consider

Is there a problem that is causing significant harms? "If it ain't broke, don't fix it." This saying isn't always true, but it is a good place to start. If you want to change a course of action, there must be something wrong with what we are doing now or something to be gained if we change. If you want us to stay the course, there must be something worse that will happen if we change.

But more than just establishing that there is a problem, you need to show that the problem is significant in some way. It will take time, money, and effort to change so that change has to be justified by achieving some benefit that is larger than the difficulties of change.

In 2008 a controversy arose in the United States about "hot fuel."[1] Gasoline stations store gas in tanks underground. The temperature of that gas changes somewhat depending on how warm the earth is. When gas gets hotter, it expands. For simplicity, gasoline pumps all assume that gas is at 60 degrees Fahrenheit. If the gas is really warmer than that, the pump will misread the amount of gas. The pump will click off a gallon, but because the gas is warmer (and less dense), the energy content of that gallon will be less than the energy content of a gallon of cold gas. The idea of always assuming the gas was at 60 degrees was that in the winter it would be colder and more dense and in the summer hotter and less dense, and things would average out over the year. But in California, where the weather is warmer, the gas was more likely to be warm than cold.

You're getting cheated! Scandal! Outrage! Various consumer advocates were quoted expressing their desire for the motorist to get their money back. What to do? Refit all the pumps with some expensive gadget to compensate for changes in temperature? Give drivers a rebate? Tax the gas companies?

Well, first, we might ask just how big this problem is. "Millions of dollars a day" we're told. But buried deep in the article is the real datum we need to know: Gas expands 1 percent for every 15-degree temperature change (diesel fuel expands 0.6 percent per 15 degrees). And the actual fuel temperature in a California summer? About 72 degrees, less than 15 degrees. So you are losing just a little under 1 percent of your gas on a hot day. If you don't inflate your tires properly, your mileage can decrease by 2 or 3 percent. If you leave your windows open when driving on the freeway, the increased drag will lower your mileage by more than 1 percent.

In other words, the game isn't worth the prize. The problem isn't significant enough to worry about. We have much bigger problems. Fix the big problems first.

Is there a necessity for change: Why will the current policy not solve this problem? Some situations will cure themselves, some do not. You may need to show that the current

---

[1] "Hot fuel adds to pain at the pump," *Los Angeles Times*, May 23, 2008, p. C1.

policies in effect will not fix the problem, and change is needed. During the beginning of the 2008 financial crisis, there was talk that no action was needed because markets were self-correcting. If prices were out of line, if a bubble of speculation had occurred, the market would correct itself in time, bad companies would go under, their workers would find jobs at better companies, and everything would go forward.

Change can be blocked for legal reasons, but also due to economic structures or social attitudes.

Sometimes that is true, but the 2008 economic downturn was so severe that policies for our financial system had to be designed on the spot to address the problem and fix it.

What is your plan? You have to have one. You need more than a goal; you need a specific plan for what you are going to do. In the scope of a typical classroom paper, you probably cannot go into great detail, but you should at least have some idea of what you are talking about. Almost all countries around the world have universal health insurance for their citizens, but the way in which that is accomplished varies quite a bit. It therefore isn't enough just to advocate for universal coverage; you need to say something about what your plan is.

There have been complaints for fifty years and more about the budget deficit of the U.S. federal government. All sorts of people want to eliminate it and want to claim that their opponents have no desire to eliminate it. But in those fifty years, there has seldom, if ever, been put forward a plan, with actual numbers and specifics about how to produce a balanced budget. Some plans have been put forward with claims to reduce spending, but, upon examination, they typically turn out to just have a line with some label like "Cut waste, fraud, and abuse" or "Eliminate unnecessary programs," but with no explanation of how that would be done or what would be cut.

Other plans are specific but involve massive cuts to programs without considering how that would impact the economy.

A related problem is when a policy claim is advanced with no plan whatsoever. Innumerable organizations have held press conferences or produced documents with a "call for action" in them. People gather, speeches are made calling for action, demands are made for action, but what specific action is demanded is often not specified. Or the action requested is some variation of "no": We are urged to "stop the [budget] cuts," stop layoffs, or stop something, but it is seldom clear what action is proposed as a replacement for the action they oppose.

Indeed sometimes you will find such groups actively opposed to providing a plan. When asked what their proposal is, they will claim that is "not their responsibility" and that politicians or leaders have that responsibility.

How much does your plan cost? Who pays? Who benefits? "There is no such thing as a free lunch." Nothing is free, especially, the saying goes, free advice. Everything costs something. Policies that advocate "free" things (free tuition, free health care) usually mean "free at the point of purchase," because the actual costs are moved into general taxes or paid for in some other way.

It is certainly possible to advocate that a certain policy should be funded differently than it is now, and there is no reason at all you can't advocate for some funding to move from being paid for by a user fee to having general taxes pay for it. But that doesn't make the policy free. You must discuss the costs of implementing and maintaining your policy.

You need to consider the costs of implementing your plan and the cost of operating your new policy. If you are going to build something that will eventually wear out, you need to think about the costs of eventually replacing that.

Likewise, you need to add up the benefits that will occur from adopting the plan.

There are a class of arguments we could term the "Wouldn't it be wonderful if ..." plans. Wouldn't it be great if every kid learned a second language, if every college student got a scholarship to travel abroad, if every newborn had free health care, and if textbook authors got paid ten times as much as they get now. Well, yes it would. But how much does it cost to do those things?

There are many aspects to the costs of a plan. Here are a few common ones that are often not made clear.

- The difference between **income** and **profit.** Income is all the money you take in. Profit is what you have left after you pay expenses. Some plan might increase the income of an organization but increase expenses by even more.
- The difference between **cost minimization** and **profit maximization.** They aren't the same. Sometimes you need to spend money to make money.
- The difference between **operating expenses** and **capital expenses.** Does football make money for the university? It might cover its year-to-year running expenses of salaries and equipment and travel but likely does not cover the capital expenses of building the stadium and practice facilities.

Specificity: The proposal is a great idea. Can it be defined? There are a number of ideas that are good, even unexceptionally good in and of themselves, but simply cannot be defined precisely enough to form the basis of laws. We don't want "hate speech" in our communities. But what is it, exactly? Is attacking Israel's policy toward Palestine hate speech (a form of anti-Semitism) if you get excited enough? Is telling blonde jokes misogynist? Probably not, but what if you do it all the time and after you've been told to quit? Does your intent matter? Will we have to provide a list of exactly what is and is not considered hate speech and hope no one can adapt the language to work around our list?

Likewise, what is an "excessive profit"? We don't like large companies exploiting situations to make huge profits off our misery, but what is the definition we'll use?

However, a difficulty in defining terms doesn't have to stop you. Sometimes we go ahead because some terms that are hard to define (like "intent") are just so important we have to use them. But laws are regularly tossed out by courts because they were so vague that a person could honestly not know if they had violated the law.

So, in building your arguments, you need to at least address any definitional problems that might arise. You may need to discuss how those problems will be dealt with as your project goes forward over time.

Will your plan solve (or significantly improve) the problem? Proving that there is a problem and then proving that you have a plan is still not enough. Will your plan actually fix the problem? Efforts to stop smoking, underage sex, or activities that lead to HIV infection often are based on education. If you educate people, they won't do certain behaviors. But if the behaviors are driven by hormones, social pressures, or deep personal drives, people may do things they know are wrong.

There is clearly a need to ensure that people do not get on airplanes with bombs. So good security measures are justified. But, the question is about some particular rule: Will this proposed rule in fact reduce the danger of terrorism on airplanes, or is it irrelevant? And if it does reduce the risk of terrorism, is it the best and most efficient way to do so? What is needed is some very serious discussion about what plan would actually solve the problem for the least cost and inconvenience.

Your proposed policy has to actually solve, or reduce, the problems you are addressing.

The proposal is a great idea, but can it be enforced? Even if your idea is well defined and actually solves the problem, you may have problems enforcing your plan. The United States tried banning alcohol in the 1920s: a plan that was clear and well-defined. But it simply could not be enforced. Likewise, efforts to stop prostitution, people entering the country illegally, or the smoking of marijuana also seem to be largely futile. You certainly can argue that these issues might be so important that efforts to reduce them are vital nonetheless, but you can't ignore the issue of how your plan will be enforced.

However, even a vital moral necessity does not exempt a policy proposal from careful analysis. Is the cost of imperfect enforcement worth the gains achieved?

After Your Plan: How Will People and Society Adapt If This Proposal Is Adopted? Will That Adaptation Undermine Your Plan?

The United States passed campaign finance reform, and now there is more money in politics than before: The contributors adapted their actions and found ways around the prohibition. Building an anti-immigration fence may just send immigrants to a different part of the border or to get in the country in different ways. Building roads to relieve congestion can cause people to build houses and businesses along the roads leading to more congestion.

In a previous section we discussed unintended consequences, and here we are dealing with the same general idea in a different context. What we want to highlight here is not that we didn't comprehend the dynamics of a system but rather the specific human adaptability to changed circumstances—to initiate new behavior to get around obstacles.

In constructing a policy argument, you may need to assess what motivations people might have to get around your proposed policy. Will there be massive incentives to change behavior? Will those behavioral changes help or hurt your plan? Can you design a plan that is less likely to be subverted?

Some cases where a significant change in behavior after a policy is adopted might include the following. Perhaps they would be good examples to investigate just how significant the change in behavior might be.

- Physician-assisted suicide of patients in extreme pain or with no chance of recovery. As long as it is illegal, it may happen clandestinely but most likely only in very justified cases. If it is made legal, some fear it will become easier, occur more often, and cases will arise when the physician is pressuring patients into it.
- Why do we screen the stereotypical "little old lady" at airport security? Has such a person ever been a bomber? Or why does the flight crew have to get screened? But suppose that all women over 70 were exempted from security measures. How long would it be before terrorists either recruit such a person or fool one into carrying a bomb on board?
- Historically, a woman had to face daunting barriers to report, and see through, a prosecution of someone for rape or sexual misconduct. Thus, false claims were thought to be extremely unlikely. "Why would someone put themselves through all that if they weren't telling the truth?" it was said. In recent years, efforts have been made to reduce the stigma about reporting these incidents and make us more aware of how often these crimes occur. Does that then reduce barriers to making a false claim? Some think this has happened, that an increase in false claims is to be expected, and so we can't just assume a claim is true. But what is the evidence? Is there data to show whether or not false claims have increased and, if so, by how much?

A MODEL FOR CONSTRUCTING A POLICY ARGUMENT

There is no one way to construct a policy argument, but if you are having problems getting started, consider a paper where your paragraphs might be organized as follows:

- There is a significant problem. It is causing these harms ...
- The problem isn't going to go away ...
- To solve this problem, we should do this (specific and well-defined) thing ... (your proposal)
- This plan will solve the problem because ...
- This plan will produce these benefits, which are larger than the costs ...
- We will be able to enforce the plan, and it will not be circumvented ...

Obviously you have to scale this to your task. If you're writing a twenty-page proposal, then each of those bullet points becomes an entire section. And in any case, you should revise the sentences to use language appropriate for your particular proposal. We also haven't included all of the points discussed up to now; this is the bare-bones outline of an argument. But maybe it can help you get going.

RESPONDING TO POLICY ARGUMENTS

At various points along the way, we've discussed how you can respond to aspects of a policy argument. However, there are some general strategies to consider. With a policy claim, you have more options than just disagreeing with the claim.

- Check to see that the proposed **policy includes the elements** listed in the previous sections. If you are responding to a plan that, for example, did not include costs or omitted major impacts, you can focus on the problems.
- Suggest the current policy only needs **minor repairs** to achieve most of the same benefits. In this strategy, you agree that a problem exists, but you argue that you can fix the problem by improving the present system rather than changing it. You'd likely try to argue that the costs of a minor fix are much lower than the proposed alternative.
- Propose a significant **alternative plan.** In this approach, you agree that a problem exists and that it needs a major change from the current course of action, but you propose a plan very different from the plan being proposed. You may use this strategy when you agree that there is a problem, but you disagree about the cause of the problem.
- **Redefine the problem.** In this approach, you may well ignore the proposed plan and go back to the analysis of the problem. You locate the root causes in something different from what your opponent did. Perhaps the problem identified by your opponent is, in your view, only a symptom of a different, underlying problem. By redefining the problem, your opponent's plan becomes irrelevant and doesn't need to be addressed in detail.

COMMON FALLACIES AND PROBLEMS

In addition to the issues discussed in the previous sections, there are some specific fallacies that affect policy arguments.

Trying to Solve a Policy Issue by Only Debating Value Arguments

The authors grew up in a farm state. Every election cycle it was the same thing: "Mr. Politician, how will you solve the farm crisis?" "Well, my fellow citizens, farmers are the heart and soul of America. Family values. The family farm is precious. I stand in support of the family farm. Salt of the earth. Heartland values. Wave the flag. Yada, yada, yada."

Okay, so what are you going to do? What do you propose? No answer.

We have no objection to the value that a family farm is a good thing. But that, in and of itself, is not a policy. Arguing for a value does not address the practical questions that a policy argument must deal with.

It's worse than that. A focus only on values may actually mislead us on policy in some cases. "Illegal" and "immoral" are not synonyms. Read that again. Not everything that is immoral can be illegal. And not every illegal thing is immoral. And that is not just a cynical view of the world. It is a necessity.

Consider the question of enforcement and then ask yourself why most countries do not have a law against adultery. Almost everyone, including people who commit adultery, agree that it is wrong. Imagine how that law would be enforced. Would police be sent undercover into singles' bars to check if people were really married? Would we charge the NSA to read our email, looking for messages with keywords that signified a likelihood of illicit activity? And even if we just let people lodge complaints when they were cheated upon, would it be a good use of tax money for prosecutors to spend time on this rather than some other crime?

If we were to ban abortion, would we actually put women in jail for having one? Or arrest them while still pregnant because we had reliable information that they were planning an abortion? Force women to give birth by holding them in jail until they did? People who oppose abortion rights seldom explain in detail what they would actually do if their policies were adopted.

Trying to Reject All Value Dimensions of Public Policy in Favor of "Practicality"

If only looking at values is wrong, so is rejecting all value aspects of policy. Actually, attempts to reject values and focus on practicality or profit are often smoke screens for simply preferring one value above all others. The view that the only duty of a company is to make money is certainly a value statement. The debate over Wal-Mart and its impact on a community cannot proceed without consideration of what values our economic entities should follow.

Values have a legitimate role in many policy discussions. Debates about universal health care or the need for Social Security can certainly involve value arguments about duties to the less fortunate or beliefs about what sort of society we want to live in. Opponents of universal health care or those who deride Social Security are promoting the value that each person should stand on their own and that all failures or suffering are the fault of the individual, and it corrupts individual character to do otherwise.

Not Putting Quantitative Values on Impacts

We've discussed at several points the need for specifics in policy arguments: costs, benefits, numbers affected, and so on. But it's worth looking again at the extent to which we advocate for something we think is good, but we don't say how good.

Nutritional and health claims are often examples of this. "Lowers cholesterol" but by how much? "You fall asleep quicker." "Enhances mood." By 1 percent? Five percent of the time? The problem is again the issue of trade-offs and cost. Is the benefit big enough that we'll even notice? Is it big enough to be worth the cost?

Consider how quickly this can slip past us. Consider this sentence extracted from an appeal:

> "Overconsumption of sodium often leads to higher blood pressure as well as heart problems."

Sounds like a perfectly reasonable thing to say. Nice and precise. However, there are three critical quantitative issues that are totally ignored. First, how much consumption is "overconsumption"? Does that amount vary between men and women or due to age or weight? Second, how often do these heart problems occur? Does the rate of occurrence depend on how much overconsumption is done, or does an amount over a certain value just trigger the impacts? And third, how severe are these problems? How much is the increase in blood pressure? A percent or two? And is that increase significant? What kind of heart problems does this produce? And what are the impacts of those problems?

The (Sometimes) Fallacy of the "Slippery Slope"

The slippery slope argument is of the form that "If you accept this, you have to accept that." Once "the camel's nose is inside the tent, the rest will follow." More specifically, this is found in arguments like "If you accept homosexuality, how can you reject group marriage or bestiality?" "If you let Pakistan and India acquire nuclear weapons, how can you stop Iran from getting them?"

Slippery slope can be a valid rejoinder to a policy proposal in some cases, but you can't just assume it is true. What has to be investigated in each case is whether or not there are forces that will cause the slope to be slippery, so to speak. If one thing occurs, does it change conditions in society so that the next thing is easier, or are there other factors at play that will prevent that? Sometimes slippery-slope arguments depend on an assumption of logical consistency—but many things in practice are inconsistent. Nations may acquiesce in one country getting nuclear weapons but be very hard on some other country.

CASES OF COMPLEXITY

Policy claims are everywhere, but if you are looking for examples where the complexities of the issues we've described in this chapter make decision making harder, we suggest the following as a few examples.

> *The death penalty.*   This is often debated purely in value terms. Does someone deserve to die? Should we match death for death or opt to refrain from it. But what is the goal of having the death penalty? Is it punishment—the murderer inflicted this amount of pain and so should suffer it? Is it deterrence—a way of stopping others who might commit a murder? Or is it retribution—our sense of justice demands this?

But behind this are practical questions. Does it deter crimes? And there is a fundamental practical question: Do we execute the right people?

> *Alternative energy.*   Wind, solar, ethanol, wave energy, hydropower, and others. Should we convert our economy to rely on these options? First up is a very significant value argument: Should all this be left "to the market" or should the society, acting through government, direct how resources should be allocated?

And if it is inevitable that the government does influence what energy sources are used, there is a huge set of practical questions. How should this influence be made: tax credits, subsidies, taxing pollution or carbon, loan guarantees, direct purchase, or even direct orders to use a type of energy?

What weight should we give the risk of climate change if we don't act? How do we decide between short-term pain and long-term gain? Should we change slowly with the risk of multiple conflicting approaches going on at the same time or gain efficiencies by acting quickly?

And what is clean energy? How do we measure that? It's not just pollution out of the tailpipes of our cars or wasted electricity in our houses. The energy used to produce clean energy sources and recycle them has to be included.

Many values lurk behind these decisions. Is the earth there to be used, or should we preserve it? Is the good life one where you "live large" or live simply?

Different audiences are involved as well. Jobs in farm country is a strong argument for ethanol derived from corn, but probably doesn't carry great weight with consumers of energy in cities. Producers, researchers, local officials, business leaders, and others will all have different perspectives driven by how they will benefit or be affected by policy changes.

CONCLUSION

So, what should we do about sex offenders on Halloween? Maybe nothing, maybe a number of different things. What is the problem, really? Our fears for our kids? Our queasiness at sexual misconduct and our wish that these people would simply disappear so we don't have to deal with them? Maybe we need to do a better job of sharply distinguishing truly dangerous offenders from those who are unlikely to reoffend. Perhaps we need to ask why the neighborhood as a collective entity doesn't watch over all the kids on Halloween night. Or maybe we need to be out with our own kids that night.

The authors of this book take no official position on the vexed question of Halloween safety. But they do wish you would think about it—as an example of the complexities that arise in policy discussions. This little example highlights the role of illusion and fear and wishful thinking that are involved in all policy questions, be it a question about spending a trillion dollars or about if getting drunk tonight will affect your life.

Yet, the role of Pathos cannot be dismissed. The Halloween question also makes us realize that policy should not just be about mechanical summing of profit and loss but is also about our legitimate hopes and dreams for our children, our desire to live in a safe and comfortable community, and our need to have some way to come to terms with our inability to remove all danger from our lives.

As advocates you have a duty when making policy arguments to not simply orate in favor of some unobjectionable "goodness" but to do the work to discover how that "goodness" can be implemented in a world of limited resources, irrational behavior, and unavoidable choices. That is the sort of leadership a democracy needs from its citizens and that a democracy needs its citizens to demand from its elected representatives.

SUMMARY OF POLICY CLAIMS

Description

Policy claims advocate a course of action, as implemented in a law, regulation, rule, cultural practice, or personal behavior.

Explicit form

"We (should/should not) do X." "We (should/should not) continue to do X."

Implicit forms

Can include statements like
"We ought to ..." "I recommend that we adopt ..." "It would be good if we ..."
"Let's do this ..." "I don't want to change."

Examples typically developed as policy claims

"We should revise the packaging on our product within the next six months."
"The United States should adopt a program of universal health insurance."
"This is the house we should buy."

Issues and Aspects

- Are always built on value and fact claims.
- Require consideration of various practical issues.
- Are not just about public policy or politics.

Study Questions

- Describe a policy claim in one sentence.
- Name some common fallacies associated with policy claims.
- What are the components you need to have if you argue for a policy claim?
- How are fact and value claims related to policy claims?

Kairos: The Context of Your Argument

INTRODUCTION

A man stands in the middle of a crowded theater just after a horror movie has pushed an audience into feeling scared. He shouts out "Fire!" at the top of his lungs, pointing and looking scared. There is no fire, but the crowd lurches toward riot. Another man goes running down the street looking for someone to call 911; he tells them there is a fire in a house nearby. He galvanizes people into action, and some children are saved. A black man used the "N word" to playfully address another black man. A white woman throws the same word at a black man on the street to express contempt. A comedian uses the "F-bomb" in his stand-up routine to a roar of laughter. The same words spoken during a Sunday School class cause a scandal.

> "The most stringent protection of free speech would not protect a man in falsely shouting fire in a theatre and causing a panic. It does not even protect a man from an injunction against uttering words that may have all the effect of force."
>
> *Gompers v. Bucks Stove & Range Co.*, 221 U.S. 418, 439

> "The question in every case is whether the words used are used in such circumstances and are of such a nature as to create a clear and present danger that they will bring about the substantive evils that Congress has a right to prevent."
>
> Justice Oliver Wendell Holmes, Jr., for the U.S. Supreme Court
> *Schenck v. United States*, 249 U.S. 47, decided 3/3/1919.

A long time ago, the Roman writer Quintillian observed that what words mean involves more than just the words.

> . . . the same remark will seem freedom of speech in one's mouth, madness in another's, and arrogance in a third. (Quintillian, 2002 , 9.1.37)

Your argument is not just the words and images you present; it is also impacted by everything that surrounds your presentation. To enable analysis, we divide "everything" into consideration of the *audience* that you address, the *medium* that

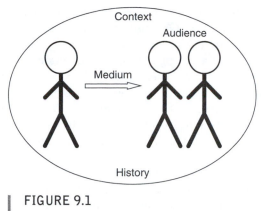

FIGURE 9.1
Communication as Contextual.

conveys your argument, the *occasion* (time and place) in which you deliver your argument, as well as the *history* of previous communications between advocate and audience. The combination of these factors is sometimes termed *Kairos*—the fourth of those Greek words that describe the dimensions of your argument. We'll also term it the *context* of your argument.

Our thesis is that as advocates, we have to be aware of these issues. We have to do so because the context inevitably affects the persuasiveness and the meaning of our communication. The same words are not heard the same way by everyone nor heard the same way by the same person at two different times.

Assessing these contextual factors will give us guidance to make choices about which specific points to include in our argument, how to sequence our various points, and what tone or style to use to clothe them.

AUDIENCE ANALYSIS: WHO RECEIVES YOUR ARGUMENT?

There is more than one audience. By this banal-sounding statement we simply mean that communication is typically intended for a specific group of people, not for people in general and not just to hear ourselves talk. Peruse a magazine rack at a newsstand or bookstore. There are likely magazines about domestic news, foreign news, business, fashion, various hobbies, movies, fitness and health, travel, cars, the arts, music, pop culture, poetry, computers, religion, crafts, and other categories. Within each of these categories, there will be magazines reflecting different points of view.

We think of these magazines as being different from each other, but turn that perspective around and think of the difference among the buyers of those magazines. Each separate category implies a different audience. Imagine the audiences for each magazine on the newsstand standing in front of it. Of course, someone who buys a newsmagazine might also buy a woodworking magazine. But the audience of people who buy the woodworking magazine is thinking about different things than the audience who purchases the newsmagazine—even if many of the same people are in both audiences.

And what makes those audiences different is far more than that one is "interested in woodworking" and that the other is "interested in the news." One audience will be interested in news about changes in what can be harvested from forests, the other about changing gas prices. One audience will care about the safety of wood-working tools, the other about the cost of health care.

But, we are not at all claiming some simplistic notion that these audiences are "opposed" to one another. The audience reading the newsmagazine isn't likely to be offended by the woodworking magazine; it is just not interested in it at the moment. Each real person is a combination of many interests. Each real person will work, relax, peruse a hobby, have a view on the world, grieve, and be happy at various points in life.

So, each message is going to have a particular audience.

The audience is not like you. The next thing we have to tell you, gentle reader, is this: You're not the center of the universe. You may not even be orbiting the center of the universe. One mistake communicators make is to assume that their audience is just like themselves, assuming that everyone sees the world like they do—in effect having an "audience of me." We've all encountered people who could not imagine the world from any other perspective than their own. Sometimes such people have a vision compelling enough that they can persuade others to adopt their position, but more often they simply miscommunicate and in a way that is annoying. We don't appreciate people who seem not to be listening to us.

First and foremost, in understanding the audience, is not to try to argue with them about what they should be, but to try to accept them the way they are.

Does that mean denying yourself? No. Of course, you have to "put yourself" into your argument; you should communicate in a way that is authentic to you and what you believe. Certainly, if your argument sounds false or fake to you, it is a sign that you need to change something. But, we hope, part of who you authentically are is that you respect who you are communicating with and desire to communicate clearly and persuasively.

It is also worth remembering that crafting an argument is not quite the same as a creative work of art where originality and the unique personal voice of the author are highly valued. When we approach art (as part of the audience), we expect to have to make an effort to engage the work. Part of what makes creative writing hard and wonderful is the way the author takes us inside their unique perspective.

In contrast, a persuasive communication differs in emphasis: It is up to the advocate to reach out to the audience. You want your audience to do something for you: to change their view of the world. Therefore you have to accept the duty of learning about them first. However, that doesn't mean there is no creativity to making an argument. There is art and the satisfactions of creativity involved in the process of making a good argument, in selecting words that have an impact, in arraigning your points for impact and clarity. But fundamentally, your objective is to persuade. Since that is your true desire, understanding who you are engaged with should be in line with what you want.

Aiming at an Audience

You are aiming at a specific audience in your mind. But do you reach it? Consider a number of possible targets:

- The actual audience. These are the people who actually hear or read your message, the people it does, in fact, reach. But is that who you aimed at?

- The ideal audience. Maybe you don't know who is going to read your argument. In that case, it might motivate you to do better if you imagined your audience as open-minded, rational, perceptive, good-natured people who are interested in knowing the truth and making good decisions.
- The intended audience. This is the group you are trying to write for. It differs from the actual audience in that you may be mistaken in your assumptions about who is going to read your work. It differs from the ideal audience in that you may realize that you have to address false beliefs your audience has or prejudices that might block your message.
- The implied audience. This audience is identified by reasoning backward from the text. We look at the text and look for clues about what the author intended. Historians and literary critics will do this with older documents when we don't actually know much about the author or the situation that prompted the writing. The intended and implied audience may differ if the author makes a mistake or doesn't write effectively.

These terms give you some tools for talking about your goals and for assessing your writing after you've completed a draft.

The Audience You're Not Aiming At

Sometimes differences between actual and intended audiences are not the result of mistakes but are intentional. An author is aiming at one group and hoping or intending the argument to be private to one group. So, unlike the magazine example we gave at the beginning, in this case you want certain groups to *not* see what you are arguing to another group.

There certainly are cases when limiting the audience is legitimate: a lawyer talking to a client, two people in an intimate relationship with each other, a coach talking to their own team, people discussing a personnel issue at their organization. But there are cases when this isn't legitimate. Every month, it seems, brings some example where communication "escapes" from its intended audience and gets out to a group it wasn't intended for. Be it an email that someone forwards to the wrong people, or a politician saying something to one group that contradicts or is deeply offensive to another—it happens.

One of the more spectacular examples of this is the secret speech of Nikita Khrushchev. He was the head of the Soviet Union in the 1950s. In 1956, at a major gathering of senior officials of the Soviet Union, Khrushchev blasted the former dictator Stalin. Criticizing Stalin was taboo, unheard of, and certainly dangerous for an ordinary citizen of that country. For several hours Khrushchev gave chapter and verse of the abuses perpetuated by Stalin.

However, even the all-powerful leader of a very closed off society in a time before cell phones and the Internet could not keep the speech a secret. Given on February 25, 1956, by June it was being reprinted in the *New York Times*. Secrets escape.

Sometimes an author works the deception by speaking in a code that some listeners will understand but others will not. The British call this "dog whistle politics"—just as only a dog can hear the whistle, only the target group will get the code. In the late 1960s, some U.S. politicians would speak of their belief in "law and order." On the surface, who could be opposed to that? But it was understood as a code for "not letting the Blacks gain too much power."

Your Audience and the Universal Audience

We have to keep a balance between two notions: that our communication will address a specific audience and also that there is a larger audience that might also hear our argument.

It can be useful to think about your communication in this way: Imagine your audience in the center of the room, while the rest of the world is around the edges of the room listening in. You have to tailor your communication to aim at the specific group, but not say anything that would offend the ideal audience we identified earlier. On his first job out of college, one of the authors received the following advice: Always write so that you would not be embarrassed to have your words reprinted on the front page of the *New York Times*. Observing this rule has saved the author many embarrassments over the years.

While this mental exercise may sound restricting or that you won't be able to say anything specific, it can help to hold yourself to a standard of integrity: You won't be pandering to one group and then to another.

Am I Addressing a Uniform Audience?

Given that a group of people are absorbing your communication, can we claim that they are homogeneous—uniform? Consider a typical college class. Investigate hard enough and you can separate each student into a separate group. There are athletes and those who never exercise, departmental majors, undeclared and non-degree students, males and females, some old and some young, commuter students and those who live in dorms. Some work, some don't. Some are conservative, some liberal, and some are tired of politics entirely. There are different religious perspectives, different attitudes about money, and they have different amounts of money. Some are into cars, others into partying, movies, a hobby, reading, and many other choices. Some have specific career ambitions, some aren't sure, some will be sure later on. And on and on.

Yet, that all are college students and all in a particular class does bind the group together so that they can be addressed for their common interests in tuition, grading policies, teaching styles, and so on. Whatever else this group is and does, part of the time they are students trying to learn a subject. That this group of people all experience your argument is also something that binds them together. By presenting an argument to them, you are contributing to creating an audience.

Sometimes a single audience for an event will have various subgroups within them. Imagine you are giving a talk as part of a panel discussion. Your audience could well include:

- Regular attendees of the group who are quite knowledgeable with the issues being discussed
- Visitors, not fully aware of the history of the issues being discussed
- People there specifically to see or support one of the presenters and not necessarily open to hearing what others have to say

- The other presenters who may react as if they've been attacked or feel competitive with your presentation

The Audience of the Future

As if we haven't found enough different audiences, sometimes it is worth thinking about how your presentation might look twenty years in the future. Your predictions and concerns might be shown to have been wrong by then, that could happen to anyone, but would what you say look foolish? That it gave too much importance to trivial or transitory things? Said you'd never agree with this, or work with that group, and then you've been forced to? This is worth a little consideration so you don't paint yourself into a corner.

So, we have identified our audience, and now we need to learn about them.

Three Dimensions of What We Want to Know

There are many facets to what we would like to know about an audience, but it can be useful to organize them under three terms: epistemology, ontology, and axiology. These are technical terms but very useful ones; we'll provide definitions as we go.

What are the audience's epistemological beliefs? *Epistemology* is the study of how we know what we know. It considers what counts as knowledge, what justification there is for a belief, and how knowledge can be validated or tested. In the context of designing an argument, we want to know how the audience decides that something is true or not. In short, what type of proof do they think is persuasive? What form of proof will they accept as valid? Obviously, then, we should try to provide a form of proof to an audience that matches what they accept. We'll demonstrate by offering some examples.

One of the authors participated in a court case where the two sides made radically different assumptions about what the jury's epistemological beliefs were. One side made their case through expert witnesses. Each witness was presented with extensive credentials so that the jury was sure to understand that this person was a real expert on the topic at hand. The idea here is that they thought the jury would understand that they themselves weren't experts and that this legal issue was a topic requiring expertise and that they would accept the word of an expert.

The other side in the case took the approach that all that was required was common sense. No fancy words, no fancy experts full of "book larnin'." Just plain folks could decide the case using common sense.

The two approaches highlight our somewhat ambivalent attitude toward experts—our different epistemological presuppositions. Sometimes we are impressed (or intimidated) by experts, and we accept their views uncritically. Other times, we can resent them, feel inferior in their presence, and then respond by aggressively defending the virtue of remaining uneducated. And should an expert seem ignorant of practical realities, act condescending to us, or throw complex vocabulary at us, we can swiftly reject them. This reflects different views of epistemology: what we will accept as proof.

One of the authors was sitting in a coffee shop and couldn't help overhearing two young women talking. They were obviously members of a Christian church most would describe as evangelical or fundamentalist. One was lamenting her failure at convincing someone of the Bible's truth. She explained that she had quoted various verses to the person that spoke to the authority and veracity of the Bible but was mystified that these had not been persuasive.

She obviously accepted the Bible as authoritative. Her epistemology was that if the Bible said something, it was true. In that world, to quote a Bible verse would be more authoritative than anything else. However, the person she was communicating with had a different epistemology. He did not accept the Bible as a source of truth and so was not persuaded by it. If you don't believe something (or someone), having that text (or person) tell you that they are telling the truth will not carry much weight.

The point is not that one was right and the other wrong. The point is that communication did not work here because the advocate was not communicating in a way that took into account the epistemological beliefs of her audience.

To get you started, here are some categories and issues to think about. Of course, each is a simple scheme, and people will have more complex views:

- Will they be more moved by a statistical study or by a compelling story?
- Will they respect tradition as carrying authority or look favorably on a "rebel" position?
- Do they warm up to outside experts, to one of "their own," to family members, or to any specific group?
- What is their attitude about the truthfulness and authority of politicians and government officials? To corporate executives? To the wealthy or the poor?
- Would personal experience trump all other forms of proof?
- Do they believe traditional media or "new" media?

If you can understand what sort of proof your audience will accept, you can adjust the evidence you use to make your presentation more persuasive.

Epistemic closure is a term that has come into popular use of late. It refers to a condition when a person or group's criteria for what they believe has narrowed down simply to whether or not the advocate agrees with them. They decide that any information that disagrees with their position must not be credible—simply because it *does* disagree. The danger of such a condition is that it is self-reinforcing. The person is closed off from new information and closed off from the process of proof.

What are the audience's ontological beliefs? *Ontology* is the study of what is real, what the concept of "being" means, what is existence. In the context of argumentation, it refers to what experiences have become "real" for your audience. Let's consider this along the dimensions of Pathos and Logos.

In terms of Pathos, we need to examine not just those things the audience gives assent to, but what experiences have had a significant impact on them. Many are affected by the Iraq war, but to those who have fought in it, the experience of combat carries very real memories that are probably different than those who have not been in the armed forces.

Nor are we just referring to extreme events like being in combat. Any significant life event, such as earning a Ph.D., holding a particular job for twenty years, getting fired, winning a championship, being married, giving birth, going through a stressful event with a group, or growing up in a particular part of the country, gives us certain experiences that carry a "reality" to us.

A friend of the authors is from Cyprus. His family was from the area now occupied by Turkish settlers. He was recently able to return for a visit and sought to visit his father's grave. When he got to it, he discovered that the headstone had been smashed by some unknown person. Most of you are not from that country, are likely unaware of the conflicted history of the island, and don't know the people involved in this story. So it's not real to you. But, on the other hand, imagine how your world would be affected if this was your parents' grave that had been desecrated. How would that affect you, change your views on political issues? It was very real to this friend.

Of course, as we mature, we should learn to appreciate that others have "real" events also and have some comprehension and even sympathy for other perspectives. But the extent to which humans do this is always uneven, and even mature people can have a significant lack of sympathy for people who have experienced different "realities." This is reflected in the way we can dismiss the pain of others as being less serious than our own or the way we assume that others could just solve their problems if they tried.

Think about attitudes to being able to stop drinking, lose weight, being an immigrant (legal or otherwise), being the only woman or minority in a group, being homosexual, or a white male approaching retirement. Consider the different realities of being from rural America or urban America or from another country, among many others. Our inability to comprehend the reality of someone else is a major block to effective communication.

This point is worth exploring. It is one thing to notice that (for example) Swedish immigrants to the United States will talk to each other differently than Vietnamese immigrants do. It is a second issue to have a Swedish immigrant addressing a Vietnamese group. In other words, cultures (and by culture we do not only mean "ethnic group") vary in their communication patterns. More than this, when we as advocates are "crossing cultures" to advocate to an audience whose reality is different than ours, then we have to be particularly sensitive to how our arguments are received.

But, it isn't just our view of other realities that is a problem. We can also use our particular experiences of reality as a weapon to prevent others from expressing their views on a subject. Often we hear something like the argument that "If you haven't done X, you have no right to comment on it." This is not a valid argument or, rather, the scope of validity claimed for it is generally too wide.

The point for us as communicators is that the ontological beliefs of our audience can be a major factor in our ability to persuade them—either a major help or a major stumbling block. In March of 2008, then-presidential candidate Barack Obama made a speech on racism in the United States. In that speech he acknowledged as real both the ontological beliefs of whites and blacks. For blacks, it was the experience of their parents suffering with legal racism and the experience of the lingering effects of racism for the current generation. For whites, it was the common familial story of the loss of culture from immigration and the experience of building a new life in America. It was close to unique for a politician identified on the liberal end of American political beliefs to refer to this defining perspective of white people. Obama's ability to connect, in this speech, with the beliefs on both ethnic groups is one of the reasons it had power.

One of the reasons the Israel–Palestinian situation is so intractable is the vastly different ontological perspectives of the two sides. To the Israelis, reality is that a civilized democracy, heir to the advancements of western culture, a culture that has made the desert bloom, is under permanent attack by a barbarian force that adopts terrorism as its primary weapon and conducts suicide attacks on civilians. Reality to the Palestinians is that they are a colonized, occupied, near-powerless society that cannot even travel on the highways within their own country without permission and is having their ancestral homes, olive groves, cemeteries, and very culture slowly wiped out of existence as the world refuses to notice. It would be an advanced problem in communication to develop arguments that would appeal to both of these audiences.

We also have to consider this issue of ontological beliefs along the dimension of Logos: What does your audience know of the issue being discussed? Do I know what they know? What do they know that I don't know? One function your communication will likely have to attend to is to inform your audience of certain things. Sometimes you have to give the background of an issue or simply present some data necessary to understand a point you are making.

But you can offend or turn off your audience here as well. If you tell them things they already know or if you refer to something as well-established truth when your audience doesn't believe it, you can cause them to stop listening to you. Also, while people often like to learn, they don't like to feel stupid. If you flaunt your learning or puff your ego because you know something they do not, they will reject your argument.

However, failing to educate your audience can also be a big mistake.

What are the audience's axiological beliefs? *Axiological* refers to values and value systems. In ancient Greek, the word "Axios" meant "worth." In the context of argumentation, we are very interested in the values held by our audience. Values are harder to change, in general, than a view of a particular fact. The values we hold can strongly influence which facts we accept.

We discussed values and value systems in the chapter on value claims and so will not discuss it here. We would simply like to draw your attention to the fact that values can be tenaciously held and that they greatly affect how our audience views our arguments.

We will give one example of what happens when you fail to really attend to a group's axiological beliefs. An article in the *Financial Times*[1] reported on a marketing effort gone bust. Montblanc, maker of high-end pens, introduced a very expensive fountain pen they called the Mahatma Gandhi. They intended to honor Gandhi's use of rhetoric and even wrapped the pen in some homespun cloth,

---

[1] Amy Kazmin, "Perils of blundering into India's cultural minefield," *Financial Times*, March 19, 2010, p. 13.

a symbol of Gandhi. But there was widespread outrage that a person who had lived so humbly and had identified with the poor was being commemorated with a limited-edition pen that very, very few could afford. It was also felt by many in India that it was offensive to use a person who is revered as an icon to sell products. The company had to make a humiliating apology because they failed to understand the values of their audience.

PRACTICAL CONSIDERATIONS

Blocks to Communication

It is worth considering what would so offend your audience that they would stop listening. Every few months there is an example of some effort to communicate that is not heard at all because the means used to communicate set off protests. Be it a college student skit that has whites in blackface to represent blacks, an extreme metaphor or image that backfires, inappropriate use of profanity or obscenity, or a personal attack that rebounds against the accuser—anything like this will cause your audience to reject the entire message. Sometimes it doesn't have to be very much to offend an audience. Use of sexist language (in some contexts) or the use of some goofy term to avoid sexist language (in other contexts) will do it.

Audiences have their prejudices, self-deceptions, scapegoats, and blind spots. You may need to challenge them directly on those limitations or educate them, but being unaware of these issues is seldom useful.

How do I use information about the audience? In subsequent chapters we will discuss the specific decisions you have to make about shaping your presentation. That is where you will use audience information. In general, though, you can think of *audience information* as an attempt to find out what warrants the audience has. Warrants, remember, can be thought of as the stock of inferences you need to connect grounds to claims. You want to use grounds that build on warrants your audience has.

Second, you want to collect things you need to explain to your audience. When you become an expert at a topic, it is easy to forget what you learned along the way and what was hard to understand initially. So, as you are researching your topic, try to notice and remember what was confusing or surprising. Especially, collect the terms, jargon, abbreviations, and concepts that you didn't know at the outset of your work. The audience might not know these things either.

HOW WILL YOU LEARN ABOUT YOUR AUDIENCE?

The Ethics of Analyzing Your Audience

Anytime you are learning about others for the purpose of persuading them, there are ethical implications. The concept can carry a stigma of cynical manipulation of unsuspecting people by tricks and gimmicks. Is it legitimate to study our audience to appeal more effectively to them?

The real answer begins by observing that, in fact, the only choice you really have is between being aware of what impact you are having and not being aware.

Whether you realize it or not, all your communication involves choices. You won't communicate everything you know about a subject, you will select what to communicate—that has an impact. You also inevitably choose an order of things to communicate; something goes first, and something goes last—that has an impact. And you will also be serious or funny, use simple language or complex, be ironic or earnest, cynical or inspirational—and all that has an impact.

Not to think about these choices is simply to remain ignorant—and to be, most likely, not as effective as you can. But there certainly are some ethical issues about how you do this analysis.

As a communicator, you stand, most likely, in some privileged role relative to your audience. You probably know more about the specific topic than your audience does or at least you know different things. You know what sources you examined but chose not to include. You know what arguments you discarded because they were too weak or you couldn't support them. You know what points you can't refute. You know what your objective is, and you have likely considered what to communicate.

By doing those things, you have thereby acquired a responsibility, a trust. The audience will typically start out assuming that you are reasonably honest and fair. The audience may take what you say at face value and not be searchingly critical. They'll likely give your sources credence. Thus you have the power to manipulate them.

This conclusion is true—if somewhat modified—even in circumstances where you are not the one with the physical power. A defendant addressing a judge, a child talking to an adult, a crime victim confronting an armed criminal—all do not have physical power over their audience and can be at severe risk. Nonetheless, those communicating in those extreme circumstances still have choices to make about how to communicate—and the urgency of a correct audience analysis becomes even more apparent.

Fortunately, such crisis situations are rare, and we can focus on more typical situations.

So, what are some guidelines for ethical audience analysis? First and foremost, you must respect your audience. Even if you are going to confront them or challenge them with your communication, you must have some hope that they will change for the better and some reason to care what their view of an issue is. If you do a formal analysis of your audience, would you show it to the people you just assessed? If you are reluctant to do so, it could well be because you were patronizing or condescending in your approach to them. Audiences often sense such an attitude—from printed arguments as much as those face-to-face. An audience should not have their vulnerabilities exploited. You should appeal to the best in them.

The value of patient listening cannot be overstated. Whether you do this by actually listening to a real live member of your intended audience or do it by careful reading, it takes time to go beneath the surface and really see the world from another's perspective. When someone takes the time to do so, it often is the case that what seemed inexplicable or silly in their views becomes clear. Now you are in a position to communicate effectively.

Second, we would suggest that your goal of communication should always offer some benefit to the audience. You care about them having an accurate view of things. Even if you are trying to get them to give you something, you want their open consent and their ready willingness to give it to you. That is very different than guilt-tripping, shaming, or manipulating to get what you want in a dishonest fashion. Remember our definition of argument back at the beginning of this book? Argumentation depends on persuasion leading to freely given assent to your position. It is hard to do that if you are really trying to take something away from the audience without giving something back.

How Do I Learn about the Audience?

For the papers you write in class, you're not likely to do full-scale sociological research. And if you are required to do that, you'll likely be taking a class that focuses on those skills. But there is a lot you can do with some informal and quick research and a little thinking about the audience. There are a number of ways to learn about your audience.

- Information from the media that your material will appear in. If you are writing for a journal, you can read other issues of the journal to get a sense of how the articles are written. This isn't just true for academic journals; it can be useful for any publication. Journals often have a formal set of author's guidelines that can answer a lot of your questions about format, but will not likely tell you the sorts of things about the audience that you want to know. This is even true if you are trying to get a letter in your college newspaper. Read other letters and see how long they are, for example.
- Informal focus groups. Consider finding one or two friends, teachers, or relatives in your target audience and just taking some time to quiz them about the issue. You can gain a great deal by even asking just one or two people about what their views on a subject are.
- Informal polls. What do students think about some subject? Is it a big deal or not? What are people wearing on campus? How often are the busses late? You might just sit someplace for twenty minutes and count. Or walk up and down your dorm floor or living group and ask ten people the same question. You can learn a lot this way as well.
- Informed speculation. If you've been in contact with the people likely to be in your audience, you can benefit just by sitting down and trying to sort through what you know about them. Apply the three areas we discussed above.

THE MEDIUM OF MY MESSAGE

The Medium Affects the Message

Reading a book (without pictures) about a place is not the same thing as examining a "coffee-table" book with large photos. And neither of those is like seeing a video of the place. A nice design for a print ad is not necessarily very effective as a Web page design. Seeing a video in a darkened theater is not the same as seeing it at home on a high-definition screen and not the same as watching it on your iPod. Watching two politicians debate on television is not like being in the room when it occurs. The medium affects the message.

You may not have the choice to appear on the radio or television, but you do have some media decisions to make. In a written presentation, you could add an image, graph, map, or table. In a spoken presentation, part of your message is conveyed by nonverbal elements such as gestures, expressions, your clothes, and even how you walk.

Recent Changes in Media

There are a number of trends in media that have led to some significant changes in how we absorb communication. Some of these changes include the following:

- Shortened attention spans. Every magazine that has done a makeover of late seems to move in the direction of shorter articles. Mass media is dominated by the sound bite or a short clip. As a result, you have less time to engage your audience than before. Movies and television shows move at a faster clip than they did twenty years ago.
- Increased visual content. More and more visual media are opening up, and video and imagery is being added to traditional media like newspapers. Ten years ago, busses did not have murals on their sides. Five years ago, few people had color printers for their computers. And the first generation of iPods displayed only words on their screens. You might not be able to add visuals to your papers but you can consider using language that is more vivid; you can think about telling stories that will leave a visual impression on your audience.
- The density of messaging, the amount of communication, seems to be increasing, leading to a declining significance for each individual piece of communication. Cell phones, iPods, television screens in airports, Blackberry devices, commercial messages in bathroom stalls, the spread of wireless access to the Internet are all signs of the increased connectivity between people in economically developed societies.
- Multitasking. It seems we handle multiple tasks (and multiple communications) at once. We talk while watching television, listen to music while working, play Sudoku in class. This means less of our attention is going to any one communication. While many instructors are conducting a valiant rear-guard action against student use of cell phones in class, we predict it will not be long before students are texting the instructor in the middle of a lecture—and the instructor will reply! Again, this puts more emphasis on being clear in your presentation. The skills of carefully demarking transitions, keeping paragraphs to appropriate length, using bullet points or other ways of laying out information can be important.
- While messages are increasing in frequency and type, perhaps our ability to block out messages is also increasing. We may not notice advertisements, corporate logos, or other messages as we formerly did.
- The globalization of communication and increased channels of communication are leading to a decline of shared cultural experiences. In the 1950s and 1960s, certain television shows were more or less watched by everyone—or so it seemed. The nation tuned in to Milton Berle or to Ed

Sullivan. The Kennedy funeral, the first Beatles appearance on U.S. television, and the moon landing in 1969—these were events that, to a considerable extent, it could be said that the nation participated in together. The rise of specialized channels of communication and us making our own lists of favorites means that there are fewer cultural references that are known to everyone.

- In seeming contradiction to the last point, it is also the case that recent communication trends also mean the breakdown of isolated communities of communication. Regularly, some person makes a comment, thinking they are speaking only to a private audience, only to find that comment on YouTube or flashing across the Internet leading to embarrassment. Think of Ann Coulter referring to John Edwards with an antigay slur at a conservative gathering, the use of "macaca" by Senate candidate George Allen in 2006, or the controversy in 2008 over the sermons of Senator Obama's pastor. These are all examples of communication that previously would have remained inside a narrow community. When everyone has a cell phone that takes video, this isn't likely to work as much.

The set of changes has been going on for a long time and can be illustrated by comparing political campaign communication. In 1858 when Abraham Lincoln and Stephen Douglas had seven debates in a race for the U.S. Senate, the opening speaker would talk for sixty minutes. Then, the other candidate would have ninety minutes to reply, with the first speaker getting thirty minutes for rebuttal. Sometimes they broke for lunch in the middle. Can you imagine anyone doing that now? It is very hard to imagine even a scientific debate among academics today relying on this extended attention span. In the first televised presidential debates (Nixon and Kennedy in 1960), each candidate had an eight-minute opening statement. No one would put up with that now. And incidentally, foreign policy dominated these debates. In 2004, the three Kerry–Bush debates had two-minute answers to questions.

More than the format, the language has changed also in the direction of shorter sentences. The complex structures of the rhetoric of Lincoln and Douglas would, we suspect, be difficult for a contemporary politician to recite, let alone create. Kennedy and Nixon used simpler language but spoke in complete paragraphs with topic sentences. Today we are in an era of slogans and one-liners.

If you think we are making much out of nothing, consider this single sentence from Lincoln's second inaugural address in 1864:

> If we shall suppose that American slavery is one of those offenses which, in the providence of God, must needs come, but which, having continued through His appointed time, He now wills to remove, and that He gives to both North and South this terrible war as the woe due to those by whom the offense came, shall we discern therein any departure from those divine attributes which the believers in a living God always ascribe to Him?

Admit it, you read that twice before you understood it. That is a long way from President George W. Bush's "I am the decider."

These changes in communication are both curse and blessing. While there is much to deplore in a culture seeming to embrace caffeine-buzz attention deficit disorder as a mode of existence, it is undeniable that much communication from a hundred years ago is hopelessly boring. Color, visuals, the interconnections of the Internet open up the possibility of vibrant communication and make the beauty of a well-done communication possible in new ways.

Use the new options, but remember, quality still counts.

How do I use this? You will likely make both written and spoken arguments. You should be aware of how they differ. In a written argument you have a number of things beyond the actual words that you can use to demonstrate your organization and help the reader understand. These include section breaks of all kinds, use of fonts, boldfacing, underlining, footnotes, tables of contents, appendices, and references that a reader might peruse.

In a spoken argument you also have a set of tools, but they are different. You have tone of voice, pauses, gestures, loudness, and facial expressions to use. You can repeat things for emphasis when you're speaking; that can be quite annoying when you read it. When speaking you have to provide reminders or even recall points previously made; when writing you can insert a cross-reference. Notice how we occasionally boldfaced a word in a paragraph to help the central point stand out.

Beyond that, spoken English is different from written English, and this isn't just a reference to dialogue between people. When speaking to an audience, you can be a little more informal, use a little humor. Much of this does not come across well in print. Spoken sentences can be shorter and need not be perfectly grammatical.

However, do not get carried away with that difference. If you want to inspire people or lift them up, some elegance, some appropriate complexity is still of use.

You should also pay attention to the length of your argument. The shortening of communication and the rise of multitasking make it even more critical that you get to the point. Someone who cannot figure out your point in the first two or three paragraphs, or who is not presented with anything emotionally or intellectually compelling in that same time, will likely tune out. If you are doing training in a company, you may have to give up dreams of an all-day seminar and think of delivering training in small doses instead.

However, please resist the sound-bite culture, and do not inflict a series of zingy, random, one-liners on your audience. People still seek quality communication that takes time to explain something or to fill in the background. People are still seeking inspiration, and while they may claim they don't want sophisticated communication, they may well be hungry for something they cannot exactly describe.

The Art of the Paper

You might think that the media for your classroom arguments is so tightly defined as to eliminate any decisions. You know the drill: "white paper, black type, double space, one-inch margins, 'normal' sized font." But in fact, even in this very restricted medium, you have a number of options to adjust the visual impact of your arguments and significantly affect the ease of communication. And we are not talking about grammar, clarity, and sentence structure.

Let us now praise the section heading. You may have noticed that we use quite a few of them. They give the reader anchor points; they let the reader go back and find things. They let a reader scan the overall flow of your argument if they are too impatient to read it all the way through. Sometimes students resist them because they feel they are "spoilers," giving away the arguments before you make them. That matters in a novel, but in persuasive writing we generally prize clarity above almost all else.

Section headings can be organizational, such as "Introduction" or "Conclusion," but they can readily be descriptive or summarize a section ("Costs: less than you might expect") or, on limited occasion, whimsical or informal ("Yes, yes, but what about the costs").

Another layout decision that aids or blocks comprehension is the length of your paragraphs. This can scale to the length of your paper, but in general, the longer the paragraph, the less coherent the thought. Any paragraph longer than half the page is almost always a sign of a stream-of-consciousness style of writing. Long paragraphs seem to make the readers eyes slide over the page with no place to fix on.

Think about adding visual content to your communication. This doesn't mean just pictures; it also includes how you lay out your words on the page. Some careful use of boldface can make your paper much easier to follow. A single, well-chosen chart, table, or image can increase understanding. But do not succumb to the PowerPoint culture of dozens of fonts and special effects with graphs that make no sense other than that it shows off your mastery of fonts.

A checklist for class paper formatting (for all of these, assume we've added "as appropriate and useful" to each bullet point):

- A title that is specific to your argument (not "Paper 1")
- Section headings
- No overly long paragraphs
- Margins are standard
- One font only or one text font and a second font for headings
- A running head with your name and page number
- A header on the first page with appropriate identification
- Judicious use of graphs, tables, and images
- Boldface key words

THE OCCASION

Communication is not just between those giving and receiving it. It cannot be understood without considering the world in which advocate and audience are embedded. In this section we'll consider the specifics of the context immediately surrounding the communication event. In the next section we'll look at what took place before the communication.

The setting or occasion matters. You know this or at least your instructor does. Each spring the call arises from students across the nation to leave the dingy classroom with its gray-beige walls and uncomfortable chairs and flee to the outdoors.

It seems like such a wonderful idea. Sun, bright colors, fresh air, the smell of new-cut grass, the contemplation of clouds, and the world filled with new energy and hope.

And it is, almost always, a disaster. Nothing can be written on the board, your papers get grass stains or just blow away, you can't hear voices above the din of the nearby Frisbee game, and too many are watching (with more than innocent curiosity) who is walking by. Few are paying attention. In any case, whatever communication was intended for that day, usually nothing much happens. Context counts.

There are background factors that shape the occasion.

- Cultural conventions. We communicate in a culture that has a series of conventions that mark things, like what communication is acceptable and what is not. Our cultural conventions about swearing, obscenity, and sexual references have changed in the direction of greater acceptance. Some cultures require greater formality or politeness or regulate how younger people address elders. There are certain conventions about how we begin and end our conversations.
- Forbidden topics. Few subjects are actually forbidden, but there does exist a category of things that we all know but do not talk about, at least in certain contexts. Sex comes to mind because despite living in a culture that drenches us in sexual images (from one perspective) we still do not talk openly either of the mechanics of the act (thank goodness) nor of its power to inspire us (unfortunately). But there are other, more subtle things that are difficult for us to talk about: economic inequality, crime among minority groups, religion. Which topics are not talked about varies by the situation.
- Outside events. Communication about a host of topics changed on September 12, 2001. The content of humor, especially satire, will change with each new administration. Small things local to your communication can affect things as well. Your audience may be distracted by something that has recently upset them or anticipating something (like the arrival of the weekend) that is distracting them.

As we move from the general to the specific, we have to ask more focused questions. Where are we? How we talk in a jury room about a particular crime is not how we talk about crime in general. A football locker room allows different forms of communication than does a church social.

Some communication situations are in and of themselves occasions when the audience expects certain things from a communicator. A very small selection of these would include:

- Opening of a conference or meeting or any sort of gathering. You are expected to welcome, to include, to acknowledge the prominent guests, to set the tone, and to provide some forecast of what is to come.
- Presenting an academic paper when those who disagree with you are present. You are expected to adopt a tone of respect for others, acknowledgment of what can be learned from others, yet, to present your views without excessive waffling.

- Writing an op-ed piece in a newspaper. You have to be entertaining as well as advocating your position. You have to take account of a very diverse audience with wide ranges of interests and knowledge of the situation. You may not be expected to use footnotes or references but may refer to one or two examples.
- Pitching a proposal to your boss. You'll have to think about timing. When would the boss be the most receptive? How can you ensure you'll get the time you need? And what do you know about their preferences for presentations: short or long? Cut to the chase or start with the background? Are there any sore spots due to previous proposals or projects or corporate context that have complicated the decision for your proposal?
- A wedding reception. You are expected to be gracious, to praise the couple, to offer respect to the two families, to be witty. There are multiple audiences here, and the crude humor that might be accepted among your buddies may not go over well with the parents and the minister.

HISTORY

What happened before your communication takes place also matters. Here we are focusing not on history in general, but on the specific history of previous communications between advocate and audience. We'll look at four aspects.

1. Personal history. We take time to adjust or "calibrate" our relationships with others with whom we have a history. In doing so, we are certainly judging the Ethos of the other person, but a history of communication gives us insight into how to interpret a new communication. Others hearing it may take it very differently if they don't know the speaker. Do they tease or tend to be serious? Do they push us because they want us to be better or because they abuse us? What gets spelled out, and what can be assumed? Did they lie to us before and that taints all our communication now? In interpersonal relationships this history can be a very significant factor in how communication is understood.
2. Institutional history. When the communication comes from someone seen as representing a company or a government agency or any organization, the history of our communication with that institution will come into play. If the last customer-support person gave us bad advice, we'll be more suspicious and less trusting of the next representative we encounter.
3. Cultural history. Some communication events, particularly cross-cultural ones, are strongly affected by the history of communication between the groups. If one group is known to be manipulative or condescending to the other, new communication can be seen in that framework, even if the new communication comes from someone who'd never speak that way.
4. History of this type of communication. If you've heard something before, you may not want to hear it again. In the era of globalized communication we now hear of "compassion fatigue" and "outrage fatigue." Having heard about a whole string of disasters, we may have been desensitized to pain and suffering and are not moved by the latest famine or war in the way we might have been 20 years ago. Some think that watching many fictitious disaster movies may have affected how we saw the images of 9/11.

ASSESSING CONTEXT: SOME EXAMPLES
Let's apply what we've discussed so far to some case studies.

The Personal Ad
The personal ad is a very specific form of communication. It is intended to display yourself at your best and attract someone. But, of course, you are trying to attract someone who is exactly what you want. Thus, how you write a personal ad should reflect the audience you are trying to attract.

Consider these two real examples of ads placed by women seeking men.

Ad 1:

APPEALINGLY THIN, beautiful inside and out, yet so much more. Embraces life, expressive, unafraid of joy. Divorced, 5'8". Adventurous in spirit, calm and quiet in manner, laughs a lot, open, deep thinker. Radiantly alive, interested in the human condition, politically liberal. Relishes third-world adventures, outdoor activities, skiing, hiking, blueberry pie, reading *The Economist*, Mozart piano sonatas. Midwestern roots, international outlook, lived abroad. Savors tapas in Barcelona, trekking in Turkey, galleries in Paris, snuggling together at home.

Ad 2:

I am intelligent, silly and playful, affectionate and strong willed. . . . I am fiercely protective of my children (boys 15 and 7). I think I would rather go fishing, or for a walk through the stockyards, or to a horse show on a "first date" than out to dinner. Or rummage through someone else's "stuff" at a flea market or trade days. Broke horses for a living when MUCH younger, am skilled at the art of tree felling, have a degree in veterinary technology, and a passion for microbiology and clinical pathology that guided me to a long career in the dairy/food industry (manufacturing).

How do these two differ? Think about what they imply about children, money, and interests. They are not interchangeable in the least: someone who wants to walk through a stockyard is generally not someone who wants to go trekking through a gallery in Paris, though there must be some exceptions. These authors are appealing to two very different audiences.

Also consider the context of a personal ad in general. It is a context where self-promotion is accepted, even required. What could sound like insufferable arrogance in a different context becomes acceptable in the context of the personal ad.

One of the ironies of personal ads is the prevalence of lying (or "creative embellishment") in them. On the one hand, we want to attract people who are impressive in some way. We want to look as attractive as we can, so there is a tendency to inflate our presentation of ourselves. On the other hand, the objective is to attract someone who actually will like us for who we really are. From that angle, lying by puffing yourself up actually means you are addressing the wrong audience.

Business: Product Roll-out

In business you may well have to make arguments for the same thing to different audiences. Imagine that you are the manager in charge of a new product roll-out. Think about how it might be different to address the senior executives, the employees, large dealers, and customers.

- The senior executives. In front of the CEO and vice presidents, you will be making a case for full funding of your product and lining up a full commitment from all sectors of the company. You will be free to discuss things that would be confidential in other contexts, such as the budget or possible problems with the product or responses from your competitors. On the other hand, you may need to be acutely aware of the political sensitivities of each of the department heads that constitute your audience. If a previous product was unsupported by a department or you overran your last budget, these will be contextual factors you will have to address (perhaps indirectly).

- The employees. You will be arguing to the employees that all the work of a product launch will lead to benefits to them. But the work comes first and the benefits are later (and may only be received indirectly), so you have a persuasive task to accomplish. Your communication with them may be both written and spoken if the company has multiple offices or is fairly large. Despite whatever confidentiality agreements exist, any "all company" communication is effectively public. That typically leads to such communication being excruciatingly bland and viewed as an annoyance by the employees. Thus this audience has an epistemology of disbelief about the truth-claims in corporate announcements. So can you get to the point quickly, make it short and snappy, and tell them something they can actually use?

- Major dealers. You will be making a case to them not about how the product will make money for your company but rather how it will make money for the dealers—which should be two goals in alignment with each other, but often are not. If they have been pushed around or had their discounts cut, they will be upset. They will want to know if you are really going to support them fully, if your tech support is up to speed, and if they can get product samples, among other things. The ontology of this group is that they see themselves as "out on the front lines" and see "corporate" as somewhat removed from their reality. Can you convince them that you see their reality?

- The customers. You will make a case to them to buy the product or you will help design such appeals. Customers are totally uninterested in the internal dynamics of your company. It's not real to them, not part of their ontological beliefs. So they aren't going to find stories about that very interesting—other than sort of juicy gossip you really have no business sharing. And they are well aware that you make money when they buy your product. Therefore, they are very skeptical of your claims; their epistemology is not to accept as true claims made by someone who is trying to sell them something. You can be upset about the attack on your honesty, or you can use this fact by developing product demos (so they can see for themselves) or third-party testimonials (who have no financial interest involved).

CASE STUDIES

Fighting against Kairos: Japan 2011

In 2011 a large earthquake followed by a massive tsunami hit the coast of Japan. Among the devastation was damage to six nuclear reactors. For weeks the world watched as operators struggled to keep the plants under control. We saw gas explosions at the buildings, releases of radioactivity, and fears of an extensive meltdown. It became a powerful moment, recalling two previous nuclear accidents at Three Mile Island and Chernobyl.

This context became, in many people's minds, a persuasive argument against nuclear power. It was proof by Kairos. It seemed to many to be absolute proof, beyond all arguing, that nuclear power was dangerous, a killer, a mega-disaster just waiting to happen.

But how persuasive should this moment have been? Consider what it took to knock out these plants: One of the most massive earthquakes ever, beyond design limits for the plants, a tsunami with waves over 40 feet high that knocked out the backup systems that would have kept the plants under control, forty-year-old plants that were not in compliance with contemporary standards, and the plants located near the epicenter of the quake. This last is no small point, for Japan has many nuclear reactors, and those located farther from the epicenter had no trouble completing their shutdown without incident.

The Pathos dimension of this Kairos appeal cannot be denied: "Nuclear" is a word with scary connotations to most of us; radiation, an invisible killer, is particularly scary. The thought of radiation damage persisting for generations and spreading over a large area raises the stakes further. These situations also bring to the fore our fear that governments are not being honest with us.

If you are an opponent of nuclear power, the temptation to ride this moment and point to it as irrefutable proof is almost impossible to resist. But if the plants had a higher seawall or more backup options, none of this would have happened. That's the only adjustment proponents of nuclear power would need to make to completely answer the argument this moment makes. In other words, using this moment works emotionally, but would likely not be very persuasive after emotions cool.

That is the danger of strong moments.

On the other hand, moments such as "9/11" or Pearl Harbor or a major personal event can motivate us (or a country) to do more than we might have expected.

Waiting until a Favorable Context

During the U.S. Civil War, President Abraham Lincoln had decided to issue a proclamation freeing slaves in areas that were in rebellion against the government. However, the military situation was not favorable, and Lincoln's secretary of state counseled against releasing the document.

> Mr. President, I approve of the proclamation, but I question the expediency of its issue at this juncture. The depression of the public mind, consequent upon our repeated reverses, is so great that I fear . . . it may be viewed as the last measure of an exhausted government, a cry for help . . . our last shriek, on the retreat. (Seward, in Goodwin, 2006, p. 468)

Lincoln accepted this point and delayed releasing the Emancipation Proclamation until after the Union victory at Antietam.

INTEGRATING THE DIMENSIONS OF KAIROS: WHAT IS THE PERSUASIVE TASK I FACE?

All right, you've figured out who your audience is, what they think, what they know and don't know, now what? We'll try to put this information together by using it to inform us about what persuasive task we are facing when we make our specific argument to a specific group. By *persuasive task*, we mean what you are trying to convince the audience of—and the answer to that needs to be a bit more specific than just "to accept my argument."

To sort this out, let's simplify the multitude of situations you could face down to five situations on two dimensions. We'll consider audiences in terms of their support for you (favorable, unfavorable, and mixed) and then consider audiences in terms of their passion for the issue (engaged, unengaged).

Audience Views

The supportive audience

This seems like the easy case: they already agree with you – what could possibly go wrong? Quite a bit it turns out. Let's enumerate some risks you face in this situation:

- You get lazy. Praise is nice, but nothing motivates like a challenge. If you think this presentation is "in the bag" you're likely to get sloppy.
- You work hard to persuade them of what they already believe: and this is boring.
- You pander – you promise things to this group that you can't deliver on.
- You get carried away and argue things you'll be embarrassed to have others learn about.

But getting a grip on what your task actually is will help avoid these problems. If you're not trying to persuade them to agree with you – what are you trying to persuade them of? There are some options.

- You need to motivate them to action. They agree with you, but you want them to do something.
- You need to educate them about some aspect of the problem. The support the same position as you, but they don't know what you've found out.
- You want to equip them to deal with opposition. "Now, our opponents will tell you this, but actually . . . ."

The opposing audience

Here you have an obvious challenge, you want to change their mind. What are the risks?

- You offend or turn-off the audience the moment you start so they never really listen to your argument.
- You become defensive and thus do not come across as authoritative.

- You anticipate their rejection, act like it is inevitable, and so cause it to happen.
- You try to abuse them into loving you. That is, you yell at them for being hostile to you.

You know what your task is, but how do you go about it. Keep this in mind:

- Think how you might find some points of agreement to build on. When we discuss models of argument presentation in chapter eleven, you will get some tools to assist you to do this.
- Remain calm. Or as they say, "never let them see you sweat."
- Study carefully what you've discovered about their epistemology, their ontology and their axiological views. You are looking for a "way in" – to find what they will find persuasive.

The mixed audience

- By mixed, we don't mean "indifferent" – we'll discuss that below. When your audience includes a variety of views on the argument there are some special risks.
- You become convinced that someone will object to everything you write and so you wind up feeling that there is no argument you can make that would be effective.
- You decide to ignore the people who disagree with you.
- You decide to ignore the people who agree with you.

You have some opportunities due to the mixed audience:

- The mixed audience is a particularly good forum for advocating a "third way" solution to the problem. Take good parts of each side's view and form them into a new compromise proposal. You can stand "above the battle" and advocate for consensus.

Audience Commitment

The passionate audience. An audience that cares deeply about the topic, regardless of if they agree or disagree with you, poses some special risks:

- You haven't done your homework, and the audience knows more about the subject than you do. Even if they agree with you, a committed audience demands expertise from authors they read.
- The audience can be closed off to new insights or just want advocates to confirm what they already know.
- If you try to discuss details or nuances of the issue or suggest caveats or try to caution them, a passionate audience can see that as a lack of commitment on your part.

With a passionate and well-informed audience (not always the same thing), you need to recognize that and do something with it.

- You can more easily motivate them to action. They may have come to your piece prepared to do something, but they need to know what that is.

The uninterested audience. An audience that does not care about the issue and is not informed about it poses some risks:

- In order to get them to care, you start exaggerating to get their attention. In spoken presentations, advocates often start raising their voices and getting more extreme because they are not feeling any response from the audience.
- You become timid, apologizing for bothering them.

   Don't mistake lack of knowledge for opposition. You have some options here.

- It becomes more important to explain why the issue is important. You need to intrigue them with something interesting or get them upset at something that is unjust. So in addition to arguing that "You should do X," you have to first persuade them that "You should pay attention to X." This issue will also come up when we discuss Introductions in the chapter on argument presentation models.
- You need to examine the ontological views of this group. Why is this issue not real to them? Is there a related issue that is real? Could the issue become real to them if something were to happen to them?

CHANGING THE CONTEXT

We must be clear that "knowing the context" of your argument does not mean the same thing as "adopting the context." There always has to be room for being countercultural, for opposing the context or challenging it. But even when you do that, *especially* when you do that, you have to be aware of what the context is.

In general, you can ignore the context, use it, or reframe it.

Sometimes the context is just not of major significance, and you should more or less ignore it. Sometimes the contextual influences are so mild that calling the audience's attention to them is counterproductive. A flickering light, noise from the elevator, a minor error—things like these should probably be ignored. A minor distraction becomes a major one if you obsess about it in your presentation.

Using the context means that you will employ aspects of what is going on to frame your message. You adopt the language of the situation. "When in Rome do as the Romans do" went the old saying. So you adjust your argument to fit in.

Reframing the context means taking the situation and transforming it through your communication. A funeral is a significant example of that. All of the communication, be it in a religious service or in informal conversation, is intended to reframe the grief at loss into pride or commemoration of the life lost, offer respect to someone who has given up their life, and provide means for those grieving to move back into normal life.

There have been particular instances of communication that have reframed cultural conventions. Examples would include Richard Nixon's 1952 Checker's speech or John Kennedy's 1960 address on Roman Catholicism as a candidate. Natural history writer Rachel Carson's 1962 book *Silent Spring,* about the dangers of DDT, convinced many that pollution had consequences. The movie,

Arguments We Don't Ever Want to Hear Again:
"All those people understand is force."

"There is no other way of bringing the English to their senses. They belong to a class of human beings with whom you can only talk after you have first knocked out their teeth."

Adolph Hitler to Joseph Goebbels, quoted in John Terraine, *A Time for Courage* (MacMillain, 1985), p. 479

"These people hate America and all it stands for! The only thing that these barbarians understand is force!"

Blog comment referring to Iranians, Sept. 2009

"The only thing these sand [expletive] understand is force and I'm about to introduce them to it."

Comment of senior officer in Iraq, quoted in *Cobra II*, Michael R. Gordon and Gen. Bernard E. Trainor

[Africans have to] "be ruled with an iron hand in a velvet glove" and if they failed to understand the force of it "you must take off the glove."

Baden-Powell, quoted in Piers Brendon, *The Decline and Fall of the British Empire, 1781– 1997*, p. 145

"These people must learn submission by bullets— it's the only school."

Commissioner Sir Arthur Hardinge, speaking of Kenyans, quoted in Piers Brendon, *The Decline and Fall of the British Empire, 1781–1997*, p. 357

This argument disrespects and diminishes the audience; indeed, it reduces the audience to something less than human. Notice how the speakers dismiss the values and reality of the world of their audience. There is no attempt to understand why the audience is behaving in a certain way, and it projects the speaker's world onto the audience.

And it is also worth noting that in many of the cases cited here, the speaker's side lost, was beaten, or expelled. So the perils of not understanding your audience can, on occasion, be fatal.

An Inconvenient Truth, featuring Al Gore's presentation on global warming, changed the national conversation on this topic.

But reframing is not ignoring or overriding. In general it takes a sensitive analysis of the current situation in order to change it. Often what you do is look for aspects of the current situation that are not emphasized, are forgotten, and bring them to the fore.

CONCLUSION

Thinking about Kairos in all its aspects really demonstrates how communication cannot be taken in isolation. Of course Kairos does not determine the meaning of communication, but it can change it significantly.

SUMMARY OF KAIROS

Description

The set of factors around a communication; its context.

Issues and Aspects

- The advocate can be speaking to a different audience then intended.
- Recent changes in communication practices tend to accentuate short, overlapping messages.

Study Questions

- Name and briefly describe the four dimensions of Kairos.
- What are the three aspects we want to know about our audience?
- For a given occasion, can you describe how it would shape your communication?
- How can you adjust the format of a class paper to enhance your communication?

Ethos: Developing Your Credibility

INTRODUCTION[1]

The University of Minnesota's basketball program had not been doing well of late. So, in 2007 they fired the coach and lured Tubby Smith, an experienced and highly respected coach, away from the University of Kentucky to be the new coach at Minnesota. "Instant Credibility" screamed the local sports pages. If they'd hired someone who was an absolute genius but had never coached before, that would not have been the headline. And if they'd hired someone who had an outstanding reputation but had not actually produced any winners in the last ten years, the headline could well have been the same, but it would have been wrong.

Ethos is one of the most odd of the topics we consider in this book. The factors that determine it, and the nature of problems with assessing it, are such that it is very temping just to tell a series of stories and marvel at the ins and outs of this subject. But we have to aspire to more.

> Furthermore, mark you, the man who wishes to persuade people will not be negligent as to the matter of character; no, on the contrary, he will apply himself above all to establish a most honorable name among his fellow-citizens; for who does not know that words carry greater conviction when spoken by men of good repute than when spoken by men who live under a cloud, and that the argument which is made by a man's life is of more weight than that which is furnished by words? Therefore, the stronger a man's desire to persuade his hearers, the more zealously will he strive to be honorable and to have the esteem of his fellow-citizens.
>
> Isocrates, Antidosis 278, ca. 350 BCE

Ethos, one of the three forms of proof identified by Aristotle, may sound like the word "ethics" or "ethical," and your ethos does have (or, should have) quite a bit to do with how ethical you are. But it will be less confusing for you if you

---

[1]The authors are indebted to Dr. Jeremy Rose, Department of Communication Studies, the University of Minnesota, for sharing freely of his research on credibility and persuasion and gratefully acknowledge his assistance with this chapter.

associate the word *credibility* with this topic. Credibility is about being believed. We need to assess how believability (the credibility, the ethos) of the advocate is won and lost and how that affects the persuasiveness of the presentation.

Why do we need to deal with credibility at all? Shouldn't we just assess the validity of the arguments being presented? Many of you were probably told in high school to ignore the person and focus on the argument. That is good advice in many situations, but we have no alternative other than to assess credibility. We don't have time to check out or demand proof for everything we are told. If we ask someone for directions, we seldom demand proof of the accuracy of their instructions; we trust that people are honorable enough not to deliberately deceive a stranger. We (typically) accept what doctors, lawyers, and professors tell us—until they've given us a reason not to believe them.

Oprah Winfrey, for example, commands credibility with her fans. There are many stories about how a product's sales boomed from being endorsed by her. People trusted her judgment.

Sometimes credibility is crucial. A crime has been committed, and all we have is an eyewitness. Do we believe them? A child says he did or didn't do something—that's all the parent has to go on. Should they believe them?

You apply for a job. The company needs to decide if you are representing yourself fairly, because that is a key piece of evidence for what sort of person you are. If you've never held a professional job before, you need some references with great credibility to vouch for you.

People in the film industry can wish to have "indie cred," meaning that they are respected as people making films for artistic purposes and not just money. People in certain communities seek "street cred" for being authentically a person of the neighborhood.

But credibility as a field is difficult to study. There is no accepted theoretical framework for discussing credibility, no equivalent of the Toulmin model. Research in the field has as much to do with psychology as anything else.

In this chapter, we have three objectives. You should develop your ability to (1) enhance your own credibility as an advocate, (2) assess the credibility of other advocates, and (3) (when appropriate) attack the credibility of other advocates.

UNDERSTANDING CREDIBILITY

Defining Terms

It will be useful to define some terms at the beginning. These concepts are often used in discussions of credibility. We use some of these terms, but knowing all of them will help you understand other academic writings on Ethos that you encounter.

- Source credibility and message credibility: An audience evaluation of Ethos depends on their view of the communicator apart from anything being communicated (*source credibility*). But it also depends on their judgment of the content of the communication (*message credibility*).
- Primary and secondary credibility: *Primary credibility* is the Ethos you gain or lose "on your own." *Secondary credibility* is making reference to the work of others (quotations, citations) to gain credibility. We'll discuss the

very useful strategy of a communicator "hiding" behind sources with higher credibility to raise their own credibility.

- Internal and external credibility: *Internal credibility* is about how you can provide proofs of credibility to the audience; *external credibility* is about having other advocates testify on your behalf. (Note: These advocates are not providing testimony about your specific argument—that would make them a source you are using (see "secondary credibility" above), rather, they are specifically recommending you as a person.) In a corporate context, internal credibility has been used to refer to a company's internal controls on some process (such as evidence that can be provided to prove certain practices are being followed), and external credibility refers to audits by outside parties and testimony from independent sources.

We appreciate that these pairs can be confusing or sound very similar. Note that *source* is used in two different ways in the first and second pair. Sorry, but that is the way the profession discusses these concepts. Each pair has its use in disentangling the components of credibility.

Who Has to Demonstrate Ethos?

Our primary concern is about the individual making a communication. Most of you readers are individuals, we suspect! However, it is certainly possible to apply this analysis to some collective entity when that entity is viewed by the audience as a unit or a single communicator. We are thinking here of when an organization issues a communication on behalf of the entire organization and the audience is evaluating that communication as if the organization has a single level of credibility.

For example, statements on global warming by the Intergovernmental Panel on Climate Change are given great weight because that organization is seen as widely inclusive of the best climate scientists and that its publications are backed by the organization as a whole. Other examples would include recommendations from Presidential Commissions, Blue Ribbon panels, findings of agencies, and so on.

This collective view may also be of value in business when contemplating consumer attitudes toward brands and evaluating decisions about forming (or reforming) a brand. Sometimes companies, when faced with a product that has lost credibility in the market, decide to drop the product and produce a new one (even if it really isn't new) in part to assist consumers (or fool them) into forming new views of the credibility of a product. That may be easier than trying to rehabilitate a product's credibility. Sometimes all that is necessary to "reset" brand credibility is to change the name. So Philip Morris wanted to shed its association as a producer of cigarettes and changed the name of some of its corporate units to Altria. Blackwater Security wanted to remove their negative association with actions in Iraq and rebranded itself as Xe.

In some contexts the actions of individuals are seen as actions of the organization, and credibility of the organization can determine views of individuals. In 2010, the Roman Catholic church suffered a loss of credibility as word emerged of not only misconduct by priests, but also the effort to suppress reports of it and to avoid punishment of offenders. Actions by individual priests were seen as reflecting on the collective identity of the church. And likewise, the reputation of innocent priests suffered by being identified with an organization some had come not to trust. The same dynamic occurs with police officers. When a police officer is seen to be abusing their authority, it isn't viewed as just an issue for that one officer, but affects the public's view of the police in general.

Is Our Discussion Prescriptive or Descriptive?

As authors we have a choice: Should we describe how people *do* gain credibility, or should we openly defend (and prescribe) what we believe to be right and proper and advocate how you *should* attempt to gain credibility? As communicators, you have the same choice. Do you want to know what works, or will you do what's right and be content with what occurs?

Similar dilemmas affect all of the issues in this book, communication in general, and, indeed, all of human life. But they seem more obvious when discussing credibility.

If we are describing how credibility in fact works in the world, we have to acknowledge the irrational, the incongruous, the inexplicable. All sorts of people have credibility who shouldn't have it. A person is regularly on television advocating that cancer can be cured by techniques no evidence supports. A U.S. senator claims that global warming is "the greatest hoax of all time." Various television pundits for finance, health, or religion got there on the basis of being convincing and not on their knowledge. People are running organizations that have no clue how to do so. And many people give credence to some who run for president or sometimes even vice president, who lack the mental acuity to organize a bake sale. Feel free to add your own examples.

Likewise, there are plenty of people who should be respected and listened to who are ignored. The band you saw at the bar last night could well have been better than many on the radio. Unknown blog authors can be much more insightful than those with a national audience. Cream does not always rise to the top.

On the other hand, if we are to adopt the prescriptive approach and tell you how you ought to go about making your communication credible, then we'd have to be clear what principles underlie those judgments.

So, what we will have to do is a little of both. As a communicator, you have to be aware of what works and what doesn't. But you also have to have ethics. The values of always telling the truth as best you know it, respect for the audience, and a belief that the purpose of communication is to make the world a better place, would be a good set of values to start with.

Fortunately, in most cases, you can take account of what does work without compromising your principles. You can adjust your tactics of how you do your presentation (to use what the audience finds effective), in many cases without having to lie or deceive anyone. In the chapter on argument presentation, we discuss some of the approaches to doing this.

Who Makes the Decision on Credibility?

Credibility is a decision made by the audience, but discussed as a property of the advocate.

Don't get confused on this—we (and everyone else) will write about the "credibility of the advocate," how you "have to think about improving your credibility," and that "your reputation can be hard to change." All this is useful to get an advocate focused on this issue. But credibility is a decision made by the audience—and unmade and remade—and sometimes just refuses to be made in any way we like.

When we write about how you should raise your credibility, we mean you should be aware that part of the persuasive task is to be aware of this and that credibility is one aspect of persuasiveness.

Credibility Depends on Context

Since credibility is a decision made by audiences and there is more than one audience, it means that there can be more than one decision about credibility for a given advocate. Advocates often have credibility with one audience and none with another. A professor of agriculture may have a lot of credibility in academic circles for his careful and well-researched writings, but none with a group of farmers ("Has he ever gotten manure on his shoes?"). This is but one example of how intelligence can be a determent to your credibility, unfortunately.

But credibility is also context-dependent in a different way. It is dependent on which claim is being made. Kate Moss is a supermodel who got into trouble for drug abuse in 2005. Keith Richards of the Rolling Stones, a noted drug user himself, opined that she was doing too many drugs. If Mr. Richards tells you that you are doing too many drugs—you are doing too many drugs. His credibility on that particular question is quite high. On the other hand, were he to be advocating for legalization of all drugs, his credibility on that question would be considerably lower because he'd be seen to be arguing in his own self-interest.

Credibility: What You Bring to the Argument and What You Demonstrate in the Argument

Credibility decisions are made by the audience based on what sort of reputation the advocate has, but also on how the presentation is made. They may use what they know about you to decide how much weight to give your words, but they also use your words to decide what they think about you. A powerful argument can be diminished by an arrogant (or hesitant) presentation. This duel dimension is one reason discussions of credibility can become so tangled. This distinction is what was referred to above as *source* and *message* credibility.

One of the authors once went to a worship service to hear a guest preacher. This man, a Catholic priest, was dressed in old clothes. There was a hole in his red sweater. He spoke in a monotone, reading his sermon word for word. He held a pen in one hand and used it to check off sections of his talk as he hunched over the pulpit. Despite violating all sorts of rules for how you show credibility in a speech, the entire congregation sat in rapt silence for the entirety of his sermon.

Why? This was Father John Cortina from El Salvador. The congregation knew that he had come from the remote villages where he had been shot at, received death threats, been threatened with arrest and torture many times, and denied any support from the government officials. Thus, he had tremendous credibility to speak of justice, of commitment, and of being faithful in the face of trouble.

The Bottom Line

The audience makes a decision: to add or subtract from the persuasiveness of your argument based on how they regard you. You can influence that decision by work you do before you begin your presentation and by how you structure your presentation.

MODELS OF CREDIBILITY

We've been arguing that the audience makes a decision about your credibility. We need now to try to dig into that decision and discuss what the dimensions of the decision are and what evidence or criteria they use to make the decision.

Dimensions of the Audience's Decision

While there is no universal theory of credibility, many writers on this topic suggest that the audience makes decisions about (a) your expertise and (b) your trustworthiness. We are going to suggest adding a third term—your authority—to this.

Expertise: Does the advocate know the truth? When the Bush administration began to torture people in its custody, some interrogators from the military and the CIA spoke out against the practice. They said it didn't work and that they, in their expert opinion, wouldn't use it to find out the truth. Because they were seen to be experts, this view was persuasive with many, but, unfortunately, not with the Bush administration itself.

Trials often have expert witnesses who have to be qualified in some way as people who can speak on the forensic data, on the psychology of the defendant, some technical subject or other issue. Beyond that, we consult doctors, lawyers, councilors, financial advisors, college admission specialists, and perhaps even professors, looking for an expert who will know the answer and tell us what the facts are.

And all of us make informal and quick decisions about who to look to for advice on the best restaurant, the quality of a band, how to find parking near campus, and a host of other questions.

Trustworthiness: Does the advocate tell the truth? But, knowing the facts, knowing what is and is not going on, is of no use to us if the advocate is misleading us. Richard Nixon's expertise on U.S. politics was unrivaled—but he lied to us. Henry Kissinger was a master of diplomacy, but we were not sure we could trust him either.

This works the other way around also. Many are taken in by people who seem to care about us, only to discover that they do not know what they are talking about. Trustworthiness seems to be in better repute currently, rather than expertise, and so ads for everything from doctors to car dealers will stress how nice they are, how much they smile at us in order to create in us a feeling of trust—we can let our guard down with these people, we think. But a doctor still needs to know medicine, we hope.

We might devote an entire section to the impact of sexual revelations on trustworthiness. We'll use Bill Clinton as an example for something else later, but think of Elliot Spitzer, Newt Gingrich, Gary Hart, John Edwards, and many, many others. Such revelations lower the ability of many to trust them as advocates for their views.

Authority: Can the advocate define the truth? This third category is a little more subtle, but, we feel, captures a key aspect of how we make decisions about credibility. There are people who hold offices or positions that give them the right to decide what truth is for some specific question. You ask a traffic policeman if you can park here and the person tells you. Most of the time, you're not deciding if that particular person is an expert or if you can trust them; you're going off the fact that they hold a position that grants them authority over this issue.

What is the law of the United States? The Supreme Court tells us. Of course, you can say they are wrong, but nonetheless, when they rule, that has authority to decide the question for us.

Cardinal Ratzinger wrote a number of books. When he became Pope Benedict, the words in those books acquired additional authority for many people. It wasn't because the arguments got better and not exactly because becoming pope made him a better expert or revealed his expertise and trustworthiness to us. There was something about being pope, holding that office, that made the words special to many.

The Milgram experiments also illustrate this. Stanley Milgram, a Yale University psychologist, conducted experiments in the early 1960s when he asked volunteers to administer negative reinforcements to people taking tests when they gave the wrong answer. Volunteers had controls they used to administer electric shocks to the test subjects each time they made a mistake. The volunteers could hear the test subjects, but were visually separated from them. At first the shocks were mild, and the test subjects response was mild also. As the wrong answers continued, the volunteers were told to increase the level of the shocks, and volunteers heard the subjects giving louder and more anguished responses—or so they thought, because in fact, no actual shocks were being administered.

The experiment pitted the internal moral beliefs of the volunteers that hurting people is bad against the authority of those running the tests who were telling them to administer more and more painful forms of punishment. Volunteers had never met these people, had no way of assessing their expertise and trustworthiness, but in most cases they went on causing (what they thought) screams of horrible pain, just because someone in authority told them to do so. Indeed, more than half the volunteers administered a shock they were told was 450 volts. Sometimes they were allowed to hear the test subject banging on the wall or to have all response from the subject stop (as if he or she was unconscious or dead).

This, as well as inadvertent societal experiments about obedience to authority conducted by the Nazis, and more recent examples from a variety of tyrannical governments, suggests that we give a great deal of credibility to those who seem to have some position of authority, and this can override our judgments about their actual expertise or trustworthiness.

And, lest you think this is a legacy of an authoritarian past, the *New York Times* reported near the end of 2008 that the Milgram experiments had been recently rerun by another researcher—and the results were the same (Cohen, 2008).

Implications for Your Arguments

Of course, audiences do not calmly sit and debate each of these three dimensions separately. The components can be hard to disentangle—we assume that people who have authority actually have had to prove expertise to get there, for example. But, in trying to sort out credibility decisions and in assessing the words people use to defend their decisions, we think you will find these three terms to be helpful. Ask yourself if you have any problems communicating your expertise and trustworthiness. Consider what you could do to enhance those dimensions. Later in this chapter we'll offer additional suggestions.

Criteria Used by the Audience

So what does an audience use to come to those three judgments we just listed? It's tempting just to give a long list of the factors involved; the list of things that people actually look to for making decisions about credibility is quite long. We'll try to summarize.

Audience characteristics. As we've argued in a previous chapter, knowing the audience is critical for developing your argument. Certain aspects of the audience affect how they look at credibility.

- Low expertise (in the audience) means the audience relies more on the credibility of an expert advocate. An audience that is not themselves an expert on an issue or thinks they are not experts, will be less able and less likely to judge your arguments or pick them apart. Instead, they will (of necessity, to some extent) look to find a trustworthy and expert advocate. They will be less inclined to argue with what they hear.
- Low identification with an issue means the audience relies more on credibility. An audience that is not engaged with an issue does not want to do the work of sorting out the facts. They're more willing to simply trust someone that sounds credible.

Criteria "Outside" the Presentation

- Goodwill and regard leads to trustworthiness. If an advocate manifests "goodwill" to the audience—smiles at them, welcomes them, shakes hands, puts an arm around the shoulder, offers comforting words—this goodwill, this friendliness, seems to communicate that "I can be trusted." This can be done in print as well by a preliminary discussion before the actual argument is given.
- Credentials and qualifications lead to expertise. What has this person done? Have they published books, received a degree or a credential, been accepted by a gatekeeping body, had a relevant life experience, or done something to acquire a credential that shows that they are an expert?
- Arguing against interest. Sometimes this dynamic is encapsulated in the phrase "Only Nixon can go to China." The phrase refers to how Richard Nixon, a lifelong anticommunist crusader, had the credibility to start talks with China and travel there in 1972 when the U.S. government had no official contacts with mainland China. Other leaders might have been reluctant to do that for fear of being called "soft" on communism, or an "appeaser," or "naïve." Nixon's history of tough attitudes to communism insulated him from that charge. His actions were against his long-term position. The analogy of this in argumentation is when we find an advocate pushing a position that would hurt them financially or be detrimental to his or her political party—a liberal endorsing a conservative position, a man defending feminism, a rural person holding up the value of urban life, a general arguing for peace, and so on (and, of course, the reciprocal examples as well).
- External credibility, as defined above. The testimony of those we trust can be a powerful aid to giving (or withholding) credibility as every student who has sought letters of recommendation knows. This goes throughout life as well in the way we always try to find a contact who can give us credibility with another ("So-and-so told me to call you").

Criteria "Inside" the Presentation

- Nonverbal dimensions of spoken arguments. Your gestures, voice, accent, even your dress, personal appearance, and how you walk can contribute to how people regard you.
- The language you use for your argument. Are you formal or informal? Do you use academic prose or what you might find in a mass-market magazine? Do you use swear words or slang?

For both of these, it is more or less impossible for us to give a list of how to judge your impact from these aspects because it depends so much on the particulars of the audience. Further, sometimes you gain by matching your audience and sometimes you gain by being something your audience admires or respects.

If someone in a three-piece suit with an upper-class British accent is speaking to a county fair in a rural part of the United States, one might think the audience would laugh at the speaker or have contempt for them since they were so different. On the other hand, if that speaker praises the local area and discusses how many know of the fame of this region—the audience might well decide that this is a very wise person indeed.

Further, a speaker who exactly mimics the speech and prejudices of an audience might come across as fake if they've too obviously put on those attributes for the occasion. All we can tell you to do is to think about these aspects and decide what would work and what you can do authentically.

- The structure of your argument. In the next chapter we'll discuss various models of how to present your argument. These can impact your credibility.
- How you treat opposing views. One way to judge an advocate is to see if they are fair with opposing views. Do they avoid insults, treat the opposing advocate with respect? Do they get the opposing argument accurate? To be sure, if your audience doesn't like the opposing advocates, then making fun of them or insulting them will likely get a laugh and enhance your status, but it's not really developing a good argument.
- Conformance to audience views. It is always more work to change your perspective than it is to retain the one you've got. If you change your mind, you have to face all the people you've expressed an opinion to and deal with potential conflicts and confusion. If you change one viewpoint, this may interact with other viewpoints, meaning you have to change more opinions. It is easier, then, for an audience to resolve potential conflicts by downgrading the credibility of people who disagree with them and increasing the credibility of those who do agree.

Note that this can be done totally innocently and for seemingly good reasons. If you've studied a position, thought about it, read about it, and then formed an opinion, you naturally conclude that your opinion is based on good judgment and is accurate. When you encounter someone who holds the opposite view, it is then a logical conclusion to assume that this person has not thought as carefully as you have about the issue and has bad judgment—and thus to consider that the person is not credible and you can dismiss their argument without really evaluating it.

From that, you can see that asking an audience to change its mind on an issue it has already formed an opinion about will take some work. You'll have to have good reasons for it and explain how the audience will gain by changing its mind.

TIME AND CREDIBILITY

Credibility has an odd relationship with time. In much of this book we are implicitly evaluating a static situation—what does an argument look like at a particular instant in time? Of course, arguments progress over time, but it is useful to evaluate what is going on at a particular moment.

Credibility, however, seems to be almost inevitably a "lagging indicator." By that, we mean that views of credibility seem to lag behind the data that one should use to decide on credibility. A team has a history of winning at the highest level and gets a reputation for being a good team. Time marches on, and whatever made them a winning program goes away. Several down years ensue—but commentators will still call them a "great program." Based on what?

Senator John McCain won a reputation with people of both parties as a "maverick," based, in part, on his espousal of campaign finance reform, his opposition to the use of torture, and opposing "pork barrel" entitlement programs. However, that reputation for independence persisted through most of his 2008 presidential campaign even though he no longer defended those views. He had voted with President Bush a very high fraction of the time and had publically embraced (both figuratively and literally) Bush and neoconservative opinions.

It is also true, however, that our view of an advocate's credibility should take into account our experience with the advocate over time. And it is also true that we should test people (and magazines and other sources) before we give them credibility. Thus our judgments about credibility are going to have to wait until we have a track record and so will lag behind. This is particularly true with the new Internet world where "Anyone can be a pundit." By all means, take advantage of the great information on the Internet, but remember to judge which writers over time are proven correct, which apologize and correct their mistakes, and which demonstrate sound judgment.

Regaining credibility after it is lost can also be a difficult example of how reputation persists. There are examples of people rehabilitating themselves after some mistake but it takes time, and it's not clear what actually brings the rehabilitation process to an official end.

One (unusual) example of this is the case of John Profumo. He was a junior minister in the British government in the early 1960s. In 1963, Profumo, who was married, got involved with a women who, while not exactly a prostitute (Profumo never paid her for sex), was certainly made "available" by a man who was brokering the services of a series of such women. Further, this same woman, Christine Keeler, had sexual relations with a man at the Russian embassy in London who British security services knew was a KGB agent, a spy. Profumo never passed confidential information to Keeler or the agent, but since he dealt with issues of military policy, once rumors of the affair surfaced, it became a scandal. Profumo lied in a speech in the House of Commons, denying the affair, and when this was proven a lie, he had to resign in disgrace.

Unlike today, when such a person might simply brazen it out, write a book, or appear on talk shows, Profumo took a job (literally) cleaning toilets in a charity in a poor district of London. He refused publicity and declined for years to take any leadership position in the charity. Eventually, he did fund-raising for the charity. In 1975, he received an award from Queen Elizabeth for his successful fund-raising work. A photo of her shaking his hand became a marker, a sort of official stamp that his reputation had been restored and he was welcome back in society.

Life seldom provides such clear markers of a reputation restored as Profumo had, although similar dramas play out all the time. Note that it took twelve years in this case.

Our culture is more "flexible" in regard to personal credibility and tends to allow notoriety to substitute in part for credibility. Someone caught today would probably feel less shame. Governor Eliot Spitzer, forced to resign in 2008 after being caught using prostitutes, was by 2010 hosting a national television show.

ISSUES WITH CREDIBILITY

People often give or withhold credibility for reasons that do not make sense. As an advocate, you have to be able to detect and respond to these fallacies and also be aware of how people may judge you unfairly for some of these reasons.

Popularity as credibility ("Everyone is doing it.") This is sometimes called the fallacy *ad populum*, the "herd instinct," or the "bandwagon effect." This refers to confusing popularity with wisdom. "New York Times Best Seller!" screams the tagline on a book. This shows the book is a best seller, but the best books are not necessarily popular, and being popular does not make the book good.

"Four out of five dentists surveyed preferred …" That was an advertising slogan used for several products at various times during the 1960s and 1970s. It relies on you giving authority to dentists about teeth and your mouth—not an unreasonable assumption. So this one might carry some credibility, *if* the specific statement was true and not misleading in some way. A consensus of experts, properly surveyed, can be valid.

But popularity is often not a good guide to what to do. Peer pressure for choosing clothes to wear, partners to date, what music to like, what things to drink, or how to behave can be very misleading and even harmful. During each academy award season, poll after poll attempts to predict not who *should* win, but who *will* win. Decades ago there was a saying in business: "No one ever got fired for buying IBM." This meant that IBM computers were very popular, and no one could criticize you for going with the popular choice—even if it didn't work out.

Agreement as credibility ("He agrees with me, he must be smart.") This is another way of stating the problem we discussed above under the criteria for how audiences come to judge your credibility. As we wrote there, it's just less work to give a high reputation to people who agree with us. See the discussion of epistemic closure in the chapter on Kairos.

Newness as credibility. Products put the word "New!" in little red circles on their boxes. We're drawn to the latest thing, the newest fashion, the current trend, things that are "fresh" or "innovative." We want "new ideas" in politics, not those "old solutions" (like liberty?). And while some things decay with time and some ideas no longer fit new circumstances, ideas are not bread, with a limited shelf life. You have to examine, in each case, if the newness being invoked is really a benefit or a distraction.

Passion as credibility. Excitement is catching. An advocate who is excited about their topic, who expresses themselves with energy and excitement, can lead us to get excited as well and give them more credence than we should. We assume that their passion comes from being "blown away" by what they are advocating. However, passion can be an act, or the advocate's judgment can be faulty. In other words, they really are excited, they aren't lying to you, but their reason for being passionate is not persuasive.

Price as credibility. We assume that prices are rational—a better product will cost more. While it would seem normal to prefer to pay less for whatever we are buying, there are undoubtedly instances when the mere fact of paying a lot of money for something increases its value in our minds. This seems the only explanation for the high-priced "bottle service" in dance clubs—the attraction, the thrill, is posing as a high-roller because you can pay out that much money.

Identity as credibility ("They're just like me.") Of course, since we're so perfect, anyone similar to us must be perfect also. And we can more easily relate to people like ourselves, we speak the same language, we look at the world the same way. But honesty and dishonesty, wisdom and stupidity, follow no group lines. Of course we want a leader to understand us and to be able to identify with "ordinary people" (Harry Truman had this reputation) but leaders don't have the same job that we do. You wouldn't choose a brain surgeon, a pilot, or a designer of bridges because they had the same socioeconomic background as you—you'd want them to have qualifications and experience at the job.

Likewise with advocates, their identity with your situation is useful if they are asked to analyze your situation, but identity is no substitute for discernment. Some people, apparently, voted for George Bush because they could more easily see themselves having a beer with him (despite him being a recovering alcoholic) than they could imagine sitting down and shooting the breeze with John Kerry or Al Gore. But we elect a president to do something more than drink beer.

Personal authenticity as credibility. By *authenticity*, we mean specifically that elusive quality that we think some people are "real"—they are who they present themselves to be. Ronald Reagan seemed to be "real." One of the authors knew someone who had spent an hour with Reagan and who glowingly reported that he was "just as common as an old shoe"—meant as a genuine compliment. No airs about him, he didn't think he was better than anyone else.

Authenticity indeed is a valuable quality in a neighbor or a friend. It becomes a valuable asset to a competent advocate because it can be an indicator that the person hasn't lost touch with the reality of day-to-day life. Some arguments suffer because while they sound technically correct, they still are unrealistic or assume things about how people behave that are unlikely. So we are led to trust the judgment of someone we think is real—it's a marker for being trustworthy.

So authenticity is good, but it isn't the same as good judgment. It can be a fallacy to assume that a person who is who they present themselves to be is also a person who makes good judgments about the world. Authenticity can be associated with ignoring others or being self-absorbed.

And, more to the point, authenticity might be a marker for trustworthiness, but trustworthiness isn't the same as expertise. Just because someone is honest doesn't mean they're accurate.

On the other hand, there are reasons to desire a leader, especially one far above us, to have authenticity or share identity with us. We hope that means such a person knows how big policy decisions affect ordinary people and will be inclined to give weight to such issues.

Benefit as credibility ("He told me I'd be rich.") "You can buy real estate for no money down!" "This pill makes the pounds just melt away." Someone who tells us that if we buy a certain stock we'll become rich or that a certain product (they just happen to be selling) is a bargain can sucker us in. We want to benefit, we hope to find some way to become rich or gain something, and we can be vulnerable to pitches based on that. Nor is this limited to money. Social status or sex can also be the implied benefit.

Loyalty as credibility ("Of course our side is right.") Every election cycle there are some amazingly stupid arguments put forth and earnestly repeated in the mass media. Can people actually believe that living next to a country gives you expertise about it? Or that having a certain middle name makes you a terrorist? Or that failing to reply to a damaging attack and passively watching your approval fall is proof of your Jedi Master political skills? Well, perhaps.

But, some of this is certainly driven by a desire to defend our own side. Our team was attacked, admitting any weakness is bad, and so we have to say something. And sometimes the best we can come up with is something ridiculous.

It actually turns out that admitting a particular weakness but defending your larger position, does work and can even gain you credibility for being honest (see Chapter 14), but we don't always trust that to work.

The halo effect ("I know about this, so you should trust me on that.") If somebody has credibility in one area, we often give them credibility in other areas—when we shouldn't. Now, of course, it is logical to suppose that someone who has proved excellent in one thing might bring that quality of judgment to something else. But it doesn't always work that way. A scientist who is an expert in one field can turn out to say some embarrassingly stupid things when venturing outside their field.

We see this fallacy in use all the time with celebrity endorsements. Why exactly is a baseball player or a movie star credible to advise us on cars or toothpaste? But there is no doubt such is effective. Mike Rowe has a well-deserved reputation for down-to-earth honesty for his work on the wonderful television show *Dirty Jobs*. But he, absent any other data, did not decide to endorse Ford trucks based on some detailed comparison testing. The Ford company hopes your affection for Mike will make you buy their products.

We readily detect this fallacy when a celebrity works for a political campaign— at least when the celebrity works for a candidate we don't like—we're much more forgiving when they endorse someone we like.

This is also a problem involving heroes. We admire people who've done something brave, heroic, or who have performed well. But that shouldn't give them credibility automatically in other areas. Rudy Giuliani did perform admirably as mayor of New York City in the days after 9/11; most would agree. But he hadn't been a generally successful mayor, and, when he ran for president, the holes in his knowledge and the defects in his character came to the fore. He tried to run a campaign based, to an amazing degree, on simply reminding us at every occasion that he'd been mayor of New York City on 9/11. It wasn't enough.

A more sensitive case of halo effect involves soldiers and their views on the war, or police and their views on social issues, or similar cases. Take soldiers. Of course we have ample reasons for admiring someone who is willing to put their life on the line for something they believe in and to protect the country. Nothing wrong there. But being nineteen years old and getting shot at does not make one an expert on geopolitical realities, nation building, foreign cultures, or (in many cases) even counterinsurgency strategy. That a soldier supports the war or opposes the war is only useful to the extent that they have thought about it and can offer good reasons for their view. They are experts on their own experience, credible authorities on what it is like to be in combat, but not necessarily on the larger issues.

The problem is that rejecting the view of a hero seems like you are attacking the hero, and people don't like that. You will have to proceed carefully and make sure that no one can credibly claim you've disrespected the hero.

The Reverse Mussolini fallacy. The authors confess that they would include this fallacy even if it almost never occurred, just for the chance to write the name. This fallacy is best described by a sort of syllogism, but first you should understand that one thing commonly thought about the World War II era Italian dictator Benito Mussolini is that he "made the trains run on time." In other words, he organized a people with a reputation for not being organized. (As to whether this is historically accurate or not, the authors have no idea.)

The fallacy goes:

"Mussolini made the trains run on time."

"Mussolini is a bad person."

"Therefore, trains running on time is a bad idea."

You might think of this as a sort of reverse halo effect—a black cloud effect. A person's low credibility is being used to undermine an idea that should be evaluated on its own. If an evil person came up with a cure for cancer, would we use it? What if some research on human reactions to stress came from Nazi concentration camps. Would we use that? Perhaps we should—if only to partially redeem an evil (while making sure we pay tribute to the victims while we use what was learned from their pain).

Personal experience as credibility ("I've done it and you haven't, so you don't know.") A parent has lost a child to a dread disease, to a drunk driver, or to a convicted child molester, and now is campaigning for a change in the law. We sympathize with their loss, but did their experience make them an expert on the policy issue at hand? Perhaps it galvanized them to study the issue and become an expert—that would give their views validity. But going through a tough or painful experience does not in and of itself make you an expert on the policy implications of changes in laws, the wider social implications, or other larger aspects of the issue.

This is somewhat similar to the discussion of heroes in the section above on the halo effect. A person has acquired a sort of protected status that insulates them from criticism, or we fear we would look bad for criticizing them.

DEVELOPING YOUR CREDIBILITY

Before the Argument Starts

We said that credibility was what you brought to the argument and what you demonstrate in your argument. How can you change what you bring to the argument? If you are speaking or writing today to an audience that has never heard of you, then perhaps not much. But you might have more to work with here than you think.

If you have some time before you will make your argument, you can ask yourself if there is anything you can do to enhance your credibility as an advocate for your position. If you are going to argue about homelessness, can you volunteer for a homeless agency for a few days? If you are going to argue that it is easy to save energy, can you reduce your own energy consumption first?

If you are going to be advocating to an audience that does know you, are there any problems with their view of you? Has there been a previous argument that has put them off you? Is there some business you should take care of in order that they can really listen to your argument?

In the Argument

There are a number of general considerations that apply to almost all presentations. Some of those were discussed above in the section describing how audiences made up their minds. There are some further points to be made however. You don't want to do anything that distracts from your presentation by calling attention to yourself (but we will discuss below how to use your personal experience to your advantage). As a rule, you don't want to make the argument about you, most of the time, but to highlight your argument.

In many presentations, the ethos of the advocate is not a major part of the argument. In these cases, the advocate wants to present in a way that does not raise any issues of their credibility. So the use of correct language, grammar, and spelling avoids credibility concerns. Adopting a professional tone, or a tone consistent with the situation and audience, is also helpful.

You do have to be consistent: Your presentation cannot be at odds with your primary claim. At a district political convention in Minnesota in 2008, it was time for people to come to the microphone and announce the names of their special interest groups they wished to form. The chair announced firmly that the rules allowed you to announce the name of your group and hold up a sign for identification but you could not make any speeches promoting your group. Halfway through, a man approached the mike and launched into a tirade about the lawless activities of the Bush administration, which continued over the chair's gaveled objections. The name of his special interest group: "Restore the rule of law." Hummm—you want to restore the rule of law and the first thing we see you do is break the law? Not good for his credibility.

Advocates have this problem more than you might suspect. Some extreme environmental groups, committed to reducing pollution, burn houses or condone those who do. Some Muslim groups, in order to object to the accusation that they are violent, burn down religious buildings. Some people, urging others to love them, yell at those whose affection they seek.

But what if you don't have any credibility to use? You're inexperienced or inexperienced compared to your audience, or you have no personal connection to the issue. In this case you might be vulnerable to being attacked (fairly or not). You shouldn't try to bluff, but you can make your lack of personal credibility almost an asset. You do this by framing your argument as "Don't take my word for it, look at the facts." You highlight very credible sources, you document everything. Your stance is that of an open and unbiased person with nothing to hide.

But how do you bring your personal experience into the argument? Let's suppose you do have a story to tell. You're writing on drunk drivers and you had a narrow escape yourself, or you are writing on abortion and you've had one, or you are writing about a particular sport that you play. This personal experience can be a strong plus if used well.

First, you can't fall into arrogance and commit the "personal experience as credibility" fallacy we discussed above. You have to understand the limits of your personal story and not claim too much. You want to strive to offer the reader the best of both worlds: You've got personal connection to the issue *and* you've got the facts and the authorities also. One approach is to use your personal experience in the introduction (see the next chapter) to draw the audience in and to get them interested. You tell your personal story with vivid details and some drama and then transition to more general facts and data.

Another approach is to discuss the issue generally first and present the facts and figures. Then, you use your personal experience to drive the general point home. The audience will then connect your one story to the larger world that you documented with your sources. You told them there were a thousand kidnapped children and then you told them about your experience or the experience of your close friend. The audience then thinks about how that pain and fright affects many kids.

Regardless of if you use your personal story at the beginning or at the end, you do not let it stand alone, and you do not try to use it as a weapon to silence opposition.

Your level of personal credibility also affects the evidence you need to supply. If you are going to assert something that sounds reasonable, the audience will often just take your word for it. If you're going to claim something that the audience finds hard to believe, they will look at your credibility much more closely.

ATTACKING CREDIBILITY:
THE AD HOMINEM ARGUMENT[2]

If you knew one argumentation term before you started reading this textbook, it was probably the term *ad hominem*. It means "against the person" and is a reference to arguments that attack your opponent—seeking, in essence, to lower the credibility of the person on the other side of the argument.

If you haven't heard the specific term, you may have heard the phrase "Attack the argument, not the person." And, most of the time, that is very good advice. Our arguments would go better, we'd live better, if we had fewer personal attacks. However, two problems require us to discuss ad hominem arguments. First of all, you might be the victim of one, and so you need to know how to defend yourself. Second, there are some situations when an attack on the credibility of your opponent is fully justified—it may even be required.

Types of Personal Attacks

To deepen our understanding of this issue, we're going to present seven different types of personal attacks. We'll discuss when they are valid and when they are not valid. And then, after that, we'll summarize.

1. The **direct** or **abusive** attack. This is a pure attack on the character of the person without any particular reference to the arguments being made by the person. It's attacking Bill Clinton by making crude remarks about his sexual habits or attacking Hillary Clinton's looks or Ann Coulter's looks. It's any manner of insults directed at people for being foolish, stupid, ugly, crude, or whatever. When is this form of argument invalid? Just about always. Theoretically it might be valid when the character flaws of a person are so severe that we simply do not want to be associated with the person in any way. Perhaps pedophiles and Adolf Hitler might fit this category, but, even then, we might ask if we'd really reject a totally legitimate argument from one of those people, just, and only just, because of who made it. There is no doubt that we do reject arguments just because they come from disreputable people, but should we? Nonetheless, the abusive attack is almost always a fallacy and should be rejected.

2. The **circumstantial** attack. This is an attack based on circumstances related to the argument that the advocate is making. It can be called the "practice what you preach" attack. So, a person tells you that smokers are bad people—and then you find out they smoke also. An environmentalist is discovered to be living in a house full of rare Amazon woods. New York City Mayor Bloomburg was a big public advocate of mass transit. Why, he argued, I take the subway to work myself. Yes, he did—only it was discovered that he had himself driven in a two-SUV convoy a number of blocks to an express subway stop instead of walking a few blocks to the local stop nearest his house.

---

[2]This section draws in part on the work of Douglas Walton on ad hominem arguments, including his book, *Arguer's Position*. Dr. Walton is not responsible for the particular analysis and examples used here.

In these cases, attacking the person is valid because they have made representations about themselves or have made arguments about how people should behave that they themselves do not follow. So you can point that out in an argument. Many leading public officials get driven to work, but if the official claims to do something else or makes fun of people who get driven to work, then it becomes legitimate to attack them.

But you cannot overreach here. There was a bit of controversy when it was discovered that global warming advocate Al Gore lived in a house that used a lot of electricity. His credibility was attacked for that. (Gore blunted the attack by pointing out that he paid for offsets that purchased an equivalent amount of alternative energy.) However, it would not be valid to claim that global warming itself was a fraud just because Al Gore didn't totally practice what he preached. You can attack him for his behavior and you can suggest this means you shouldn't trust him, but the global warming argument doesn't stand or fall on the credibility of any one advocate.

In short, the circumstantial argument is invalid when the person being attacked has offered legitimate reasons for their view. The attack can be valid when the person being attacked is offering their personal credibility as part of the argument.

So, go back to the argument about Bill Clinton having sex in the Oval Office with someone who wasn't his wife. If you think that everyone is entitled to a private life and that private life is irrelevant to the performance of a public office, then you'd regard attacks on President Clinton on this subject to be an abusive ad hominem argument. On the other hand, if you think that the president also has some responsibility as a moral leader, then you would regard the attack to be circumstantial and valid. But it would only be valid to attack President Clinton when he was exercising moral leadership; it wouldn't refute his arguments on some specific issue.

3. The **bias** attack. This is a contention that an advocate has a hidden agenda, a conflict of interest, a stake in the outcome that affects their ability to be an unbiased authority on the subject. It is common to use the word "bias" to mean "anyone who disagrees with me," but the word actually means that there is something unfair about the opponent's position.

So, a person who is wrong is not biased. Bias means a defect in the decision-making process, not just a wrong decision. The biased person didn't fairly judge the issues before making a decision.

So what is also involved here is the difference between being an advocate for your own interests and being a disinterested advocate. That's a key distinction: There is nothing wrong with advocating your own interests, as long as you make it clear that is what you are doing.

Examples of true bias are things like someone presenting themselves as an independent public policy think tank and attacks global warming, but doesn't tell you that they were set up and funded by oil companies. Or it is someone telling you that the economically correct way to treat capital gains is not to tax them at all—but neglects to mention that all their income comes from capital gains and so they'd pay no tax at all if the proposal was adopted.

So it is valid to launch this attack on someone posing as an impartial advocate who makes an argument that depends on their claim to be trustworthy, but doesn't tell you of their conflict of interest. It is invalid to make this attack when the advocate has been either (a) open about their conflict of interest or (b) does not use their own credibility as part of the argument.

We need to explain that. Consider the first situation. Let's suppose the oil-company-funded think tank is open about where their money comes from. Are they still disqualified from advocating a position? No, people can argue for their own interests. Students can argue for a reduction of tuition, professors can argue for raising their own pay. What they can't do is to hide their financial interest in the outcome of the argument.

The second point is also key. The oil company think tank, if they want to be persuasive, need to understand that they will not be considered trustworthy with their audience because of their financial interest. Therefore, they need to avoid arguments that rely on them claiming expertise and instead find other sources to make their points for them.

4. The **tu quoque** attack. This attack is to accuse your opponent of doing the same thing they have accused you of doing. Back when Osama Bin Laden was still doing interviews, a (rather brave) reporter asked him if he financed terrorist camps. His reply was that the United States had invited representatives of the Irish Republican Army to the White House, had dropped nuclear bombs on Japan, and killed many children in Iraq. "You are the biggest terrorist," he said. He didn't answer the question about his own activities. Bin Laden was making a tu quoque attack on the interviewer.

    Before we assess whether this is valid or not, note the differences between the circumstantial attack and the tu quoque attack since they can seem very similar. In the circumstantial attack, person A makes a claim X and the opponent contends that A does not follow X themselves. In the tu quoque attack, person A claims that person B does X, and person B replies that person A also does B, and so person A cannot attack B for doing the same thing.

    Now, back to Bin Laden. Those who found Bin Laden's attack valid said that the West, and the United States in particular, was claiming moral superiority over Bin Laden because he was a terrorist, so Bin Laden's accusations of terrorist activity by the West could be valid. A double standard was being applied, like back in the 1960s when some whites called blacks violent for marching and protesting when whites had not objected to acts of violence against blacks.

    Those unimpressed with Bin Laden observe that his reply was a fine way of avoiding answering the question and was essentially nothing different than the "He did it first" defense of a three-year-old in a sandbox, which has been greeted, from time immemorial, by the parental reply that "Two wrongs do not make a right."

    And that is the actual risk of making a tu quoque attack—that the outside observer of the argument will simply think that both you and your opponent are wrong. So if you are going to make this attack, you need to frame it clearly as an accusation that your opponent is applying a double standard.

5. The **guilt by association**/honor by association attack. The guilt by association attack is when you associate your opponent with some person who has low

credibility. In the 2008 election, people who did not like Senator Obama tried to link him to Bill Ayers, Rev. Wright, and others. Those who did not like Senator McCain tried to link him to President Bush. Some who didn't like Sarah Palin tried to link her to questionable behavior by her husband Todd. Guilt by association was covered above in the Reverse Mussolini fallacy. What we will add here is that guilt by association can be valid if you can prove the link between the two people is significant and ongoing (or if it has ended, that the person has not changed since then). If the association is trivial or wasn't chosen by the person, this is not a valid attack.

Honor by association is the opposite, and it is not really an attack on credibility, but rather a fallacious attempt to claim credit by association. It can be harmless fun: You claim bragging rights in the office because your favorite team won. Sometimes it is less amusing.

6. The **genetic** attack. This attack is to find something unsavory in the origins of your opponent (or their idea) and try to link that to the present. Let's suppose that marriage originated as a way for men to mark certain women as their property and to alert other men to leave them alone. Does it then follow that your impending marriage is evil because of that? Not really. The man who invented the Kwanzaa festival, Ron Karenga, served time in prison in the 1970s for torturing two women. Does that mean the festival is tainted or something that shouldn't be celebrated? No. Hitler was involved with the creation of the Volkswagen. That doesn't mean you can't buy one now.

This attack is the temporal version of the guilt by association attack. And like that attack, this one is only valid if the connection is continuing or essential to the character of the thing being attacked.

7. The **"poisoning the well"** attack. This attack is to present negative information about your opponent before the argument begins. What is key here is that the attack is done first, before the argument even officially begins. You don't want your opponent to receive a fair hearing, so you poison the audience against them before they are even heard. Because of that, this attack could be made by using any of the other six forms.

However, there is a form of this that is worth highlighting. Some attacks are of the form that would tend to permanently poison the audience. Examples would be when you allege that your opponent's job or position in life would mean that "Of course they will say that." "He's a priest. Of course he's going to say God exists." "He's a man. He's got no right to criticize what a feminist says." "Only a black person can speak about racism." This, in a sense, is an accusation of bias (of the form we discussed above). What makes it insidious here is that many think that certain accusations of this form are automatically true and therefore there is no way to refute the attack.

The Bottom Line

Well, this is a long taxonomy of personal attacks. Can they be summarized? Is there a bottom line here? Yes, there is:

- You can attack someone's credibility if, and only if, their credibility is part of their argument.

In other words, if they are offering themselves as experts, you can examine if that claim is true. If they are claiming to be trustworthy, you can offer evidence that such is not the case. Likewise, people can attack you if you are making credibility-based claims for your position.

But there is a warning here also:

- Your attack should be connected to the argument and limited to issues raised in the argument.

In general, there are too many personal attacks—far too many. Sometimes ignoring them is the best response. If you decide to make such an attack, you should limit the scope of it and document it the same as you document any other claim. Insults without evidence are never arguments, remember?

Responding to a Personal Attack

If you are attacked, how should you reply? Consider just two possibilities.

Person A: "You're a jerk!"

Response 1: "You're an even bigger jerk!"

Response 2: "You just made a personal attack. That's not how people should behave."

Response 1 is quite tempting. It might even be justified, after all. To make a personal attack is to be a jerk, in many cases. But the problem with Response 1 is that now we have two people making personal attacks, and those watching, who just don't like fights, are likely to blame both people.

Response 2 calls attention to how the first person has violated the rules of polite argument.

CASE STUDIES

The Tylenol Crisis of 1982

In September of 1982, several people in the Chicago area died after taking Tylenol pills from bottles that had been laced with cyanide. Investigation quickly ruled out any sabotage or negligence in the production of the pills. Johnson & Johnson, the company that made the pills, acted quickly and aggressively by issuing warnings to the public not to consume Tylenol, recalling their product, and offering to exchange suspect capsules for replacement capsules. During the crisis, the public lost faith in Tylenol, and its market share dropped dramatically. But within a year, after the introduction of a more heavily sealed package for Tylenol, the consumption of the product had rebounded.

Here we have an example of credibility of a corporate brand and the credibility of the company that owned it. Because the problem did not occur at the factory, Johnson & Johnson could have taken the tack that they were not to blame. They could have been defensive, been legalistic, or issued statements that their product was of high quality. However justified, this "stonewalling" would not likely have been effective. There would likely have been a "guilt by association" effect where consumers would not separate the company from the problem—and certainly would not have separated the product from the problem. It was a correct analysis to understand that their credibility was at stake.

Further, they recognized that a crisis is an opportunity to demonstrate character and in particular an opportunity to demonstrate to the public that they cared about those who consumed their products. It was a critical moment when the public would form opinions about the company. By being out in front they won praise, and their credibility was enhanced.

The Curious Case of Governor Sarah Palin

Love Governor Palin or laugh at her, her candidacy for vice president with Senator John McCain in 2008 brought forth a veritable cornucopia of material for students of credibility. Why was she added to the ticket? Theories included that she would appeal to conservatives or to women in general or Hillary Clinton supporters in particular. This is an example of the "credibility as identity" we discussed above. The theory is that people will vote for someone based on an identity of personal story, rather than agreement on positions. Throughout the campaign, the effectiveness of this identity politics was widely debated. Conservatives did seem to identify with her, women not so much.

Her public identity as a "hockey mom" and "one of us" took a hit from the story of the $150,000 wardrobe. Interestingly, her first response to the revelation of this story was to say that this was not who she was. The image of identity (being just like us) would trump the actual facts.

Her lack of experience and her absence of foreign travel became an issue as well. Many thought this detracted from her credibility. Others, it seemed, liked her specifically because she was not well informed. They found her trustworthy because of her beliefs and did not place high value on expertise. Thus, the trustworthy dimension outranked the expertise dimension in the minds of many.

Indeed, it sometimes appeared that her lack of expertise actually enhanced her trustworthiness with some people. She wasn't contaminated by contact with experts and elites who were viewed negatively by those who liked Governor Palin. Those elites did not share any "identity" with the audience and weren't considered authentic, so their disapproval of Palin was to the benefit of her. The more that these people attacked Palin, the more credibility she gained with some.

Arguments made for her expertise, including that she commanded the Alaska National Guard or that Alaska was adjacent to Russia, are examples of the "loyalty as credibility" fallacy we identified. They could not be taken seriously as positions, but were offered by people trying to find something to say in her defense. It backfired, however, as these positions were widely subject to satire.

Because the nation had little experience with Gov. Palin, her performance in interviews became more important. Thus her credibility would depend more on what she could demonstrate while making her argument (as opposed to what she could bring to the argument). Her early interviews with Katie Couric proved very significant when she came across as incoherent and uninformed.

Supporters of Governor Palin thought it was unfair to give such weight to her bloopers when Senator Biden, running for the same job for the Democrats, also had a long tradition of saying "off the wall" things. But Sen. Biden had a long public record, so his reputation did not have to rise or fall on just a few things he said. Palin was in a different situation.

Remember also what we said about advocates with little credibility of their own to offer. She might have benefited by taking a more humble stance and not pretending that she was on a par with people who'd been in the national spotlight for decades. A more even-tempered approach, a willingness to focus on the issues she had some acquaintance with as a governor, and to even admit a lack of experience in some areas might have won her praise. In other words, behaving credibly might have won her credibility.

But finally, her story also points to how credibility is a "decision made by the audience." Or, in this case, a multiplicity of audiences. People looked at the same set of data and came to radically different answers about her. And they still do.

CONCLUSION

You can affect the decisions that your audience makes about your credibility. And how you present your case also has an impact on this. Even young advocates without expertise in a subject can present a credible case if they manage their presentations with an eye to doing so.

SUMMARY OF ETHOS

Description
The credibility, or believability, of the advocate, as assessed by the audience.

Issues and Aspects
- Credibility is a contradictory subject with many inconsistent features.
- Ethos is a decision made by the audience but discussed as an attribute of the advocate.
- While there is no generally accepted theory for Ethos, it can be broken down along the dimensions of expertise, trustworthiness, and authority.

Study Questions
- Under what conditions can you legitimately attack the credibility of an advocate?
- If you are going to make an argument on a subject when you do not have any significant personal credibility, what strategies should you employ?
- Describe some common fallacies with Ethos.
- How can you legitimately use your personal experiences in an argument?

Presenting Your Argument

INTRODUCTION

How do you present your argument? How do you decide which way you will structure what you communicate? What will you present first, and what will you hold to the end? What will you include, what will you leave out? These questions are addressed in this chapter.

The key insight is that the answer to these questions is affected by both the *content* of your argument and by the *context* of your presentation. So we needed to know what sort of claim we were making, and then we needed to know about the audience, the media, and the occasion, before we can discuss how to order your presentation.

> "Words differently arranged have a different meaning, and meanings differently arranged have different effects."
>
> — Pascal, Pensées, 22

But, we must be clear at the outset that these choices have nothing to do with saying one thing to one person and something different to someone else. It is unethical to shift your convictions to pander to your audience. Rather, the choice you face is this: Out of all the things you could legitimately present and all the ways you could present them, which will you choose? And once you've chosen, in what order will you present your material?

While there are potentially an infinite number of ways to present your argument, certain ways of doing so, call them *models*, have become well-known.

First, we describe the classical model of how to present an argument, followed by an examination of a number of other common models. Then, we will consider the various impacts and advantages of the models.

THE CLASSICAL MODEL

This model is termed classical, because it goes back to the time of Rome and ancient Greece. A Roman rhetorician, Quintilian, who lived approximately 35 to 95 AD, wrote a lengthy handbook for argumentation called the *Institutio Oratoria*. In the book, he has given an extensive description of this model. Over time the model evolved slightly and became a standard. It, or derivations of it, are still commonly used to present arguments. The model has a number of distinct parts and a particular order to those parts. We will go through each part in order. There are Latin and Greek names for the parts that we will include to help you connect with other descriptions you might encounter, but it is fine to use the English names.

Parts of the Model

Introduction In Latin this was called the Exordium, in Greek it is the Proem. It is the front door of your argument, the first thing people will read or hear.

> The sole purpose of the exordium is to prepare our audience in such a way that they will be disposed to lend a ready ear to the rest of our speech. The majority of authors agree that this is best effected in three ways, by making the audience well-disposed, attentive and ready to receive instruction. (Quintilian, 2002, 4.1.51[1])

Introductions are not summaries. Please note that. In this model, the content of the introduction is *not* a short version of your argument (that comes later). The objective of a classical introduction is to do what Quintilian wrote: to put the audience in a receptive frame of mind. That goal is achieved not by describing your argument, but by intriguing the audience. Compare these two beginnings.

> Summary: We can increase product sales by 20 percent by expanding into the African market. This is because that market is not well-covered by our major domestic competitors.

> Introduction: Fifteen-year-old Mwaka has a problem. He has a question about his homework and needs to ask his friend about it for the assignment due tomorrow. But, that means a three-mile walk to his friend's house and then three miles back. If only they had those new, inexpensive, cell phones. But, they are not yet available.

Introductions have a different purpose than summaries. The rhetorical goal of an introduction is not to persuade the audience that your claim is correct. Rather, the goal is to persuade the audience to listen to your argument.

Introductions are often a story or a description of some incident. If you are describing something that affects thousands of people, you might introduce your appeal by telling us about one particular person that is affected by the problem. It is an odd aspect of human psychology that reading about a thousand deaths has little impact on us, but reading about one particular death can move us to tears.

---

[1]H. E. Butler, Loeb Classical Library, (public domain), cf. http://penelope.uchicago.edu/Thayer/E/Roman/Texts/Quintilian/Institutio_Oratoria/4A*.html

Introductions intend to draw us in, and using Pathos is a common way to do that. Telling us about one particular person makes us feel the impact of the problem and makes us interested in learning more about the issue.

There are a number of criteria that make for an effective introduction. First, it must connect to your argument. That seems obvious, but you do hear introductions that only link to the main presentation by a catch phrase or seem to be just something the author thought was interesting. A good introduction focuses attention on the subject and motivates the audience to want to know more.

Consider the tone you want to use, such as light or serious, humorous, forceful, indignant, or pleading. In particular, consider the tone of the rest of your piece in relation to how you want to begin. Sometimes you may wish to set a particular tone in the introduction to set up your main argument; sometimes you may want to do one thing in the introduction and then transition to another approach in the body of your argument.

Is there some immediate, obvious difficulty with having your audience focus on your issue? If on September 12, 2001, you wanted to publish an article advocating more tourism to the Middle East, you'd need to deal with what had happened on the previous day. In fact, the attack in New York City might be a good reason to argue for more knowledge and contact with the Middle East, but it would have been a fatal error to ignore the terrorist attack in your introduction.

Should you invoke your own character? There are some situations when you need to address issues of Ethos in your introduction. Perhaps you are a college youth addressing a group of middle-aged combat veterans. In that situation, there might be some skepticism about your credibility. You would likely need to address that in your introduction.

And an introduction should be a small fraction of your presentation. If half of your paper is an introduction, then there is something wrong.

Let's consider some examples.

> When Curlin chased down the Kentucky Derby winner Street Sense to capture the Preakness Stakes, his owners bounded to the winners' circle at Pimlico Race Course. They were an eclectic bunch that included a winemaker, a computer magnate, an investment banker and two lawyers. (Drape, 2007, p. 1)

In this brief example of an introduction, the author sets the scene; he leads you mentally to the end of the horse race. He tightens the focus to the winners' circle and the people in it. And he alerts you that the owners are unusual. So far, there is no statement of a problem and no conflict, but somehow you are expecting that one is about to develop. And indeed it does. It turns out there is a dispute over who owns this valuable horse and, thus, who is entitled to be in the winners' circle. So the writer's use of that particular image in his introduction is designed to lead into the discussion of the dispute. The writer uses your interest in races and their winners to draw you in to a particular situation where something is in conflict. It's an effective and compact introduction.

Introductions do not need to be stories.

> At any violin recital the performer's challenge can be simply stated: How do you combine two hours, four strings and an unforgiving box of wood to achieve transcendence? (Eichler, 2004)

Here the writer sets up a strong contrast between a flat statement of time, "four strings" and a "box of wood" on the one hand and "transcendence" on the other. There is a second contrast between the "simple" question and the profoundness of the dilemma posed.

A forceful sentence that grabs your attention can be a fine beginning.

> Bond investors are living in a world where nobody eats or drives. (Staff, *The Economist*, 2007)

This was the first sentence of an editorial about the arcane subject of indexes of inflation. Measures of "core inflation" (that excluded food and energy) were compared to inflation indexes that used all consumer products. The author is upset at the lack of common sense displayed (in his view) and so his abrupt, challenging opening signals his tone. By being so blunt, it conveys that this (otherwise technical) subject has real consequences.

A question can serve as an introduction.

> Does privacy exist any more? And if so, do public figures have a right to it? (Thornhill, 2007, p. 7)

This was the beginning of an essay about how the media should respect (or not respect) the privacy rights of leading politicians. Both examples take their issue and state it in a form that commands your attention and makes you wonder about it.

Consider the question of the proper tone for an introduction:

> "Since many have undertaken to set down an orderly account of the events that have been fulfilled among us, just as they were handed on to us by those who from the beginning were eyewitnesses and servants of the word, I too decided, after investigating everything carefully from the very first, to write an orderly account for you, most excellent Theophilus, so that you may know the truth concerning the things about which you have been instructed." (Gospel of Luke 1:1–4, New Revised Standard Version)

This is a famous introduction. It's famous in part because of its style and tone. In Greek, it is a very elegantly written sentence, two balanced clauses of three phrases each. It's elegant Greek, and copying of formal conventions of introductions for its time signal to the reader that the author is a serious, educated person who should be taken seriously by serious, educated people.

We mentioned that introductions can be used to address questions the audience might have about the author:

> "When in the Course of human events it becomes necessary for one people to dissolve the political bands which have connected them with another and to assume among the powers of the earth, the separate and equal station to which the Laws of Nature and of Nature's God entitle them, a decent respect to the opinions of mankind requires that they should declare the causes which impel them to the separation." (U.S. Declaration of Independence)

The authors explicitly acknowledge that those who hear of a declaration of political independence will desire some justification from those taking this important step. Rebellion is a serious matter. They gain credibility by admitting that they need to justify their actions. People wrote in a more formal way in 1776 than they do now; nonetheless, the stately, elegant tone of this introduction signals that the authors are serious, sober people. They are not ranting, not out of control. Rebels are often accused of being out of control or of being intemperate, so the authors here try to counter that impression.

If it is not too confusing to have a conclusion about introductions, let's remember that an introduction is not the same thing as a summary or forecast of your argument (see that section below). Advocates do often try to summarize their claim and reasons in the first paragraph but we are trying to warn you away from assuming that. Notice that all the examples we gave of introductions were aimed at drawing you in to the significance of the topic, not in trying to lay out a series of claims you should adopt. Arguing is not the same thing as appealing. Of course, in a very short piece, you may need to do more in an introduction than just try to show how fascinating your topic is, but think of the introduction as something to draw them in, get them interested, not as something they have to adopt.

Background In Latin, this is termed the Narratio, the Narration, or the statement of facts. Today, we'd more likely use the term *background*. In order for the audience to understand your case, there is likely to be some information they need to know. This information isn't directly part of your argument, rather it gives context. So you might explain why there is a problem or explain some history. You could include definitions of terms, abbreviations, and concepts that the audience won't be likely to know or address or any common confusions that might interfere with understanding your argument.

When you research an issue, you learn things about it. But your audience didn't do all the research. After you have worked on an issue for some time, it is easy to forget why it was confusing. Try to keep track as you are researching for a presentation the items that puzzled you on first encounter. Those things will probably puzzle your audience also and should be explained.

In a short presentation, a separate narration section may not be necessary. In a two-page paper, this shouldn't be more than a paragraph or two. Regardless of how long your piece is, you should not spend more time here than is necessary because you risk losing the audience's interest. It's tempting to include all sorts of interesting things you found while researching your topic, but be careful. Is everything you've included relevant to proving your case? If your introduction was effective, you've "bought some time" with your audience, and they will listen to some background or history because they anticipate that something interesting will be coming.

This section has a parallel in a common technique of fiction. You've read novels that start with a big crisis, a fight, a death, or a significant event. Then, in the second chapter the author sends you back in time to show you where and how it all began, and you begin the story that you know will lead you to the crisis.

If you will have several different aspects to your argument, they may each have different sets of background facts. You may therefore consider dividing this section and including the particular facts relevant to a particular aspect of your argument when you make that portion of your argument.

Here is an example of providing background information in a short essay urging more attention to a group of tropical diseases.

> "Experts formally refer to them as the 'neglected tropical diseases,' or NTDs. They are hellish infections whose combined impact on disease, disability and death rivals the impacts of AIDS, tuberculosis and malaria, yet they are far less known, partly because they are diseases that afflict only the poor in the tropics." (Jeffrey D. Sachs, "The Neglected Tropical Diseases," *Scientific American*, January 2007, Vol. 296, Issue 1, p. 33)

The author introduces the abbreviation, NTD, which he will use throughout the article. He provides some information on how severe the diseases are, who they affect, and why you might not have heard of them. Some of this supports his argument for more research, but most of this paragraph is background, information you need to understand his argument.

Proposition   In Latin, the Propositio. This is your thesis, your claim. You need to state this succinctly and clearly. This seems hard for some to do. Either there is a desire to be coy or indirect and not be blunt about what you are arguing for, or advocates in fact aren't clear themselves about what they are arguing. If you are finding it difficult to state in a sentence or two what your central claim is, that is a warning sign that you need to think out your argument some more.

Sometimes, advocates think that being too direct is a bad thing, arguing that it gives too much evidence to your opponents or that it is more artistic and clever to be indirect. This is a misreading of the genre of persuasive communication. This isn't poetry you're writing; it's an argument to persuade someone and you want to make it easy for them to understand you. Actually, we'd argue that poetry also aims to persuade, but the objectives of that genre demand a radically different technique.

Again, your claim should be one sentence long and no longer.

Forecast   In Latin, the Partitio. You may have heard the advice that you should "Tell them what you are going to tell them, tell them, and tell them what you told them." The forecast is the first of those three. Here you give an overview of your argument. It is different from the introduction in that in the forecast you describe the specific grounds you are going to offer in support of your argument and briefly outline the evidence you will offer. In the introduction you focused on drawing the audience in; by contrast, here you give them a roadmap to what will follow.

This needs to be as brief as it can be and, in a short argument, may only be a sentence or two or omitted altogether. Once again, short is more useful than long-winded.

Forecasts often have this form: "I am going to offer three reasons for why you should adopt my view. The first one will be . . . The second will be . . . The third will be . . . ."

You want to phrase your forecast so it is clear that you are *going* to prove this later, not that you are offering proof now.

So, use this: "I will prove that this is obviously true."

And not: "This is obviously true."

The second form leads the reader to expect some proof or a citation to a source, and when you don't give one, they can think you are just making wild assertions. So make it clear that this is a forecast of what you will do.

An example:

> This article examines the effectiveness of leadership targeting based on a dataset compiled by the author. It shows what factors determine whether leadership decapitation will be effective, and it concludes that the death of Bin Ladin is unlikely to weaken the al-Qaʻida terrorist group. (Jordan, 2011, p. 10)

The final paragraph of the Introduction section of this chapter is a forecast for the chapter.

It would be quite typical to merge the proposition and forecast sections, especially in a short paper.

Presentation In Latin, the Confirmatio or confirmation. This is where you present your case, giving the grounds and evidence to support the grounds. You might explain the warrants you are using if necessary. In other words, the Toulmin model fits into this section.

This is typically the largest section of your presentation, probably more than half of the material. If it's not, there is likely something wrong—either you don't have enough to say or you have been too wordy in the other sections.

Typically you have several reasons or grounds you want to present in support of your claim. Be sure to clearly label each and consider them in sequence, not mixing them all together.

The structure of this section is discussed more fully in the next chapter.

Rebuttal In Latin, the Confutatio or Refutatio. This is where you deal with opposing views. You have to summarize the opposing view and give reasons why you do not think it valid. Note that we have an entire chapter devoted to rebuttal. But we will summarize some of the issues here that relate to the classical model.

First, you have an ethical obligation to fairly summarize the opposing view. Twisting the opposing position to make it look ridiculous can become the "straw man" fallacy. You also have an obligation to take on the strongest of the opposition arguments, not the weakest. In addition to these ethical obligations, there are also strong practical reasons for treating opposing views as carefully as possible. Your audience may be familiar with the opposing arguments, and if they discover they cannot trust you to present them accurately, the audience will decide not to trust you on the things they cannot check. Your objective is to persuade people, and so you want to win over your opponents, not bludgeon them into silence.

Moreover, you can gain credibility as an advocate for dealing fairly with your opponents. Character is demonstrated in adversity, the saying goes, and by keeping your tone professional while describing opposing arguments, you demonstrate that you are in control, that you are not insecure or threatened by dealing with opposition.

If misrepresenting your opponent's arguments is one fallacy, ignoring them is another. Nothing is so frustrating to a genuinely undecided observer of an argument, someone who really wants to figure out the truth, to have one side or both just talk past each other, ignoring what each other said. The suspicion is natural that if you are ignoring an argument against your view, this means you probably don't have a good reply for it.

You may also wish to concede the validity of some of the opposing arguments. No real argument is entirely one-sided; there is almost always some valid reason against as well as for a position. Trying to win every single aspect of the argument lowers your credibility because it shows you don't have good judgment.

Of course, it is possible to concede too much. On the one hand, we do live in a sort of "take no prisoners" culture where any sign of reasonableness can be misconstrued as weakness. (It should come as no surprise to be told that the authors take a dim view of this.) On the other hand, sometimes advocates are so timid and afraid of starting a (conflicted) argument that they just agree with almost everything because, well, there is something to be said for it. But the art here is to not simply accept another viewpoint, but to put it in context and perspective. Typical ways for doing this would include the following:

- You accept an aspect of your opponent's argument, but argue that it is less significant than some factor in your own argument. For example, "Yes, taxes on this group of people will go up in some circumstances, but that will be countered by how my proposal lowers taxes across the board."
- You accept an aspect of your opponent's argument, call attention to your own fairness in doing so, but then argue that other dimensions of your proposal are more important. For example, "Yes, a commitment to honest dialog requires me to admit that there is a point here. But I think it is, on balance, less significant than all the benefits of my proposal."

But there is more to arguments than just two opposed sides that we have to choose between. The rebuttal section is a good way of showing how your position includes the best of other views and avoids their problems. You can do that by following any of these methods:

- You may take an aspect of your opponent's position and include a modified (and improved) version in your own proposal. For example, "The proposal to bomb selected businesses is good, as far as it goes, but my proposal is that we bomb everything."
- You may show how your position lies between two extreme positions and has the benefits (or avoids the problems of) both. For example, "While advocates want to expel all immigrants and opponents want wide open borders, my proposal will . . ."

In subsequent chapters we will discuss various forms of reasoning. We will also present various ways of attacking those forms of reasoning. That will help you form a rebuttal argument.

Conclusion In Latin, the Peroratio. Here you summarize your argument, trying to integrate all that you have said. This section might include a call to action. It can be a section that brings Pathos to the fore. It can be effective to return to the images and examples used in your introduction. If in your introduction you told us about one person affected by the issue, return to that person's story and tell us about what happened in your conclusion. If in the introduction a person was waiting for a heart transplant, the conclusion would be the time to tell us they died because your proposal hadn't been adopted.

Conclusions, like introductions, do not need to be stories. Lincoln's Gettysburg Address ends this way:

> It is rather for us to be here dedicated to the great task remaining before us—that from these honored dead we take increased devotion to that cause for which they gave the last full measure of devotion—that we here highly resolve that these dead shall not have died in vain—that this nation, under God, shall have a new birth of freedom—and that government of the people, by the people, for the people, shall not perish from the earth.

In this conclusion, Lincoln deftly reminds you of the sacrifice of those that died in battle, what they were fighting for, and urges his audience to fight (in their daily lives) for the same things.

Perhaps you can summarize your argument with a pithy saying that you would like to be remembered. One of the more famous examples was how the lawyers defending O. J. Simpson used the refrain "If it doesn't fit, you must acquit" as a quick way of reminding jurors about a misfitting glove and summarizing their argument for acquittal.

A key mistake advocates use is to introduce new topics or ideas here, hoping to sneak them past the audience. This is neither ethical nor persuasive.

The one new topic you can address in a conclusion is to look ahead. You can discuss what further work needs to be done, what data should be collected, or what you might extend your argument to in the future.

The Model in Summary

Having now come to the conclusion in our description of the classical model, it is appropriate to give a conclusion about the model. The classical model can seem obvious, and it is commonly used. Perhaps it is an obvious structure because of its inherent logic or perhaps it appears obvious only because it has been in such long use in our culture. In any case, mastery of this form should be a requirement. It contains all the parts you might use in an argument and is very easy for the audience to follow. It's a good model to consider as your default option.

This model works by being very transparent. Everything is right out in the open for the audience to see. And that brings us to the concept of *signposting*. A common problem for both students and published writers is failing to provide markers (signposts) for readers to advise them of what is going on. As you write, you need to signal to your readers each change of section. You can do that in two ways. First, by starting paragraphs with strong transitions ("The first of my three reasons is . . ."). Second, do not overlook using section headings, even in a short paper.

TABLE 11.1

The Classic Model for Presenting an Argument

Formal Name	Contemporary Name and Description	Issues
Exordium (ig-zor-de-em) (Lt., Gk: Proem)	**Introduction:** Prepare the audience to hear your argument (Pathos). Lead them to want to listen now (Kairos). Often a story, a striking question, a bold claim that will intrigue the audience.	Not a summary. Must connect to the argument and not just by a catch phrase. Acknowledge any difficulties. Invoke your own character. What tone should you take (the same as the rest of your argument or a contrast)? Don't guilt-trip. Cannot be too long.
Narratio	**Background** or Narration: The statement of facts: things the audience needs to know, definition of terms, abbreviations, jargon Any common confusions that need to be addressed.	Don't lose them by too long a narration. Put everything here or divide it up among the arguments in the confirmation.
Propositio	The proposition, the thesis, the **claim.**	State as succinctly and clearly as possible. Do you have one or more?
Partitio	**Forecast** of what you talk about: Tell them what you're going to tell them.	As brief as is useful. Omit in a short piece.
Confirmatio	**Presentation** of your case (subclaims, grounds, evidence, warrants, backing as required).	Expect it to be more than half of your presentation.
Confutatio, refutatio	Summarize opposing views. **Rebut** main claims from opponent. Concede to valid opposing arguments.	Must deal with the strongest opposing arguments. Smearing your opponent can and should damage your ethos. Conceding obviously valid points your opposition has made is not a weakness.
Peroratio (per-oratio)	**Conclusion** (Pathos): Summarize but also integrate your argument.	Do you have a pithy saying you want to have remembered? Must be consistent with what you have said so far. May return to the images used in the exordium. May include a call to action.

Classic-lite

The full-blown classic model is seldom used, especially in shorter presentations. However, many ways of making an argument are drawn from simplifying the model. In school, you may have run across this model:

Introduction

Point 1

Point 2

Point 3

Conclusion

In this model, the introduction probably includes your claim and any background information is folded into the "point" sections.

Here's a more general version of the same thing:

Introduction

Claim and Forecast

Presentation

Conclusion

Sometimes in business you write a memo using something like this:

Claim

Bullet points

Conclusion/Summary

In this version you are writing to people who already know the topic (hence no background section), who have been part of a longer conversation and so don't need to be persuaded that this is an important topic (hence no real introduction).

OTHER ARGUMENT STRUCTURES

There are several other commonly used ways of presenting your argument. We will present several, but we are certainly not claiming that these are the only ways you can present an argument.

Pathos-centric

In some writings on argument, this model is referred to as a "pathetic appeal." This is grammatically correct; the model is an appeal to Pathos, the emotions. However, the term is confusing since it can also be taken to mean a "sad and weak appeal." Thus, we will term this a *pathos-centric* form of presentation.

In a Pathos-centric model, the argument is typically presented by a story or a series of examples that paint a picture and emotionally draw in the audience. So, instead of presenting, for example, statistics about risks to pregnancy, you might tell a story about three women friends who had difficult pregnancies, one of which resulted in the death of the woman. You'd describe her fear, how she felt about oncoming death, and describe the pain and anguish her loved ones experienced.

Pathos-centric does not mean exclusively a story. To continue the example, you might present the story of the three women and then weave in statistics on how common this sort of problem is. But Pathos-centric is more than just *starting* with a story; to be Pathos-centric, the bulk of your presentation has to be done in a way that puts emotional issues at the center.

Wildlife stories on television often use this model. They are told by following an animal throughout a year. You see the cute baby animal in the spring, its first steps out on its own, the struggle to live on its own, the terror of dodging predators, and so on. You come to identify with the animal and feel what it feels. During the course of the story, the narrator typically adds background facts that put the story in context. This is very different than a presentation that would use the classical model and present a thesis statement about animals and give several reasons for it.

Inspirational speeches, sermons, a letter to someone who is grieving: These are some occasions when we'd expect a Pathos-centric appeal.

In the classical model, the introduction is often an appeal to Pathos. But after the introduction, the classical model does not emphasize emotions. In a Pathos-centric appeal, you continue this approach all the way through.

In our culture we seem to have accepted the idea that emotions are opposed to logic and simultaneously to despise that distinction. We need to place the debate about "head and heart" on a different footing. Remember that all along we have been arguing that Logos and Pathos are two dimensions of any argument. We want to be clear that an appeal to the emotions is a form of argument and can be evaluated—and evaluated logically, in part. If you are telling a story, is it a good story? Does the story fairly represent the problem? Is the story true? Which emotions are you appealing to? Have you chosen appropriately, or are you inducing (for example) anger, when you should be inspiring?

Pathos-centric appeals are not only found in the telling of stories. Sometimes they are the presentation of claims and grounds, but in a special way. Consider this section from one of the most highly regarded works by any American politician, Abraham Lincoln's Second Inaugural Address.

> Fondly do we hope—fervently do we pray—that this mighty scourge of war may speedily pass away. Yet, if God wills that it continue, until all the wealth piled by the bond-man's two hundred and fifty years of unrequited toil shall be sunk, and until every drop of blood drawn with the lash, shall be paid by another drawn with the sword, as was said three thousand years ago, so still it must be said "the judgments of the Lord, are true and righteous altogether."

Here, Lincoln certainly is offering claims and reasons for them. But note the powerful emotions he is invoking—the violence of slavery, the destruction of war, and the cosmic significance of both. His argument is made by emotion, by arguing, in effect, that you should have certain emotions about this war. These are claims induced by the words, rather than being explicitly presented. He didn't say "People got wealthy from slavery and so there is a kind of justice in having the war take their wealth away." He puts you in a state of mind to see his claim, rather than simply telling you what he thinks you should believe.

Delayed Thesis

A delayed thesis presentation puts the claim at the end or near the end of the presentation. It may help to think of this style as taking the audience on a mental journey. You start with some situation or facts, work through the issues, and then, at the end, let your claim come out as a conclusion to the presentation.

In the classical model we suggested it wasn't ethical to introduce new ideas in the conclusion. What makes it ethical in the delayed-thesis model is that claim that you make at the end flows directly from and sums up the material you've been giving all along.

This is a helpful form for when you want to prove a startling claim that seems not very plausible.

Court decisions Decisions of an appellate court approximate this form—with an exception. The court does begin with a quick statement of their decision. However, once past that initial, often short, section, the rest of the decision follows a delayed-thesis form. The court begins by describing the facts of the case as determined at trial, then it might review lower-court decisions, and work through the various issues presented. The decision is announced at the end.

As an example, consider how Justice Thomas delivered the decision of the U.S. Supreme Court in *Bowles v. Russell*.

The decision begins with an abstract, termed a "head note," that summarizes the case and gives the verdict of the court. The main part of the decision itself begins with this:

> In 1999, an Ohio jury convicted petitioner Keith Bowles of murder for his involvement in the beating death of Ollie Gipson. The jury sentenced Bowles to 15 years to life imprisonment. Bowles unsuccessfully challenged his conviction and sentence on direct appeal.

It's true that you could argue that this is an introduction, but it really starts with a description of the facts of the case including the history of the appeal. In that description of facts is mentioned that a district court granted Bowles a 17-day extension on filing a motion, rather than the 14-day extension mandated in the rules. That will prove to be the key issue. This section ends with a one-sentence notice that the Supreme Court is affirming the appellate court decision, but it does not explain why.

The decision then goes on to consider the rules about time limits in more detail, discussing the meaning of "jurisdictional" as it applies to rules. A dense thicket of precedents and rules and cases are discussed until the majority concludes that despite Bowles filing his motion on February 26th, relying on the district judge who told him the deadline was February 27th, that the deadline was really the 24th (14 days, not 17 days), and so his motion cannot be considered. He was too late.

So, even though we do know where the court is going to end up (because of the abstract), the flow of the argument is such that the claim (*why* they will rule the way they do) comes out at the end rather like proving a theorem in math. This is a different flow than in the classical model.

By the way, four judges, led by Justice Souter, dissented, contending: "It is intolerable for the judicial system to treat people this way, and there is not even a technical justification for condoning this bait and switch."

Rogerian

A Rogerian presentation gets its name from the client-centered therapeutic techniques developed by Carl Rogers. In the argumentation field, a Rogerian presentation gives centrality to the perspectives and concerns of the audience. You would typically start by acknowledging what the audience cares about; you'd admit that you have disagreements with them (if applicable). Sometimes this is called the *common ground* approach, because you are looking first for what you agree on.

So you begin with what your opponent believes. But this model is more than a way of starting an argument. Throughout your presentation, you always keep the particular interests of your audience in mind. You avoid loaded words that might generate defensive responses in your opponents. You tailor your language to what your audience uses; indeed, you use their vocabulary and concepts to clothe your appeal. You use their values and beliefs to build your argument.

To some extent, this is good advice for any presentation. What is different in the Rogerian approach is the extent to which you do it and the effort you go through to translate your presentation into the belief system of your audience. If the classical model appears to sit in splendid isolation, a system of pure logic unconnected to any actual person (that isn't true, but it can seem that way), then the Rogerian system is like talking with a sympathetic friend who is talking just to you.

While we shouldn't treat our audience as children, it may be a helpful example to remind ourselves how we have to make arguments to children. We know there are concepts they will not understand, and we have to phrase our arguments in language they will grasp. We know they are very centered on themselves, and so arguments that appeal to the needs of others may not be persuasive; we have to appeal to their self-interest or concerns. This translation into the world of a child is an example of the Rogerian approach.

Well, okay, I look for common ground, but when do I get to make my case? In the Rogerian model, you make your case using your audience's concepts. That requires a real effort at translation.

As an example, consider how you might approach a person who is convinced that we need to strike out hard against terrorists. You want to persuade him that the war in Iraq is not reducing the risk of terrorism. A Rogerian approach would be to begin by acknowledging the problem of terror, perhaps that you agree it is an increasing problem. You might cite a recent example of a terrorist attack and explain how appalled you were by it.

As you turn to stating your position, you would agree that we need to be effective against terrorism, that you support spending money to fight terror, perhaps you supported the Afghanistan war, but you want money spent efficiently. In fact, you might suggest that you share a view that taxes should be as low as possible (if that is also a value the two of you share) and to do that, you'd argue, we cannot spend money on things that are not helpful against terror. From there, you might suggest that a stronger military approach in Afghanistan would be better than the results of the Iraq invasion.

This can all seem very slow and indirect. What is so hard, you may feel, about grasping the simple proposition that "the war in Iraq has increased the number of terrorists?" But the insight of the Rogerian model is to be aware that people's views are also rooted in value judgments and that people associate certain positions they oppose with values they do not share. So, they may believe that people who oppose the Iraq war are people who "blame America first" or people who "apologize for Muslims." Such people may hold the view that in regard to Muslims, "All they understand is force" and the like. The intent of using a Rogerian model is to be aware (and respectful) of those beliefs and to separate them from your position.

But make no mistake, the Rogerian form only works when you respect the framework of the audience. Using this approach to engage in psychological manipulation is unethical. An insincere application of this model will likely be detected by the audience and resented.

Diatribe

A diatribe is known today as a rant. This is a highly emotional, over-the-top series of polemical statements and invective. We can see examples in the style of several contemporary comedians. Dennis Miller had his famous beginning: "Now, I don't want to get off on a rant here . . ." before he would launch into a rant. Lewis Black makes arguments for traditional democratic values and ethical behavior, laced with hyperbole (and profanity).

However, don't be misled by a dictionary definition or by some of the negative emotions that are attached to the term "rant" or even to "diatribe." Such a type of speech is not necessarily out of control, abusive, or even unwelcomed by the audience. The key attributes of this type of speech are its passion, its direct confrontation of ideas it rejects, and its more flexible organization.

Diatribe as a rhetorical form has ancient roots in Cynic and Stoic philosophy. Some have identified a diatribe style in the writings in Paul's letter to the Romans and the letter of James in the New Testament.

More modern examples can be found in the stereotypical half-time speech of a football coach to a team that is behind. The coach wants to stir up the players and does so alternatively by deriding their poor performance and inspiring them to do more.

James Kunstler gives an example.

> Last evening at twilight I was driving my rent-a-car up Interstate Five north of Seattle with a vivid testicular fear of being trapped in the very metaphor of a failing society racing into a dark future. All around me loomed the monuments of an out-of-control financial credit Moloch—the tilt-up chain store boxes with their giant logos glowing against the distant craggy peaks of the Cascades (many of them active volcanoes which, like Mt. Saint Helens, might blow their tops any day).
>
> At every compass point sprawled the McHousing pods of American dream mortgage time-bombs silently blowing families to financial smithereens, and banks with them, including, incidentally last Friday, the state of Washington's own Shoreline Bank just off I-5 north of Seattle, seized by the FDIC.
>
> My way was lighted, as darkness finally stole in, by the endlessly replicated dispensaries of fast food-dom (pizza-burgers-chicken-fries-and-shakes) provoking this nation of overfed clowns to ever-greater feats of gluttony, medical catastrophe, and bankruptcy. (Kunstler, 2010)

He's making an argument, but doing so by invoking emotions with vivid comparisons (volcanoes exploding), leading you to feel that his physical journey is risky. He's angry about what is happening and piles up extreme examples to get that point across.

There are important issues about in what context this model is (or isn't) persuasive, and those are discussed in subsequent sections.

STILL MORE ARGUMENT STRUCTURES

While the models described above are common, there certainly are others that are important in particular contexts.

Specialized Models

A specific, focused, communication context can produce a model of presentation tailored to that context. Here are some examples:

Inverted pyramid This refers to the traditional way a story was written in a newspaper: a series of increasingly detailed descriptions of the argument. First you'd have one paragraph that presented your entire argument including your claim and the main reason for it. Then you'd present the argument again with more detail. Finally you'd give background information.

Two ideas motivate this model. A newspaper is read by people with a wide range of interests. Some, for example, are not interested in politics generally, but would be interested if something really significant happened. Others will devour all the political news. So, by letting readers know the whole story in one paragraph and then having more and more details as the story unfolds, they can accommodate readers of various degrees of interest. The second issue is that space is always an issue—can all the stories fit? There isn't time to edit or rewrite a story to make it a bit shorter. The inverted pyramid form means you can cut a paragraph off the bottom if you need more space and that can be done without making the story end abruptly.

A tiny bit of this inverted approach exists in the tradition of preparing an abstract for an academic paper or an executive summary for a business presentation. Neither of these is an introduction but in fact is a summary of the entire presentation with the assumption that if the reader finds the material interesting (or doesn't believe it), they will read the entire article, but many will simply not read the details.

The Five-Paragraph Field Order

In some branches of the U.S. and British military, there is a formal model for presenting an order to a small tactical unit. In one version, this has one paragraph each devoted to Situation, Mission, Execution, Administration & Logistics, and Command & Signal. There are variations, and the items included in each paragraph are also broken down in detail. Using a consistent model helps commanders make sure they include everything, and it helps the leaders of small units know that they received everything they need in one place.

ORAL MODELS

Some forms of organization of a presentation fit much better in oral than in written presentations. Speakers have the need to memorize or at least partially memorize their presentations. This can motivate different patterns of organization. One example is a *linking* model where the end of the first point links to the start of the second point. So a speaker might discuss a trip that ends at a museum, talk about issues with museums including money, then discuss his own finances.

Another model is *chiasmus*. This is a ring pattern. Consider this example:

Remember your family. Give your parents the respect they deserve. Showing respect is a way of remembering what is important. Respect the good in the world. Seek the good in the world.

That doesn't seem to immediately have a clear organization. But if you print it out this way, you can see something different:

Remember your family.
    Give your parents the respect they deserve.
        Showing respect is a way of remembering what is important.
    Respect the good in the world.
Seek the good in the world.

Now you can see that it balances an inward focus of return with an outward reach to the world. It is organized around the central concept of showing respect. Chiasmus is a pattern of A/B/C/B/A.

This pattern seems to exist in ancient texts that may have started out as oral compositions. It's not clear if those listening to such a form would recognize the form or if it is simply a help to the speaker to remember the speech.

REBUTTAL MODELS

In the rebuttal section we will describe some other ways of organizing arguments when the context is that you are rebutting a specific argument someone else has already made.

Cultural-specific Models

By leaving this to last, we certainly don't mean it to be the least. Actually, we think this is a very important concept. To fully describe the world's communication practices is far beyond the scope of this book. This book is written in the United States and written in English. We quote Greek and Roman authors, and some of the theory described here originated in those cultures. But that should never be taken as a claim that the entire concept of reasoned argument only exists in that tradition.

The models we have discussed here actually are not specific to "western culture" (whatever that actually means) but they are commonly found in it. Other cultures not directly derived from European roots—specifically Native American, Hispanic, African, African American—and nations and cultures with long histories such as China, Egypt, India, or the Muslim world (to just list a few) can have conventions of how arguments are to be made that are specific to them or to a certain context within those broader cultures.

Nor is the concept of a culture having a specific communication practice limited to ethnicity or nationhood. Various religious groups, professional societies, and other groups can develop specialized conventions for presenting arguments as well.

If you are in one of these contexts, attending to and respecting the conventions is important to communicating well. These conventions may be pieces of a full model such as the way you greet others, how you begin your speech, the order in which people speak, how disagreements are framed, or similar things. Or they may be something broader. Furthermore, learning about the diversity of how people communicate can enrich our own argumentative practices and help give us perspective. Just because some model originates in one context doesn't mean it can't be useful in another.

So, while the models we've highlighted are quite common, they are certainly not all the important models that human beings use to persuade each other.

CHOOSING A MODEL

Which model is best? The answer is: It depends. The best model is matched to your argument and to your audience and so the answer depends on those factors. We will evaluate each of the five main models on the basis of the four dimensions of an argument (Logos, Rthos, Pathos, and Kairos).

Classical Model

Logos. Logos is the primary appeal of the classical model. It is a good model when you want to place logic front and center. It does so by its entire approach, which makes for a transparent, step-by-step presentation.

Ethos. Your credibility can be enhanced by following the classical model. It enables an advocate to display precise, deep, and detailed knowledge of a subject. Indeed, should you be presenting an argument when you bring no significant credibility to the argument, you can "hide" inside this presentation style. You are implicitly saying, "Don't take my word for it. Look at the facts and logic I am laying out. Never mind who I am. Look at what the authorities I am referring to say."

Moreover, if your credibility is either suspect for some reason or has been actively damaged by something you've done, you can use this model to deflect attention away from you and onto your argument.

Pathos. While this model would seem to have nothing to do with Pathos, that isn't necessarily the case. Logic can be beautiful, cool precision can be refreshing, especially on a highly emotional subject. One of the authors attended a public discussion on homosexuality in the church. Emotions were running high, very high. The speaker began his presentation. He was precise, careful, very logical, some would say dry and pedantic. Gradually, however, the crowd calmed down and began to listen. He sorted out a number of positions, led many in the audience to reflect on the subject and transcend their visceral emotions, and regain contact with a higher set of emotions.

Kairos. The classical model is suitable for audiences that are favorably disposed or neutral to the case you are making. It is also a good model to consider if the audience is uninformed. It has obvious applications in situations of teaching, science, legal or business presentations, or any formal situation.

This model can appear inappropriate in some emotional situations when an audience needs to be inspired or comforted. In these situations you as advocate can appear to be unfeeling or clueless if you stick with a classical model.

Pathos-centric

Logos. If the classic model erroneously appeared to be only about Logos, the Pathos-centric model can be mistakenly assumed to have no logical content. On the contrary, some emotions are appropriate, some are not. Some stories support the emotional effect you are seeking and some do not. You do have to think about emotions.

However, the logical risk in a Pathos-centric model is that you overdo the emotions and leave yourself open to a rebuttal composed of that particularly logical form of humor called satire.

Pathos. Of course , a Pathos-centric model will emphasize Pathos. In particular, the goal of the model is to engage the imagination and sympathy of your audience. An issue with such appeals is which emotions are you going to invoke? Will you appeal to the lowest common denominator or the highest emotions? Both Hitler and Buddha engaged the imagination and sympathy of their audiences. The temptation to advocates is that sometimes it is easier to stir up passions than it is to ennoble and inspire.

We'd refer you back to the section on emotional appeals in an early chapter.

Ethos. The issues of credibility of the argument and speaker can be obscured by a Pathos-centric approach. The audience can be so absorbed in the emotions of the story being told that they ignore questions about the presenter. Likewise, if a story is emotionally compelling, the audience may not notice if the story is true or false or an embellished form of the truth.

But this model can be assessed along the dimension of credibility. If you present a fictional story as truth, that should not be considered a credible thing to do. If you appeal to base emotions, glorify violence, present a bad lifestyle as exciting, or similar things, it should diminish your standing as an advocate.

Kairos. Like almost no other model, the Pathos-centric presentation can create its own Kairos by reshaping the moment. Human beings seem to be wired to respond strongly to emotional appeals—if the appeal is on target. Perhaps it is connected to how we'd agree that if we find someone hurt, crying, or in distress that the right thing to do is to drop whatever we are doing and attend to the person in crisis. Thus, a Pathos-centric appeal, if done well, can almost ignore the situation and context and reshape things to their own perspective.

It is also an effective choice when the situation calls for immediate action.

Delayed Thesis

Logos.   Similar to the classical model, the delayed thesis approach is useful for putting logical appeals front and center. It naturally tends to support a structure for your argument when you build your case step by step.

Pathos.   The delayed thesis is often used to overcome emotional resistance from the audience by starting with some fact that cannot be disputed. By putting the (presumably controversial) thesis or claim at the end, you give the audience time to warm up to your idea or to even see it as inevitable. This is why this approach is often recommended for a hostile audience.

Ethos.   Similar to the classical model, the step-by-step approach of this presentation can enhance the advocate's ethos.

Kairos.   As indicated this is a model to consider when your audience is opposed or skeptical. It's a model to consider when you are advocating a claim that appears to defy common sense or is one you don't think people are going to like originally. If you were going to advocate legalizing all drugs, legalizing prostitution, negotiating with Al-Qaeda, or abolishing the automobile, to give some examples, this might be the model to choose.

Rogerian

Logos.   Rogerian presentations use logic as an emotion. By that, we mean that the Rogerian approach almost mandates a calm, reasonable presentation style. The underlying claim is that "We are all reasonable people who can work out our problems."

However, that isn't the only situation. The logic of this model is to get inside the world of your audience, whatever it is.

Pathos.   Rogerian presentations rest on the knife-edge of Pathos. They can reach the audience like almost no other form, but they can also seem fake and manipulative. If you only appear to be addressing the concerns of the audience, without really meaning it, this can backfire. On the other hand, if you want to show respect and care, this form can make it easier.

Remember that calmness and serenity are also emotions.

Ethos.   "Sincerity is everything. Because, when you can fake that, you've got it made." This satirical saying encapsulates the dilemma of the Rogerian approach. Do it for false motives and you can come across as the stereotypical used-car salesman. Do it out of utter sincerity and it can transform a situation.

Done with integrity, you command respect because you are opening yourself, becoming vulnerable.

This model has stirred some controversy among feminists. This model, despite being originated by a man, has been critiqued by some for seeming to be like the stereotypical "female" way of making an argument: nonconfrontational, accepting what the other says, looking to show empathy with a respected "other" rather than destroying a hated opponent with cold "male" logic. So is it affirming the validity of female cooperative approaches versus male confrontational approaches? Not all agree. This model has been viewed as denying the right to be angry and, in particular, anger over injustice inflicted on women. More than this, the self-denying aspect of presenting your argument in the terms of the "other" can seem like just another way of making a woman's voice invisible.

The way out of this conundrum, we think, is to stress again that the choice of model is a decision made by the advocate in response to the advocate's evaluation of the situation and is a decision about what will be effective communication. Rogerian approaches may well be useful in situations of power imbalance when a person with less power may find it an effective way to defuse the power of their audience. For that matter, we suspect that hostage negotiators may use elements of this approach as well.

> *Kairos.* Rogerian presentations must be responsive to, and are designed around, a close understanding of the situation, the moment, and the audience. Reflecting its counseling origins, this model is particularly useful if your audience is a single person.

Diatribe

> *Logos.* There may be no logic visible on the surface of this type of presentation, but it has logic nonetheless. The *reductio ad absurdum* ("reduce to the absurd") is a form of argument easy to incorporate in a diatribe as is satire. Both involve a form of logic by taking some person or position and inverting or exaggerating what they say.

Diatribes work by referring to claims, grounds, and warrants the audience has already accepted. If you're a football player, you accept the warrant that you should do your best and strive to win. A diatribe that derides you for failing to meet that standard will hit home. If you think football is pointless, you're unlikely to be moved by it.

However, diatribes are vulnerable to sliding into a torrent of insults rather than arguments. It becomes easy to pile up the abuse and make more and more outrageous claims.

> *Pathos.* A diatribe is usually intended to stir up emotions, and these are often emotions of anger, derision, or bitterness. However, it is also a useful approach when you need to motivate people or to cut through a fog of confusion to reclaim what is important. A diatribe is not well suited for conveying gentle or peaceable emotions.

TABLE 11.2

Models of Argument Structure

Argument Structure	Logos	Pathos	Ethos	Kairos
Classical Introduction Background Proposition Grounds/Evidence/ Warrants Rebut opposing arguments Conclusion	(Primary appeal) Make clear a complicated or confusing issue.	The beauty of logic. Antidote for too much Pathos.	Enhanced by displaying precise, deep knowledge of topic. Enhanced by sources that are also Logos-centric. If you have little ethos yourself, then you can draw on the Ethos of your sources and of Logos itself.	Appropriate for a favorable, neutral, or uninformed audience, a formal situation, a teaching situation, science, legal, or business context. Can be appropriate when inappropriate emotion is about to spin out of control. Risk: Can appear unfeeling or out of touch in an emotionally charged environment.
Pathos-centric Tell a story, use examples, paint a picture. Highlight emotions, human impacts of issue.	Logic of the story. Is the emotion rational? Risk: Easy for opponents to mock if overdone.	(Primary appeal) Valid when appealing to the best, highest emotions	Hidden, but story must be credible. Risk: A valid argument can fail if the story is shown to be fake.	Can create its own Kairos. Often used when a call for a decision is the goal.
Delayed Thesis (1) Show how someone got to your belief from starting at the audience's view. (2) Start at crisis; go back, explain how you got there.	Is there, but initially hidden. Revealed at the end.	"Let me show you something." Take the audience on a journey.	"You won't notice me sneaking into your brain."	Appropriate for hostile audience or audience that disagrees. Appropriate for a claim that appears to defy "common sense."
Rogerian Start by acknowledging disagreement. Emphasize how you understand their position. Use what they agree with (accept their warrants).	"We are all reasonable people."	Risk: Seen as flaky, "peace, love, dove." Risk: "I'm being manipulated."	"I take you seriously (and thus, I am serious)." Risk: Used in a calculating way to create a false Ethos. Risk: Antifeminist?	Appropriate for an angry audience that is not listening. Appropriate for an audience of one or a very homogeneous group.
Diatribe A rant	Typically, reductio ad absurdum, and satire.	Stir strong emotions. Risk: Being dismissed as out of control. Risk: Offending someone who has power to stop you.	Torrent of words conveys the author's conviction; this conviction is understood as credibility.	Appropriate to motivate a discouraged or defeated audience. Appropriate to intimidate a hostile audience.

Ethos.   The passion the advocate pours into their presentation can convey conviction to the audience, and audiences tend to like advocates that are passionate about their beliefs. Curiously, fervent conviction seems credible, even if the conviction is about something absurd.

Kairos.   A diatribe can change the moment if it is powerful enough. It can be useful for cutting through a confused situation and recalling people to fundamental issues. However, there are certainly situations that are more formal or reserved when the rough-and-tumble diatribe would backfire. If a judge appears set to rule against you, this would not be the form of argument to use to present your objection!

CHOOSING HOW TO PRESENT YOUR ARGUMENT

Over the past few chapters we've considered how to assess your audience, how your choices as an advocate impacts the credibility of your argument, and how to choose a presentation style. Now, we want to put that all together.

Few debates in America are more contentious than that over abortion. What marks this debate is the vastly different views of almost all aspects of the issue. How would you present an argument on abortion to an audience?

It's always good to remember that real people have complex positions that cut across clichés, but this is one issue where it is plausible to think of two sides. So consider two possible presentations: one in favor of abortion rights, one opposed. Consider two audiences: one favorable to abortion rights, one opposed. So there are four rhetorical situations. Can you make a good presentation in each of those four situations? The following table summarizes the rhetorical challenges you face.

	Audience in favor of abortion rights	Audience opposed to abortion rights
Advocate for abortion rights	Sympathetic audience	Unsympathetic audience
Advocate ending abortion rights	Unsympathetic audience	Sympathetic audience

FIGURE 11.1
The Classic Model.

As a class exercise, divide up into groups and each take one of the four situations given above.

However, it would be very good if each of you had to develop an argument and presentation for more than one of the four. Because abortion is so contentious and because your own view of the issue may be directly tied to deeply held moral and religious views, it is worth restating why it is a useful exercise to try to argue on both sides of an issue. This isn't because argument is a game without consequences, but rather because when you try to imagine how your opponent will argue, it helps you see the weak points in your own position. In doing an exercise, everyone knows that you are doing an exercise; you are not being forced to recant your cherished beliefs.

Audience Assessment

To prepare for this, we will assess the audience. Remember, we want to develop a sympathetic understanding of their view, not satirize it.

Abortion rights supporters We might anticipate that this group would

- Tend to be liberal;
- Place a high value on personal choice and individual autonomy;
- Be concerned about traditional suppression of women;
- Believe traditional morality stifles freedom and was more about control than morality; and
- Feel oppressed by religious conservatives (especially religion on television).

What characteristics would you add to this list?

If you are going to argue in favor of abortion rights, what is your goal for an audience that already agrees with you?

Abortion rights opponents We might anticipate that this group would be more likely to be

- Religious, especially Christian and especially Roman Catholic;
- Identify as politically conservative;
- Think that sexual activity has become too prevalent in contemporary society;
- May themselves have been at risk of being aborted by their mothers;
- Tend to define themselves in terms of family (that is, their vocation as parents or grandparents);
- Place a high value on moral choices, especially involving duty and personal responsibility;
- Think that the secular world makes fun of religion and resent that; and
- Place their concerns about abortion in a larger context of a "culture of life" including such issues as euthanasia (which they would also oppose).

What characteristics would you add to this list?

If you are going to argue against abortion rights, what is your goal for an audience that already agrees with you?

Choosing Which Arguments to Use

Now we have to consider what argument you will make. What claim will you advance, and how will you phrase it?

Arguments in favor of abortion rights Common arguments in favor include the following:

- A woman should be able to control her own body.
- This is a personal moral choice that society should not control.
- Every child should be a wanted child.
- The fetus is not a person.
- You have to permit abortion for rape and incest.
- Pro-lifers are hypocrites because they do violence at abortion clinics.

- Pro-lifers really just want to stop people having sex.
- Pro-lifers really just oppose the liberation of women.

Which of these arguments will appeal to the audience you are addressing?

Arguments opposed to abortion rights Common arguments against abortion rights include the following:

- Women who have abortions are traumatized by it.
- Abortion is murder.
- You have a responsibility to the unborn child.
- God has forbidden abortion.
- The church has forbidden abortion.
- Rape and incest are horrible crimes, but the pregnancies resulting from these are rare, and they do not justify committing a second horrible crime.
- My tax dollars should not be used to fund something I find morally offensive.
- Abortion is part of the permissive and destructive sex morals existing now.
- Abortion is part of the current trend to devalue all human life and making life serve issues of expediency and profit.

Which of these arguments will appeal to the audience you are addressing?

Choosing the Model

Now we need to take our third step: to identify a model for presenting our argument.

Which model provides the best fit of your audience and the argument you want to present? Can you explain why?

Make Your Argument

OK! Make an argument.

PRACTICALITIES

There are any number of rules of "good writing" that need to be followed to make your presentation effective. We'll just list a few that are specific to the issues of choosing a model.

- Don't advertise or telegraph your choice of model. There's almost no value in saying "I'm going to use a diatribe here." However, that is different than signposting the sections of your model so that the audience can follow your approach.
- If you are using a model that has specific sections to it, be painfully clear when you transition from one to the next.
- If you are using the classical model, don't use the Latin or Greek names for the sections. And for some of the English names, consider changing the section titles to something appropriate for your paper. People understand

what "Introduction" and "Conclusion" mean, but other sections should probably be renamed.

• Keep the relative size of the pieces of your argument in perspective and make sure that your actual reasons for supporting your argument are not buried under the other material.

CONCLUSION

With this chapter we bring to a close an extended discussion of how to connect your argument to your audience and the times. We've assessed the situation and decided what our rhetorical task is. We've examined how you as a person and the order of your argument affect communication.

In summary, we return, yet again, to our little diagram of the advocate communicating with an audience in a context. Paying attention to these factors will greatly enhance your ability to be persuasive.

Finding Evidence

INTRODUCTION

You Need to Use Better Sources

We haven't read your papers, but we know you need to find better sources, use them more critically, and cite and document them more carefully. We know this because we're assuming you are pretty much like everyone else. It is an irony of the current situation that while evidence has become much more readily available, the ability and willingness to use good sources doesn't seem to be increasing.

> "The Egyptians who live in the cultivated parts of the country, by their practice of keeping records of the past, have made themselves much the most learned of any nation of which I have had experience."
>
> —Herodotus, *The Histories,* 2.77

Why do you need to devote an effort to finding and using better evidence? It's worth spelling out the reasons.

- There are many **false beliefs** floating around. We all are confident in the truth of any number of things that we've never really checked.
- Thousands upon thousands of diligent people throughout time and from many cultures have done hard work to explore the truth and find things out. It's arrogant to think you can ignore that. You should show respect to others. And you can **use the work of others,** build on it, and contribute to it.
- It's a key way to **enhance the credibility** and persuasiveness of your arguments. You can demonstrate that you're not alone in your views.
- You get ideas from others. This isn't just direct copying, but a good source will suggest things to you, inspire new ideas and new **directions for your work.**
- You can add **color and vividness** to your writing by finding pithy sayings or sharp quotations.

You Need to Learn How to Find Good Sources

No one is born knowing how to find quality evidence. Growing up, you don't see it done well. Your elementary and high school textbooks generally don't cite many sources or show you how disputed topics should be treated.

The mass media seldom provides any model at all of how to distinguish good sources from bad. They have several bad habits that teach us bad habits. They often engage in *false balance*—providing one source on each side, regardless of where the weight of sources fall. So we'll get one person believing in alien visitation and one who doesn't. They have a belief that conflict is entertaining, and so the extreme and the flamboyant is preferred to a careful peeling back of the surface to extract the truth. They seldom spend time probing evidence or assessing conflicting data. They have short attention spans coupled with the 24-hour news cycle that combine to generate frenetic jumping to immediate conclusions and an echoing of those conclusions endlessly. And the on-air personalities are seldom people with a background in research nor are they specialists in the topics being discussed. Nor does journalism as a profession seem to teach careful researching skills.

Finally, searching for sources is work. It's hard to search things out, it takes time, you have to be careful and precise and . . . well, it is work.

The Revolution in Evidence

The way evidence is found is undergoing a transformation driven by the twin revolutions of the Internet and the digitizing of data. The Internet is making information easier to find—but it is doing that both for information of the highest quality and of the lowest quality. There is also an explosion of the creation of evidence. Now, anyone can be a blog writer, video producer, or commenter on other's activities, and that leads, again, to both the best and the worst being produced in great abundance.

The digital revolution receives less notice but may be more important. Digitizing of print, audio, and video sources allows that material to travel over the Internet and (this is crucial) be copied easily without loss of information or degradation of quality. As a result, more and more sources are now available directly online and indexed in databases.

We will explore the implications of this transformation on your arguments in the "Finding Evidence" section. For now, we should just observe that because of this explosion of sources, evidence now often floats free of those institutions that provided a warrant of credibility. So there are more situations when you cannot rely on the source of data to tell you if it is valid or not. Therefore, it is more important than ever to know how to assess evidence.

Those of us who grew up hefting the green volumes of the "Reader's Guide to Periodical Literature," and who grew bent and squint-eyed on our epic treks into the deep thickets of the library stacks to stalk the elusive species "data," tend to have little sympathy for those of you who contend you can't find any information on your topics. But we should have some sympathy, because you are awash in ephemeral data. Confronting a million pieces of information is just about as paralyzing as having none.

Due to these factors, the question of evidence—finding it, assessing it, using it—still has a critical role in forming a valid argument.

FINDING EVIDENCE

The specific activities that make up the task of "finding evidence" are in rapid change due to the twin revolutions of the Internet and the digitizing of data. However, this revolution is not complete nor is everything just "there" to be found. The skill of finding evidence is still one that you need to think critically about and to master.

Levels of evidence One way to start is to think about types of sources going from general to specific.

- *Encyclopedias.*   Don't distain these, and don't assume that Wikipedia is the only one. The virtue of an encyclopedia is that it can give you a calm overview of a topic, define commonly used terms, and even suggest your next steps. You likely have access to several online encyclopedias.
- *Reviews and tutorials.*   As a type these are hard to find, but worth it. A review article or a tutorial piece is one that isn't making just one specific point about one aspect of an issue, but rather steps back and presents a survey of the broader picture. They may discuss the history of views, point out standard sources, and give you more detail than an encyclopedia article.
- *Detailed sources.*   And of course, you want detailed sources. If you know the general topic, then you can know how to fit a detailed source into the larger picture.

The problem, of course, is that it isn't realistic to think that you can do a search in this order. What typically happens is that you go back and forth. You start with something general, dig in, realize you are confused about a point, back up, look at your general sources again, and then go back to more detailed ones.

Techniques for Finding Evidence

We'll look at four distinct ways you can look for evidence: searching the Internet, searching databases, by following clues in sources, or by asking people.

Searching the internet Most of you already do general Internet searches with Google. However valuable this is, there are issues you should be aware of.

It is not true that "all" things are online or that you can find everything that is online. Google, the current leader for searching the Internet, is a remarkable achievement. In a second or two it provides results of indexing billions of web pages. However, Google may miss as much as a third of the Internet[1]; no one seems to be quite sure. And these estimates were from January 2005, the Web (and Google) have grown enormously since then.

---

[1] A. Gulli, A. Signorini, The Indexable Web Is More than 11.5 Billion Pages, retrieved February 2, 2007, from: http://www.cs.uiowa.edu/~asignori/web-size/size-indexable-web.pdf

We will say more about using the Internet as a source in the "Assessing Special Types of Evidence" section.

Additionally, search engines only find the "indexable" web. Some websites block the "spiders" that conduct the search. Many websites are driven by databases and only construct the Web page when you request it. Examples of this would be sites that search catalogs (like a library) or present account information for you. Additionally, sites that are secured by passwords or other measures are off-limits to search engines, at least currently. So Google isn't going to give you results from classified government sites, private intranets for companies, commercial databases, and other private sites.

The content of the Internet is dynamic and growing. Sites also disappear and change, unlike a book that once published stays the same and can be referenced and checked. That is one reason that you put "retrieved [date] from . . ." in your documenting of sources.

Further, you should be sensitive to what kinds of information are less likely to be online. While we are not aware of any systematic evidence to support these conclusions, casual use of the Internet suggests that you are less likely to find the following online:

- *Older data.* Data produced after the digitizing revolution got into full swing can be put online readily, but older data has to be converted and so has only been sometimes digitized. Some older data may be online, but not fully indexed.
- Data from **non-English** language sources or from the third world. While Canada and a number of European countries are as advanced (or more) than the United States, once you venture into the third world, this is much less true.
- Data produced by **poor people**. There are, one supposes, many, many blogs and sites about rural third-world folk music. But few are produced by those that actually produce most of the music.

So, by all means, use Google or other search techniques for the Internet. Go beyond their simple search procedures and learn the ins and outs of how to use them. Just remember:

- Searching with Google is **not** enough.

Searching databases In order to do a competent search for material, you must be able to use online databases. University libraries typically provide access to an amazing series of databases that index journals, newspapers, and other sources. More and more of these now include the actual text of the documents, saving you the trouble of looking for the print sources, and allowing you to search from anywhere, not just in the physical library itself.

You need to become proficient in using online databases. Which databases to use vary by the field you are studying, but identifying two or three primary databases for your field of interest is a high priority. Don't expect that any one database will answer all your questions.

You should be aware that some skill is required to use these sources. How you form search criteria can have a significant (and unpredictable) impact on what you find. Lean on a research librarian for help in mastering these skills.

What sources are cataloged in those databases?

- *Newspapers and general circulation magazines.* The database LexisNexis (and databases for some specific newspapers) has indexed and provided full text for popular newspapers and related types of sources. This can be very useful both for finding articles, but also for evaluating the currency of a topic. How many articles were there about some topic? When did this term come into use?
- *Academic publications.* This is the bread-and-butter of these databases. Journals, reports, conference publications, and the like. You have a choice of databases that are general or those that focus on a subject area like medicine, GLBT issues, a region of the globe, or a type of ethnic studies.
- *Reviews and abstracts.* Databases can contain indexes of literature that refer to other sources. These include abstracts, book reviews, and related material.
- *eBooks.* While databases have been long oriented toward periodical literature, the rise of the ebook means that full textbooks can also be found in databases.
- *Original content.* While we focus our attention on databases as ways to find sources, the integration of material is leading to the blurring of boundaries. Some online places we might think of as "websites" are acquiring enough search capability that they can look like databases.

Additionally, databases can help your research process.

- Help for **formatting sources**. Some of the databases will print or email lists of sources in the exact format you need to cut and paste into your bibliographies. This can be a great time and frustration saver.
- **Tools for exploiting** what you've found. Databases are going beyond just giving you a list of results to a search. Some will tell you that a given source had references in it to a certain number of sources and then let you see that list. That makes the tasks described just below in the "Searching Sources" section much quicker. Some databases can do that in reverse and show you how many other sources have cited a particular source. An oft-cited source could well be a respected one or at least a source that got noticed and affected the debate.

Searching sources If there is any truth to the suspicion that humans still contain genetically encoded behaviors for hunting, one way for modern people to satisfy that craving is by hunting for evidence: Following the tiny clues can lead you from one source to another. While searches are valuable and essential, it is still essential to know how to get from one piece of evidence to another. You may not have all the money they throw around on the crime scene investigation shows, but the clues you are following are more obvious.

Techniques you should be familiar with include the following:

- *Follow footnotes and links.* A good source likely makes reference to other sources, and if the source really is good, there is a good chance that the sources it cites will also prove to be important. Some databases, as we indicated in the previous section, can do this for you automatically. One sign you have really started to understand the literature on a subject is when you see the same articles being cited over and over.

- *Follow names.* You find an article by someone and you decide it is a good article. Try searching for other things that person has written. Figure out what institution they are part of and search for other things from that institution.
- *Follow organizations and groups.* You find a really good website. Who do they link to? Who sponsors them? Who do they endorse?
- *Use interested/one-sided sources to find disinterested data.* You find an article attacking the position you want to defend—a source that isn't directly helpful. But that article may cite sources that it is attempting to refute. You may be able to use those other sources. Or, you find a source that is advocating for your position, but you determine that it is not a very good source. Again, the sources cited by this source may be of use.

Searching people When you do a search, you normally focus on sources (and the people who created them). But, think for a minute about a different group of people: the people you personally know or have access to, and think of them as sources.

- *Ask "Who would know?"* Searching for data often requires a starting point. A moment thinking about who or what kind of person would know the answer can be helpful. If you are at a university, there is a good chance that somewhere on the campus is someone who works in the area you are researching. As a student, you've got general permission to contact them and ask them for some direction.
- *Ask a librarian.* Librarians, especially research librarians, know more than just what their library has and what other libraries have. They know how data is organized and can advise on databases to search, how to structure queries, and what keywords might be helpful. As we've said, not all online searching is obvious and the various search engines use different conventions.
- *Ask an expert.* If you identify someone who is known in the field, you can try sending them an email, even if you don't know them and even if they are famous. The key is to ask a limited, specific question that they can answer quickly without having to do any research. Many like to help and can point you to a key source.
- *Ask where experts gather.* Almost any group of specialists likely has an online forum where they discuss their issues. Go there and ask for help. Ask for a good link to a good source.

ASSESSING EVIDENCE

Having found a source, you need to evaluate it. We divide those two topics up, but, of course, you do both at the same time. You consider which sources to pursue based on judgments you make about which will be likely to be useful.

We want evidence that is both *true* and *credible*. We want evidence that is accurate, of course, but we also need evidence that is "capable of being believed" or "believable."[2]

---

[2]*Oxford English Dictionary*, online edition.

Credible evidence is not exactly the same thing as accurate or true evidence. A source can be very reputable and accurate—but not thought so by the particular audience you are dealing with. The question is: How do you prove something is true to your audience? To do that, we have to offer credible evidence.

We want credible evidence both because it would be unethical to use evidence that we know is false or misleading and because using credible evidence increases the power of our argument with our readers.

How do we decide if a piece of evidence is credible? This is not a simple question, and there are no magic rules to apply. But there are a number of *heuristics* or "rules of thumb" that increase the odds that our evidence is credible. These involve the use of primary sources and then a series of tests to apply to the source, the author, and the place the source was published.

Typically, Prefer a Primary Source over a Secondary Source

A primary source directly originates the data; a secondary source cites primary or other secondary sources for its references. A person writing about their personal experience is a primary source. An encyclopedia is a secondary source. An article reporting research results done by the author is a primary source; an article summarizing research done by many people is a secondary source.

The definition of primary and secondary is not attached to the type of media but to the specific piece of evidence. An author, for example, might recount his own personal experiences (being a primary source) and also quote others (being a secondary source). A magazine might publish articles that were primary sources and also publish secondary sources.

There are several advantages to consulting primary sources.

- A secondary source may have filtered or selected from the primary source in ways that are not consistent with the argument we want to make. This is not to suggest that the author of the secondary source has been deceptive. The secondary source had its own objectives and agenda and chose from the primary source to make the point they needed to make. But our needs may be different.
- We can discover other information in the primary source that would be useful to us. A secondary source picks out a phrase or single argument to use, but it often is the case that when you track down the primary source you find a wealth of other useful information. This information can be a variety of forms. Suppose we have a reference to some event, but not many details. The primary source might give us details like the exact location, the date, things that led up to it, and other information that can assist our research.
- The primary source may give us other sources for our argument. Study the full primary source. You may find direct references to other sources. More than that, you can find references to events, people, concepts, that you may use directly or use to help focus your searching.
- We can be sure that there has been no deception. Sometimes authors do manipulate their sources (even unintentionally), and this allows us to be

certain that we are not the victims of it. One advocate quoted a court decision and made the claim that "the facts (of the guilt of the defendant) were not disputed." But when the court decision was read, it was found to have actually said: "even assuming the guilt of the defendant . . ." That is a huge difference lurking inside a subtle word choice. The first phrase means "no one tried to claim he was innocent" but the second phrase means "even if he was guilty (on the facts), it wouldn't affect our decision (about the law)." The first implies that his guilt was so obvious no one even tried to argue about it. The second says his guilt or innocence is irrelevant in this case.

- We raise our credibility. One mark of a scholar is the ability to handle primary material. It is a requirement of obtaining a Ph.D. Outside of academia, it still is the case that we respect someone whose researched the issue back to the beginning.

There are exceptions where a primary source cannot be easily used.

- The primary source may be too detailed or too technical for us to evaluate. It is relatively easy to obtain a copy of Albert Einstein's original paper setting forth the theory of relativity, but most of us will learn much more from someone who summarizes it for us in nontechnical language. Scientific articles, medical reports, technical discussions, and court decisions are several areas where this is particularly true.
- The primary source is unavailable. Sometimes we just can't get the original material, or it has never been translated into a language we speak.
- We need a summary of an area of research. If you want to make an argument about the likelihood of curing cancer in the next twenty years, and breast cancer is one aspect you are going to discuss, you could read thirty or forty scientific articles on breast cancer, interview some experts, and then reread the articles. But what you really need for a short paper is one credible article that summarizes and synthesizes the research and comes to some conclusions.

Finally, do not make the mistake of thinking that primary sources are more accurate than secondary sources. That isn't the point. A book of transcripts of Hitler's speeches is a primary source, but it's not an accurate depiction of the role of Jews in Germany in the 1930s. A history book about Germany in the 1930s would be a secondary source, but much better on the status of Jews. However, if your goal is to write about Hitler, then you need to read his speeches directly and not just read about his speeches.

Evaluate the Content of the Source

The source is more likely to be credible if it meets these heuristics:

- *The source is internally consistent.* A recent book attacking the existence of God picked a few verses out of the Bible that seemed to approve of slavery and used that to argue that the Bible isn't very moral. It then admitted, however, that there were other verses that rejected slavery. It then argued that selecting a few verses was "cherry picking" and wasn't a valid way of arguing. It either is or it isn't. Discovering a source using inconsistent rules undermines the source's credibility. Likewise you can look for inconsistent use of data. A source that uses one type of data approvingly but then rejects the same data when it disagrees with the author is not a credible source.

- *Is the source is detailed and specific?* It's easy to "rant" in general about something that bothers you. Harder is to provide specific examples, discuss the history of it, refer to the opinion of others, and offer analysis of how this issue came to be. By being specific, the source shows its command of the issue and gains credibility.
- *The source has references.* Footnotes, endnotes (or other forms of reference) mean that the author is not relying only on his own opinion or her memory. When an author uses footnotes, they "put their cards on the table" and let you see how they came to their conclusions.
- *The references check out as valid.* Unfortunately, not all authors understand evidence. It certainly happens that—either through ignorance or malice—authors provide citations that do not stand up to investigation. Before deciding that an author is reliable, you should check out a reference or two. What you want to discover is if the reference exists, if it is accurately cited, and if the evidence supports the use the author makes of it.
- *The evidence presented relates to the claim being made.* Notice if the evidence actually does support the claim. This seems obvious, but it isn't always the case.
- *Evidence is offered for the main points of the claim being made.* It's all very well to provide a host of well-documented sources for all the minor points, but to slide over the main issue. Don't be mesmerized by a host of references. Do they supply evidence for the key issues?
- *The evidence uses sources that are read by experts in a particular field, compared to sources with a mass audience.* This criterion may be hard to assess, especially if you are researching an area that is new to you. But you want to look at who the sources are that your source uses. Do they look like scientific articles and specialty books, on the one hand, or from blogs from opinion sources, popular articles in newspapers, on the other?
- *Sources can provide evidence that works against the interests of the sources* (i.e., a liberal source providing evidence for a conservative conclusion). If your source is arguing for a "liberal" conclusion and they can use "conservative" sources to support them, then their evidence gains weight.
- *Evidence can come from a wide variety of sources.* Can you tell if the author of the source you are examining is widely read in the subject at hand? Have they done a lot of research? If so, it enhances their credibility.
- *Evidence comes from a source cited by other credible sources.* Does this source appear in the footnotes of other credible authors?

Evaluate the Author of the Source

You should distinguish if a source is credible because of *what* it says or because of *who* says it. These aren't completely unrelated. An ordinary, unknown person can acquire considerable Ethos, considerable credibility, just by writing authoritatively. On the other hand, an internationally known expert can still say stupid things that shouldn't be accepted regardless of their stature. The key is to make a distinction between a source that makes a case through logic and evidence contrasted with a source that is speaking on their own personal authority. Both can be valid, but they are easily confused.

If someone gets up and says, "I saw this. This is what happened," then their personal credibility is clearly the issue, and you will have to assess their credibility. On the other hand, if they present an argument using Logos and evidence, then you assess the quality of what they've said. Of course, both are mixed in together in many cases.

The author is more likely to have produced credible evidence if the author meets these heuristics:

- *The author is known to be well thought of and proved reliable.*   As for the source, so for the author. Is this author quoted with approval and respect by others with credibility? Note that this is not just a test of popularity; it's a test of what other credible people say.

- *The author corrects their previous mistakes.*   Only in politics is it fatal to admit you've changed your mind. In most of life, we expect people to grow and become wiser as they gain experience. An author that is willing to go back and say "I was wrong," or "I see things more clearly now" has enhanced their credibility, not reduced it.

- *The author admits weak parts of the case.*   Few arguments are totally one-sided, most have some valid points on either side or on several sides. Almost all real policy choices involve some trade-offs. If an author can see those things and admit the valid issues on the other side, it is a sign that the author has good judgment.

- *The author treats opposing views fairly.*   Few things reveal someone's character better than how they describe opposing views. It's easy (and fun) to caricature them or twist them so they appear foolish. It's much better to state opposing views fairly and then rebut them.

- *The author follows the money.*   This phrase is a shorthand way of saying that the author looks at motive when he describes how people made decisions. Whether dealing with public affairs or how people behave in their neighborhoods, people tend to look out for their self-interests. An author can sound naive if they ignore that dimension. The phrase 'follow the money' specifically refers to seeing who gains and loses financially from advocating certain positions.

Evaluate Where the Source Appears

The source is more likely to be credible if the place it is published meets these heuristics:

- From a **peer-reviewed journal.** *Peer-reviewed* means that before a journal prints an article, it is sent out (anonymously) to other experts in the field who comment on it. Those comments are shared with the author and the editor, and the author must deal with any objections raised before the article is accepted for printing. While this can suppress new and dissonant ideas from being published, it provides some assurance that the article makes sense to those who know the most about the topic. This is commonly done in scientific and academic fields. It is less common (or nonexistent) in popular writing.

- From a source that is **transparent about its associations**. You won't find peer-reviewed journals that deal with popular subjects. But you can look to see if the source is being open about who funds it, what group it is associated with, and so on. Failing to find this isn't proof of a problem; many magazines just list a publishing company without further explanation.

- From a source that isn't **controlled by its advertisers**. There is always an uneasy relationship between maintaining integrity and independence, on the one hand, and the influence of those who pay the bills. Some periodicals are simply conduits for selling products or define their topic in terms of which products to buy.

- From a source with a **reputation for publishing credible evidence**. You can try to discover the reputation of the journal itself. But doing so generally involves getting an opinion of an expert (whose credibility you then have to assess) or by reading a journal for a long time and seeing how it handles issues.

Watch Out for These Warning Signs

Here are some heuristics that warn you that a source is **less** likely to be credible:

- *Sources hide the methodology used or refuse to provide primary data.* Sources that hide things should make you suspicious. Of course, there can be valid reasons for confidentiality such as personal privacy, classified information, confidential business information, and the like. But refusal to explain how data was collected or how much primary data exists are red flags. It often covers up the fact that the author has only a few anecdotes rather than systematic data or that the author has manipulated the data in some way.

- *Sources claim national security prevents them from proving their contention.* Of course, there really are things that have to be classified. Few arguments you will make would be improved if you knew the actual codes to launch nuclear weapons, the names of spies, details of battle plans, or just how good a photo our spy satellites can take. But it is often true in recent history that when public officials have used the excuse of national security for why they can't give evidence, it has been a cover for a weak argument that had little data to support it. This argument is really an appeal to use the Ethos of the politician rather than Logos to support an argument.

- *The author argues from silence.* An argument from silence is using the absence of something to prove a point. For example: "No one saw President Kennedy's body from 12:09 to 12:23 so no one can prove that a UFO didn't descend and switch bodies with an alien during that time." The fallacy is that the absence of information is often due to ignorance, not to the thing actually being absent. Sometimes, authors have to argue from silence, but they should exhibit some awareness of its weaknesses.

- *The author claims that all who have evidence to prove the case have died under suspicious circumstances.* This is a favorite of conspiracy theorists.

And they usually can list the names of those who have died—died five years later, but just, it turns out, days before they were to testify or be interviewed. Check it out, see if those deaths were really suspicious. See what those people had said prior to their deaths.

- *The author uses evidence from far right-wing or far left-wing sources uncritically.*   There is a marketplace of ideas, and there are those selling rotten fruit. Out on the fringes are those who believe that liberals have been in a 50-year conspiracy with our enemies and those who believe the government planned 9/11—twenty years ago. They are entitled to be heard and to make their case. But what they are not entitled to is to have their views accepted as credible without evidence.

- *The author uses the Westboro Baptist Church, Rush Limbaugh, Michelle Bachmann, or the X-files as a source.*   This list is incomplete and would change over time. But these sources have been shown, in the opinion of the authors, repeatedly to exaggerate their claims, pass on information proven to be false, and to grossly misrepresent the views of their opponents. Therefore, they have forfeited any presumption that they are normally credible, and you should not trust them. You can use them for ideas—that you then work to validate from other sources. Oh, and the X-files was fiction, remember?

- *The author assumes that corporations act in our best interests.*

- *The author assumes that politicians act in our best interests.*

- *The author assumes that wealthy people act in our best interests.*

- *The author assumes that corporate officials, politicians, and the wealthy never act in our best interests.*   It is a great principle of a democracy that people are judged by their own actions, not those of a group they belong to. It is also a great principle of logical thinking that "Fool me once, shame on you, fool me twice, shame on me." Corporations, politicians, and wealthy people have demonstrated certain tendencies, and those tendencies are not generally to work on behalf of ordinary people or in the best interests of the nation as a whole. This isn't surprising nor necessarily sinister: Most people most of the time work for their own interests, not the interests of others. On the other hand, it is foolish to *assume* selfish motivations in a particular instance without proof. What you should do is develop evidence one way or the other.

- *Authors use a headline of the form "X to do Y."*   This means X hasn't done Y. Newspapers often publish press releases, and this is particularly true in business coverage. These announcements are of intentions, not accomplishments. They may well be sincere intentions, but they are about the future. You should not assume that a statement "We *plan* to start doing X" means that "We *are* doing X."

- *Authors make assumptions from probability on the basis of too little evidence.* For example, you find statements like "Isn't it obvious that a reasonable person would have done this" when it isn't obvious. In a variety of ways, assessing human behavior in the absence of full data is about assessing probability. The problem is that there is a very strong tendency to wish that what was probable was exactly what you need to prove your case. The actual probability of some action requires you to know all pertinent circumstances, something you seldom know. "Is it reasonable that a father would park so far away from school when picking up his child? Wouldn't a good father want to be as close as possible?" Sure, except that parking at this particular school is a big problem or the child doesn't want the father to cramp his style with his buddies as he walks out. Hence they agreed that Dad would park a block away.

- *Authors commit the "tree with no forest" fallacy.* You will not find this fallacy listed in the textbooks, but it is a common one. It refers to isolating one piece of evidence out of thousands and blaming someone for not acting on it. The authors would like nothing better than to blame President George Bush for failing to respond in time to stop 9/11. And there is that memo that went to him entitled "Bin Laden determined to strike in the United States." Sounds like he should have known, right? Well, what we need to know is how many other memos and conversations and position papers went to the president about the likelihood of terrorist attacks, as well as how many other urgent crises were presented to him on that day. Were there claims that six other groups were going to attack? Had the last ten claims of imminent attack proven to have been false? To judge fairly, we need the full context.

How You Can Use a Source That Is Not Fully Credible

Suppose you find a source, but you understand that the source has problems. Perhaps part of it seems reliable but another part raises questions. Perhaps it has a great claim in it, but no evidence for the claim. You actually have a number of options.

- *You can use the source as a starting point for more research.* Now that you have an idea where to look, you can perhaps find another source that makes the same point with more credibility.
- *You can see if other sources will endorse this particular aspect of your source.* It can happen that you will find people who will write "Source X was often unreliable; however, on this one point he was proven correct." If you can find someone who will endorse your source on the point in question, you are in luck, but this can be pretty rare.
- *You can use the source, but clearly indicate its problems.* You might write something like "So-and-so puts forth an intriguing claim, but does not provide any evidence for it. Thus, it cannot be taken as proved without further investigation." This is not the best solution because it can seem that you are trying to have it both ways, but this may be the best you can do.

It will often be the case, however, that you will simply have to let this source go. Consider it a test of your integrity. Congratulate yourself for passing the test.

Dealing with Conflicting Sources

So you've done some research, and you have several sources, but they disagree with each other. Welcome to reality. These disagreements aren't just about interpretations but will be about facts as well. What do you do?

The first thing is to avoid the fallacy of *confirmation bias.* This fallacy is where you start with an opinion, read a source that agrees with you that you decide must be credible (since it agreed with you). Then you read a source that disagrees and you decide that source has to be wrong (since it disagrees with the source you just read). This is a hard fallacy to avoid. It's natural to reject things that seem to require us to change our mind, since if we do change our mind, we have to, most likely, change things we've written and think about other issues.

Another mistake is to just throw your hands in the air and decide that everyone is wrong or that there is no way to tell what is really the case. In the case of disagreements, you have some tests to apply:

- In the case of two competing primary sources, you will have to assess which is more credible. Compare and sift how each conduct themselves. Which is more accurate?
- In the case of secondary sources, you can see if one source seems closer to the event than the other? Is one source using better primary sources or more primary sources than the other?
- Does one source refer to the disagreements and deal with it? Let's say that source A writes: "While some sources say it was $5,000, that is because they have added X and Y. In fact, it was $3,000 in 1991 and $2,000 was added later." Source B just says: "It was $5,000." All other things being equal, source A looks like it has a better command of the situation.
- Does one source acknowledge and deal with ambiguity? So source A writes: "They paid $5,000" and source B writes: "Most people think they paid $5,000, but it must be acknowledged that source C has made an interesting case that it was $7,500." Here, source B looks like it has a better understanding of the issue.
- Keep going and find a third and fourth source that helps resolve the issue.

But maybe, you should just accept the ambiguity. Many things, especially at the edges of a topic, are unclear. Any number of historical issues are still argued. New interpretations are proposed, disputed, debated, and sometimes accepted. Being able to accept and deal with that is one mark of a mature writer and academic. So, if you come to a conclusion, after research that some issue is not currently able to be resolved, just present that conclusion in your paper. Don't apologize or act as if this is something to cover up.

ASSESSING SPECIAL TYPES OF EVIDENCE

In the previous section we discussed general principles of assessing evidence. In this section we will consider a number of special cases when the type of evidence poses particular issues for us.

Evidence That Is Translated from Another Language

Translation makes available to us the wisdom, knowledge, and data from around the world that we would not otherwise be able to use. However, you should be conscious that translation is a difficult exercise and not just a substitution of one word for another. Subtleties of meaning, idioms peculiar to one language, poetry, humor, word play, and so forth, do not translate easily. When using a source in translation you may have to try to verify that the translation is considered to be credible. There are sometimes different translations available, and when you compare them, you can be surprised at how much they vary.

There have been some significant conflicts or arguments that have turned on conflicted translations. Those interested in examples could check out the 1956 statement of Soviet premier Khrushchev that got translated as "We will bury you" or the 2005 statement by Iranian president Ahmadinejd that got translated as "Israel must be wiped off the map." Neither was an accurate translation of the meaning of the speaker.

Evidence That Comes from a Different Culture

By "a different culture" we are primarily referring to sources from beyond our own country. However, there are many different cultures within any one country—think of the difference between urban and rural, conservative and liberal, people who like sports or NASCAR or art or classical music, the communities of scientists, four-wheelers, church-goers, square-dancers, musicians, and a thousand others.

Words can mean different things in different locations. Winston Churchill recounted an example of misunderstanding in World War II because "to table" something means "to stop discussing it" in the United States, whereas it means "to consider it for discussion" in Great Britain—the exact opposite.

From that, you can see that an American using sources from Fiji or France may face issues of understanding even if the source is in English.

Using sources from beyond our own culture is a critical way that we prevent ourselves from becoming too myopic. However, as with translated evidence, there can be a number of issues that we can stumble over.

- The sources referenced by this source may not be accessible to be checked. They may come from journals that are not indexed or not available in our libraries.
- The source may make reference to local cultural conventions, slang, or technical terms, personalities or incidents that we don't know about or understand.
- The source may be bound by conventions of what can be said and what can only be hinted at and are very different from what we expect. This is particularly the case if the source is from a place where freedom of speech is restricted in different ways than it is restricted in your country.

Studies

You've seen headline after headline: "study proves. . . ." Eggs are terrible for your cholesterol, no they're not, we're too fat, no it's not our fault, this causes cancer, that causes cancer, no it doesn't. On and on. But there are some problems with believing stories about studies.

In order to achieve a rigorous result that can be duplicated by others, studies often measure "proxies" for what you really want to know. We can't test a drug on a thousand people, but we can test it on a thousand mice. We can't evaluate how happy people are by just asking them; we wouldn't be sure everyone was using the same standard. But we can ask them about a number of behaviors that can be associated with happiness.

Studies often proceed by holding many variables constant and varying just one dimension of a problem. Some real process has a hundred causes, but we have to sort out which matters. So a scientist tests them one at a time. The authors propose some modest and narrow conclusions. But then, those results get put into the popular media with wild conclusions far in excess of what the study, and those who authored it, are actually claiming.

The media also make certain characteristic mistakes over and over again with reporting scientific studies. They often drop the numerical data that tell you how significant an effect is. Some time ago there was data to support the notion that oat bran lowered your cholesterol. Maybe it did, but in the popular press there was little discussion of what *quantity* of oat bran you had to consume in order to produce what *amount* of reduction in cholesterol.

Media also regularly ignore issues of trade-offs between effects. This came to its laughable conclusion, in the case of oat bran, when someone produced "Oat bran Beer" and advertised it as lowering your cholesterol. It might well have done so, but you had to drink two six-packs a day in order to get enough oat bran to have a significant effect. Good luck with that.

To be sure you are not misled, look carefully for qualifications and limitations on what was studied. Another key tactic is to look for the story or study to be reported in a general science magazine rather than the popular press.

Statistics

We have an ambivalent attitude to statistical evidence. On the one hand we automatically ascribe authority to numbers. Yet, on the other hand, we also think you "can prove anything with statistics."

As with studies, we will consider questions of validity in the next section. Here we want to discuss reasons that might confuse you about what a statistic is actually claiming.

Numbers often separate from the context that generated them and float freely. In other words, the number represents something precise, but by the time you read it, it is quoted as referring to something else. It was 400 complaints in the original source, and then it became 400 arrests and then 400 trials and by the time you read it, it has become 400 convictions.

Understanding statistical evidence involves being able to understand some technical terms. Here are a few common misunderstandings—and these involve only the simplest forms of statistical data.

- *The three kinds of averages:* mean, median, and mode. A *mean* is the number you get from summing the numbers and dividing by the number of data points. A *median* divides the sample between two halves, with 50 percent of the numbers below the median and 50 percent above. The *mode* is the most frequently occurring data point. Each can be the appropriate number to use in different situations.

- *Nominal vs. real.* This occurs in regard to money and involves the effect of inflation. If you had $100 in your savings account a year ago and $110 now, you've earned 10 percent nominal interest. But if there was 10 percent inflation over that year, you're actually not any richer and your real interest rate was 0 percent. This is a crucial thing to take into account when using historical data involving money. Something can be "the biggest tax increase in history" only because inflation has made a dollar worth less than in the past.

- *Shifting base.* The federal budget deficit is larger. Or smaller. Government spending has grown (or spun out of control). That's terrible, or good. But our country's population grows over time also. And the economy grows as well, apart from inflation. By one measure (there are several), the federal deficit in 1945 was $47 billion and in 2004 it was $520 billion. Huge increase! But the federal income in 1945 was $45 billion and in 2004 it was $1,798 billion. So in 1945 the deficit was as big as federal income; in 2004 it was only a third of federal receipts. Likewise if you compare deficits to the Gross National Product of the United States you will get a very different chart than if you look at absolute amounts (even absolute amounts corrected for inflation).

- *Percentage changes vs. numerical changes.* If you were making $10,000 last year and made $20,000 this year, you could describe that as a $10,000 raise or a 100 percent increase. The later sounds more impressive, doesn't it? You could lord it over your friend who made $50,000 last year and $70,000 this year, because he only got a 40 percent increase. Or could you?

- *When does the trend start?* "Jobs have been lost while President Bush has been in office," "No, the recession started under Clinton." This particular dispute turns, in part, on when you start counting. Percentage gains can be strongly influenced by when you start measuring for a trend. Start a trend in 1935 at the depth of the depression and the numbers will look very different than starting the trend in 1943 when the United States was rapidly expanding its economy during World War II.

There are other issues like this, as well as much more complicated statistical paradoxes. You must be careful not to misunderstand what the statistical evidence is telling you. We're not trying to make you statisticians (though that might be a good idea); we are simply saying that "common sense" is not good enough.

Graphs and Charts

While a chart seems to be objective and straightforward, this type of evidence can be "spun" just like any other document to create an impression that is not supported by the underlying data. By choosing different ranges of data, a graph can be made to look dramatic or ordinary. Graphs can be subject to some of the same problems as statistics but with the added drama of a visual media.

See the books listed at the end of this section for some good sources of information about how graphs can be misleading.

Court Cases

The decision of a court can be valuable evidence. It is usually carefully documented, and everything in it has been challenged by one of the two sides and reviewed by the judge. However, there are several reasons why court cases can be difficult or misleading to the unwary.

- *The writing in the decision can be very difficult to understand.* The writing is complex. This is one place in our society where language has not been "dumbed down." Decisions use specialized terminology from the legal profession that have particular meanings that might be different from what the words mean in ordinary language.
- *Courts have complex rules for what evidence is allowed to be used.* These rules are partially motivated by a desire to find the truth, but they not the same as what people attempting to decide a question might use. Sometimes courts exclude evidence that is true because it may be prejudicial to a defendant. An example of this is previous convictions for the same crime. Courts, wisely, are concerned that if a jury knows the defendant has been previously convicted of the same crime they will just assume guilt rather than evaluating the evidence. But, if we are trying to write a biography of this person, we need that information.
- *It is a common misperception that courts decide on what is "right" or "best."* In fact, court decisions are not generally concerned with who is "right" in a moral sense nor do they set out to decide what is the best policy for society to adopt. Court decisions often turn on technical legal issues such as who has standing to sue or what specific precedents apply. Despite common impressions, courts do typically decide on the basis of what the law actually says, regardless if that makes any sense or if the judge personally agrees.
- *In criminal cases, there is a strong burden of proof on the prosecution to prove its case "beyond a reasonable doubt."* So a verdict of "not guilty" is not the same as proof of innocence. You might think someone was "probably guilty" but they would still be judged innocent in court.

The White Paper

A *white paper* is a colloquial term meaning a special report. It usually refers to a document produced by a government or other official agency or corporation that reflects more research and analysis than an informal memo, press release, or short statement. The term "white," it should be said, has absolutely no racial or ethnic connotations in this context.

There are some contexts (mostly governments) where the term has a specific meaning for a certain type of report that has some official standing or may officially declare a policy. Some agencies produce "green papers" that are less official or simply propose policy. In some contexts a similar sort of document might be called a "working paper."

You should be aware of this phrase, "white paper," and look for it in sources. While there are no guarantees, it often means that it is a more serious or carefully thought-out work by an agency. However, aware of the credibility the term carries, some companies are producing "white papers" now that are little more than marketing material. Sometimes they are a more technical type of marketing material aimed at a more knowledgeable audience.

The Internet

Is "the Internet" a good source? Isn't there a lot of unreliable information on the Internet? Doesn't a search engine return good sources and rubbish equally? There used to be a lot of attacks on the Internet along those lines. Sometimes people point out what fraction of web traffic is spam and porn. However, it's time to get over that issue. The Internet is more or less ubiquitous—it is a medium of information exchange, indeed, perhaps the primary nonpersonal medium of exchange now. The best and the worse are online. Would we ever say, "Are books a good source?" and expect a yes or no answer? According to Bookwire, some 375,000 English language books were published in 2004. Were they all good? Of course not, they included everything from a few that will be read a hundred years from now to total junk.

But not everyone gets that point. Several years ago one of the authors needed to access something while on a trip. He went to the local city library to access the Internet but before being allowed to do so, he had to sign a statement that he acknowledged that information on the Internet had not been reviewed by properly trained librarians who could sift for quality like they did with the materials in a library and make judicious and wise decisions about what to select. He sat down, started to use the terminal, and looked up. Across the room was the magazine rack, and the first magazine that caught his eye was *Cosmopolitan*. That had passed their quality controls and was judged a credible source by the library.

The Internet is often critiqued because it is "unedited." Why, anyone, the complaint goes, can put up anything. No one is reviewing or checking it. In response, it should be pointed out that the quality of editing and fact-checking in major newspapers and magazines leaves a lot to be desired. If you wanted to know if Iraq had weapons of mass destruction prior to the recent war, you would have done far better to research the Internet than to rely on the *New York Times,* which was consistently wrong.

Yes, much on the Internet is unedited. And, it is also true that because anyone can post material, it means the Internet is also largely uncensored. It is the contemporary realization of the concept of "the marketplace of ideas" where rival ideas compete and readers (like you) assess the varying viewpoints, decide who is right, and reward them with your clicks, your links, and your citations. This is an old concept, first expressed in a dissent by Oliver Wendell Holmes, Jr., to a U.S. Supreme Court decision that is worth quoting at length. But, apropos of what we said about the difficulty of reading court decisions earlier, don't get tripped up by his first sentence; he means it ironically. He's saying it is logical to suppress speech if you have bad motives.

> Persecution for the expression of opinions seems to me perfectly logical. If you have no doubt of your premises or your power and want a certain result with all your heart you naturally express your wishes in law and sweep away all opposition. . . . But when men have realized that time has upset many

fighting faiths, they may come to believe even more than they believe the very foundations of their own conduct that the ultimate good desired is better reached by free trade in ideas—that the best test of truth is the power of the thought to get itself accepted in the competition of the market, and that truth is the only ground upon which their wishes safely can be carried out. That at any rate is the theory of our Constitution.[3] (Oliver Wendell Holmes Jr., [*dissent, Abrams v. United States, 1919*])

In other words, the Internet is just a particular instance of what this chapter, and this textbook, has argued all along. That it is up to *you* to have the skills to discern truth from falsehood, to weigh and assess opinions, and that your ability to do so is as much a part of being a citizen of a democracy as voting.

In a hierarchy you can lie and make it stick, because higher authority will back up the lie and punish whistle-blowers. Lying is far more flagrant on the Net, but no one can make it stick, because anyone can challenge the lie directly and make their case with multiple links to corroborating sources. (Brand, 1999, p. 96)

The quotation highlights that the Internet has a self-correcting function or at least it does for evidence that is put out to the wider public. The Internet is a medium of exchange like paper or sound waves; it is not a type of a source any longer. Once again the conclusion is inescapable: You have to be able to judge for yourself who is credible and who is not.

Evaluation of Specific Sources

There are a number of specific sources that are popular with students and problematic with teachers. These are worth a few specific comments.

- *Wikipedia.* Just as with the Internet (see above), traditional researchers have a problem with Wikipedia because of its open, democratic nature. Some teachers ban its use by students. We think this is excessive. Both personal experience and some research studies have shown that Wikipedia has a great deal of interesting and valid material on it. Because so many different people contribute to Wikipedia, you cannot treat it as a single source but instead have to view each entry as a separate source. In other words, do not rely on the Ethos of Wikipedia in general, but assess the validity of each article that you want to use. Remember also that Wikipedia is not a primary source but a secondary one. Therefore, you can use Wikipedia as a source of ideas and the links in each article as starting points for more research.
- *Fox News.* This source should be regarded as you would any other opinion source. They are not an unbiased source of news, giving equal time to all sides. They are openly what some news agencies are covertly—people who advocate for a particular set of opinions. In doing so, they often give short

---

[3]*Abrams v. US*, 250 U.S. 616 (1919); dissenting opinion of Oliver Wendell Holmes, joined by Louis Brandeis. Retrieved February 3, 2007, from en.wikipedia.org/wiki/Marketplace_of_ideas. The decision was later overturned by *Brandenburg v. Ohio*, 395 U.S. 444 (1969).

shrift to opposing views and do not always represent them fairly. As we said in the credibility chapter, people (and networks) are allowed to be advocates, but we have to be aware of it.

- *USA Today.*   This is an enormously popular source. *USA Today* is noted for their heavy use of color and graphics. You need to use this source for what it is good for, not what it cannot do. It is a decent source of news about popular culture and sports and is useful for a variety of statistics. It is not a thoughtful source of sophisticated analysis.

FOR FURTHER LEARNING

Interpreting data is a complex process. The following two books are classics of the field and have many useful insights about how graphs and statistics can reveal or hide information.

Darrell Huff, *How to Lie with Statistics* (1954, Norton).

Despite how old this book is, the statistical fallacies it explains still commonly occur, and its advice is still pertinent.

Edward Tufte, *The Visual Display of Quantitative Information*, 2nd ed. (2001, Graphics Press).

Another classic but for the graphical world. Explains many fallacies that are done with graphs and suggests better alternatives.

Evidence and Your Argument

INTRODUCTION

In this chapter we continue our discussion of evidence. The last chapter was about finding good sources; this chapter is about using that evidence in your particular argument.

SELECTING EVIDENCE FOR YOUR ARGUMENT

Out of all the evidence you find, which should you use in your writings? Your objective is to use enough high-quality evidence that supports your claim and will have conviction with your readers. There are a number of factors that influence which evidence you should use.

How Much Evidence Do You Need?

Actually, it *is* possible to have too much evidence. How much evidence you need is a function of what you are attempting to write. If you are doing a literature search for a postgraduate thesis, then, yes, you need to make an effort to find *all* the evidence. That's an impossible task, of course, but you will have to demonstrate that you have made a diligent effort to identify a significant majority of relevant evidence that is accessible to you.

In many contexts, you're better off with fewer sources of high quality than a large number of average sources. Quality over quantity. If you are writing a short popular article, such as an editorial for a paper or a blog post, you may only have space to describe one source. In that type of piece you will be better served by one (or a small number) of very good sources.

There is power in citing source after source, but if it comes to dominate the presentation, a reader can get "lost in the woods" and not know what point you are trying to make. Here is a better suggestion. Suppose you have a number of sources that all provide evidence for the same point. Include all of them in the bibliography. You highlight or discuss in detail in your work one or two of the best ones, and then write something like "This point has also been substantiated by . . ." or "Other authors have confirmed this . . ." and list the authors and cite them. By describing one source in detail, you've made the point to your readers. By citing several other sources to support the first one, you've shown that the one source isn't an isolated view.

Evidence and Your Entire Argument

You have to consider how evidence fits into the overall context of all that you are writing to make your argument. First of all, of course, the evidence has to relate to your claim. Evidence does that, typically, by providing support for the grounds of your argument. If you are discussing warrants explicitly, evidence may be used to provide some of the backing for your warrant.

But, more than the Logos dimension of your argument, evidence also affects Ethos and Pathos, as we will see. As a result, we also have to consider how evidence impacts your audience.

The Ethos of a Source Depends on the Claim You Are Advancing

Suppose you have a source that is the remarks of a senior executive in an insurance company. The executive is discussing regulation of a particular insurance product. We'll also stipulate that this person does know what they are talking about; their argument is supported with data and plausible reasoning. This would be a decent source, in the abstract.

But how useful this source is depends on what argument you are making. If you are going to claim that there is too much regulation, then you can expect that someone from the insurance field will be an advocate of reducing regulation. If you were going to argue that more regulation is needed, this source would gain more credibility because you don't expect that perspective from this source. If your argument was about a technical issue dealing with a narrow aspect of regulation, then it would matter more if this was an executive with a background and credentials in that particular area compared to someone who had a more general insurance background. If your argument was about international issues, then it would matter if the source had specific expertise in more than one country.

The Ethos of a Source Depends on the Audience You Are Addressing

This is a similar point to the previous one, but looked at from a different angle.

If your article about lawsuits was aimed at an audience of lawyers, sources that were prominent and respected members of the legal profession would be very good to use—if what they were arguing was otherwise credible. On the other hand, if the audience was people angry at how they were treated by the legal profession, a lawyer testifying that "Most of the time the system works" will likely be dismissed out of hand. In that case, finding a public defender (a person your audience identifies with) or a person critical of the legal process to say things are generally okay would carry more credibility.

Sources from a Different Point of View than the One You Are Advocating Increase Credibility

Many antiwar organizations have a retired general or admiral on their board of directors. Why? Because having a military person (who we assume accepts the necessity for war in some cases) advocate against war increases credibility. Likewise, if you are arguing for a conservative point of view and you can find a prominent liberal as a source, that will increase your credibility.

This is some of the same dynamic as the previous point, but now we're looking at the source in relation to the audience, not the claim.

Evidence, the Audience, and Your Argument

The three previous points may make more sense if we combine all of them into a chart. We have a topic that can be argued for (pro) or against (con), we have the audience that, due to its own interests and orientation, is disposed to be favorable (pro) or negative (con) to the issue, and then we have the evidence that comes from a perspective (or interests) favoring (pro) the issue or opposed (con) to it.

Evidence	Audience		
	Audience's interests favor issue. (Pro)	Audience's interests oppose issue. (Con)	Mixed audience or uncommitted audience
The interests of the source would favor the issue (so we expect a **Pro** position).	Source argues **Pro**: Result confirms prejudices of audience; is thought credible. Argues **Con**: Challenges audience; can be credible. "I'm like you, I believed this, but. . .". Risks audience disputing judgment of source's interest.	Source argues **Pro**: Dismissed as "biased." Argues **Con**: A convert, considered credible.	Source argues **Pro**: Needs careful qualification as an expert; then can be persuasive. Argues **Con**: Can carry conviction due to circumstances.
The interests of the source would oppose the issue (so we expect a **Con** position).	Argues **Pro**: A convert, considered credible Argues **Con**: dismissed as "biased"	Argues **Pro**: Challenges audience; can be credible. "I'm like you, I believed this, but . . ." Risks audience disputing judgment of source's interest. Argues **Con**: Confirms prejudices of audience; thought credible.	Argues **Pro**: Can carry conviction due to circumstances. Argues **Con**: Needs careful qualification as an expert; then can be persuasive.

FIGURE 13.1
Evidence/Audience Interaction.

Of course, in real-world arguments, sources (and audiences) may agree in part and disagree in part. Sources may introduce new issues or new perspectives that do not fit neatly into this chart. But notice the symmetry to the left-hand columns of the chart. The value of a piece of evidence is a combination of audience and the Ethos of the source.

Evidence from Diverse, Independent Sources Increases Credibility

In the example above about lawsuits, suppose you can support your evidence with evidence from a lawyer's organization, a judge, a public defender, a historian, and an ordinary citizen who wrote a book about juries. That would carry more credibility than a paper with sources from six different trial lawyers—even if the lawyers were objectively better sources. Now, that doesn't mean you can use bad sources just because they are from diverse points of view, but, when choosing among credible sources, you should keep this factor in mind.

Likewise, to continue this example, if you could provide evidence from a law journal, a popular magazine, a national newspaper, a journal published in another country, and a sociology journal, that would give more credibility to your work than quoting six law journal articles—assuming all your sources were credible on their own merits.

However, this diversity only improves your credibility if the sources are truly independent. If you have six sources, but five clearly got their information from the sixth, that is not as impressive as six independent sources.

And we want diversity of perspectives, not really diversity of published sources. So six trial lawyers might be fine if one worked for a corporation, one a big law firm, one a public defender, one was self-employed, one was a government prosecutor, and one was retired—and they were from different cities.

Evidence That Directly Addresses Audience Concerns about Evidence Should Be Sought

If you know that your audience will have concerns about evidence or if you know they disregard some types of evidence, then you need sources that discuss not just their conclusions but the state of the evidence for their conclusions. If you are writing about frivolous lawsuits, for example, you are probably aware that on at least a couple of occasions, oft-cited examples of frivolous lawsuits have turned out to be urban legends without foundation. There was the story about a man putting his Winnebago on cruise control while driving, got up to make a pot of coffee, crashed it, and sued, winning a lot of money. That story was false. But it might make an audience wary about another claim.

Knowing this, you need to insulate your argument against claims that the examples you site are fake by also providing more than normal amounts of proof of their veracity.

Using Evidence in Your Introduction

The classical model formally begins with an Introduction; other argument forms may well begin with one. It is often a story or example that appeals through Pathos to create a bond with your audience. Here, the credibility of the evidence may be even more important than other places in your argument. A powerful introduction can stir deep emotions in the audience. Should it turn out that the story you use is false, or significantly distorted, your entire argument can be lost with your audience—even if you provide a powerful Logos-based argument in the rest of your work.

You Have an Ethical Obligation Not to Omit Information That Affects Source Credibility

You have a great source, but you know that two years after this was written, all the data was discredited. You have important statistical evidence, but you know the trend ended a year later and is no longer happening. You have a source that claims to have surveyed all the important sources, but you know there are significant disagreements in the literature.

In each of these cases, you cannot use the source, no matter how persuasive it would be. Or, if you do use it, you have to include the additional information and use the source carefully only in the area in which it is valid.

You have an ethical duty to your readers not to deceive them. This is independent of any practical worry that you will look bad if your readers find out you tried to "spin" them. Each time someone covers up what they know or deceives an audience, the overall credibility of the "truth-finding" process goes down. And we are all the losers for that.

Summary Criteria

How we use evidence affects the persuasiveness of our argument. We have five standards we want to meet:

- *Credibility:* You enhance the Ethos of your work. This is achieved by not plagiarizing and by giving credit to others for their ideas. You demonstrate to your audience that your sources are credible.
- *Clarity:* Your readers understand clearly what the evidence says. This is achieved by picking sources that explain things your audience is not likely to understand. Sometimes you also need to set up a source by explaining a term they may use.
- *Transparency:* You allow people to check your work. This is achieved by providing citations that allow readers to find the same evidence you did.
- *Efficiency:* You don't use more space than you need to or distract your readers by irrelevant information. This is achieved by selecting specific quotations from your sources.
- *Recency:* Current information is typically better than older sources. (This is more likely true for secondary sources. Primary sources are going to be older.)

HOW WELL IS YOUR ARGUMENT SUPPORTED?

We've been talking about many different ways that an argument is or is not well supported by evidence. We offer here a "ladder" of ways that evidence could support your argument. In this list we aren't considering the types of evidence the sources might offer, just how you are using them. Try to move yourself from the lower rungs on the ladder to the higher one.

1. An assertion by the advocate.
2. An assertion by one source.
3. An assertion by one source together with giving the credentials of that source.

4. Citing the evidence provided by one quality source.
5. Citing the evidence provided by more than one quality source.
6. Citing the evidence provided by one or more quality sources with additional evidence that the relevant community of experts agrees with these sources.

By "citing the evidence provided" we mean that the source provides more than an assertion and has made an argument itself with supported claims.

CITING EVIDENCE

What to Cite

Not everything needs a citation in your text and a source listed on your page of references. While there can be gray areas, there are some simple principles to use. Provide citations for the following:

- *A direct quotation.* Any time you use a phrase of more than three words from a source, you must put it in quotes and provide a citation for it.
- A **specific term** that has been recently coined.
- A **concept or general idea** you got from a source. If you gain a key insight into your topic from a source, you can't claim that as your own. You need to cite the source of the idea, even if you've never directly quoted the author.

Do not provide citations for the following:

- **A phrase that has entered the culture** and is in common use now. It's common to take a well-known phrase and twist it. So the movie title *No Country for Old Men* becomes a title for an article about getting rid of old cars: "No Country for Old Cars." You don't need to cite the movie. Which phrases need to be cited will change over time.
- **Well-known concepts** long in circulation. You don't need to provide a citation to Einstein every time you talk about the theory of relativity or to Newton when you discuss gravity. Sometimes authors provide a "courtesy citation" in this situation as a way of paying homage to an author.
- **Common knowledge.** These are things generally known and not in dispute. You do not need to provide a reference to prove that the sun will rise in the East, or that the United States has presidential elections every four years, or that the baseball world series is a best-of-seven competition. Be careful, however, to note that what is common knowledge can be context dependent. There are things, for example, that would be common knowledge among a group of musicians, but would also be unknown to the general public.

Plagiarism

Don't do it. Don't come close to doing it. In theory, that should be all that would need to be said about using the work of others without giving credit. However, more does need to be said, if for no other reason than that evidence suggests that plagiarism is a rampant problem. One source cites research that between a quarter and a half of college students have, at various times over several decades, admitted to have plagiarized or cheated on an exam (Hart, 2004). It is widely thought that the rise of the Internet and (more to the point) the rise of cut-and-paste capability on computers has made plagiarism easier and thus more tempting.

There are some points to consider:

- *Being on a website does not make the information free to use without attribution.* There is a notion that anything you can find on the Internet can be used for free and even without acknowledging its origin. This is not true. Copyrighted information does not lose its copyright protection by being posted on the net. Even if someone else has copied protected information, the information is still protected.
- *Using (without quoting) the words of others is plagiarism even if you cite the source.* If you put a quote in your work but fail to put quote marks around it—that is plagiarism, even if you close the quotation with a citation to the author. This is probably unintentional, but it is still plagiarism because you are giving the impression that those words were written by you and not the cited author.
- *Don't engage in indirect plagiarism.* Source A writes something. Source B uses it but doesn't credit source A. Now you quote source B and cite source B. Indirectly you've plagiarized. Sometimes this can be accidental, but just because someone else violated copyright or plagiarized does not make it open season for you do to it also.
- *Being caught at plagiarism does have consequences to your credibility that can follow you for years.* The academic community runs on a chain of results, one researcher or thinker using and expanding on others. There is no worse crime for a professional to have faked data or to have copied someone else's results without attribution. Doris Kearns Goodwin, a respected writer and commentator on presidential history, was shown in 2002 to have failed to attribute some passages in her 1987 book (Harvard Plagiarism Archive, 2004). Despite the absence of malice, her otherwise good reputation, and the age of the complaints, she had to resign from the Harvard University board of directors and the Pulitzer Prize committee, and suffered sustained public embarrassment.
- *The consequences of plagiarism for you as a student can go far beyond the paper.* If you get caught, you may fail the assignment or receive a zero on it. But for more significant plagiarism offenses, you could fail the class. Depending on the policy at your university, the issue may not simply remain a private one between you and the instructor. It can involve a formal hearing, a mark on your record, and consequences to your academic progress.

How to Cite

Citation styles Over the course of an academic career, students may encounter a number of different style guides such as those promulgated by the Modern Language Association (commonly known as MLA), the American Psychological Association (APA), Kate Turabian's *A Manual for Writers of Term Papers, Theses and Dissertations* (Turabian), and *The Chicago Manual of Style* (Chicago).

There are others set forth by the American Chemical Society, the Council of Science Editors, the American Medical Society, the Modern Humanities Research Association, the Associated Press, and the Society for Biblical Literature, among others.

It will perhaps not be merely churlish to say that advocates of a particular style can resemble medieval theologians in their ferocity and conviction of the correctness of their particular style above all others. This is particularly a burden for students whose academic journey takes them across multiple departments and multiple styles.

However, failing to conform to the rules of whatever community you are writing to will inevitably cause your work to be downgraded, and your ethos as a communicator to be diminished. You must determine what style guide applies to your particular writing, you must follow it, and you must follow it carefully.

Style guides contain many things: what abbreviations are standard, citing of documents particular to their field of work, and others. We are most concerned here with citation style in documents and with how you should list your sources. Even if you know you will be using a more general-purpose style, such as MLA, you should still consult the specialty guide that pertains to your area of work.

Note that this is another area where the Internet revolution is having an impact. All these guides were originally designed for the citation of printed references and are now (and have been) adapting to deal with the variety of Internet material. The Internet rapidly creates new types of material (no one had rules for citing blogs in 2002 or websites in 1990, for example) and style guides are changing to keep up. MLA has, for example, changed its mind on how to cite web sources more than once. Be sure to consult a current version of your guide and consult the online resources for your style guide as well.

Handling quotations Yes, you can use quotations.

Some students are reluctant to actually quote a source. We're not sure where that comes from, but, yes, you can use quotations. This doesn't detract from your credibility or imply that you can't create your own words.

> "[T]o quote is to continue a conversation from the past in order to give context to the present. To quote is to make use of the Library of Babel; to quote is to reflect on what has been said before, and unless we do that, we speak in a vacuum where no human voice can make a sound."
>
> Alberto Manguel, *The Library at Night*, p. 224

You can quote everything from a paragraph or two down to an individual word. Yes, sometimes, just quoting one word from a source will be useful. Consider the difference between writing:

"The spokesperson expressed her strong opposition to the idea."

and

"The spokesperson was 'dismayed' at the idea."

Even using a single word can give you the ability to express a stronger view than you might otherwise be able to justify. It allows you to bring in vividness from the original source to your writing.

On the other hand, you should really pause before quoting an entire page of a source. Very long quotes or page after page of quotations from a single source give the impression that you have nothing to say. Doing so can also violate fair-use provisions of copyright law.

The Practicalities of Citing Evidence Properly

There are a number of situations that require you to have a good technique for making a reference. While this is the sort of detail that you would normally find in an English style guide, we want to discuss it here because how to do this has implications on your credibility and persuasiveness.

In particular, we will focus on the use of quotations. You should be able to correctly handle the following situations.

- *A quotation cannot be changed in any way.*   You cannot change "he" to "he/she" or change insulting or racist language. You may choose to omit parts of a quote, you can replace the word with something in a bracket, but you cannot change the words the author used.
- *Proper length.*   You have to quote enough to show the main points, but not include interesting, but irrelevant points.
- *Indenting vs. in-line quoting.*   Style guides have rules for when a quotation goes in-line and when it becomes long enough that you must put it in a separate, indented paragraph. Note and follow these.
- *Use a helpful lead-in to set context.*   When a quotation is removed from its original context, its meaning can shift. The role of providing a brief lead-in is to correct that so that the reader obtains the same meaning they would have received from reading the quotation in its original context.
- *Any lead-in word or phrase cannot slant the quote.*   A lead-in is not intended to spin the meaning of a quote.
- *Use ellipses to focus and remove distractions.*   Parenthetical asides in the original can be removed, but be careful not to remove important qualifiers on the claim.
- *Use [sic] to indicate mistakes in the original quotation.*   This marker tells the reader that any misspelling, punctuation problem, or factual error is in the original and not introduced when you put the quotation in your paper.
- *Use bracketed words to restore context.*   A quotation may have referents in it ("he," "the author," "it") that make no sense when the quote is removed from its context. You can use bracketed words to restore those referents.

Fitting Evidence into Your Writing

By lifting a quotation out of a source and putting it in your writing, your audience is only able to see the source. You have to be sensitive to what gets left behind.

- Use evidence with awareness of **uncertainty**. You think this piece of evidence is true, it has some support, but there are concerns about it. You gain credibility by frankly reporting these concerns and not assuming more than you should about the credibility of your evidence.

- Don't forget to establish the **credibility of your source** with your audience. Your source has thirty years of experience, has won awards, is considered a leader, but your audience won't know that. You can often qualify a source in a half-sentence, a parenthetical expression, as you introduce the quote.

"As the famous psychologist, Dr. A, said . . ."
"Mr. B., winner of the XYZ prize for his lifetime of work on . . ."

Quoting, paraphrasing, summarizing You have a choice of how to report the arguments of a source. You can quote them directly, letting them make the argument to your audience for you. Or, you can not quote them, and recreate their argument in your own words. Depending on how much you condense their argument, that might be called paraphrasing or summarizing (if the condensing is more severe).

Lean toward an exact quotation in these circumstances:

- The actual quote is **startling or unexpected.** People might not believe it coming from you.
- The quote is very **well written, pithy, or conveys significant emotions.** Don't try to compete with good writing; share it with the world.

Lean toward a paraphrase of a quote in these circumstances:

- To avoid **digressions or rambling.** The source took four sentences to say what could be done in one.
- When the original wording is **offensive** in some way. You shouldn't paraphrase to cover up a problem, but you can do it when the offense would introduce a side issue or is irrelevant to the truth of the source.

Lean toward concisely summarizing a long argument in these circumstances:

- Quoting would **unbalance** your writing. You can't quote for an entire page from one source when you're writing a three-page paper.
- To focus on **the conclusion.** The source may have gone into the history, the background, nailed down evidence questions—all of which is useful—but not relevant for what you're trying to prove.

Don't forget that you can combine these. Sometimes it is very effective to summarize a long argument and then end it with a short quote from the source.

Quoting errors Make sure to avoid these problems:

- Turning a **quote of a quote** into a direct quote. Your source, A, writes: "Source B thinks point C," and you cite A as having said C. Now you've misquoted A and failed to properly credit source C. This error is more common than you might think.
- Misunderstanding the **role** of a quote in the original. Your source, A, has a paragraph summarizing a common view and then goes on to rebut it. You quote A (accurately!) but now it looks like A holds the opposite view from what they actually do.
- Misunderstanding the **tone** of a quote in the original. Your source was being sarcastic or ironic, and you quote them (accurately!) in a way that the tone is missed.

- Properly **qualify** your evidence. A common error is to use a piece of evidence to claim more than it actually does. The evidence supports what men in California believe, you uncritically apply it to what men and women around the world believe without providing a reason why you think it can be generalized. This can occur because you lift a quote but not the qualifying information that was several pages back.

LISTING SOURCES

What citations do, of course, is refer your readers to your list of sources at the end of your paper. While this seems like a housekeeping list, a poorly organized list does detract from your credibility by communicating that you are careless about evidence. A quick checklist of things to follow:

- Start the list on a new page.
- Use the proper name for the list as specified by the style you are using.
- Alphabetize the list.
- Is each cited source listed?
- Is each listed source cited somewhere in the body of the paper?
- Use a hanging indent format (the first line at the left margin, subsequent lines indented 0.5 inch.
- Web sources are named and sorted by author or title, not by URL (but include the URL if your style guide says to.
- Don't number your list or use a bullet in front of each entry.
- Use the same font as the rest of your paper.

CREATING EVIDENCE

The conduct of surveys and interviews is a significant subject in its own right and goes beyond the scope of this book. We will touch here on how to report and use information that you have developed yourself for use in short, informal argumentation settings. The objective: to produce evidence that would pass the standards of the previous sections.

The key concept is to document. When you use a source, you can refer to it; when you create your own evidence, you have to provide additional documentation.

Yes, you can create information We'd encourage you to think about how you could approach people to ask a question or two. You may not think you know anyone, but if you reflect on who do you know at the university, your hometown, or family, you may well come up with someone who knows someone and can get you an introduction.

Don't just think about national leaders or famous people, but it is possible to interview city officials, county prosecutors, local business executives, and similar people. Many leaders are flattered to be asked about their jobs and interested in helping a student. If you get rebuffed? Well, you're no worse off than when you started.

There are certain ethical considerations about interviews. You must identify yourself and the purpose of your contacting them. Make it clear that you want to quote them. If you want to record the interview, get permission in advance. For the purposes of a class paper, taking notes is probably enough.

You can cite this information as personal communication (if you interviewed a specific person) or conduct an informal poll.

Personal communication The term *personal communication* is typically used to describe any sort of evidence gathering that is directly between you and another person. You interview a professor, you have a conversation with a knowledgeable person, you exchange emails with someone: You can use this as evidence. Indeed, this can be very helpful evidence because you can drill in on the exact issue you are trying to understand.

Each such encounter should be added to your list of references in a format consistent with the style guide you are using. Then, you cite it in your work as needed. For an informal paper in a class, that is probably all you need to do. If you are doing a formal research project, your notes or other primary documentation of the conversation may need to be retained to substantiate that you had the conversation.

Consult the style guides for the mechanics of how to document these.

Informal surveys and studies For a class paper you may find it useful to stand on the street corner and ask people questions as they go by, ask ten store owners their views, or survey your class on an issue. Again, you can document this as your style guide indicates and use it in a paper. You will typically need a two- or three-sentence description of exactly what you did.

Again, the sort of informal documentation we are describing here is suitable for an informal paper. It's not sufficient for a Ph.D. thesis or professional article. But, you should be encouraged to look beyond the evidence you can find and feel empowered, where appropriate, to generate evidence yourself.

Using yourself as a source Are you a source? You can be, but, of course, the question is: Are you a good source, and can you prove that you are?

You may have studied some subject or it's been an interest for some time. You've become knowledgeable about it. Can you explain that or document it in some way? But you need to be careful. That you've followed, for example, a particular sport for many years and played it doesn't mean you've been a student of the game's history, coaching techniques, finances, or its social place in the culture. If you think that is harsh, just look at the stars of the sport—are they experts on any of those particular things?

This risk is that you don't have a good perspective on what you know and what you don't know. Have you talked with anyone who is an acknowledged expert to sharpen your views? At worst, your own involvement might let you quickly identify very good sources.

Perhaps you've had a significant personal experience—served in the military, been in an accident, had a family member with a serious illness, or so on. This may well allow you to tell a compelling story and share with your readers the emotional impact of the event. But again, that doesn't necessarily give you a balanced view on what *everyone* who has gone through that experience thinks or the range of experiences they've had.

Remember how we said that a story (to communicate Pathos) combined with statistics or broader evidence (to give overall perspective) can be a powerful combination if done right. Consider using your personal experience in combination with evidence that allows you to generalize from that experience.

TEN THINGS THAT AREN'T TRUE

To illustrate the need to research and check facts carefully before beginning an argument, we offer ten examples of where popular opinion is incorrect on the facts.

1. Al Gore did not claim to have invented the Internet.

The story may have begun with a statement by Declan McCullagh in March of 1999 when he said "It's a time-honored tradition for presidential hopefuls to claim credit for other people's successes. But Al Gore as the father of the Internet?" He quoted Gore from a Wolf Blitzer interview the week before as follows: "During my service in the U.S. Congress, I took the initiative in creating the Internet." McCullagh repeated the claim later that month (Wired News, 1999).

From there it has become a staple of right-wing propaganda. But both Gore's actual remarks and his role in technology development point to something different.

Gore's comments were accurately quoted—and produced no reaction from Wolf Blitzer at the time (CNN, 1999). The key question is the modifier "in the U.S. Congress." From the context, Gore seems to be claiming that he was a leader in the Senate. And there, Gore has a point. Gore was an early advocate of the possibilities of the Internet. Even McCullagh had to admit that in 2000, when he noted that all the way back in 1994, Gore was speaking about the "information superhighway" and raising issues about antitrust and universal access. Indeed, Vint Cerf, someone who might actually claim with some justice to have invented the Internet, noted that Gore had been holding hearings on the Internet back in 1986.

In 2005 Al Gore received a "Webby" Lifetime Internet Achievement award "in recognition of the pivotal role he has played in the development of the internet over the past three decades." The award was presented by Vint Cerf.[1]

2. Crime in the United States has not been rising over the past several decades.

Do you think crime in the United States has increased or decreased over the past few years? What do your parents think? In late 2009, Gallup found that 54 percent of Americans rated the problem of crime to be either "Extremely serious" or "Very serious," although few rated crime as the most serious problem facing the country. Anecdotally, one might think crime was out of control from watching the local television news that seems to regularly lead with a violent crime ("If it bleeds, it leads").

"2009 change in crime rate: down 4.4%
Percentage who think crime went up. 75%"

Harper's Index, May 2010, quoting the FBI and a Gallup poll

---

[1]Press Release, the Webby Awards. Retrieved 1/2007 from www.webbyawards.com/webbys/specialwin.php

How much crime is there in the United States? We can measure that in one of two ways. First, by adding up the crime data from various police forces. The Federal Bureau of Investigation publishes annually a Uniform Crime Report. This tell us what crimes were reported to or detected by law enforcement. The second approach is to survey people and ask them if they were the victim of a crime. The Bureau of Justice Statistics in the U.S. Department of Justice administers the National Crime Victimization Survey. Not all crime is reported to the police. On the other hand, some reports to the police are false. So, looking at both data sources is worthwhile.

The 2008 edition of the report *Crime in the United States* shows that, comparing 1989 to 2008, overall violent crime rates are down 30 percent, murder is down 35 percent, rape down 20 percent. Property crime rates are also down, with auto thefts being just half of what they were in 1989.

Turning to the National Crime Victimization Survey, they report (combining their data with the FBI reports) that the total violent crime rate in the United States has declined by about 50 percent between 1993 and 2006 and appears to have stabilized since then.

3. One million children do not go missing each year.

Losing a child is very traumatic and affects all of us, even those without children. And we judge criminals who kidnap children among the lowest of the low. Thus, we want to attract attention to this issue. For years, claims have been circulating that "a million kids go missing each year." Websites that deal with missing children commonly refer to the U.S. Department of Justice (more specifically to the FBI's National Crime Information Center) and their report that, for example, in 2004, the names of "834,536 missing persons were entered" into their database. 800,000 missing kids in one year! Pretty alarming.

However, what organizations do not emphasize, but what is also reported by the federal government is that during the same year, 844,838 (10,000 more) missing person records were cleared, and at the end of the year, the FBI had a total (from all years) of 109,531 open missing person records with 58,081 being children under 18. 58,000 *total* is a long way from 1,000,000 a year. What is going on?

A publication of the Office of Juvenile Justice and Delinquency Prevention suggests some of the reasons. Many children are missing for less than six hours before they are found. This alone clears several hundred thousands of the cases each year. Second, not all missing persons are children, but they are a majority of them. And finally, a distinction needs to be drawn between children who go missing briefly for accidental reasons (got separated from a parent in a public place) as opposed to children who are victims of stranger kidnappings.

The fear that a stranger will kidnap a child is an understandably strong one. The National Center for Missing and Exploited Children gives similar statistics to the ones cited here and cites a 2002 Department of Justice figure that 115 children were abducted by strangers in the United States in 2002.

So, what does this prove, and what doesn't it prove? Have we argued here that nothing should be done about missing children? No, we've said nothing in support of that. Have we proved that the problem is trivial? No, we have not.

What we've shown is a failure to properly keep definitions clear. A "missing person" is not the same thing as a "child gone missing," a "child that doesn't return," a "child kidnapped," or a "child kidnapped by a stranger and murdered."

And now we can offer some informed speculation about what causes this problem. It is in no one's interest to lower the number of *reported* missing children. (Everyone is interested in lowering the number of *actual* missing children.) The more people that are affected by your issue, the more attention and money you can get for it. Combine that with people's general lack of skill at handling statistics, and you have a recipe for number inflation.

4. Social security will not disappear in ten to twenty years.

It is often said that the national program of pensions for elderly (Social Security) will go bankrupt or will run out of money. So, those of you who are college-age now are told not to count on this being around for your retirement. From that comes a resentment about why young people should pay into a system that will not benefit them later. Value arguments swirl around the system as well, with some thinking that retirement should be each person's own responsibility and not a collective goal of the society.

Social Security is not like a retirement fund such as an IRA (Individual Retirement Account). In those accounts, an individual contributes money, it earns interest over time (often tax-free), and when the person retires, they withdraw money. What another person does has no direct impact on a person's funds.

Social Security, by contrast, is financed by taxes levied on those who are working. This money goes into a trust fund, and benefits are paid out of the fund. If more money comes in than goes out, there is a surplus that year. If not, there is a deficit.

Information on the financial performance of the fund and estimates for the future are contained in the annual reports by the trustees of the program.

For many years the fund ran a surplus, and in 2010 had about 2.8 trillion dollars in it. However, the ratio of those working to those on retirement is in a very long-term trend of decline. As fewer are working (and paying into the fund) and more are in retirement (taking money out of the fund), the surplus will decrease (if nothing else is changed).

The number of people who will be retired twenty years from now can be estimated from the number who are twenty years away from retirement today. Likewise the number of people born this year helps predict how many will enter the workforce eighteen years from now. There are a number of other factors, of course (immigration, death rates, change in working habits, among others), but this is one area where some decent predictions about the future are possible.

Prior to the economic recession of 2008, the fund was expected to go into deficit in 2018. That wouldn't mean the end of Social Security; it would just mean the cashing out of money from the trust fund. Some have said this won't happen because the money in the trust fund is "just bits of paper" or just "a promise." However, these "bits of paper" are U.S. Treasury bonds and are as safe as anything we have.

A different problem arises as the trust fund itself becomes depleted. Prior to the economic recession, it was estimated that the fund would be depleted sometime around 2040. Even that wouldn't mean the end of Social Security; it would mean about a 30 percent cut in benefits to break even or obtain a subsidy from the general budget of the federal government.

The 2008 recession has made all these estimates worse. More people are out of work (and not paying taxes) or took early retirement. If the economy recovers, these estimates will get better again.

But, of course, these estimates are all based on doing nothing. There are all sorts of things that could be done. In 2012, only the first $110,100 of a person's income is subject to the Social Security tax; that limit could be increased. The age of retirement benefits could be increased. Taxes could be increased, benefits could be slowly reduced.

There are other means of affecting these estimates. More economic growth would help, more young immigrants to the country would also help. Under some scenarios of more rapid economic growth, the fund never runs out of money, even with current demographic assumptions.

In some ways, a bigger threat to the program is the "Everyone is responsible for themselves" view referred to at the beginning. Social Security is a program that is based on a value of seeing all citizens as belonging to a community. It requires people to value the overall health of the community. In particular, it depends on a value of general respect for elders as a group and a view that "We don't like living in a culture that lets elderly live in poverty."

To the extent that values of community and respect of elderly are replaced with values of individual self-reliance, societal support for the program might decline.

5. Eskimos do not have 23 (or 42 or 150) words for snow.

This was an urban legend that was often cited to prove the superior discernment of a native culture compared to the clumsy majority. It is not true as a question of fact, nor would the fact have substantiated any moral claim, nor would the moral claim need the fact.

This myth has been exploded in several places; even Wikipedia has a good takedown of it.

As to the facts. Eskimo (or Inuit) languages use a system of creating compound words by suffixes. An entire English phrase can be said in one compounded word. So, one could say Eskimos have an infinite number of words for almost any concept, just as English has an essentially infinite number of phrases and sentences.

And what of the significance? People who deal with a topic have more concepts for it and hence (in English) more words for it. Civil engineers have more words for bridge, wine aficionados have more words for wine, and ski patrol officers likely have more words for snow than most of us do.

And finally, a desire to respect and admire the Eskimos, or any other culture, is not dependent on comparing them to ourselves—in our terms. Better to spend time understanding how the world looks in their world. The Eskimo languages seem intriguing in their own right.

6. Railroads are not on the verge of extinction.

Most Americans would assume that railroads are about to go under. The reason they think so is likely to be an example of an "argument from sign" (see the appropriate chapter later in the book) that turns out to be fallacious.

When people think of railroads, they think of passenger trains, and passenger trains are largely dead in the United States. Only Amtrak survives, and it is in a constant struggle to get enough in subsidy from the government to continue. While Amtrak on the East Coast operates on frequent schedules and offers speedy service, for the rest of America, we think of one half-empty train a day—and a train occupied largely by the elderly, the poor, or students, not businesspeople in a hurry.

In other words, we take passenger trains as a sign of the health of railroads. But, in this case, the sign is deceptive. In fact, railroads are booming, and it is because of the shipment of freight in general and coal and container traffic in particular. Over the last twenty years before 2010, the fraction of all freight shipped on railroads has actually increased from 30 to 40 percent as they have taken business away from other modes of transport. Railroads have made mammoth investments in additional track, locomotives, and cars also. And while this boom has occurred, rates have declined, safety has improved, and energy efficiency has increased.

7. Kansas is not flat.

Permit the authors (who grew up in Kansas) a personal diatribe. It is a commonly stated proposition that Kansas is flat, an unending and undifferentiated plane without hills or valleys. Not true. Kansas is neither flat in absolute terms nor does it outrank all other states in "comparative flatness."

Kansas has a wide area with ranges of rolling hills of several hundred feet in elevation in its eastern third. These diminish into gentle swells in the western part of the state. So, no mountains, but Kansas does not deserve a reputation for being "flat" compared to other states. Downstate Illinois, the Dakotas, and parts of western Minnesota are far "flatter" in absolute terms than even western Kansas.

But why the attention to Kansas in this regard? Why does it attract attention compared to other flat landscapes in the United States? It is an interesting case study of cultural conventions.

And three for you to investigate We can't do all the work. Here are three commonly believed propositions that we strongly suspect are false. They might make good topics for papers, either to establish the basic facts or to investigate why false views are so widely accepted. Add more ideas of your own.

8. **The number of lawsuits is not rising rapidly.**

9. **Sex offenders do not always commit new crimes within a short period of being released.**

10. **The budget of the U.S. federal government cannot be balanced or drastically cut by removing "waste, fraud, and abuse."**

Rebutting Arguments

INTRODUCTION

The Problem

All throughout this book, we've been discussing argument as an effort to persuade an audience, and we've discussed both how to make various types of arguments and how to recognize when they've gone wrong. But now we will focus on the "back and forth" communication between an advocate and another advocate who disagrees.

As with everything else, rebuttals are often done badly. A discussion between two people on opposite sides of an issue can readily turn into an emotional shouting match where insults, escalating accusations, and the potential for ruptured relationships can occur. It's also the case that the process between two (or more) advocates can get sidetracked into side issues that do not affect the main question.

Because of that, some fear the process of debating or engaging with another advocate. While that concern is based on the reality of human disagreements, it is also the case that the process of debate can be a great opportunity for all involved to make progress toward better understanding of an issue.

Two terms are important to know: **rebut** and **refute**. They are not synonyms, even though they are sometimes used as though they were.

To *rebut* an argument is to respond to an argument. It is the name applied to whatever is offered in reply to what an advocate has said.

To *refute* an argument is to overcome it, to disprove it, to show that it is false.

The Opportunity

Of course it is true that, purely in terms of winning and losing, understanding how to engage an opponent is vital. We'd all like to win more arguments. And we'd like to win with our audience, convincing them that our view is more valid than our opponent's. How you handle opposition is one very important way that your audience decides on your credibility and worth as an advocate.

But beyond that, the give-and-take of responding to arguments is a major way that you sharpen your position and come to understand how others may mistake what you meant to argue. Working on responding to opposing arguments gives you a chance to learn better approaches to your topic and to improve your case and your understanding of the issue.

STASIS THEORY: WHAT ARE WE ARGUING ABOUT?

The Theory

One of the first things to establish in an exchange is what, in fact, is in dispute. Many debates, even rather friendly ones, turn out to involve the two sides "arguing past each other" and not really engaging the same issues. On the other hand, it is certainly a legitimate move for one side to argue that the issues are different than the other side thinks.

From classical times, the discussion about what is in dispute has been termed *stasis theory*. Over time, some very technical classification schemes have been developed to analyze the various issues that could be in dispute. We don't find those schemes to be very helpful or very general in their applicability. However, it can be the case that a specialized area of argumentation may have developed a classification scheme for various issues, as, for example, the way legal disputes can isolate issues of "standing"—who has the right to be a party to a lawsuit.

Instead of these classification schemes, we will look at a number of common problems of stasis.

Locating the Central Question

Climate change, or global warming, is a significant issue, but what exactly is in dispute? That the climate is changing? Or, if you accept that the climate is changing, is the issue whether or not humans caused the change? Or that the change is something we should attempt to counteract? That some specific policy (e.g., cap-and-trade or a carbon tax) should be adopted? In various contexts, all might be useful to discuss. But it does seem that, given the consensus of science that change is real and human caused, we should be spending more time debating if we should and how we should counteract climate change. Thus, people who insist on going back and debating if it is real can be effectively preventing a discussion about how to deal with it.

But, insisting on a shift of grounds, a shift of the location of the dispute can be a perfectly legitimate move to make. At a student debate about affirmative action, the side defending the policy located the dispute around the question of justice and fairness. The side opposing affirmative action shifted attention to practical issues of how best to overcome these problems, arguing that current policies were not effective. The team in favor of affirmative action then has a choice. They can argue both points and claim that affirmative action is both needed to promote the value of justice and that it is the best practical approach. Or, they can try to show why the issue of effectiveness is not relevant or is of less import than questions of justice.

Some issues seem noncontroversial because they have *no obvious opposition.* That "X is important," or should get more funding, or should be a concern to more people, are common forms of these issues. This situation might arise when the topic is that a certain animal makes a good pet or that some disease needs more research or that a social issue should be given attention by students.

It's unlikely you'll find someone arguing directly opposite to these propositions. It is unlikely that someone will claim that some disease is unimportant or that we should ignore some issue that harms people. That doesn't mean there is no controversy. What you might find is someone arguing that money is not available or that other diseases are even more important. In other words, an argument isn't necessarily "symmetrical" with one side saying "yes" and the other side saying "no."

Another type of dispute is between arguments about the *internal consistency* of a position contrasted with arguments about the *premises* of the argument. A headline describing a politician's view once said, "time to get serious about the budget deficit; we need to cut taxes." There is a question of internal inconsistency since cutting taxes increases deficits, not reduces them. That is different from the question about the premises: Is cutting the deficit a high priority right now? Both sorts of issues can be relevant in an argument, but be clear about which is which.

Evading the Question

Have you ever read an article that seemed to be a brave defense of some position and wondered, "Who actually would disagree?" Perhaps it was an editorial opposing crime or a piece warning us of secondhand smoke (when we have already banned smoking near others). Sometimes writing like this is just an accident but sometimes it is a way of avoiding tricky issues. If you orate about how bad crime is, then maybe no one notices that you have no actual ideas about stopping it.

Sometimes it can sound like an issue is in dispute, but, in fact, the way it is being discussed is a way of avoiding the real issues. An article on net neutrality went on at great length about issues of bandwidth and how providers of bandwidth needed the freedom to charge customers whatever they wished, but never discussed the question of freedom of speech—that if the Internet is the primary means of conducting public discussion, then restricting access involves restricting freedom of speech, and hence there is a societal interest in ensuring access (but not necessarily free access) to the Internet. That is a crucial issue, and to ignore it means the debate does not engage the real question.

Some forms of evading the question are common. One is called "wrapping yourself in the flag." This is when you portray yourself as a staunch patriot and bravely defend your country with the implied claim that your opponent isn't quite as good a patriot as you. However, the actual issue in dispute is rather unlikely to be about patriotism or about your patriotism in particular. Quite often, such a move is just avoiding the real issue.

Finally we should offer something for your instructors. If you wrote a paper about a subject dear to your heart, it can be hard to hear a critique from your instructor. But look closely. Are they saying to you that "Your position is wrong" or are they saying "You were not persuasive." The latter can easily be misheard as the former.

Misstating the Argument: "Straw Person" Fallacy

A common fallacy of rebuttal is to misstate your opponent's position. Done either intentionally or accidently, it derails the argument.

One way is to divert attention by introducing an irrelevant issue that you imply that your opponent has raised. For example, there is a debate over the rules being used at airport security; some object to them as ineffective and intrusive. The defenders of the rules might reply that "Keeping the flying public safe is our highest priority." But this is defending what no one has attacked. No one wants airplanes to blow up, and the issue in dispute is clearly not about the priority of safety. The actual issue in conflict is that the rules didn't really enhance safety.

Arguments about national security seem to invite a certain type of straw person fallacy, when one side says some aggressive action is wrong or ineffective and the other side accuses them of "wanting the terrorists to win." Nobody wants that. You can argue that some policy will make terrorist attacks more likely, but that is very different than accusing someone of actually promoting terrorism. Similar straw person attacks revolve around accusations of "not supporting the troops."

The left can do this also. When Obama had first become president, Rush Limbaugh took some heat for seeming to wish that President Obama would fail—he then was accused of wanting the nation to suffer. But it seemed that all Limbaugh was saying is that he thought Obama's policies would be bad for the nation and therefore did not want them to be implemented.

This form of the straw person is also known as the *fallacy of representation*. In other words, you have misrepresented the views of your opponents. A related straw person fallacy is the *fallacy of selection* when out of all that your opponent argued, you pick the weakest thing to reply to. This often comes up when someone has made a serious argument, but also put in some funny aside or made some sort of offensive comment. Then the opponent zeros in on that and ignores the comments that are more substantial.

Dealing with Chaos

> It is much easier to refute a bad argument than to refute a truly dreadful argument. A bad argument has enough structure that you can point out its badness. But with a truly dreadful argument, you have to try to reconstruct it so that it is clear enough that you can state a refutation. (Searle, 2009, p. 89)

Sometimes you encounter an argument that is just very poorly made. It's hard to understand what their point is or how the logic of their position works. For example, consider these remarks made by a former candidate for the U.S. Senate from Delaware:

> "Today marks a lot of tragedy," O'Donnell, who lost her recent bid for a Delaware Senate seat despite strong backing from the Tea Party, said Tuesday night during an appearance in Virginia.

> "Tragedy comes in threes," O'Donnell said. "Pearl Harbor, Elizabeth Edwards's passing and Barack Obama's announcement of extending the tax cuts, which is good, but also extending the unemployment benefits." (D'Aprile, 2010)

Exactly where would you begin to disagree with this? The length of time between the first and latter two events? Why is extending unemployment benefits an evil on a par with a foreign nation attacking us? Would you wonder if she was serious? Or if she'd been accurately quoted?

The temptation in this sort of case is to sort out the argument for them and spend your time and energy fixing the opposing position or recasting it so that you can deal with it. The quotation from John Searle suggests that sometimes that is a good thing to do. If there is some benefit to doing so that you can identify, then go ahead.

But there is a danger that what you wind up doing is looking confused yourself. You get lost trying to follow a lost argument and then those watching the debate think the problem is that you can't understand your opponent. So, should you just go ahead and try to refute the opposing view? This also has a problem. If your opponent has made a number of contradictory claims, then when you refute one of them, you might well support something else they've said.

What might be a better approach is to back up and point out the internal contradictions and inconsistencies of their argument. This puts the onus back on them to reply by sorting out their case.

Who Are We Arguing With?

Part of stasis is to be clear about who we are arguing with. There are two potential audiences here. If you are in a discussion with another advocate, then one audience is that advocate and your goal is to persuade that person. But you and an advocate may be in discussion in front of an audience. Now there are two audiences, and convincing one may be in conflict with convincing the other.

You may be getting irritated with the other advocate, but if you lose your cool, you could turn the larger audience against you. Too bitter an argument and the audience can tune both sides out.

This situation arises even if there is no direct confrontation between you and another advocate. If you are writing an article about a topical, current issue, you are probably writing it to the larger audience, while being aware that this audience has been informed by another advocate whose views you want to rebut.

The Benefits of Dealing with Stasis

Not all arguments are a fight to the death. And sometimes you yourself are confused about what your point is or what you need to prove. A discussion with someone who has a different perspective can help clarify and strengthen your position. Having a friend play "devil's advocate" and take a position against what you are arguing can be a good way to find problems in your argument.

THE BURDEN OF PROOF

How much work you have to do, how much evidence and the reasons you need to provide is affected by who has the burden of proof in an argument. The terms *burden of proof* and *presumption* are two sides of the same coin. They are easiest to explain first in terms of criminal trials.

In the criminal justice system, the defendant, the one accused of a crime, has the "presumption of innocence"; we treat them as innocent until enough evidence has been presented to prove them guilty. Thus, the prosecution has the "burden of proof." That means that when the trial begins, the prosecution has to be the first to make an argument. We don't ask the defendant to prove themselves to be innocent; we require the prosecution to prove guilt. If their presentation of the case is weak or full of errors, it is possible (but not that common) for the defendant to be acquitted at that point without having to present any proof at all. If, after both sides have presented their case, the evidence is divided, the defendant still wins.

So the person with the burden of proof has to make a bigger effort. They are the ones who have to come forward first, prove what they are saying, to overcome the presumption that the other side has.

Outside the legal arena, there is no official determination of who has the burden of proof in an argument. However, there are some guidelines that can be offered.

- Those arguing against the majority view, or against a view long held generally, have the burden of proof. So, in the global warming controversy, since the overwhelming majority of those with professional skill in the relevant science have decided the climate is changing, the burden of proof is on those who are climate change skeptics.
- Arguments that depend on a change in our understanding of the laws of physics have the burden of proof.
- Arguments for things that are very rare or not typically seen. Since in general, whatever evils we think governments do, they very seldom organize secret plots involving hundreds of people to kill thousands, those arguing that the Bush administration organized and planned the 9/11 attacks have the burden of proof.

Note that who has the burden of proof is *not* determined by who is right or who has morality on their side. Burden of proof has nothing to do with who is right. It has to do with who is assumed to be right or expressing the "normal" opinion.

Another way of trying to sum up who has the burden of proof is the expression "Extraordinary claims require extraordinary evidence." That is saying that the more unlikely, the more extreme, the more startling your claim—the more evidence you need for it.

One of the authors read about how there were more than 100 eyewitnesses to an event that occurred several hundred years ago. That seems like more than adequate proof for the truth of the event. Except that the event was how a religious leader could levitate. A truly extraordinary claim. So perhaps 100 eyewitnesses are not enough to supply adequate proof in this case.

The Tactical Value of Trying to Assume the Presumption

Since it is work to have to take on the burden of proof, one tactic in an argument is to try to make your opponent assume the burden. For example, arguments about gay marriage can often make this claim. Those against gay marriage point out that thousands of years of human culture have never allowed it. This paints gay marriage as one of those extreme positions that, they argue, should require extreme evidence to overcome.

On the other hand, those defending gay marriage will often invoke the notion of discrimination. You are treating gays unequally, they argue, and our presumption is that unequal treatment is always wrong. So they then try to get opponents to overcome the burden of proof.

Both positions have an element of truth to them, and this can show that the burden of proof may be in different places for different aspects. The weight of human experience should count for something, but, on the other hand, we've changed our minds before, and the evils of war and slavery have also been in human culture for thousands of years. As for discrimination, well, we discriminate all the time between classes of people if we believe there is good reason to do so.

Be wary of being put in the position of assuming a burden of proof that isn't really yours. If you opponent makes some "out there" claim—don't immediately start assembling reasons why they are wrong. Instead, ask them to supply the proof.

Consequences for Disputed Questions

When the evidence on an issue is divided, how we decide the debate can hinge on who we decide has the presumption. At the time of writing, evidence about the danger of cell phone usage causing disease appears to be divided or at least in dispute. Assuming, for the sake of this example, that it is unclear. Consider two claims:

C1: "Cell phone use has not been proven dangerous."
C2: "Cell phones haven't been proven safe."

Both statements are true. They start from different assumptions about who has the burden of proof in the argument. Do you use a cell phone unless it has been proven dangerous (presume they are safe)? Or do you stop using your cell phone until it has been proven safe (presuming it is dangerous)?

A Special Case

The age-old argument about the existence of God seems one that almost entirely turns on what decision you make about burden of proof. Is the question to prove God's existence beyond a doubt or is it to prove the nonexistence of God beyond a doubt? Both seem equally hard to do.

WAYS OF RESPONDING

There is more than one way to reply to an argument. In this section we're going to give you some ideas of constructive ways to respond. We'll resurrect our "smoke and fire" argument from the Toulmin chapter, but also give you a more real-world example. To make it a little more interesting, we'll assume that you made your argument, you encountered a reply (that we'll term "R"), and you are now offering a defense (termed "D") of your original argument.

Approach 1: Rebut Directly (with Evidence or Reasoning)

If this was your argument:

> C: "There is a fire!"
> G: "I see smoke."
> W: "Where there is smoke, there is fire."

And you got the reply:

> Reply 1: "I don't see any smoke."

You could make a direct defense of your original ground by offering more evidence:

> Defense 1: "I have five witnesses here that see smoke."

Notice that this direct way of "going at" your opponent's view is *not* a simple "Yes it is"/ "No it isn't" exchange. You are offering *additional* evidence; you're providing more proof, not simply restating what you've already said.

Consider a second example:

> Reply 1b: "There is no evidence for climate change."
> Defense 1b: "Sure there is. Look at these sources."

Again, the defense is not to just repeat a previous claim but either to attack the evidence against your claim or to offer more proof in favor of your position.

Approach 2: Reject the Reply as Irrelevant

> R2: "You always say there is a fire."
> D2: "All that matters is that there is a fire now."

The reply may or may not have some justification behind it, but it introduces issues that do not directly impact your original argument.

> R2b: "It is very cold this year, thus global warming is false."
> D2b: "One cold year does not refute a long-term trend."

Again, this reply doesn't overturn the original argument, even if it were true. Climate change is based on a long-term trend, the "noise" of one year, or one month, is irrelevant.

Approach 3: Qualify the Claim to Exclude the Impact of the Reply

> R3: "I remember a time when there was smoke and there was no fire."
>
> D3: "Yes, smoke can sometimes not be associated with fire, but it is true most of the time."

In this case, the reply is true, and it does affect your claim. You claimed a bit too much and got dinged for it. The proper reply in this case is not to defend your broader claim; it is to qualify your claim. You can accept the truth of the reply and still defend your position.

> R3b: "Some parts of the world are getting cooler."
>
> D3b: "Yes, warming does not mean all parts of the world will get warm. There is variation, but overall the world is warming up."

Somehow the idea has been put about, or simply assumed, that "warming" of the average surface temperature of the world means all areas will warm equally. But this was a bigger claim than actually needed to be made. There will be change, but the models predict that some areas will get colder while the overall average temperature increases.

Approach 4: Move to a More Sophisticated Position That Includes the Reply

> R4: "That isn't smoke; it is steam."
>
> D4: "Well, there is some steam, but I also saw smoke, so there is still a fire."

So our warrant now is: "Where there is smoke (even if there is also steam) there is a fire."

This is a bit like approach 3, but here, what we're doing is not so much to limit our claim as to expand it to include a more sophisticated model of what is happening. Now we're not just looking at smoke, we're including other things in our analysis. It makes our claim a little more complicated and maybe makes it sound less forceful, but it does mean we've come to have a slightly more nuanced view of the world—and that's good.

> R4b: "Tree ring data has noise in it and doesn't always give a consistent result."
>
> D4b: "Yes, that's true, so we should now include ice core data, ocean measurements, and other data that gives us a better picture of what is going on."

Approach 5: Concede Validity of the Point, but Maintain Your Argument on Other Grounds

> R5: "That smoke is coming from a smokestack."
>
> D5: "You're right, but our heat detectors are also going off in places other than the smokestack."

If your argument had multiple reasons to support it, then when it turns out that one of your reasons is wrong or is much weaker than you thought, you should be able to continue to develop your argument with other data. In other words, do not think you must simply defend every single thing about your case. It is not a defeat to admit you were wrong about something: It is progress. You can concede a point but keep on going.

Of course, given the propensity for people to make personal attacks, you may well get attacked on this one weak point by an opponent who is trying to focus the debate on your mistakes. But you can refrain from compounding one mistake by another and simply keep coming back to your other arguments.

This situation doesn't just come up in an actual debate. You will encounter it as you research and develop your arguments. You start off with some ideas about why your position should be adopted. But as you research, you discover that one of those reasons is wrong. We get attached to our beliefs, and it can become hard to let them go but it is necessary. Don't get trapped into just defending every single thing about the view you are trying to advocate.

> R5b: "There were exaggerations in Al Gore's *An Inconvenient Truth*."

> D5b: "Apparently so. But our argument doesn't rest on that movie, and, in fact, we are only using the pieces of evidence from that movie that have held up over time."

Approach 6: Change Your Mind!

> R6: "We're burning that field intentionally."

> D6: "Okay, you're right."

Every semester some student is in crisis. They've started to research some position they want to make, and as they got into it, they realized that they were having more sympathy for the other side. Eventually, they realize they really believe the opposite of what they started out to promote. Will this cause them to flunk?

No, it won't. Changing your mind is not a failure; at least it is only a failure if you're running for political office, apparently. In normal life, changing your mind because you got convinced of something is not a failure; it is growth and progress. You should do it more. More people should do it more often rather than getting backed into a corner and defending a lost cause at all costs.

> R6b: "You used to say that the world was going to cool off, not get warmer."

> D6b: "It's true that some people for a short time believed that, but the evidence was never very strong, and with much better evidence in hand, everyone has changed their mind."

Of course, once you admit you were wrong once, many shallow people will jump on you and insist that since you were wrong before, "How do we know you aren't wrong again? Huh? Huh?" As in so many situations in life, behaving maturely doesn't always lead to fame, power, wealth, and many sexual partners—at least not in the short run. However, it can be a nice way of finding out who else around you is and is not is mature, since the mature people will likely admire you for your maturity. Select your friends accordingly.

PLACING AND FRAMING YOUR RESPONSE

From more general considerations of approach, we now turn to the question of how a rebuttal will fit into your actual, written argument. First we'll look at where to put it—first, last, or other choices—and then we'll get down to the level of individual paragraphs and talk about how to compose your reply.

Strategy: Where Should You Discuss Opposition Arguments?

There are a number of different options for where in your presentation the rebuttal will go.

In the classical model that we discussed earlier, the rebuttal goes *after the presentation of your case*. You introduce your argument, give the background, present your evidence and data. Then, after you've done that, you take up opposition arguments and attempt to reply to them. The idea is that you get the audience thinking about the issue in your terms, and then you can fit other objections into that. There is a certain logic to this; it seems somehow "normal" to make your case and then say that not everyone agrees—and turn to that. We can sort of expect that arguments are made this way. However, it is not the only choice.

There are some situations when you should *put it first*. If the audience is preoccupied with a significant concern about your argument and you don't address it right away, they may not pay attention to your presentation of your case. They are just sitting there, thinking "Right, but what about …" and never give your case a chance. This might be the case if you were advocating more tourism to the Middle East right after a terrorist attack, if you (or your main source) had just suffered some major attack on your credibility, or if an opponent had just introduced some counterargument that seemed to be very powerful.

There are some cases when you may want to *divide up* your treatment of opposition arguments. Let's say that your case revolves around three grounds: G1, G2, and G3. And let's say there were good reasons why you would want to present your grounds in that order. You are planning to discuss opposition arguments made against G1 and G3. If you put your case first and then deal with opposition arguments, it means the audience has to remember what you said in favor of the first issue when you get around later to dealing with opposition arguments. In this case, it might make more sense to order your presentation as follows:

G1: [your evidence in favor]

R1: [describe opposition arguments related to G1]

D1: [defend your position on G1]

G2: [your evidence in favor]

G3: [your evidence in favor]

R3: [describe opposition arguments related to G3]

D3: [defend your position on G3]

You can certainly combine some of these options. Suppose again, you're going to offer grounds G1, G2, and G3 but now you'll deal with opposition arguments around the topic of G1 and G3 (as before), but you've also got a fourth opposition issue to deal with. In this case you would proceed as we just outlined, and then, after you've finished your case, add:

R4: [describe opposition argument]

D4: [give your response to this objection]

There is one more way to approach this. Sometimes you *organize your entire argument around a reply* to a position. This might come up if you were writing a rebuttal to someone else's position. You want to look at each of the points the other person made and reply in the same order. So you would bring up each of the points the advocate made and present your rebuttal of each. You would use the organization of their work to organize your reply.

Even in this case, however, you might want to raise larger issues the advocate didn't address or shift the ground of the argument. You'd have to decide if it was more effective to discuss that before or after you worked through their argument.

Tactics: Signposting and Formatting

Your audience has been reading your case for your position, but now you're going to explain a contrasting opinion, respond to it, and then continue with another part of your case. You have to guide the audience through these changes of direction. If you don't, they can easily think that you've changed your mind midstream or have started to make contradictory arguments.

First, when you transition to describing the opposing position, one that you need to explain but not endorse, you have to provide a very strong "signpost" to the audience, and you do that by a very explicit transition. That transition is, at a minimum, a new paragraph with a strong transition sentence at its beginning. More often, you'd signal the change by a new section heading. That section heading doesn't have to be something bland like "Opposing Arguments"; you can use something that describes the particular issue relevant to your topic.

Even if you do use a section heading, make sure you start that first paragraph with something very clear like:

"Not everyone agrees with the position I've been developing."

"To be sure, there are dissenting opinions."

"A major attack has been made on this view by ..."

You then follow that start with a description of the opposing argument. Don't slant this with loaded language; be neutral in your description. While you may respond to a position you know is a common objection, be careful about just referring to what "many say." It's much better if you can find a specific source that disagrees with you and quote them or at least cite them. This makes it less likely that you're doing a straw person fallacy by responding to an invented opponent.

When you start to explain your objections to this opposition argument, you need to start a new paragraph and again signal that you're changing direction, with something like:

"This argument isn't persuasive ..."
"I do not agree with this because ..."

You must then actually respond with new reasons, additional evidence, or something that extends your original argument. We sometimes see replies like, "However, I still believe that ..." and then there is nothing to follow it up. We hope you don't just "believe" your point of view as if digging in your feet were some type of virtue. You should offer evidence to explain why we shouldn't find that opposition argument persuasive.

The Value of the "Little Courtesies"

It certainly is tempting to abuse your opponent, either bluntly by name-calling or more subtly by little words that diminish their arguments, but, in general, it's better to be courteous. Any reader who is genuinely undecided is looking to find people who are experts, who sound persuasive and believable. Treating your opponent with politeness actually increases your credibility with this sort of reader.

In particular, things like attacking motives, insults, and so on may be fun and certainly can score points with readers who agree with you. But the smarter your audience is, the weaker that sort of response looks.

A Checklist for Your Rebuttal Section

If you are writing a paper where you explicitly deal with an opposing argument in one section, this checklist may assist you.

- You have addressed the strongest arguments against your position, not the weakest.
- The rebuttal section is set off by a heading or another strong separator.
- The rebuttal section begins with wording to alert the reader that you are describing a position other than your own.
- You quote or cite a specific opponent, not just what "many say."
- The opposing argument is described fairly and without abuse.
- There is a reply to the opposing argument that is substantive.
- The reply is set off to clearly alert the reader that you are again expressing your view.

REBUTTALS THAT AREN'T ACTUALLY REBUTTALS

There are a number of types of common responses that are offered to arguments that aren't really rebuttals at all. That is, they appear to be responding to the claims being made, but they are really just evasions.

Falling into "Yes, It Is"/"No, It Isn't"

It isn't just comedy skits and angry people who wind up arguing in the manner of "Yes, it is"/"No, it isn't." Sometimes when confronted with a reply, advocates just seem to retreat into a fortress and restate their position. Sometimes it is accompanied by a profession of faith: "I still believe . . . ." This is not really a rebuttal at all. Even if the opposing argument was not very cogent, you still need to reply with new material.

Think of that Monty Python skit we quoted in chapter one. It makes a good point that argument is not just repeating your position and getting louder each time.

Non-Denials That Appear like Denials

When Martha Stewart was indicted for financial misconduct, she, according to a story, posted on her website the following: "I want you to know that I am innocent." Is that the same thing as saying "I am innocent"? We have no idea what she intended to communicate. But, it has been suggested by those who watch these things that it is not uncommon for people to try to make you think they have denied something when they haven't.

The theory is that many people do not want to lie and so look for ways to communicate "no" (when the truth is "yes") without actually saying "no." What follows are a few variations on this.

"I refuse to dignify that question by an answer." A person of respectable reputation is asked a question about some disreputable activity they might have done. And the reply is given "I refuse to dignify that question by an answer" or "I find

---

Arguments we don't ever want to hear again:

"If I have to explain it to you, you wouldn't understand."

This gets on our list just for general condescension and rudeness.

Somebody doesn't understand something. They see something of a logical hole in someone else's argument. They ask a question or raise a challenge. And they get told that "you wouldn't understand."

Like a lot of insults, it works only because we agree that it does. It's a put down, it embarrasses the recipient, and they can feel inferior.

But, what does it actually mean? It often seems to mean that the person doesn't know how to explain whatever "it" was. They are just making an assertion. What was important to them was having status, to be an insider with special knowledge in contrast to the person who asked the question.

that argument to be insulting and inappropriate." These answers do not even deny the accusation; they try to rule the accusation out of bounds before the debate starts.

This nonrebuttal can be rhetorically effective if the question got asked in a context where such questions are not generally asked or if the person being accused enjoys a reputation for moral probity.

A variation is when the person replies: "I can't believe you would think that about me." They are, again, appealing to their reputation as proof against accusations of a specific wrong. This reply tries to move the accusation beyond the pale, to suggest that the accusation is so implausible as to be not worth even responding to.

"That's not our policy. "/"I'm just following orders." You go to complain about something unfair, perhaps something a store or an official did. You explain why it was unfair. And the reply you get is: "Our policy doesn't permit us to do . . ." That just means: "We've decided to be unfair, and we're not discussing it with you." Of course, policies are often made for a reason, and perhaps there is a reason why they must act unfairly to one in order to be fair to many, but you would at least hope that the person you deal with could explain all that instead of hiding behind a policy.

As a tactic, what this response does is to deflect your anger someplace else and onto someone you can't talk to, most likely.

It seems akin to a phrase with a more sinister history: "I'm only following orders."—which has been used at points in history to justify why some person did a very evil act.

"That fact is offensive" A discussion was being had about the effect of religion on behavior. Someone referred to a study showing that regular church attendees give more to charity than those who don't. A deeply offended reply came back to the effect that "I find it deeply morally repugnant to suggest that groveling submission to an imaginary being leads people to support poor people."

Well, maybe the person was indeed offended, but do churchgoers give more money or don't they? That's a factual issue; it is either true or not.

The issue here is that we do tend to link moral and emotional conclusions to certain facts and link them so firmly that even mentioning or raising the possibility of certain factual situations is deemed to be endorsing the moral wrong. So some issues such as the rates of crime, or comparative test scores among minority groups, or terrorism by certain groups, or faults of one's own country, to give some examples, can be factual issues whose mere discussion is freighted with too much emotion for some to allow.

The attitude or reputation defense Someone is accused of doing some action and the reply is: "I've always been opposed to doing that." Yes, but did you do it this time? People fail to follow their beliefs; they say one thing in public and do the opposite in private. So this isn't as big a defense as people think.

It can be valid to offer this defense if there isn't much evidence. It's very hard sometimes to "prove a negative." So if you're accused of doing something bad three weeks ago Wednesday, and you can't remember what you were doing and there isn't going to be any physical evidence, what can you say? In this case you may have to place the weight of your argument upon your credibility. What you are then arguing is that it wouldn't be probable that you did this act because of what you believe.

The "I'm working hard" defense Some one is accused of doing some job badly or failing to meet their responsibilities. They reply by saying that "I am working very, very hard. And I deserve some credit for how hard I'm working, how long my hours are, how little I'm being paid . . ." and so on.

However, if you're doing the wrong thing, working hard at it is not the point.

"False balance" fallacy This is one often seen in our news media. They want a debate on if the world is round or not. So they get one person saying it is round and one saying it isn't. Look, a "fair debate." Except it is not; the one person is a crank, the other represents the overwhelming majority of informed opinion. Or there is a war in which one side kills scores of civilians and the other side occasionally kills one or two. So we condemn both sides equally, being "fair." Except that isn't fair when one side accounts for 80 or 90 percent of the civilian casualties.

Sometimes the media goes to extreme lengths to engage in a false "balance." A story about corruption or criminality by an official in one party will be "balanced" by a "both sides do it" and reference to some older story from the other side—or sometimes by no evidence at all that the other side does the same thing. Or they will give an equal amount of space and airtime to two crimes: one from each side of the political debate, even though one issue is much more serious than the other.

The "I'm sorry if I hurt you" defense Nonrebuttal rebuttals happen in interpersonal settings also. One person does something that upsets another, the second objects and demands an apology. And the reply is "I'm sorry if I hurt you" or "I'm sorry you felt hurt." Neither is really an apology. Sometimes, to be sure, the desire is to preserve the relationship, and the "if I hurt you" line is a way of implying that good relations are more important than who is right or wrong. But more often than not it is a way of dodging responsibility. "I regret if anyone was offended by my remarks," is not the same as "I made a mistake." This happens in corporate settings as well, when a business says something like "We regret if any customer suffered." See an example at the end of the section.

The "Oh, you're always doing that" fallacy We've saved a personal favorite for last. You'll have to admire this one, because the respondent actually admits their opponent's case is valid, while convincing everyone else they have refuted it. It goes like this. One person makes a case, probably a case they've made before. Let's say it's a case about the need to deal more forthrightly with smoking. And you get a response like this:

> "You are always going on about smoking. It's always the same thing with you, over and over, it's all you can talk about, mentioning this, telling us about that. I'm just so tired of it, man, talk about one note. Booooooring."

So, this is intended to make the person feel bad; it's another put-down. But what did they really say? Basically all they claimed is that the advocate has consistently offered a case for something.

Was this really the best defense they could come up with? We often see replies that leave you wondering if (a) that really was a denial and (b) was it really the best you could do? The *New York Times* had a story about a woman caught up in the mortgage crisis. She'd paid her mortgage on time consistently, but bank records at Wells Fargo had gotten confused. They said they couldn't find it, they said they didn't own it, the story kept changing. It went to court, and the court proceedings dragged on for years.

> Over almost seven years, Wells Fargo employees swore [in court] to three different stories about the note on Ms. Green's property. When asked two weeks ago how this could be, a spokeswoman for the bank said, "We regret any difficulties our customer experienced in this circumstance. This is the kind of situation we seek to avoid, and we are working on this customer's situation to reach a solution." (Morgenson, 2011, p. 2)

What's your judgment on this response? In one sense there is nothing to complain about, the bank is saying they weren't happy with what they did, they want to fix it. But the reply has the air of a nonresponse to it. It doesn't really admit wrongdoing, it isn't an apology, and there is no promise of when or how they will make the customer whole for her agony. The tone is abstract, detached, emotionless.

We don't know for certain, but we'd suspect that lawyers made sure nothing was said that would commit the bank to anything. Safe. How different it would be for a senior executive (not a spokesperson) to come out and say "I'm mad that we shafted this customer, and I'm going to land on people with both feet until we get this fixed."

In the short run, the spokesperson's response is the safe one. In the long run it probably is another little example contributing to people's lack of trust in institutions (including the courts: seven years?).

BEYOND WINNING AND LOSING: WHERE REBUTTAL TAKES YOUR ARGUMENT

Much of this book (witness the previous section) is about a two-sided argument where one person advocates a position, and the other disagrees. Or, we've discussed an advocate in a more-or-less one-way conversation with an audience that he or she is trying to persuade.

These perspectives are useful to help isolate issues and help you start to sort out making arguments. They are training exercises, from one perspective.

However, there is more to argument than this. Let's consider a real situation. The presenter is discussing the role of right-wing parties in modern European politics. He makes a case for a particular explanation about why some right-wing parties succeeded and some failed. He has data; he is offering measured, limited claims; and he gives support for his contentions.

After his talk there is a question-and-answer session. One person pushes for a more precise definition of "right-wing." Another questions which countries were included and excluded and how this might change the conclusion. Yet another raises the issue of how the model might or might not apply to the right in U.S. politics. To each of these questions the presenter responds. In a sense he concedes a few things and defends a few more.

But in another sense, to describe this as an argument between two sides does not capture what is going on. The people in this discussion are not motivated by "winning" and "losing." They are all motivated by a desire to understand this aspect of European politics. As the speaker was plausible, reasonable, and interesting, no one really is trying to defeat him so he would change his mind on the entire topic. Instead they are exploring the various dimensions of the issue.

What happens in these sorts of encounters is that people, regardless of whatever "side" they were on, come out with a more informed perspective on the issue. They know more than when they came in, they've made some contacts with new people, and they leave with a more nuanced, more complex, and more complete picture of what is going on.

So everyone "wins."

Consider another example. As this textbook was being written, we authors had many conversations. How should this topic be discussed? What order should things go in? Should we bring that up? What is the best example to explain this?

Given the definition of "argument" we started with, these conversations were arguments. We each changed our minds on a number of things. One of us went in thinking one thing, but the other convinced us to change. But we would both probably be hard pressed to remember who "won" more often. We both won, and, we hope you won, since the book got better as a result.

Both of these suggest that discussing your ideas with another person, even someone who has a very different perspective, can be valuable. What can you gain from this?

- Improve your **evidence**. Someone may tell you that your source for a claim is weak, and they think you should use a better source.
- Drop **ineffective parts** of your case. You've offered several reasons; a person persuades you that one of your points is not helping your case, and you should drop it.
- Understand **how people read or hear you**. You think you were being perfectly clear, but you discover that what you said was really ambiguous in ways you didn't think about. After feedback, you can fix this.
- Make a better **connection with your audience**. It's always hard to see things as others will. Someone who reads and reacts to your argument can point out what you might not get.
- Learn what you need to **explain to your audience**. You can discover what terms or concepts are unfamiliar and if you've pitched your argument at the right level.
- Learn about **other solutions**. You all agree that something has to change, but they persuade you to adopt a better plan.
- Learn about **diverse impacts**. You've focused on how one group is affected; they show you how another group is affected.

And there is this:

- Make **stronger arguments.** It is not just muscle and will that are strengthened by competition; so too are arguments. In having to defend yourself against opposing views, you sharpen up your views, you come to see the weak points in your case, and you become motivated to change them.

And even though we wound up with a competition metaphor, that is actually not what this section is about. All those benefits can be obtained by just letting a friend read what you've written and give you some constructive feedback.

And like the two examples that started this section, the objective of this interaction is not for you to lose; it is for you to gain, to win a better understanding of the issue.

Beyond two sides Almost every issue has a lot more than just two sides, just yes and no. We'll discuss this again in the argument by dilemma chapter, but it is worth saying more than once. If we are going to change how health care is delivered in the United States, there are scores of different aspects of a plan to consider. If we're trying to decide if a certain trend in movies is morally good or bad, there are many angles to consider the problem from.

As communities debate issues, they assemble views out of a maze of various concepts and ideas. At any given moment all of them are in play. In this "marketplace of ideas," their interactions, if the principles of this book and other advocates of reasoned discourse are followed, will lead to everyone having better ideas. Everyone wins.

FAMOUS REBUTTALS

Two from Thucydides: The Mytilene Debate and the Melian Dialog

Two debates that have remained well-known in Western culture both come from the writings of the ancient Greek historian, Thucydides.

In 427 BCE, a revolt on the island of Lesbos led by the city of Mytilene was defeated by Athens. After the surrender, a debate took place in the assembly at Athens over what should be done. Tempers ran hot, and it was voted that all the men of Mytilene would be executed and the women and children enslaved, a not unusual fate for a defeated city in that day. A ship is dispatched to carry the order to the Athenian commanders at the island.

After the first debate, some had second thoughts, and another assembly was called for the following day. Two speeches are recorded from this debate, and their themes echo down to the present day. On the one hand is the "You must be strong to be respected" view and the frank advocacy of Athens as an imperial power, defending its empire and rule because it is the stronger. On the other side is the view that harshness will provoke a reaction of hatred, and it would be advantageous to be merciful.

The assembly votes to overturn its harsher ruling of the earlier day, and a second ship is dispatched to try and overtake the first one before it has time to arrive and implement its order. There is a dramatic and vivid account of this chase, with the second ship arriving at Lesbos just in the nick of time.

The second famous debate occurred eleven years later in 416 BCE. The island of Melos was a colony of Sparta but was neutral in the war between Sparta and Athens. Athens launched an expedition against the island. Confronting the islanders with overwhelming force, they offered them a stark choice: surrender, pay tribute, and live, or be totally destroyed.

The Melians say that such a choice is unnecessary, they are not hostile to Athens, Athens will look brutal if they attack a weak island. Athens contends that they cannot fail at what they have started, that if they fail to reduce Melos to surrender, they will look weak and lose credibility as a superpower. The debate goes through several poignant rounds with the Melians arguing on the grounds of justice and right, the Athenians playing power politics.

In the end Melos refuses to surrender and Athens attacks. Melos still refuses to surrender. Athens in short order conquered the island, killed the male population, enslaved the women and children, and planted their own citizens on the island.

So the Melians lost their island and their lives. But did they lose the debate? The debate didn't end with the battle; it has continued down through the centuries. All those from Athens that were there that day are now dead, and the larger community of those who believe in justice and reasoned discussion tend to think that Melos was right and this act of brutality and ethnic cleansing made Athens the loser.

Lincoln–Douglas Debates

In 1858, the Illinois senate race was between Abraham Lincoln and Senator Stephen Douglas. In an era before mass media, the two conducted seven debates at various locations in the state. The debates are notable for their impact, not so much on the Senate race (which Douglas won) but on debates afterward.

While these debates are often praised, they are seldom read. They are not always models of reasoned argument. They are full of insults and straw person attacks. They can seem very slow to come to grips with the issues. They also represent two people struggling honestly to find a way out of a looming national crisis. Because there were seven debates, each advocate developed and extended their arguments.

Lincoln practiced and developed arguments that he would use later. The debates, and his ability to go toe-to-toe with the more famous Douglas, enhanced his reputation and national standing. While he lost the immediate campaign, it led him to success later.

Prime Minister's Questions

Every Wednesday when the British parliament is in session there is a period allocated for members of parliament to ask questions of the prime minister. The tradition has evolved over time, but has been going on in some form since the 1880s.

While any member can attempt to be recognized to ask a question, there is a fixed set of six questions allocated to the leader of the opposition party.

Within the form of the question, there is a sharp debate with a skilled opposition leader making points and calling the prime minister to task. A skilled prime minister uses this time of questioning to get his case out to the public.

It is lively theater with constant shouting from the other members, insults delivered in witty style, and a no-holds-barred atmosphere of organized chaos. Americans who are used to their presidential debates will see several differences: including the use of printed notes, the short responses that directly clash with what others have said, and the role of the Speaker who directly and sometimes forcefully intervenes to keep the debate within the rules.

Other countries with a parliamentary tradition, such as Canada, also have similar institutions.

Debate Programs in High Schools and College

Across the United States there is a sport involving tens of thousands of high school and college students each year with tournaments, practices, teams, championships, but without coverage by the media (and without much money or any cheerleaders): debate.

Each year one or more topics are debated in a variety of formats. The number of speeches on each side vary as does their length. Sometimes the debaters cross-examine each other. Some formats involve head-to-head competition between two protagonists, some involve teams of two people debating another team. Over the course of a tournament, debaters have to argue both sides of the issue. Rounds are judged by other coaches and sometimes people from the community.

It's a rich source of experience in the issues discussed in this textbook: researching evidence, determining what claims to make, and how to respond to the claims of others. It is also one of the few sports where men and women compete against each other on an equal footing.

And yes, both of your authors were, and are, passionately involved in this activity.

CONCLUSION: REBUTTAL AS A WAY TO TRUTH

Rebuttal and Your Ethos

How you handle opposition to your argument is a key way that people judge your credibility. You can enhance your reputation by showing that you care for the truth more than just whatever position you were advocating. If you've treated opposition positions with fairness, it makes it a lot less painful if you later have to admit you were wrong about something.

It's easy to just rant or blather on about the total rightness of your own position. By engaging with others who have written and commented on the issue, you show that you are part of the long process of approaching the truth a little more closely. You situate yourself in the larger conversation that has gone on about an issue. And thus you gain the credibility of others involved in that conversation.

Are you a member of any Internet discussion group? Which of your members has the most respect from the others? Is it the one who never concedes anything and jumps all over those who disagree? It is far more often the one who demonstrates an ability to engage others and respond with evidence and reason—someone adept at rebuttal.

Done Right, Rebuttal Is Beneficial to Both Sides

Regardless of if the exchange is pleasant or conflicted, the process of rebuttal allows both to sharpen their arguments and gain knowledge. What makes this process work is the "little courtesies" we spoke of above: showing respect to the others in the debate, acknowledging good points, and toning down your temptation to more verbally violent replies.

SUMMARY OF REBUTTING ARGUMENTS

Description

The process of responding to arguments by another advocate or advocates.

Issues and Aspects

- Rebuttals often involve disputes over which issues are in dispute, not just disagreements about support for a particular point.
- Some rebuttals don't engage the substance of the other advocate's position.
- Many issues, perhaps most, have more than two sides to them.

Study Questions

- What is the difference between rebuttal and refutation?
- What is a straw person fallacy?
- What does stasis theory refer to?
- What are some of the benefits of engaging in debate over your position?

Introduction to Forms of Reasoning

With this chapter we begin a deeper look at how claims are supported. Claims are supported by the grounds and warrants of an argument, and we will study seven different ways you can supply support for a claim. We call these types of support *forms of reasoning*.

We looked at types of claims before. Now we will examine different forms that grounds and warrants can take. Each of the forms of reasoning can be used with any of the claim types. Another way of conceptualizing this is to think of a two-dimensional grid. We'll let you fill this out as we go along.

Are there only seven forms of reasoning? Probably not. While a large number of arguments can be analyzed with these seven types, we are not claiming that this is an exhaustive list.

One more bit of nomenclature. We speak of "a fact *claim*" but an "*argument* by sign". The claim is not the argument; the claim plus the form of reasoning makes it an argument.

The Relationship of Claim Types and Forms of Reasoning

(This section may be confusing before you study any particular form of reasoning. We suggest you look at it once and then come back to it after you've studied one or more forms of reasoning.)

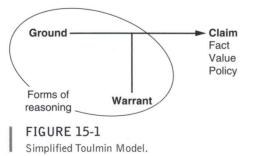

FIGURE 15-1
Simplified Toulmin Model.

	Types of Claims		
	Fact claims	Value claims	Policy claims
Forms of reasoning	Proof by logic and evidence.	Evaluate against the criteria of a value system.	Offer a plan that addresses inherency, significance, cost, enforcement, and other issues.
Definitional arguments: "X is a Y."			
Argument by example: "The generalization Y is true."			
Argument by analogy and parallel case: "X is like Y."			
Arguments from cause: "X causes Y."			
Argument from sign: "X is a sign of Y."			
Arguments from dilemma: "Either X or Y."			
Argument from authority: "X is an authority on Y."			

FIGURE 15-2
Forms of Reasoning Grid.

Studying forms of reasoning typically involves us in a two-step process. A form of reasoning is offered in support of a claim. One step is if that form of reasoning, if valid, would support the claim. The second step is to show that the form of reasoning is valid.

We can diagram this with Toulmin:

C1: [Our ultimate claim.]

G1/C2: [Support for Y, using a form of reasoning.]

W1: [How this form of reasoning proves our claim.]

C2: [Support for Y.]

G2: [Evidence that this form of reasoning is true in a particular case.]

W2: [How that evidence would support the form of reasoning.]

This is a bit abstract, but we're providing this to alert you to what will happen in the chapters on the various forms of reasoning. The first triad draws our attention to how the form of reasoning—if valid—would support our real claim. The second triad focuses us on the internals of the form of reasoning and if it is valid or not in a particular case.

We will discover that in some cases, C1 will never even get expressed in the argument (analogy and dilemma are two common examples). In these situations, the advocate believes that by expressing G1/C2, it is obvious what C1 would be. But, to analyze the argument, we have to make C1 explicit.

Another source of confusion is that while C1 can be a fact, value, or policy claim, C2 may be a different type from C1.

So you'll see statements with a "C" by them, and it might not always be immediately clear why some form of reasoning isn't just another type of claim (like fact, value, policy). But if you think about the network we've laid out above, you'll see how it all fits together.

Definitional Arguments

INTRODUCTION

The first qualification for judging any piece of workmanship from a corkscrew to a cathedral is to know what it is. (C. S. Lewis, Preface to *Paradise Lost*, in Witherington, 2001, p.1)

We regularly put things (and ideas and people) in groups and categories. And we regularly debate if we've assigned the right category or if we should object to someone else's categorizations.

Is Pluto a planet?
Is frozen yogurt a type of ice cream?
Is the snail darter an endangered species?
What is an "imported product"?
Who is a terrorist?

But where do these definitions come from? Can we change definitions? How do we decide if we've got the right categories? These are the issues that definitional arguments deal with.

Definitional arguments include a variety of types, as we will explain in the next section. They all involve supporting a claim by arguing that one specific thing belongs to a more general class of things. This form of reasoning includes both specific arguments about assigning things to categories everyone accepts but also arguments about the categories themselves.

Definitions are not just something "you look up in the dictionary." Definitions are agreed upon by a community; they are socially constructed. But that does not mean they are arbitrary or beyond critique and defense. Some definitions are better than others, but the standard of "better" depends on the context and needs to be openly examined.

Definitions are also not simply clinical or technical either. They carry emotional connotations that have to be attended to. Pathos is definitely involved here.[1]

TYPES OF DEFINITIONAL ARGUMENTS

The explicit form for a definitional argument is:

"X is a Y."

There are, however, three distinct ways this argument gets made explicit. We present them briefly here, and they will be discussed throughout the chapter.

Labeling. This is applying a term to someone or something without any discussion. It's usually just a straight accusation. "He's a terrorist," or a "liberal," or a "racist," or any one of a number of things. There is generally no discussion. The term carries persuasive force by itself or is assumed to.

Arguments about categories. This is like the previous type, only now we are explicitly discussing the pros and cons of putting something into a particular category. But the category itself is not the issue. Everyone involved in the debate accepts the definition of the category; the focus is on debating if "X" does or doesn't belong in "Y."

Arguments about definitions. Now, the focus turns to the "Y" of our explicit form. The argument might have been started because of a particular "X" we wanted to classify, but the real argument turns out to be about what is and is not the standard or criteria for "Y." Do we have a good definition? Is it the right definition? Does it properly categorize the particular issue at hand and also stand up over time?

As we often say, reality is more complex and doesn't always fit our categories. Actual arguments can flow from one type to the other. Sometimes an advocate needs to try to move an argument from one of these three types into another type. Before we explore that, however, we need a theoretical framework.

DEFINING A DEFINITION

The adjacent quote from Justice Stewart is a famous one. It is a sentiment that we've likely expressed at one time or another about something that we know is real, but is hard to pin down. How do you define love? Or what makes a movie good? However, with all due respect to the justice, we do have to try to explain how we can define our definitions.

> "I shall not today attempt further to define the kinds of material I understand to be embraced within that shorthand description ["hard-core pornography"]; and perhaps I could never succeed in intelligibly doing so. But I know it when I see it, and the motion picture involved in this case is not that."
>
> —Justice Potter Stewart, concurring opinion in *Jacobellis v. Ohio*, 378 U.S. 184 (1964)

---

[1]This chapter draws on the work of Edward Schiappa in *Defining Reality: Definitions and the Politics of Meaning* (Southern Illinois University Press, 2003).

ARGUMENT STRATEGY

First Draft of an Argument Strategy

If we think about some category of objects and what makes it a category, we might naturally think about what the objects all have in common. What attributes do they share? We'd then formulate that as a statement like:

1: "All Y have attributes $Z_1, Z_2, \ldots Z_n$."

With that established, we can make an argument about the particular object in question:

2: "X has attributes $Z_1, Z_2, \ldots Z_n$."
3: "Therefore, X is a Y."

As straightforward and obvious as this might appear, there is a serious problem here. Consider this example:

4: "All dogs have four legs."
5: "My cat has four legs."
6: "My cat is a dog." (!?)

Second Draft of an Argument Strategy

So, clearly, just identifying what all the objects in the class have in common is not enough. There are two ways to fix this problem. We'll call them the *syllogism fix* and the *practical argumentation fix*.

The syllogism fix is to translate the model into deductive reasoning:

7: "All items with attributes $Z_1, Z_2, \ldots Z_n$ are Y."
8: "X has the attributes $Z_1, Z_2, \ldots Z_n$."
9: "Therefore, X is a Y."

When we try this on our cat example, we see the difference immediately.

10: "All things with four legs and a tail are dogs." (Oops!)

That's not going to work. So we know we need to refine our definition. The problem isn't with the logic in statements 7, 8, and 9—that is internally consistent. The problem lies in our specific example. But even if we fix that and get a better definition for dogs, there still is a problem. However logically sound this approach to establishing a definition, this fix is useless for practical argumentation. If we already know that statement 7 is (or is not) true, we've already looked at all the "X"s that could be part of the "Y," and so we don't need the rest of the argument.

So, let's consider the practical argumentation fix:

11: "Y is well defined for the purposes of this argument by the attributes Z_1, $Z_2, \ldots Z_n$."

12: "X has attributes $Z_1, Z_2, \ldots Z_n$."

13: "Therefore X is a Y."

And again, our dog example is useful:

14: "The concept of dog is well defined for the purposes of this argument by the attributes of having four legs and a tail."

Now we know we have a problem. "Four legs and a tail" can't properly distinguish the different animals. We'd need a more precise definition before we even discuss a particular animal and where we should assign it.

But, even if we give a more precise set of criteria, will this theoretical formulation work? "Well defined"? "For the purposes of this argument"? Sounds rather vague and subjective, doesn't it? Actually, what this formulation does is bring to the foreground the points of contention in definitional arguments. By highlighting those issues, we gain insight into how definitional arguments work and don't work. We'll flesh out those issues in the following sections.

But first let's look at some examples. We'll go back to using the Toulmin formulation.

DEFINITIONS IN THE THREE TYPES OF CLAIMS

Fact Claims

C1: "Mr. Smith is a burglar."

G1a: "Mr. Smith's fingerprints were found inside the broken door of a business."

G1b: "He did not own the building and did not have permission to be there."

G1c: "Goods from the business in the building were found in his home."

G1d: "These goods have been identified by the owner to have been stolen."

W1: "Burglary is committed when someone does all of the following: (a) breaks into a building without the consent of the owner and does so (b) not for an emergency, (c) not to execute a lawful search, (d) not to evict a tenant, (e) with the intent to commit a theft."

A criminal trial is a form of definitional argument of the second type we identified above (arguments about categories). The definition of "burglar" is given in the legal code and explained by the judge. It's not in dispute. What is in dispute is if the defendant meets that definition or not.

Value Claims

C: "Ms. Wu is not a good Christian."

G: "Ms. Wu says she has not accepted Jesus as her personal savior."

W: "Only those who have accepted Jesus as their personal savior can be considered good Christians."

Do you want to quarrel with this conclusion? If you're an atheist, you may say the entire dispute is irrelevant to any proper judgment of the moral work of Ms. Y. If you are a moderate or liberal Christian, you may want to use a different definition of "good Christian"; you agree we need one, but you dispute some of the attributes.

In this case, we've got an example of the third type of definitional argument we described (arguments about definitions). What is in dispute is what criteria define the term "good Christian" in this context. We'll have more to say on this type in the next section.

Policy claims

C: "We need to expel Ms. Garcia from our hobby club."

G1: "She has missed the last three meetings in a row."

G2: "Our constitution requires that members cannot miss more than two meetings in a year."

W: "Club constitutions establish the definition for membership."

The club constitution provides attributes of what makes someone a member. In this case, the purpose of the definition is only for the club's use. The definition has no particular value outside the context of the club. Other clubs could set different definitions of "member."

WHERE DO DEFINITIONS COME FROM?

"A person is the measure of all things: of things which are, that they are, and of things which are not, that they are not."

—Protagoras in Plato, *Theaetetus*

Not from the Dictionary

Where do definitions come from? For too many students, they come from the dictionary. Need to explain a significant concept in a paper? Just look it up and paste in the definition. Dictionaries are very useful books, but they may not be as useful as you think for your papers. What do dictionaries do? They record how words are *actually used* in a culture at a particular time. Some dictionaries trace the evolution of words over time, but the key concept is that dictionaries are *descriptive*, not *prescriptive*.

Dictionary definitions seldom address the contentious issues that society is debating. Try looking up a few such words, and you'll see that a general purpose dictionary doesn't really help all that much.

But a general dictionary does have its uses. Much of the time, what we want to do is make sure we are using words the way most people use them so we can communicate without confusion. The dictionary is good for that.

If we're really involved in a debate about the issues around the meaning of a word, looking at a specialty dictionary is a better option. Law, medicine, theology, and other fields have created special-purpose dictionaries that would be useful to consult for an issue in a specific field. There are even dictionaries of obscenities, slang, colors, and those aimed at specific groups.

More than this, sometimes professional organizations produce a specific definition of a key term in their field. We'll look at a definition of "planet" that produces some controversy later in the chapter.

The point is to understand what a dictionary is useful for and what its limitations are.

We do disagree The dictionary can create the impression that everyone uses the same definitions all the time and that just isn't the case. It's not just slang terms that have different meanings for different people, but different groups of people use different terms. Dictionaries don't always record those.

CHANGING OUR DEFINITIONS AND CATEGORIES

We do change our definitions of things and the definition of consequential things. What about the term "rape." That should be pretty well defined; it's a very old concept, one that transcends a particular culture, and we know what it means, right? How could that definition change?

But—can a husband rape his wife? The law, and custom, used to say no. If a woman agreed to be married, then she'd agreed to have sex. She had, in fact, permanently given up her right to say no to that one man. We don't think that any more. Can one man rape another man? The laws on rape used to specifically say that it was forced intercourse by a man of a woman, so there was no legal concept of homosexual rape. That has also changed. And can a woman rape a man? That used to be thought impossible, both as a question of physiology and as a question of practice. Indeed, people used to laugh at the idea of it. But it's not impossible, and now the law admits of that possibility.

The underlying incidents probably haven't changed, but our view of what they should be called has changed (both our legally codified view and our social view). Our definition of rape has changed.

Is alcoholism a moral failing or a disease? Fifty years ago, it was thought to be a moral failing. Many stand-up comics had a "drunk act" playing a character who acted drunk for the audience to laugh at. Now we tend to think it is more of a disease—other than when people are driving a car, in which case we're convinced it is a moral failing. And few find it as funny as the culture used to. There's probably some disagreement here among us as to how to classify this behavior or maybe we're not totally consistent.

The Reality of "Social Construction"

What we are trying to point out is that things as fundamental as a definition do not just fall from the sky. Definitions get decided and accepted, or disputed, by the culture and get redefined over time. This happens either consciously or unconsciously.

Consider the term "normal" and its partner "abnormal." This gets used both as a descriptive term (what is common or uncommon) and as an evaluative term (what is right and what is wrong). How many ways has that term changed over time? What careers for women are normal? Is homosexuality normal or at least "accepted"? Is it normal to have a cell phone? To have sex outside of marriage? To go to church on Sunday? To have a tattoo? To wear causal clothes in a formal situation? The list could go on for some time.

Who Gets to Decide on a Definition?

So if definitions are disputed and changed, who gets to decide? Various definitions have been decided in various ways: experts debating and coming to a consensus, the courts, and by a majority of people slowly accepting a term over time.

But who should decide is clearly not universally accepted. In some examples below we'll see situations where the decision about who should decide is itself up for dispute.

"WELL DEFINED" FOR WHAT CONTEXT?

So, definitions can be argued over. But what issues shape those arguments? Our proposed definition of definitions said we wanted criteria that were "well defined" for the "purposes" of a particular argument or a particular context.

The idea here is that depending on the context, we might want different criteria to define a term. It might be useful, however, to start with some examples of how terms fail to be well defined.

Interests Presented as Objective Definitions

Can you invent a disease? That hardly seems likely. We might discover more about how the body works, we might realize that we were mistaken about how some part of the body failed, but how could you "invent"—intentionally invent—a disease?

However, it appears that you can. In recent years we've seen a wave of advertisements alerting us to various conditions. These have included such things as insomnia, sadness, minor allergic reactions, and, something called "social anxiety disorder." Likewise, if you read an old book, you may run across diseases such as "consumption" or "gout" that don't seem to occur now, and again, it is because we've changed our definition.

The attention paid to social anxiety disorder arose in parallel with the marketing of drugs that are aimed at treating it. "Depression"—we've had that word as a concept for a while, and there have been antidepressant drugs for years. But social anxiety disorder seems more akin to being shy or being uncomfortable in public settings. In other words, in times past, this was regarded as a normal feature of some people, like being outgoing, or athletic, or intellectual. It might have been recognized as something that people should work at overcoming, but it wasn't seen as a disease.

What's the difference? Someone has a financial incentive for people to see this as a condition that medical science can fix—and can fix by purchasing products they sell. Don't misunderstand us. We're not claiming that no one was shy before, and we're not suggesting that some people weren't miserable because of it. We're arguing that the urge to push the definition of this as a disease was not motivated by a dispassionate conviction that it was rational to do so. Somebody stands to make money if society sees this as a disease. Someone's interests favor pushing a certain definition. Examining three books on the use of drugs to treat mental disorders, a reviewer concludes that:

> First, [the authors] agree on the disturbing extent to which the companies that sell psychoactive drugs—through various forms of marketing, both legal and illegal, and what many people would describe as bribery—have come to determine what constitutes a mental illness and how the disorders should be diagnosed and treated. (Angell, 2011, p. 20)

There have been a number of such issues over the years. Is the tomato a fruit or a vegetable? That went through the court system in the 1890s because income to various groups was at stake. Are Jell-O shots a beverage? A bar caught selling them to minors claimed they were not a beverage, and thus they weren't promoting underage drinking (the court decided that Jell-O shots were a beverage).

The problem is not that someone has interests, but that you hide them. It is the same concept we discussed before under the topic of "bias." You are allowed to argue for your own interests, you are allowed to find a need and make money filling it, but to hide your interests is deceptive.

Asserting Authority: Definitional Hegemony

Who gets to make a definition? That is a more complex question than might be expected. Certainly one way to control a debate is by being able to define the terms in play or to claim for yourself the right to define them.

A long-running dispute in the United States is over the definition of the term "wetlands." How tightly or expansively that is defined will set rules for how land may be used. It might seem reasonable to argue that experts should make this definition. People who are students of ecology and biology or hydrology and who understand the role of water in an ecosystem would seem to understand best how to make this definition. Their definition of wetlands is more expansive than what farmers and other landowners want to use. Those groups favor a narrower definition.

In this case, it can be easy to frame the argument in one of two ways. One way is to see this as a bunch of exploitive and insensitive people (the landowners) standing in the way of science (the ecologists) and trying to decide a scientific question by ignoring science. On the other hand, it could be seen as ivory-tower intellectuals (the ecologists) arrogantly deciding to deprive citizens of their own land.

As before, there are interests at stake. The argument over the definition is not being conducted just out of intellectual curiosity. The economic well-being of landowners and the long-term costs of cleaning up the environment are in play. If ecologists can insist they can define the term, then they are in position to win the argument by excluding the views of others who stand to lose money. If landowners claim the right to define the term, then they can avoid having to deal with a number of issues about environmental damage.

It's not right to screen out the interests of the landowners and pretend that their position is motivated only by money whereas the ecologists are only pushing a dispassionate "objective" definition. Because other people are impacted financially by this definition, one group cannot claim the right to define terms in a way that adversely impacts the other.

It would be more honest if we openly discussed the issues of how protecting the environment may produce dissimilar impacts on different groups and addressed how we can make a more fair process.

Reductionism

In the book, *Zen and the Art of Motorcycle Maintenance*, Robert Pirsig presents a definition of a motorcycle that begins this way:

> A motorcycle may be divided for purposes of classical rational analysis by means of its component assemblies and by means of its functions. If divided by means of its component assemblies, its most basic division is into a power assembly and a running assembly. The power assembly may be divided into the engine and the power-delivery system. . . . The engine consists of a housing containing a power train, a fuel-air system, an ignition system, a feedback system and a lubrication system. . . (Pirsig, 1974, p. 73)

Well, that's not wrong, is it? So what's the problem? If all you knew of motorcycles was this definition, would you want to ride one? (And that is the point the author was making by this ironic definition.)

This is an example of *reductionism*: the idea that the true definition of something is found in the lowest-level definition of it. So we have the idea that love should be defined by chemical processes, that desire for children is the work of the "selfish gene," and so on. This is a form of the "part for the whole" fallacy when you assume that what is true for the parts must also be true for the whole.

Remember, we said, "well defined for the purposes of this argument." There could be several different purposes. This reductionist definition of a motorcycle is probably well suited if our purpose is the organizing of parts for our inventory of spares or for setting out a manufacturing process. It's not well suited for the purpose of discussing the role of the motorcycle in American culture.

Circular Definitions

It's time to discuss another classic student error: using the word to be defined in the definition of it. A popular quiz question for one of the authors is to ask students what the phrase "correlation is not causation" means (if you don't know, don't worry. It is covered in the chapter on causal arguments).

Far too often what comes back is something like: "It means that just because two things are *correlated* doesn't mean that one *caused* the other." Well, we probably know what they meant.

This is circular. It doesn't get us any farther along toward understanding the concept. This error seems to happen when we've so associated the concept with a particular word that we can't unpack it in our heads.

Naming as Reality-Shifting

We've been arguing that names matter—that what we call something does impact how we see it. In a subsequent section we're going to talk specifically about the Pathos appeal of certain "loaded words." Nonetheless, we also have to discuss those situations when an argument over what to call something is a diversion from the real issues: when changing the name is thought to do the work of changing the underlying reality.

Years ago a friend of one of the authors was complaining about a book. The novel was confusing, odd things were happening that made no logical sense, sometimes there seemed to be magic occurring, but it was clearly not a science-fiction or fantasy novel. "Well," another friend said, "the author is a surrealist."

"Oh," the first person said, nodding, "I get it; that makes sense, I understand it now." Then she started laughing at herself. The book was just as confusing with the label as it was before. What difference did it make to give a label to it?

Does the library have different things in it if it is called a "resource center"? If you are losing your job, the source of money that keeps you going, does it matter if you were "fired," "laid off," "sacked," "downsized," "rightsized," "outplaced," or are now "between opportunities"? The agency that was the "extension school," and then became "continuing ed" but is now "adult ed"—does it teach different things than it used to?

Well, it might matter a little bit, but what we are identifying here is the tendency in some cases to use name changes as *substitutes* for substantive change. So the focus becomes on the name change—but then nothing else much changes.

Examples of this are plentiful in business when new names are always being generated to repackage the same concepts.

Definitions, Respect, and Political Correctness

When the issue of "empty" nomenclature change is concerned with terms for groups of people, the level of emotion rises, and many issues run together that need to be sorted out. Over the past decades our names for groups of nonwhite citizens, for those whose sexuality wasn't held up as the ideal, or for people whose bodies departed from "the norm," have gone through several generations of changes.

Most of us have now come to agree that a series of these changes are an unreserved good. Terms like "black" and "African American" replaced "colored" and "the N-word," "disabled" or "physically challenged" replaced "crippled," as just a couple of examples. In each case a term that all involved knew was intended and understood to be very derogatory was rooted out and a more neutral term used instead. Progress.

But controversy has arisen about a continuing series of changes. Should "disabled" now become "differently abled" or "special"? Should "aboriginal" become "first peoples"? What should people with vision difficulties be called if not "blind" or "visually impaired"? And given how these terms evolve, we may not be up to date on all of these.

Some object to the energy devoted to this continuing round of changes by calling them examples of "political correctness" or "PC." A term that is not neutral but negative. And others argue that the very term PC is itself an example of racism or oppression, and why shouldn't these people get to decide on their own names?

As we said, several things are going on here at once. Most of us would agree that people should have, within some broad range, the ability to name themselves. Why the qualifier? Suppose some town decided to name itself "the best town," or a group of people named themselves as "special people." It would be easy to imagine a white supremacist group naming themselves as people who attack nonwhites and using a very negative term for those they hate. That certain high schools and colleges wanted to use mascots with names of other ethnic and cultural groups was offensive to many. So there are limits to the "you can name yourself" concept.

Also, we might want to distinguish between a name and connotations of worth. Some with physical issues dislike the term "disabled" because they are fiercely determined to live a full and exciting life, and they resent the implication that being in a wheelchair (for example) means that they can't do that and should be regarded as poor unfortunates and looked upon with pity. This seems to combine two issues: a description with attributions of worth. The people involved are concerned that others will take the bare statement of fact—"X has a condition"—and turn it into a devaluation of them—"X's life is less rich."

Where some resentment about PC comes from is the idea that groups can constantly change their names and then berate others for being hateful or racist for terms that the group using them had no awareness of. A recent example from the U.S. census might illustrate this.

Prior to the 2000 census, officials aware that our names for groups were in constant flux, conducted research where they asked people to name themselves. They didn't say "Pick from this list"; they said, in effect, "You tell us how you identify yourself." A group of older nonwhites said they saw themselves as "Negros." The census put that on the form as an option along with "African American" and "Black." The census bureau did not repeat that research for the 2010 census, and the presence of the term "Negro" on the form was judged offensive by some.

Now, it is one thing to say the census erred by not staying on top of this issue and updating their forms. It is another thing to accuse them of intentional disrespect and perhaps yet another to escalate that to the charge of racism. To do that, you need more evidence than just the presence of the term on the form.

Historically the term "Negro" was a positive one, replacing less respectful terms such as "colored"—Dr. Martin Luther King Jr. used it repeatedly in the "I Have a Dream" speech as a self-identification. Time has passed, and many now view the word as antiquated and offensive, a reminder of slavery. The friction arises with people who don't study this issue every day, weren't aware that this term has now been judged to be offensive, aren't sure what specific offense is taken, and are sensitive about the claim that simply failing to stay current means they are now active racists.

The categories used in the U.S. census for ethnic and racial identification have changed frequently. In 2000, for example, people were allowed, for the first time, to indicate they belonged to more than one racial category.

But we'd like to draw your attention to one specific aspect of name-changing.

Can changing the name for a group be a diversion? Energy can go into changing a name from one recently used term, without much negative history, to another term as a replacement for discussing continuing areas of discrimination, funding programs to compensate for disadvantages, addressing laws and social practices that have disproportionate effect on certain groups and so on. The name change can be granted as a way of avoiding substantive change.

Wherever you find yourself on this issue, our fundamental point is this: Don't assume that a name, a label, is either meaningless or, alternatively, carries all the meaning. Observe how it is being used, what it means to various groups, and assess whether in a particular case, the name change will change reality. Neither dismiss names as pointless nor assume that is all you need to attend to.

THINKING ABOUT CONTEXTS

Context and Purpose

We've been hinting that a single "thing" might have two or more definitions depending on context or that we might need different definitions depending on our purpose.

We've referred to changes in perspectives on alcoholism previously. If our goal is to help people stop being an alcoholic, it seems that looking at it as a disease or an addiction seems more useful than berating people. On the other hand, if we're talking about operating a motor vehicle, then our disapproval of such action and holding people responsible for it means we look at things differently. That's not necessarily a contradiction.

"Race" has little use in biology; it may even be meaningless in that context. Socially, we have to say, the term has had significant meaning.

We made a brief reference before to a court case about Jell-O shots. A bar in Iowa City, Iowa, got caught (with the help of teenagers going undercover) selling Jell-O shots to minors. "No fair" the bar contented—these aren't a beverage, not a "drinkable liquid" (according to one definition of a "beverage")—and so the law banning serving alcoholic drinks to minors was not violated. What's of interest here is a quote from the administrative law judge, Laura Lockard:

> While there might be some debate in another context as to whether Jell-O is a food item or beverage, in this context . . . the Jell-O shots served by the licensee were alcoholic beverages. ("Jell-O Shots," 2010)

Note: "in another context." If the issue was what food handling rules applied to drinks vs. solid food, perhaps it would matter. If the issue (as it was here) is serving booze to minors, the distinction is not relevant.

Did you know that the U.S. government has defined "acts of God"? That seems a bold thing to do. In 1979 there was in the Federal Register (the place government rules get published) a lengthy paragraph with a very precise definition of the term "acts of God." The definition boiled down to "weather and sea conditions greater than one standard deviation above the historical mean for the place and season." So the federal government decided enough with theological debates, we'll settle this? Not really. Insurance policies often contain provisions for "acts of God," which is a specialized term in this context meaning "things that are pretty unusual." For purposes of deciding on claims and payouts, this needed to be more exactly defined. The context here has nothing to do with theology or religion at all, actually.

Over the past few years there has been an ongoing dispute about which company the U.S. Air Force should buy a new plane from. The Air Force decided it needed a new plane for midair refueling, and both Boeing and Airbus companies bid to supply the plane. In much of the press, this was billed as a dispute between a "domestic" company (Boeing) and a "foreign" company (Airbus). And indeed, Boeing is headquartered and has manufacturing plants in the United States while Airbus is based in Europe.

But Boeing outsources work all over the globe, and Airbus, as part of their bid, promised that certain parts and assembly would be U.S.-based. In terms of the number of jobs for Americans, it was argued, there was essentially no difference between the two companies.

So what context should rule here? Is it that the U.S. armed forces should prioritize loyalty to a domestic company? Or should we count jobs to decide which company was the most American? Perhaps we might even consider which company made a better plane. But, of course, what is in dispute is what "better" means in this context: Is it speed, carrying capacity, endurance—or is it issues like jobs for Americans or corporate ownership?

In a globalized economy, where companies move work all over the world, does the definition of "domestic" and "foreign" companies make as much sense as it used to? If you buy your "foreign" car from a dealer owned by someone in your own country and get it repaired by someone from your own country, and it contains parts built in your count—just how much different is that from buying a "domestic" car with parts in it from foreign countries?

Specialized and General Contexts

Some definitional issues seem to pit a specialized context (such as the scientific community or the courts) against a general context of the public at large. One can argue that the specialized community would have priority if the issue at stake is entirely within that community. In other words, if the issue is "Did so-and-so break the law?" one might well give the presumption to the courts in their decisions. But if the question is, "What is the proper punishment for some behavior?" then everyone has a right to participate in the discussion and to debate what should be the case. One can also respect the expertise of the specialized community, but not grant their views immunity from critique.

But specialized communities do have needs others may not care about. What is the definition of "a year"? How hard could that be? It's 365 days unless it's a leap year. That's good enough for most of us, but not for specialized groups such as geologists and astronomers. Is a year the time it takes the earth to come back to the exact same point in space on its orbit? The days in a calendar year don't exactly work out for that. And the earth's orbit slows down about a half second each century so the exact number doesn't even stay the same—which matters if you're talking about millions of years.

THE ROLE OF PATHOS

At several points above we've alluded to the role of emotion in definitions, and now we need to look at it more directly. This most affects those arguments we called "labeling" (the first type) earlier in the chapter.

One of the authors ran into this problem over the name of a test he was going to give. Was it a "test," an "exam," the "final," or merely a "quiz"? Apparently some anxiety had been generated by calling it an "exam," which carried much more significance with students than intended. A "quiz" was less threatening than an "exam."

What exactly is the difference between a "violin" and a "fiddle"? You play country music on a fiddle but never classical music. No doubt the cost of violins for symphony orchestras is much higher than the cost of a simple fiddle, and there is likely a difference in sound quality. But the two names carry very different emotional weight as well.

Consider the positive emotions assigned to "natural" or "organic" in distinction to "artificial." In the section at the end of the chapter we explain a bit about a dispute between Spenda and Equal over what is and is not "artificial."

The emotional content of definitions has some interesting consequences as we'll now discuss.

Winning without Arguing

There is no doubt that sometimes people use labels as their entire argument.

If you have a lot of money when you die, your heirs may have to pay some tax on it in order to take over the assets. What is the name for this tax? For decades it was known as the "estate tax." Somewhat expected in that the sum of assets of someone who dies is termed their "estate." People opposed to this tax renamed it the "death tax." Well, that's terribly unfair, isn't it, paying taxes to die? Who'd be in favor of that?

But that's just a label, not an argument about why the tax on 1 or 2 percent of the biggest estates is wrong. Not to be outdone, those favoring the tax decided to call it "the Paris Hilton Tax Break." Ahh, who would want to give her a tax break? But that is equally a label. Once again, a claim is not an argument. You need reasons.

People who want certain heath-care options suppressed call it "socialized medicine" and have for decades. No one wants to be a socialist, even if they're not sure what it is. Likewise there are the terms "radical," "liberal," "fascist," and others that seem to have little precise meaning, but plenty of negative emotions associated with them.

People who use force to oppose a government—are they "rebels," "freedom fighters," "guerrillas," "criminal elements," or "terrorists"? Well, there are differences among those who oppose governments just as some governments are legitimate and some tyrannies, but notice the emotional weight we assign to those terms.

So, when a group does oppose a government with force, is that an "uprising," a "revolt," a "civil war," a "rebellion," just "chaos," an example of "lawlessness," or best seen as a "humanitarian crisis." These terms assign various levels of agency and value to the participants.

"Material support for terrorist organizations" is a kiss of death, but what behavior merits this term being used? Giving money to a charity that operates in the same territory as armed rebels? The term implies that the person has really helped along someone nefarious, but what did they do?

The definition of "terrorist" itself is fraught with issues. Can a government commit a terrorist act? Some definitions exclude actions by government. If the target is a military one, in theory that is not an act of terrorism, but some will call it such nonetheless. If the agent doing the act is from a militia group or acting alone (like the person who flew his plane into the side of an IRS building), the term terrorist tends not to get applied. Why is that? Observing this, one person cynically suggested that the term terrorist means "swarthy opponent of U.S. foreign policy." That's too much to agree with.

Abortion is another field with a large set of emotional terms. What exactly is aborted? A "fetus," an "unborn child," a "zygote," a "person," or, in one memorable article by a woman who didn't want to be pregnant, a "parasite." Are the parties to abortion debates "pro-choice" or "pro-abortion," or "baby killers"? Is the other side "pro-life" or the advocates of "forced pregnancy" because they are "women haters"?

The point here is not that these terms are meaningless or random. Rather, we are urging you not to just accept the emotional weight of the terms, but to investigate if they are valid. In general, we'd suggest that "labeling" arguments are seldom valid or are less valid than people think. You should be conscious of the categories being used and ask if the same standards are being applied to everyone.

Changing the Level of Emotion

People can intentionally choose terms to raise or lower the emotional level of a debate. This seems to be particularly the case when someone does not want to acknowledge some emotionally painful event. That the Pentagon described a suicide at Guantanamo prison as a "self-injurious behavior incident" seems likely to be an intentional effort to mute the pain of the issue.

Death is another topic with a range of terms of different emotional connotation such as "passed away," "crossed over," and "departed."

Mystification and Excluding

Experts, or people who want to be considered experts, can use technical vocabulary as a way of excluding others. The implication is that if you don't know these terms you shouldn't debate the issue. Using a series of technical terms can be an effort to position yourself as wiser, on the inside, as in command of the issue. Everyone from social workers, psychiatrists, academics, perhaps especially academics, can do this.

Of course, any community that studies a specialized area develops specialized vocabulary and makes finer distinctions among things. A bridge is a bridge to most of us; civil engineers need many terms to describe different types of bridges. That is perfectly reasonable. What we are pointing to is when this vocabulary is being used as a weapon to push others out of a conversation.

FOR FURTHER STUDY

We briefly describe some interesting cases of definitional arguments that might be worth your further study.

Is Pluto a Planet?

In 2006 the International Astronomical Union gave its first formal definition of what a "planet" was. To be a planet in their view you needed to (a) orbit a star, (b) be round (to some definition of roundness), and (c) dominate your orbit, that is, have, through gravity, cleared out other objects in the same orbit. Pluto failed criteria (c) and hence was demoted to the status of "dwarf planet" along with Ceres and Eris.

This issue is fascinating for several reasons. The first reason is the following.

Who cares?

Seriously—a rock over a billion miles away is put in a different category. How could that affect your life? But people did care, a lot of people. Astrologers didn't accept the definition. The state of New Mexico didn't accept it (the person who discovered Pluto is associated with New Mexico). Schoolchildren wrote in protest. It spawned a new word, "to Pluto" someone or something, as in "I got Plutoed by that test and flunked."

If you explore this issue, some of the concepts we've discussed would apply here:

- Who gets to decide on this? Is this properly a decision for astronomers as the relevant experts, or does this decision go beyond purely internal scientific matters?
- Why is there an emotional connection to this particular planet? This would seem a fine example of a name change without consequence. Why do people not see it that way?
- Why do we even need such a definition? What context needs this definition?

What Is and Is Not a Sport?

This issue arose for the authors due to a spirited class discussion about competitive dance. Is that a sport? Well, what exactly is a useful definition of sport? Competition? Physical effort, and, if so, how much effort? So would NASCAR qualify? What about chess or bowling or curling or poker or competitive eating?

Some of the criteria offered for a definition are not that serious. One student wished to ban sports when you wear glitter or smile all the time (probably aimed at synchronized swimming).

Some of the issues around this question:

- Contexts and purpose. There are several here. The university needs a definition to decide on funding, granting travel privileges, and excusing people from classes. A court needed a definition to decide on Title IX issues (and said one of the criteria needed in this context was a governing organization). The Olympics dumped women's softball because their context demanded that a sport be played by enough countries to be truly a world competition. Other contexts wouldn't need that as a criterion.
- Does the terminology "sport" grant a degree of social status that people aspire to? Certainly, your authors can't be the only ones who wished for high school debate to be granted the lofty status of sport, equal to football and basketball.

Finally, we bring up another candidate sport, totally, you understand for purely scientific purposes. There are several organizations pushing for inclusion in the Olympics of the ancient, but not entirely honorable activity of pole dancing. Well, they'd wear clothes probably. As an exercise, can you design criteria for defining sport that exclude this, but include all the things you want to include?

What Is the Definition of Death?

Another topic that turns out to be harder than you'd think. Is it the ending of a heartbeat? Or "brain death," where there is no activity in the brain but the heart and lungs are still working? It may make a difference where neurological activity is going on, in what part of the brain. How do you decide if there is not enough brain activity to count? And it seems that each passing year brings about an ability to revive people after longer and longer periods of time. Apparently, humans have some primitive ability to enter a sort of suspended animation state, at least for a limited time.

Among the issues here:

- Who can decide that someone is dead? In many jurisdictions, EMTs do not have the formal ability to do so; that decision must be left for a physician.
- The legal system needs a clear decision to deal with issues of an estate or remarriage of someone whose spouse is dead. There is a concept of "legally dead" when someone has gone missing for a long time.
- Religions may need a different definition that may become more problematic as the ability to revive people for longer periods is developed.
- Are people put in cryogenic storage dead?

"Natural" vs. "Artificial" Sugars

The "artificial sweetener" (the term in quotes for reasons that will be apparent later) Equal uses the ingredient aspartame. This substance has a very different molecular structure from sugar. Splenda, another "artificial sweetener" uses sucralose (not sucrose, which is a "natural" sugar). Sucralose is made by taking sucrose, removing three hydroxide (OH) groups, and adding three chlorine atoms. Splenda uses the slogan: "Made from sugar, so it tastes like sugar." They claimed to be "natural" and implied that Equal is "artificial." Splenda was sued by Equal for misleading advertisements (cf. Hoffmann, 2007).

So what is "natural" and what is "artificial"? Small changes to a molecule can lead to big differences in how the molecule is used by the body. Just because two molecules look similar when diagrammed doesn't mean they'll behave similarly at all. Should we use the form of a molecule or its constituent atoms or its effects?

This issue raises the question of what defines "natural." In a sense, almost none of our foods are really "natural" in that they all have to be harvested and processed to some extent. Even if you wash a piece of fruit or let it ripen on the tree, you've intervened to change it in some way. How much change, how much intervention, makes something "unnatural"?

Second, this case points us to the preference we give to the concept of "natural." Why is that exactly? Dirt is natural. So are germs, cancer, feces, and HIV. War and fighting might be pretty natural to humans. Chlorine is natural, but we don't want to drink it. Pasteurized milk is certainly not "natural."

Yet, advertisers are confident that saying "no artificial ingredients" is a universal good thing to promote in their products, especially if they also claim their product has "natural goodness."

What words can be used on food packages are regulated, in part, by the U.S. Food and Drug Administration. They have set forth requirements that foods have to meet before they can be labeled "high potency," "good source," "low calorie," "light," "sugar free," and many other terms.

Casey Martin and the Definition of Golf

Another sports example raises a number of definitional issues. The golfer Casey Martin was born with a circulation disability that made his legs fragile and prevented extensive walking. If he were to try to walk the length of a golf course, he'd be at serious risk of breaking his leg. So he used a golf cart instead of walking.

He had a successful college career and won a pro event on the NIKE tour. He wanted to compete at the highest level in PGA events and had the skills to qualify, but the PGA requires that golfers walk. They refused his request for an exemption, and he sued.

The background for his suit is the Americans with Disabilities Act. This law required that "no individual shall be discriminated against on the basis of a disability in the full and equal enjoyment of the . . . privileges . . . of any place of public accommodation." Further the ADA required that people make "reasonable modifications" to public accommodations unless doing so would alter the "fundamental nature" of such accommodations.

The person claiming access must be those who are engaged in "enjoyment, of the goods, services, facilities, privileges, advantages, or accommodations." This sets up a distinction between customers and clients on the one hand who must be accommodated and employees and independent contractors on the other who do not have the same rights.

This case raised a series of definitional arguments.

- What is a "public accommodation"? The law provided a very long list including golf courses.
- Is Mr. Martin, or any golfer competing in a tournament, a "client and customer" of the golf course, or is he more like a performer in a play and the public watching are the clients and customers? So does the law's listing of a golf course really mean those who play for pay at a public course and those who watch pro tournaments rather than the athletes competing?
- Is letting him walk a "reasonable modification" of the rules of golf, or is walking part of the "fundamental nature" of golf? This point got considerable attention by the courts. Martin insisted the essence of the game was making shots, and how you get from shot to shot was irrelevant. The PGA insisted that fatigue is a factor in how the game is to be played at the highest level and brought in Arnold Palmer, Jack Nicklaus, and Ken Venturi to testify to that fact.

- We've presented this as a type-two definitional argument (arguments about categories) but maybe there is a case for casting our focus wider and turning it into an argument about definitions. Is the formulation of the ADA correct? What policy should society have toward inclusion of disabled people at the highest level of competition? That takes the decision out of the courts and puts it in the realm of social policy.

The case also raises the issue of who makes the definitions. One might think that the PGA should be able to set rules for its own game. Does the PGA have to play "fundamental golf"? Suppose the PGA just wants to invent some crazy rules, like making all the golfers wear clown shoes or only use three clubs. Why couldn't they do that? But, on the other hand, suppose the PGA decided on a rule that only white people could play the game—we wouldn't allow them to do that, would we?

The U.S. Supreme Court eventually decided that Martin could use a cart in a 5–4 decision that produced one of Justice Antonin Scalia's legendary forceful dissents.

If you want to study this case in more detail, we recommend you read both the Court's decision—you can find it at 532 U.S. 661 (2001)—and the concluding chapter of *Defining Reality*, by Edward Schiappa (cited at the start of this chapter).

CONCLUSION

Definitional arguments are common and a necessary form of arguing. We need categories to organize and make sense of the world. But we hope you've gained in awareness of how they can be arbitrary or accepted uncritically or how people can hide behind them to disguise what interests are at stake.

SUMMARY OF DEFINITIONAL ARGUMENTS

Description

Seek to support a claim by arguing that a specific thing is part of a more general class. This form of reasoning includes both specific arguments about categories but also more general arguments about how we frame and categorize the world.

Explicit Form

C1: "X is a Y."

G1: [evidence that X meets the criteria for Y]

W1: [what the criteria are that define Y in this context]

Examples that would be typically developed as a definitional argument:

- "Eris is a dwarf planet."
- "He is a murderer."
- "The definition of burglary in present law is unclear and needs to be changed."

Fact Claim	Value Claim	Policy Claim
C: "Competitive dance is a sport." G: [list attributes of a sport, show how competitive dance meets those attributes]	C: "Competitive dancers are as admirable as athletes." G: [because competitive dance meets all the attributes of a sport]	C: "The university should extend financial benefits to competitive dance like other sports." G: [because it meets all the attributes of a sport]

Argumentation Strategy

- Articulate a definition of Y by enumerating the attributes that will define Y.
- Defend why those attributes are relevant in the current context.
- Demonstrate that X has those attributes.

Issues and Aspects

- Disputes over what is the proper definition are sometimes not surfaced.
- Use of words with unacknowledged Pathos appeals.
- Matching a definition to the needs of a particular context.

Study Questions

- What are the three types of definitional arguments?
- What are the issues with using dictionaries to prove definitions?
- What are the issues involved in deciding who can determine a definition?
- Why can there be more than one useful definition of a term?

Argument by Example

INTRODUCTION

Someone wants to prove that CEOs of large companies commonly make over 20 million dollars a year. "Why," they say, "consider that Mr. X got $25 million, and Mr. Y who received $40 million, and Ms. Z who was paid $32 million. You see, CEOs are getting more than 20 million dollars."

The speaker has given three examples and then contended they prove a general statement that "CEOs typically make more than $20 million." This is (an example of) argument by example. Argument by example is presenting a series of specific examples in order to support a general statement.

Argument by example is *inductive reasoning*. A series of particular instances are cited to prove that a generalization is correct. The flow of the argument is from the examples to the generalization.

In terms of the Toulmin model, argument by example looks like this:

C: "The generalization Y is true" *or* "Y is true."

G: "X_1, X_2, X_3 ... X_n are instances when Y is true."

W: "The examples given are true, typical, and sufficient."

What are the standards (the warrant) for the examples (the grounds) that give us justification for a particular claim? We'll explore that in this chapter.

First, we will describe this form of reasoning and then examine its use in both informal everyday situations and the more structured use in statistics. Then we'll be in a position to discuss the ways it can go wrong and to examine some contemporary uses of it.

UNDERSTANDING ARGUMENT BY EXAMPLE

Argument by Example Is Different than Illustrating an Argument with an Example

As you've progressed through your education, teachers and textbooks often presented a model, a theory, or a general description of an idea. This could be a mathematical theorem, a model of a social process, a legal principle, or any number of other concepts. It would be common after that for you to have been given a real-world example of the process in action. You'll see this in popular writing as well.

While this is quite often a good idea, it's not really argument by example. It's using an example to illustrate or explain an argument you are making by other means. If a math textbook describes a formula, it may then work out an example using the formula. But that example doesn't prove the formula; instead, the illustration helps you understand the formula.

Illustrations like this can be very valuable to give some specificity to the argument—it helps take an abstract concept and make it real. Illustrations also can be a way of giving your argument an emotional appeal that the formal theory might lack. That was what we were doing in the chapter on models of argument presentation when we discussed how an introduction to an argument can be used to give an illustration that gives emotional appeal.

However much these illustrations add to your argument, it isn't what we mean by argument by example.

Argument by Example Is Inductive Reasoning

Consider the following:

> "I saw a pig yesterday, and it was pink."
> "I saw a pig a week ago, and it was pink."
> "I saw a pig two weeks ago, and it was pink."

After a while, you would tend to come to the conclusion that pigs were pink. How many pigs would you have to observe before you could decide that the generalization "All pigs are pink" had been proven? Ah, there's the problem.

Inductive reasoning (such as our pig scenario) can establish some probability that our generalization is right, but it is not formal proof. We've not made an airtight case to prove that all pigs are pink. We've not proven that a pig couldn't possibly be some other color. We've not delved into the genetics of pig color, done tests in the lab, and worked out a chain of reasoning that would disprove the existence of nonpink pigs.

If we can prove that we have looked at every single pig in the entire world, and they were all pink, well, then we have proven our case, but then the proof is rather useless. If I've already seen all the pigs, then the generalization doesn't save any work.

The interesting case concerns what fraction of the pigs in the world would I have to observe (5 percent? 30 percent?) before I can, with some degree of confidence, extrapolate to my generalization about all pigs. And this brings us back, as we so often do, to the question of qualifying your claim.

What Claims Can Your Examples Support?

Suppose your claim is of the following form:

C1: "Y is always true."

This would be like our claim above: "All pigs are pink." In this case, only one single counterexample, just one white-and-black pig can do us in. As long as we've failed to examine every single pig, we could be at risk of this claim being false. Consider another claim:

C2: "Y is true most of the time."

In this case ("Most pigs are pink") we can probably feel confident about this generality if we've looked at "a lot" of examples, but not all of them. If we've looked at 50 percent of the pigs in the world and over 90 percent of them were pink, then we've got a good chance to persuade you about the rest—and save you the trouble of looking.

The subject of just how many pigs you'll have to look at, but also the question of how you can estimate a number for "most of the pigs" (60 percent of them? 90 percent?) is the aim of statistics, and we'll come back to that topic later in the chapter.

Consider another claim:

C3: "Y can be true."

In this case, you really only need one example to support it. It's the flip side of C1. See one pink pig, and you can prove that pigs can be pink. This can be interesting if someone maintains that "Y can't be true" or that "Y has never happened." But most of the time, they will simply reframe their claim to "most" or "almost always."

C4: "Y is unusual, but does occur."

This is likely what someone who says C3 actually might mean: Y is true some small fraction of the time. It might be rare, but it does happen. So, just what do you need to prove this ambiguous claim? That could be contentious. A few examples are needed, some assessment of the frequency of occurrence. Perhaps some good statistics.

A second situation In practical terms, argument by example can get used in a different way. Sometimes we have a case, a situation in front of us. We want to apply a generalization to that situation, but then, the argument moves into a discussion of the generalization.

A new movie has come out. It features an older male star and a much younger female star as the love interest. You offer the generalization that Hollywood is constantly doing this. So, now you have two claims. First, that this movie at hand fits a generalization, and then second, that the generalization is valid. In the course of a discussion, both claims would get debated. To prove the generalization, you'd offer examples of other movies that had the same situation. If the two stars were not that far apart in age, you'd have to defend that the current movie fit the generalization. But you'd still have debate about the validity of the generalization, and that is what makes this an argument by example.

In a later chapter we'll discuss argument by parallel case. In that situation, you will be comparing two movies to each other and not defending a generalization. That is a different form of argument.

INFORMAL REASONING BY EXAMPLE

In this section, we will discuss the way argument by example is used in day-to-day conversation. In the next section we'll discuss more rigorous uses of argument by example.

Defending our generalization depends on the examples we give. A great deal turns on the specifics of those examples.

Providing Sufficient Examples

The fallacy of "hasty generalization" The fallacy of "hasty generalization" is one where you move too quickly from a limited number of examples to a generalization. This has a number of aspects to it.

Are three examples enough? In many situations, we do things in threes. A lot of stories and humor involve three instances with the third one supplying the punch line. When it comes to proof, one example is clearly not enough, two sounds like a small amount, but by the time we get to three we seem to be ready to be convinced.

Of course, three examples are hardly enough to prove any really useful generalization. But you might be alert to situations where providing three significant examples seems to provide persuasion.

If someone wanted to convince you that we had a problem with bridges collapsing in the United States, and they gave you three significant examples of bridge failures in recent times, you could well think that we had a serious problem. Or if someone could give you three instances of high school students killing fellow students, that sounds like a problem with teen violence.

What is happening here is that the examples are of shocking things, things we think should not occur at all. So we're willing to conclude that three examples proves that this rare thing isn't as rare as we hoped.

But do three bridge collapses in the entire country in the past year mean there is a likelihood that you will be killed by driving over a bridge when it collapses? No, that—quite different—generalization "You have a significant risk of being killed by a collapsing bridge" is not proven by three examples. But we might assume it was proven.

We bring this up so you can start to be a bit wary of this situation. Three examples, in many cases, should not be considered enough to prove a generalization. Let's look at this a little more closely.

Examples Are Typical but So Are Counterexamples

Suppose someone wishes to prove that college students are degenerate and lacking in maturity. Forget three examples! They give you five or six or seven examples of wild frat parties, plagiarism, binge drinking, dishonesty in relationships, and more. Maybe they add to that with some statistic about how there were hundreds of similar examples across the country. Sounds bad.

Now suppose someone wishes to prove that college students are wonderful, moral, self-sacrificing people with a commitment to social service. So they provide five, six, or seven examples of service projects, organ donors, community activists, students working their way through college, prize winners, and the like. And they back it up with a statistic about hundreds of other examples. Sounds better.

The issue here is that in any given year in the United States about twenty million people are enrolled in colleges and universities. So it isn't surprising that there are hundreds of examples of bad behavior and hundreds of examples of good behavior. Five examples or 105 cannot prove any generalization about "what the typical college student" does.

The same problem happens when someone wants to prove that there are "too many frivolous lawsuits" or "an epidemic of teenage runaways." Be suspicious about a few examples being offered when the population of potential examples is very large.

Examples Confirming a Suspicion

In many cases we're not really coming to the situation without any preconceived ideas. We've heard of shootings at high schools, but we've not kept track of how many they are. So when we hear three recent examples, we add that to our preconceptions in our heads and conclude that there is a real problem.

Sometimes, it seems the example is offered more to remind us about a generalization we believe but have not thought about recently, as opposed to proving something we've not thought about.

Implications for Your Arguments

In many instances, a few examples just cannot prove the generalization—but, as we indicated, a few examples are often taken as proof. The real fix for this situation is statistics, not more individual examples. But in informal argument by example, you may not have ready access to statistics.

Being responsible about arguing means that you should give some attention to the size of the population you are drawing your examples from—for example, how many college students there are if you are trying to generalize about college students.

And if you are on the receiving end of an informal argument by example, you may counter someone else's argument by pointing out that a few examples a trend does not make.

Providing Representative Examples

We not only have to provide enough examples, we have to provide examples that are typical.

Atypical examples Before everyone knew about the dangers of smoking and lung cancer, sometimes someone would object to the link between the two. "Why, my uncle smoked like a chimney," they'd say, "and he lived to be a hundred." We are happy you had your uncle around for so long. But, one example can't refute a thousand in the other direction.

Think again about the types of claims we were discussing above. One example might disprove the claim "Everyone who smokes gets lung cancer," but no one was claiming that. One example cannot disprove the claim "People who smoke have a significant risk of getting lung cancer."

Misled by a vivid example Vivid, shocking, or extreme examples are particularly prone to mislead us. Periodically an illegal immigrant to the United States murders someone. "Proof," we hear, "that those people are criminals!" But there are roughly eighteen thousand murders a year in the United States. If there are roughly twelve million illegal immigrants in our population of over three hundred million, and if they murdered people at the same rate as our citizens, then illegal immigrants would be killing about six hundred people a year. One or two examples doesn't prove a generalization that "Illegal immigrants are all murderers" or that they are "worse criminals than citizens."

A Muslim man walks into a medical facility on an army base and starts shooting, killing thirteen people. This is a horrible crime and a clear example of terrorism. But does it prove that "Muslims are terrorists" when there are, perhaps, five million Muslims in the United States? It is such a shocking and extreme example that we get worried about that. But it is one person out of five million.

These are isolated events, but we, paradoxically, live in a media environment that is typically made up of the depiction of extreme events. The media rapidly focuses on and gives ample publicity to the extreme. "If it bleeds, it leads" has been a description of local television news coverage for some time. Murders, fires, crime in general, bad celebrity behavior, sex scandals, weird behavior, corporate failures, pets doing odd things, rants, and similar extreme events make up a significant part of media coverage.

Nor is this extreme focus limited to nonfiction reporting. Our dramas contain a rate of murders, adultery, deaths, fights, betrayal, crimes, unusual diseases, zombies, drug use, and superheroes that would drive any actual person mad who had to live through it.

Well, this is hardly unexpected: No one is going to watch a news show that reports that most people went to work today and quite a few ate dinner at home, watched television, and then went to bed, perhaps with someone they're actually married to.

But the point is that we absorb this "commonality of the extreme," think that it is typical, and thus do not have a good mental picture of what really is typical and what is unusual.

Misled by the first example You come onto your college campus for the first time. You encounter a maintenance worker who is rude to you, yells at you for some silly fault. You may well conclude that all maintenance workers at that campus are rude. You then avoid them in the future, so you never encounter any who are nice, helpful, or just interesting. Your generalization survives for years.

The first example we encounter of some class of experience may unduly shape our response to subsequent experiences. It gets worse if we modify our behavior based on the first. So since that first worker was rude to us, we start snapping at the next ones we meet, being short with them, avoiding them. And, surprise, we get negative responses back, thus confirming our first example.

Selecting examples that agree with our preconceptions We buy a car. It wasn't what we started looking for, but we liked it, and we bought it. We'd never thought about that model of car before, never noticed it as we drove around. But now? We see that model of car all the time. It seems to be everywhere.

The point is that we are not simply blank, impartial, recording devices for what we encounter. We are filtering our experience all the time. By the time we reach adulthood we have already accumulated a whole series of generalizations that guide our interpretation of events. We see more vividly those examples that confirm our generalizations; we tend to downplay those that contradict them.

So, if we are a member of a group, we'll notice stories and incidents that support how great that group is. We'll remember the instances that confirm our beliefs; we'll tend to ignore the examples that don't.

We have to be aware of this tendency. It comes out when we actively start arguing for a generalization. We have to monitor our tendency to assert those generalizations and work to find actual examples that will really support them.

EXAMPLES AND GENERALIZATIONS

What Does This Support?

We've been implying so far that experiences plug into generalizations in some sort of unambiguous way. But the truth is that any given experience can be used to support a range of generalizations. Consider the example of an illegal immigrant murdering a citizen. Consider how that example could support a whole range of generalizations:

- "Illegal immigrants are criminals."
- "Illegal immigrants are desperate."
- "Citizens need to be more careful about who they associate with."
- "Officials in the city (or the state or county) where that took place are clueless."
- "We need to secure the border."
- "You need to vote for people who will secure the border."

- "We need better gun control."
- "Illegal immigrants have no way of supporting themselves and so turn to crime."
- "Drugs lead you to crime." ("Drugs" could be replaced by "alcohol" or "not being religious" or any other detail that was part of the story.)

And the specific details of that crime could lead to another list, equal in length, of generalizations that could be taken from a specific example.

This comes into play when we are going to give our examples. Perhaps, if we haven't chosen wisely, our examples could support some entirely different generalization than the one we want. Someone wants to prove that we are being way too hard on celebrities who just want to have fun. So they cite someone who has failed rehab that we are making fun of, someone who got busted for having too many painkillers that the media is hounding, and someone who ran their car into a tree that is now the butt of jokes on the late-night shows. Hey, the person says, they didn't harm anyone but themselves and we need to ease up.

But the first example was arrested for driving drunk, the second stole money intended for their children, and the third has had three accidents and just missed hitting someone. So maybe those examples might prove that celebrities are out of control.

What Comes First?

The order that you present your examples can also be a significant factor in how persuasive they are. Your examples are not likely to all be equally strong or equally clear. It's probably best not to start with the weakest of your examples or with the one that could point to several different generalizations. On the other hand, it also might not be best to have your examples get progressively weaker as you go on.

It's hard to give definitive advice given all the options, but a good example to start with would be one that is very clear, doesn't have a lot of ambiguous features to it, and serves to start your readers going in the direction you want them to.

What Should You Include?

"An example" is not just sitting there in a nice box for you to take out and plug into your writing. What details will you include about the example? How much description will you include? Which details are key, which irrelevant, and which might actually undermine the point.

It should go without saying that if you omit some crucial detail that your persuasiveness is greatly undermined when that comes out. A weight loss commercial featured a fairly well-known fitness competitor bragging that she'd lost twenty-five pounds on the supplement being promoted. She had lost that weight it was true—because she was pregnant and had given birth during the period being described. A pretty important detail that totally changed the value of this example.

Think about what details will confirm that this is an example of the generalization you seek to prove. Think about how those who disagree with you may seek to discredit the example, and perhaps you can preempt such criticism.

STATISTICS: FORMAL ARGUMENT BY EXAMPLE

Up to now, we've been discussing how argument by example is used in day-to-day life, in short arguments, and typical speeches. But there is a methodology of being systematic about collecting examples and deciding what generalizations can be supported; that is the field of statistics.

What is the difference between statistical analysis and the informal process we've been discussing up to now? Statistics imposes rules for how examples are collected and a mathematical process for deciding what generalizations ("hypothesis") can be supported.

"Anecdotal Evidence"

Our informal, haphazard collection of examples that we do in ordinary life is a collection of anecdotes, individual stories.

In the statistical world, that unsystematic gathering of data is referred to as *anecdotal evidence*. This is not a compliment. In fact, the phrase is usually used to dismiss an example as useless. Nor is the scientific world impressed by a group of informally collected examples. "The plural of anecdote is not evidence" is another common phrase.

There are two problems with informal collections of anecdotes. First, they were probably not carefully documented. They can't be verified or the specifics about them cannot be examined. As a result, they are probably not all from the same set of circumstances. And then, we can't be sure that they are a fair selection of events. If you have ten examples and eight have some characteristic and two don't, you can't conclude anything from that because you're not sure (or can't prove) that the examples are representative of the entire population.

There are some things you can use an informal collection of examples for, and in a subsequent section, we'll take another look at what we can prove from these anecdotes.

Polling, Sampling, and Systematic Data Collection

Suppose we do want to know what people really think or how many examples of bad or good student behavior there are. We have two options. We can do a carefully constructed survey, or we can search published literature for previously collected data.

Polls and opinion surveys are a staple of our modern life. Even local elections seem to have several polls apiece. Reputable agencies that conduct polls are careful to ensure that everyone has an equal chance of participation. If they are calling to get your opinion, then they have to ensure that people who only have cell phones and no landline are equally likely to be included. They are concerned that various subgroups—such as age ranges, gender, ethnic groups, geographic location, or income—all have an equal chance to be surveyed.

Reputable polling agencies also pay close attention to how they ask questions so that they are neutral. If they have to give you a list of names to pick from, for example, they will likely rotate the list so no one gets an advantage by being first or last.

When these and other conditions are met, it really is the case that a sample of a few hundred can predict the views of a much larger group. Statistics classes will show you how the math works, but by making some reasonable assumptions (which most researchers accept), if you sampled four hundred people out of the United States (and did so with the scrupulous standards we've described above), you could be 95 percent confident that the results you received were within plus or minus 5 percent of the true value. Should you want to be 95 percent confident that the results were within plus or minus 2.5 percent, you'd need to sample about fifteen hundred people.

This conclusion is not simply a mathematical theory. It has been tested in real-world applications and found to be valid.

Surveys are not always done with such care. One of the authors worked for a company that had a major tech support operation. They regularly surveyed their customers and reported very high rates of satisfaction with tech support—a result the author found hard to believe from observing the operation directly. Eventually it was discovered that surveys were not sent out to all customers who had called in. If the customer was very angry or the call had become a shouting match, no survey was sent. The director of tech support defended this practice—"They're angry!, They're not going to give us an unbiased view." So the results of this poll were not accurate because they "undersampled" those who thought the tech support operation was not very good.

While in this case the error was innocent and not intentionally deceptive, in some cases deliberate deception is intended. The practice of "push polling" presents responders with a very unequal set of choices to push the result in a desired direction. So people asked about a competitor's product might be asked "Would you buy a product that has not been endorsed by any major organization?" in the hopes of pushing the answers. One of the authors got a survey in the mail from an agency of the Democratic Party that had this question in it:

> "Do you believe that congressional Republicans will seek to obstruct further progress by gumming up the gears of government as they did after the 1994 elections?"

This would be funny if people didn't try to use the conclusions of such polling for serious purposes.

The care needed to get good answers is why online polls that you can volunteer to take are generally worthless. Even if a lot of people respond, you don't know who answered and if they are representative of the entire population.

Some of the questions we were considering in the previous section do not admit to easy polling of people. We can't ask a sample of bridges if they've fallen down or ask people if they have committed a terrorist act.

We can, however, perform a careful search of published data and attempt to show that our data is comprehensive. We could look at a database of newspaper articles for stories about bridges collapsing. We could see if state transportation departments have annual reports with records of failure. We could find academics who collect this sort of data. We could take all that data, correlate it, and come up with a list of bridge failures that we could plausibly argue was comprehensive. Then, we could go back to the transportation departments for a record of how many bridges there are in total.

If we did all that work, we could, with some degree of confidence, state a number of generalizations about bridge failures. But how exactly could we decide just how confident we were? That is the realm of *hypothesis testing*.

Testing Hypothesis

A hypothesis is a claim, a generalization. We want to test our claims against the data and be able to state if the hypothesis has been confirmed or not. In a statistics class you'll spend a good deal of time sorting through what you can and cannot claim.

But there will always be some degree of uncertainty about our claims. We've mentioned several times in this book that you must make decisions with imperfect information and without perfect certainty. In certain statistical questions, we can put numbers to that uncertainty. So, in our bridge example, a researcher might conclude something like "We predict that over the next five years we have a 95 percent confidence that there will be between three and six failures of bridges of a certain type" (as usual, we just made up those numbers). So by doing the proper math, the author is giving you a prediction of a range of possibilities and telling you how likely it is that reality will wind up being between that range.

When polls are reported now, it is common to hear that "The results have a margin of error of plus or minus 2 percent" or some similar formula. This is another way of saying that there is a very high degree of confidence (often 95 percent) that the actual results are within that range.

While statistics are based on a mathematical foundation that is widely shared among researchers, this is nonetheless based on a set of assumptions that may not be correct in all circumstances. As always you should probe back into how surveys were done.

Between Anecdote and Statistics: How You Can Use Examples You Collected

You can become good consumers of statistics and adept at detecting weak conclusions. But, you are still going to be doing informal arguments by example. Can you make them more reliable by using or collecting a limited amount of data? Yes.

Your campus is about to build a new sports stadium. You suspect students don't care, or you hope they don't. Can you prove that? You've had a few conversations, and you know what a few of your friends think. In fact, you know that four friends don't want the new stadium, but one does. Can you use that to claim the student body opposes the stadium?

No, there are some problems here. Your friends are not a random sample. If you oppose the stadium, you may well move in a subgroup of students that are more likely to be opposed.

Okay, well, you decide to stand outside the student union or whatever building contains student groups and ask people. You stand there for twenty minutes on a Tuesday and get five more views. But what about students on MWF class schedules? Or who commute and don't eat at the cafeteria? Well, is there a reason that they might think differently? If you'd stood outside the sports complex and asked athletes on their way out, well, that is not a fair sample of the entire student body any more than you'd get by standing outside the offices of the Communist student group, assuming you still have one.

But suppose you wander around the campus over a couple of days and collect twenty-five more opinions to add to the five you had. Let's consider two cases. In one case our vote is now 20 to 5 either in favor or opposed. In the other case it is 14 to 11 for one side.

You can argue that you've made some effort to give students of different groups a shot at answering. In the 20 to 5 case, you can say that there is some degree of confidence that students strongly come down on one side or the other. But you can't use the 14 to 11 case as anything other than evidence that students are likely divided on the issue. That's just too close, and your methods were not careful enough to make a claim about what the majority thinks.

In other words, such informal gathering of views can give you a general idea. But you have to be careful not to go too far with it and only draw the most general of conclusions.

HOW ARGUMENT BY EXAMPLE CAN GO WRONG

Examples Are False

It should go without saying that your examples actually have to be true. We've devoted our attention to discussing whether or not valid examples would support a particular conclusion. But your examples have to be true or at least not actively misleading. Remember the weight loss example earlier when the person had been pregnant? That was an example so misleading as to be deceptive. Ronald Reagan used a story about a "welfare queen" who had bilked the government out of a vast sum of money. The real story was a minor case of fraud that the government had detected and caught.

A British newsmagazine (Parris, 2010, p. 27) told a story about how a train had hit a cow and how it took three hours before the proper permissions from the various agencies could be found to simply shove the cow down the embankment and proceed. The writer was gearing up to write an outraged article about this, yet another example of how political correctness and absurd "safety at all cost" bureaucratic procedures had fouled up our lives. The writer then told, with mock sadness, of how his imagined column fell apart when he got the event log from the railroad and discovered that it took time to find someone to put the badly wounded cow down, more time to find someone who was willing to dispose of the cow and with the gear to move the heavy animal, time to inspect the train for damage, and time to inspect the rail-line side fences for holes that might have admitted other cows. In the end, he discovered that everyone was working like mad to restore service, and there was nothing amiss.

Within any group of people, stories will circulate about this person or that, about the boss of a company, about the people in the next department over. We have a tendency to exaggerate stories and to fill in the blanks with things that fit our preconceptions.

Examples Are Not Congruent with the Generalization

A student was writing a paper about how great his fraternity was. To prove that generalization he offered a series of examples of famous people who had been members of his frat nationally over the past decades. It was, in fact, a very impressive list of people.

But it doesn't prove the frat is great. It might prove his frat recruits great people; it might prove that you should join his frat to meet the future greats. But unless those people became great *because* of the frat, it doesn't really prove his claim.

Examples Are Not Independent

You hold a focus group to discuss a new movie, and the group votes unanimously that this is a bad movie. But, when you watch the tape of the group it turns out there was one very loud, very dominating person who hated the movie, and it appears that everyone else just went along to avoid an argument.

If you get twenty examples, but ten actually are the result of one action, then your examples are not really independent, and you have less evidence than you think.

Examples Are Not Really Similar or the Underlying Situation Has Evolved

You've gone on four job interviews without success; you conclude that you'll never get a job, you're always going to fail. But, on the first interview you discovered your resume had some holes in it, and you revised it prior to your second interview. On the second interview you realized you needed different clothes, and you bought them for the third interview. On the third interview you realized you were being too passive and resolved to come in with some questions to ask, even some tough questions that you tried out on the fourth interview and realized you needed to dial it down a bit before you went out again.

In other words, you're learning each time, getting better at interviewing, and the generalization "I'll never get a job" is not supported by these examples of rejection because the "I" who is interviewing is not the person who went out on the first interview.

CONTEMPORARY ISSUES

Recent movements that increase our awareness and concern about respecting all groups of people raise issues about argument by example.

Pattern Recognition and Racism

You buy a car, and it turns out to be a lemon. Your friend bought the same brand of car, and it was also unsatisfactory. That's probably all the information you need to decide that this brand of car is bad, and no magazine review of car quality is likely to change your mind. You buy one product at a store and find out later it was more expensive than in another store. It happens again. You decide that store is too expensive and never buy there again.

A lot of human learning comes from recognizing patterns and responding to them. Coaches scouting the opposition are looking for tendencies—patterns. People attracted to another group are looking for clues that identify which members of the other group are nice or interested.

But what about patterns with people? Generalizations about groups of people are more contentious and fraught with larger consequences than other such patterns. Views that this group are druggies, that group is terrorists, that other group just wants sex, this group is responsible for the violence in the world, that group is lazy, this group will be criminals—it goes on and on.

Why are these patterns different than the patterns we use and rely on all the time?

Well, first of all, the patterns may be false. That's one thing to keep in mind. We may be engaged in projecting fears or poorly understood situations onto a group that is just feared because it is different, "the other" who we just don't deal with every day.

Second, the pattern may be just not very descriptive of the group. More than one commentator has said something like "All terrorists are Muslim, but not all Muslims are terrorists." It would have at least approached accuracy if they would say "More than half the terrorists are Muslim, but less than 0.0001 percent of U.S. Muslims are terrorists." That's not quite as snappy a saying, but it does point out that the generalization of terrorism and Muslims, while capturing one aspect of reality ignores a larger reality of the vast majority of that group.

And then, there is a third issue, which is probably the nub of the problem in regard to stereotypes. Let's look at an example a little closer to home. A teacher is asked for an extension on a deadline due to a story the student tells them, but the story is discovered to be false. It happens again, and so the teacher announces to subsequent classes that, from now on, no excuses will ever be accepted. The teacher complains to other teachers about the untruthful habits of students. Other teachers chime in with similar stories. So, the generalization seems to be supported: "Students are prone to offer invalid excuses." Why exactly is this going to be considered unfair—and not just by students?

We have a fairly strong value that people should be judged as individuals and not as groups. We don't think groups should be punished for the behavior of individual members of the group. But, we also violate that value regularly, but almost always for people in groups we don't belong to. Our group should be judged as individuals, but "those people" are responsible for their disreputable members.

One way of looking at racism is that it is a judging of individuals not on their own behavior but on that of the group. Even if 50 percent of the members of group X are criminals, we should allow the next member of group X we encounter to be who they are—and not assume they are a problem.

While this is an ideal, in many practical cases we just don't have the time or want to run the risk. There are plenty of real-world situations when this ideal of individual judgment runs into practical problems. A ninety-five-pound woman knows that most men are not rapists, but should she walk down a dark, empty street with a two-hundred-pound man she doesn't know? Her hesitation is not totally irrational, even if it is very annoying to men who would never harm a woman.

Of course, let's be clear: Much racism is not generated by arguments by example gone wrong, however it may be expressed that way. Racism, ethnic hatreds, and misogyny have other roots that go well beyond issues of argument structure. But they are expressed in arguments, and so we are commenting on that.

G. W. Allport (1979) wrote of these issues: "a differentiated category is the opposite of a stereotype." He was pointing to one way beyond stereotyping examples without attempting to deny verifiable facts. A stereotype is of the form "All of them do that" or "Those people are like that." A differentiated category is one when you understand that some activity may be done by some members of a group, but you are aware that others do not do it, some may do it all the time, others only once in a while.

This situation is also an example of the *part for the whole* fallacy. Men are taller than women; that is a valid generalization. But not every man is taller than every woman, and if a particular man complains about how woman are taller than he is, you can't "refute" his experience by referring to the generalization.

Collection and Use of Personal Testimony

Over the last forty or fifty years we have increased our awareness that certain groups were not part of the collective conversation or at least not in the same way as others. Certain voices are not heard as oftens. The list of such overlooked voices typically includes the poor, women, disabled, homosexuals, and various ethnic groupings. In some cases who is being overlooked is specific to a situation such as children and how schools are working, entry-level employees of a large corporation, people who've lost their houses to banks, and so on. What all these groups typically share is that they, on the average, have less power and thus less ability to be heard.

There are now more efforts to pay attention to obtaining the views of such groups. Critically, one can hear calls to privilege individual testimony of members of a group over views of people who are not in the group. This issue involves many argumentation issues but we are going to focus on one aspect here. What can you learn by collecting and analyzing a series of personal testimonies?

You decide to collect the experiences of women in graduate school, blacks working for a white boss, sergeants in the armed forces, or another similar under-surveyed group. You sift their stories and look for trends. You sum up their answers. What can you conclude from this data?

First, let's say that such first-person testimony from those otherwise ignored is a valuable thing to have. How wonderful it would be if we had transcripts of interviews with slaves in Rome, peasant farmers in Russia on the brink of the revolution, homosexual priests in the Middle Ages, cleaning women in Victorian Britain, slaves in the American south, Native Americans at the time Europeans first came to their country, prostitutes from the American frontier west, peasants displaced by Stalin, or any one of hundreds of other groups who generally don't leave behind books and sets of papers and letters. It would make our histories much richer, fairer, and more accurate.

But it seems with every change comes the risk of an overreaction. And so, just because some group has been ignored and is oppressed does not require us to treat them as infallible observers. They can be self-interested like others can. They also live and form opinions based on one perspective and have limited access to the reality of different lives. In this they are similar to others.

In other words, we are reacting against the notion of the *infallibility of the oppressed*, while defending the necessity of listening carefully to the oppressed. As we've said time and time again here: You have to check.

It may help to sort out these issues if we imagine that you collect the testimony of thirty people concerning an event they experienced. Twenty tell you that "X happened" and ten say it didn't. Consider a number of possible generalizations you could make:

C1: "A majority of this group believe that X is true."

Your data does support this claim, assuming you've done a good job of designing your survey.

C2: "X is true."

Here is where problems can start. Logically, this claim also requires, in addition to your collected data, a judgment that the people in this group are reliable observers, will tell the truth, and are in a position to know the truth. Our political viewpoints are likely to strongly influence our views of who is telling the truth.

C3: "About a third of this group is in denial about what happened."

In this case you not only need other evidence to prove that X is true, you are also making assumptions about the reasons for why some people answered as they did.

When you are collecting data about discrimination, injustice, sexual misconduct, economic pressure, racism, and similar strongly felt issues, it can affect us as observers. In the case of C2 and C3, we may be right, but the tendency (on both sides) is to assume.

Consider a second issue. What types of data could you collect from a group of people? It might include the following:

- Narratives of what happened
- Descriptions of what others told them
- Statements attributing motives to others
- Giving general conclusions about this type of situation

The reliability of these types of evidence can vary significantly. Someone may be very accurate about what happened to them, mostly accurate about what people told them, very inaccurate about the motives of others, and clueless about the larger issues of a social system. And it is worth remembering that there has been plenty of research to show that eyewitness testimony can be very inaccurate. People can know what happened to them, but not why it happened. And people who are not listened to have a habit of escalating their rhetoric as they get frustrated by not being heard.

These issues are brought sharply into focus when we consider interactions of a disadvantaged group with those who have an advantage, and we are asking both sides to comment on that interaction. If we used to always assume the oppressed group was wrong, now we can assume (for certain categories of groups) that the oppressed group is always right.

So, once again an example. Group E runs things, group G is suffering from it. A spokesperson for group E says "There are no problems here." You survey G and find that:

C1: "75 percent of group G has a story of being treated unjustly by someone from group E."

That same spokesperson for Group E says, "But those people are just trying to excuse their failures. We've never seen these problems." Who do you believe?

It is a huge mistake to form your conclusions of such interactions without listening carefully to members of the powerless group—and that mistake has often been made and continues to be made. But while you'd take seriously what people from that group say, it is also a mistake to take it uncritically.

The president of a company will often feed you a long series of illusions about how marvelous their company and leadership are, illusions the janitor can puncture readily. But the janitor does not see the competitive environment, what financing issues there are, and is likely to value fully funding janitorial services above product development.

Once again, as we have said before, we're not telling you who is right and who is wrong. We're reminding you that our emotions can affect our willingness to probe for the truth and that you should always ask questions and check.

Another Look at Stories and Narratives

We argued before that anecdotes are not evidence. But, there is also a concern with the value of *narratives*, individual stories. Are we claiming they are really useless in contrast to data? We need to distinguish some cases. Suppose you hear a story about how Mr. X did something terrible to a subordinate. And let's assume this story is quite likely to be true; it's not just a rumor or something thirdhand. And now consider two claims:

C1: "Mr. X is a bad person."
C2: "Mr. X did something terrible."

The story supports C2; that much is apparent. Does it prove C1? That depends on a warrant: Does one bad thing prove a person is bad? That's the issue we raised before: Can one example prove a generalization? The issue is that C1 sounds a lot like this:

C3: "Mr. X does bad things all the time."

One story can't prove C3. But if the one incident is bad enough, it could prove C1. But we confuse C1 with C3 sometimes.

Also, we assumed this story was true or quite likely to be true. Another reason people are suspicious about single stories is that they are often not exactly true. Words have been changed, context dropped, and the intensity of an action increased in the retelling. Part of the suspicion about anecdotes is not about the validity of personal experience, nor any fear of emotion, but just caution about how stories get changed as they get retold.

FAMOUS ARGUMENTS BY EXAMPLE

Al Gore and *An Inconvenient Truth*

An Inconvenient Truth is a documentary film, released in 2006, that was based on a presentation that Al Gore had been making for some years. He argued that climate change was real and was caused by human action. There is a variety of evidence presented in the movie, but probably the evidence that people may most remember are the "before and after" pictures of glaciers.

A series of photos are shown that present dramatic images of how glaciers have retreated. They are a series of examples that, in the minds of watchers, support a generalization that "The climate is getting warmer." Many found this a compelling proof.

This illustrates the difficulties of such arguments. There are a lot of glaciers in the world, thousands in fact. Is it possible that Mr. Gore just picked a few that supported his argument? He didn't, but it is perfectly legitimate to ask the question and to look for a more comprehensive set of statistics about the status of glaciers all over the world. In a movie he couldn't present a photo from even half of the world's glaciers. Further, there are some glaciers that seem to be stable and some that are expanding. Does that prove Gore is wrong? No, not if a majority of glaciers are retreating.

Glaciers advance and retreat for a number of reasons, not just because of climate changes. So a full analysis would have to involve looking at various mechanisms that affect glaciers and trying to estimate their relative effects. Of course, glacier scientists have been doing that for years.

Those who monitor glaciers agree that there is a significant, worldwide shrinkage of glaciers.[1]

The 1948 U.S. Presidential Election and Election Polling

One well-known failure of a formal argument by example was the 1948 presidential race between Truman (the Democratic candidate) and Dewey (the Republican candidate). Dewey was widely predicted to be the winner, but he lost. A premature newspaper headline, held aloft by the gleeful Truman, resulted in an iconic image. What happened?

In the run-up to the election, opinion polls were showing a lead for Dewey of 5 percent or more. Apparently, polling agencies, less driven by the 24-hour news cycle than they are now, simply stopped polling too soon. They also had not been

---

[1] "Global Glacier Changes: Facts and Figures," World Glacier Monitoring Service, www.grid.unep.ch/glaciers.

as careful as they should have been about keeping their data collection fully random so that every voter in the United States had an equal chance of being polled. The newspaper headline resulted from a strike that required the paper to go to press earlier than it might have otherwise done. If they'd been able to wait just a few hours more, the true results would have been obvious.

There have been other failures and disputes about polling. One of the most spectacular was in 1936 when the magazine *Literary Digest* predicted that the Republican candidate, Alf Landon, would be an easy winner over then-President Roosevelt. Since that poll was based on over two million responses, it seemed pretty likely to be accurate. What happened of course was a lopsided election—for Roosevelt won forty-six of the forty-eight states in one of the biggest landslides in presidential election history. How could a poll of two million people be so wrong?

Sampling. The magazine polled its own readers, those who owned automobiles, and those with telephones. And in 1936, and especially due to the depression, those lists were all heavily weighted toward those with money. Poor people vote differently than rich people and that was the difference.

Polling disputes have not gone away. In 1982 the California gubernatorial race was between Los Angeles mayor Tom Bradley (a black man) and California Attorney General George Deukmejian (a white man). Bradley was ahead in the polls for most of the race, but lost narrowly. The "Bradley effect" was a hypothesis that argued that some white voters who would not want to be seen as racist would tell pollsters they favored the black candidate but would actually vote for the white one. Whether or not this actually occurred in the 1982 race, or has occurred since, is controversial. However small the impact might be, the term is regularly used in media accounts (Payne, 2010).

The U.S. Declaration of Independence

People sometimes remember how the declaration begins: "When in the course of human events …" or the famous, and still thought-provoking, "life, liberty and the pursuit of happiness." But few read farther along to notice the catalog of examples given there of the injustices King George inflicted on the colonies.

It's a long list, and according to one serious historian of the declaration, not everyone then or now is exactly sure what specific incident all of the examples refer to (Maier, 1997). However, they were widely accepted at the time and provided a powerful rebuttal to those who suggested that the colonies had nothing to complain about.

A Generalization Proven by an Exception?

Consider this quotation:

> Creatures are not born with desires unless satisfaction for those desires exists. A baby feels hunger. Well, there is such a thing as food. A duckling wants to swim: well, there is such a thing as water. Men feel sexual desire: well, there is such a thing as sex. If I find in myself a desire which no experience in the world can satisfy, the most probable explanation is that I was made for another world. If none of my earthly pleasures satisfy it, that does not prove that the universe is a fraud. (Lewis, 2001, p. 106)

This is a fascinating example of an argument by example. Fascinating from an argumentation perspective at least. Lewis has observed a regularity with one exception. His generalization is that "means of satisfying desires always exist." He cites three examples. He points out that there is at least one, and maybe other, desires that cannot be met. Rather than that undermining his generalization, he argues that it proves we haven't inspected the data closely enough and that there really are means of satisfying those other desires.

To some, this will sound like just bad argumentation. What he's really proven, they'd say, is that his generalization is false.

On the other hand, consider what happens when scientists observe some generalization, one that has a lot of examples to prove it so, but then they observe an exception to the generalization. It isn't uncommon then for scientists to temporarily put aside their views on the generalization and look more closely at the exception. Perhaps our data is incomplete or we're mistaken.

So, it's not absurd for someone to wonder about a desire that seems to be deep-rooted but without a means of satisfying it. Our desires to go on living, to have our work remembered, our "ache for transcendence" (as one theologian put it), or feeling that there must be more, that the universe must have a larger purpose than we can see—these can't be dismissed out of hand.

What Lewis's example really suggests, in terms of argument by example, is that *anomalies are worth investigating*. If you have a generalization with an odd exception, studying the exception and thinking more carefully about the form of the generalization may be the precise place where you can advance your understanding of an issue. You may come up with a more precise generalization or realize that your generalization was misleading.

CONCLUSION

Argument by example has long roots in our culture. Despite it being unable to provide a formal proof for our views, it is often all we have. Thinking about the way this form of reasoning is used in careful statistical analysis can be a good starting point to help us make our informal uses of it more rigorous.

SUMMARY OF ARGUMENT BY EXAMPLE

Description

A series of particular instances are cited to prove that a generalization is correct.

Argument by example is inductive reasoning.

Explicit Form

C: "The generalization Y is true" *or* "Y is true."

G: "$X_1, X_2, X_3 \ldots X_n$ are instances where Y is true."

W: "The examples given are true, typical, and sufficient."

Common Variation

"Y is a generalization supported by examples X_1, X_2, X_3 ... (from the past; or noncontroversial)

"X_n is a (current or disputed) example of Y."

Examples

	Fact Claim	Value Claim	Policy Claim
Claim	"Cheaters often get caught."	"Cheating is wrong."	"You shouldn't cheat."
Grounds	"Look at these people who got caught [list several prominent or recent examples]"	"The Bible says it is wrong, the Qur'an says it is wrong, and the vast majority of people say it is wrong."	"Look at the bad things that happened to [list some examples] when they cheated."
Warrant	"Examples are sufficient to prove the generalization."	"A consensus of moral authorities establishes moral rules."	"If a policy has led to bad things in the past, you should reject the policy."

Argumentation Strategy

- Assert a generalization.
- Give examples in support of the generalization.
- Defend that these examples are sufficient to establish the generalization.

Issues and Aspects

- Proof by inductive reasoning cannot be 100 percent certain.
- The quality and number of examples is often inadequate to prove the generalization.

Study Questions

- What are some common ways this form of reasoning can be invalid?
- What are the problems with using an anecdote or story to prove a generalization?
- How can you use some informal data collection to improve your arguments for a generalization?
- What are some of the properties of a valid statistical argument?

Argument by Analogy and Parallel Case

INTRODUCTION

> "You cannot step twice into the same river."
>
> —Heraclitus, 6th cent. B.C.E.

Heraclitus is not making an observation about rivers; he is using our tangible experience of rivers to make an argument about life—that things are always in flux and even if things seem unchanged, they have changed. He's arguing by using an analogy. How does this form of argument work?

This chapter covers several related forms of reasoning under the broad title of **argument by analogy.** This wider subject will include our discussion not only of argument by analogy proper, but also of **argument by parallel case** as well as **argument by precedent.** Just to make things a bit more complicated we will also discuss a type of argument presentation called **extended analogy** and distinguish all of these forms from the situation where an advocate simply uses an analogy in ways that is not involved in supporting their argument.

As always, the reason for these distinctions is that the various forms of reasoning operate in different ways, and argument fallacies and failures occur because, among other reasons, a type is misused.

The standard terminology used to describe this area of argumentation is not entirely consistent. We'll try to be clear about what specifically we are referring to as we go along.

Language is full of evocative phrases, startling images, and interesting comparisons. First we have to sort out which of these are really arguments by analogy and propose a set of types. Then we'll look at each of the types: how they work and how they can fail to work.

WHAT ARE WE TALKING ABOUT?

Culture and Analogies

While everything in this text is imbedded in a specific time, language, and culture, many of the examples we use in this book could be translated into another language or situation and remain reasonably pertinent. With the form of reasoning we're exploring in this chapter, however, that is not the case. Much of its power is very specific to a certain time, a certain subculture, and to English as a language. Other languages certainly do use analogies, and there are analogies known from ancient times, but specific analogies are usually (but not always) bound to a culture and a time.

If your native language is not English or if you are from a different cultural context, you may find many of the examples we use here to be hard to understand. Hopefully, you or your instructor can find other examples that will illustrate the concepts, and you can contribute examples from your background.

A Practical Taxonomy

Our language has a plethora of ways of using images and comparisons and has a number of terms to describe them. We need to sort them out and decide what is important to us.

To begin with, in most high school English classes you were introduced to the terms "simile" and "metaphor." And, if you are like most of us, you remember that one of them uses "like" or "as" and the other doesn't. But you probably don't remember which one it was (simile uses "like" or "as"), why that made any difference, or if there really was a difference. More than that, English has shorthand expressions, taglines, dead metaphors, frozen metaphors, illustrations, figures of speech, catachresis, metonymy, allegories, and parables, among others. There are various elaborate classification schemes to sort these out.

We will adopt a practical taxonomy of all of these concepts, one that focuses on their uses in an argument. And, our apologies to English teachers, but we really don't think the inclusion or exclusion of "like" or "as" makes any difference at all to the meaning or persuasiveness of the analogy.

We will divide the use of imagery in language into three broad conceptual categories: tag lines, illustrations, and analogies (proper).

Some uses are simply *taglines*, a shorthand way of expressing a concept. When we say, "The stock market crashed" or "It was raining cats and dogs" or something "ground to a standstill" or that we "got off on the wrong foot," we are, in a sense, making an argument by analogy. But the analogy is not really part of the argument. Someone may argue that it is only raining a little bit and not heavily, but they are not very likely to complain about your choice of imagery. In this category would also go *frozen metaphors*. For example, "to crash" could perhaps be defined as "to hit the ground or an immovable object at a high enough velocity to inflict serious damage." But we've used the image "the stock market crashed" so often, that now, one of the meanings of "crash" is "a significant decline in prices, especially of the stock market."

A second type of analogy that will not concern us is the *illustration*. These are real analogies, but they are not at the heart of an argument. Jack Canfield and Janet Switzer, in *The Success Principles*, write:

> Unfortunately, in too many business, educational, and other settings, there is never an opportunity for feelings to be expressed and heard, so they build up to the point that people have no capacity to focus on the business at hand. There is too much emotional static in the space. It's like trying to put more water into a glass that is already full. There is nowhere for it to go. You must first pour out the old water to make room for the new water. It's the same with emotions. People can't listen until they have been heard. (2006, p. 330)

He starts with the notion of emotions building up. He illustrates that by making the claim "Unstated emotions are like static." But immediately he switches to another analogy "Unexpressed emotions are like filling up a glass with water." This second illustration he extends a bit, but the last sentence of the quotation is his real point: "People can't listen until they have been heard." After the section we quoted, he goes on to write about this and provides a number of examples of where this occurs. That is his real argument, a generalization supported by a number of examples. The water glass and static are illustrations that just kick off his argument.

But, aren't they analogies? Yes, but the issue here is their role in the argument. Suppose you started arguing with Mr. Canfield that a person with unstated emotions is not a glass filled. You might say that a filled glass is not something you think is going to explode; it doesn't feel like something frustrating. It's not an evocative analogy, you claim. In this case, we suspect he'd quickly drop the illustration and offer you a different one. You can dismiss his analogy—it doesn't affect his main point. The analogy isn't really his argument—it illustrates his argument. It's very important to offer a reader concrete illustrations of your point, but we need to focus on analogies that are carrying the argument.

So finally, we come to *"analogies proper."* We are concerned with the use of comparisons that are the core of the argument, that are intended to persuade people. And as we said at the beginning of the chapter, we'll analyze these under the following categories:

- Argument by analogy (sometimes called *figurative analogies*)
- Argument by parallel case (including the special cases of argument by precedent and historical analogy), sometimes called *literal analogies*
- Extended analogy—a model of argument presentation

And yes, we are aware that the word "analogy" is being used for the overall category and one of the components of the category—normally a bad idea. Actually, it's even worse, because "extended analogy" normally involves not analogies but parallel cases. But that's how these terms are generally referred to in English.

Before we proceed, a brief summary.

SUMMARY OF THE CHAPTER

Description

"Argument by analogy" covers various ways that we make comparisons between two things: something we agree on and a second thing that we want you to regard in some way as you do the first.

Arguments by Analogy

This includes several types. In explicit form, they include the following:

- Analogy: "X is like Y," where X and Y belong to different classes of objects. Also termed *figurative analogy*.
- Parallel case: "X is like Y," where X and Y belong to the same class of objects. Also termed *literal analogy*.
- Precedent: "X is like the previous case Y," where X and Y belong to the same class of objects.
- Extended analogy: An argument presentation model that is structured by comparing two things.

Issues and Aspects

- Does not include every use of an image in language, but only those cases where the comparison is a significant part of the persuasive force of the argument.
- Are typically specific to a language, culture, and time.

Study Questions

- Can you name and distinguish the various types of analogy arguments?
- Given an argument by analogy, can you tell what specific type it is?

FIGURE 18.1
Chapter Summary.

ARGUMENT BY ANALOGY

An *argument by analogy* (or a figurative analogy) compares two things from different classes of objects and asserts that one is "like" the other. To support that argument you offer grounds that show that the two objects are similar "enough" to be compared. You count on the audience to share your view of the second object and to impute key attributes of the second object back to the first once they are seen to be similar. The argument is effective with your audience when the object you are making the analogy to is one that has a significant impact.

Analogies are between two things that are in different classes of objects. We'll explain that below.

The explicit form of this argument is: "X is like Y." We could also argue that "X is not like Y."

How It Works

Linking two objects Argument by analogy makes a claim by comparing two things that are really not alike. For example, a job is typically associated with duties or obligations, a set of tasks, or work—but not with Ferris wheels, merry-go-rounds, or roller coasters. The two objects are in different classes. Yet, when we hear someone say "My job is like a roller coaster," we don't have a lot of trouble understanding what is meant.

What's going on is more complex than a simple C/G/W triad. We'll describe it, use the diagram below, and then give you a full Toulmin model as well.

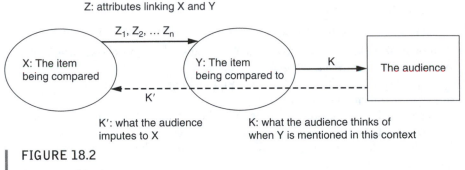

FIGURE 18.2

Structure of Analogy.

So, here is how argument by analogy works. You make a statement of the form:

"X is like Y."

and what you are intending is that the audience should regard X like they already regard Y. You hope that when people think of Y they immediately have some reaction to it. This form of argument works by making a connection between the objects (so you accept the analogy), then transporting some attributes of "the Y" back to "the X."

In the diagram above, the "something" is the attribute K. When you invoke "Y" in the context of the argument, you expect the audience to think of an attribute of Y, the "K." Then, because you've compared X to Y, you want them to impute that attribute back to X.

That's how you'd make your initial claim. But, how would you prove the analogy? To defend your analogy you will have to explain why regarding X like we regard Y is valid by showing they do have something in common. That would mean giving some attributes (the $Z_1, Z_2, \ldots Z_n$) that connect X and Y.

This may become clearer by looking at some examples. Suppose someone says: "That car is a joke." And we'll assume for now that you hear this claim as an analogy. Hearing that claim, you might go through a thought process like this:

> A joke isn't very serious; it makes you laugh. It's not something you use in a serious or formal situation. But "joke" also means something absurd, ridiculous, and something you laugh at. He means to make a claim that his car is so defective, or odd-looking, or run down that it would make you laugh to see it.

Of course, you don't really work through a process like that in your head. Data from *Star Trek: The Next Generation* might, Spock from the original *Star Trek* might (and still not laugh), but you don't. However your brain organizes its processes, we are not conscious of how we make these connections. But somehow we draw a connection between the two things and then transfer back from the second thing some feeling or view of it to the first thing.

We do become conscious of it when it breaks down. "Working for my boss is like working for a drill sergeant" is something you quickly grasp. Suppose instead, someone said, "Working for my boss is like being in a washing machine." We stop, because this makes no connection in our heads at all. We ask what they meant. And we expect them either to make a bad joke ("He goes in circles for thirty minutes, then he quits") or that the person made a mistake. Later, we'll look in more detail at how these comparisons can break down.

Using the Toulmin model

We've implied a couple of times that the statement you make in this argument isn't really your claim. You say, "X is like Y," but your real claim is more like this:

C1: "Think K about X."

G1/C2: "X is like Y."

W1: "K is the aspect of Y that is most prominent in the context."

C2: "X is like Y."

G2: "X and Y share attributes $Z_1, Z_2, \ldots Z_n$."

W2: "Objects who share attributes $Z_1, Z_2, \ldots Z_n$ are adequately similar in this context."

Let's work through two simple examples in more detail. Our original statements would be:

"That car is a joke."   "Sam is a pig."

First, let's reformulate these as explicit comparisons to make clear we are doing an analogy:

"That car is like a joke."   "Sam is like a pig."

Next, we need to think about what we are really trying to prove here. For each of these cases, we could restate the claim to "unwind" the analogy.

"That car is embarrassing and contemptible."   "Sam is crude and unkempt."

We used two terms in each claim to emphasize that there is a cluster of feelings we want to apply to the "X" of our argument (the car or Sam). We're doing this a bit backward in that you'd probably have the feelings of contempt for your car first and then come up with the analogy. In any case, we can now develop our grounds to support our claim.

G1: "The car is embarrassing."   G1: "Sam is crude."
G2: "The car is contemptible."   G2: "Sam is unkempt."

For each of these grounds we'd have to provide evidence to support it. The evidence might look like this:

G1: "The car is embarrassing in that ...   G1: "Sam is crude in that ...
its style is out of date,   he burps in public,
it makes a lot of noise."   he tells off-color jokes."

and of course, you would have more. Your evidence might be disputed, and you would have to explain in more detail (by giving examples of Sam telling offensive jokes, for instance).

And behind all of this are warrants. The warrant here is our common understanding of the implications of the analogy.

W1: "Something embarrassing or   W1: "A 'pig' in this context is
contemptible is a joke."   something crude or unkempt."

In a paragraph above, we wrote of stated and unstated claims. You are used to the idea that warrants are not always stated in arguments; analogies have a second layer of unstated issues. We'll frame these examples in the terms used in the summary above. You make a stated claim: "My car is a joke." "Sam is a pig." But you're really arguing an unstated claim: "My car is embarrassing," or "Sam is crude." So we'll lay this out and help you see how it works; we'll use language as close as possible to the explicit form in the summary.

Stated claim: "That car is like a joke."
Ground: [evidence that the car is "embarrassing" and "contemptible"]
Warrant: "Things with the attributes 'embarrassing' and 'contemptible' are 'jokes'."

Unstated claim: "That car should be an 'object of derision'."
Unstated ground: "An 'object of derision' is what people most associate with jokes."
Unstated warrant: "Similar objects share attributes."

Of course, no one talks that way. But hopefully, you can see the mechanism now. A forward comparison (X to Y) is made openly, and we count on the audience to make a reverse comparison (Y to X). But—depending on the specific analogy, we may have to defend both connections.

We'll discuss some more "real-world" examples below, but there are some other issues to attend to first.

Persuasion and Pathos

One reason for choosing to make your case via analogy is for the persuasive power a powerful comparison can have. And in many cases, the power comes from an appeal to Pathos: The attribute we want to import back to our item is a feeling. Go back to the "That car is a joke" argument. Let's suppose we are going to refine our argument to specifically address the issue of gas consumption. Gas is increasing in price; being efficient is important again for cars. If you have a car that uses a lot more gas than the typical car, that is going to hurt you financially.

But if you were to say to your friends, "My car uses gas inefficiently," there wouldn't be much emotional connection. Even if you said, "I have to spend a lot of money because my car uses gas at a higher rate than most other cars," we would understand but probably not get any sense of urgency. Instead, if you made the analogy "My car uses gas like a drunk on a bender," people would know how you felt about it. The analogy gives this point some emotional impact.

Emotions can inspire or degrade. Consider a couple of famous quotes or, at least, quotations from famous people.

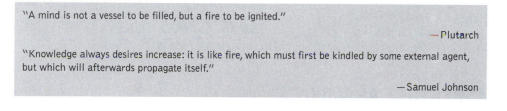

"A mind is not a vessel to be filled, but a fire to be ignited."

— Plutarch

"Knowledge always desires increase: it is like fire, which must first be kindled by some external agent, but which will afterwards propagate itself."

— Samuel Johnson

Well, of course, your mind is not really "on fire," there is no visible combustion producing heat and consuming flesh. However, we can't help but think of other playful ways that language makes a connection between images associated with combustion and your mind. "He was doing a slow burn." "That sparked an idea." "He was fuming." "Smoke came out of his ears." "You were on fire today." Shakespeare began his play "Henry V" with the words "Oh, for a muse of fire that would ascend the brightest heaven of invention!"

In the use of analogies, there is an element of art here, of image, of literary effort. One of the functions then of a good argument by analogy is to add some emotional resonance, some Pathos-based appeal to a case. And, as we'll see below, that can be one of the ways the argument falls into fallacy.

But just because analogies work at an emotional level does not mean they cannot be assessed and analyzed. Consider all the fire images we listed. "Doing a slow burn" means that the person is angry. That is a very different analogy than saying "I was on fire (with creativity)." The images may use the same general notion (fire, burning) but they do not convey the same thing nor can one be substituted for the other.

The comparisons of the mind to fire are intended to inspire both teachers and learners to see their activity not as a dull round of facts, tests, and papers, but as part of a noble and worthwhile passing on from one generation to the next the excitement of learning. Easier to do via analogies.

On the other hand, insults are also typically appeals to Pathos. You can compare people to a snake, insult a woman's appearance by calling her a cow or a horse, insult a man (who calls women those things) by terming him a dog; you can dismiss someone as an insect, attack them as a monkey, cockroach, or gorilla, belittle them as a puppy or a poodle, term them aggressive by calling them a pit bull or deriding their passivity as sheep—just to use some animal analogies.

Another key aspect of the persuasive force of analogies is that they are often pithy or use some memorable turn of phrase. Some examples are given below.

Example

"Every man has his moral backside, which he keeps covered as long as possible by the trousers of decorum." (Lichtenberg, 1990, p. 17)

Regarding work in Baghdad to try to build up Iraq as the war progressed. It was "pasting feathers together, hoping for a duck." (Ricks, 2006, p. 204)

"You only learn who has been swimming naked when the tide goes out – and what we are witnessing at some of our largest financial institutions is an ugly sight." (Warren Buffett, in Norris, 2008)

In this pithiness lies a danger. Analogies are seldom developed. And it is easy to mistake cleverness of language for persuasiveness of ideas.

ASPECTS OF ANALOGIES

Creating Meaning and Finding It

It would be a mistake to give the impression that there is some stock of comparisons and your job is to find one that exists and prove it applies to your analogy. In fact, people make up comparisons creating new analogies all the time. Poets and writers have been doing it for thousands of years. The analogy of the government working through difficulties being like the "ship of state" sailing through storms, taking on water, finding calm seas, is an old one. It may have been created by Alcaeus, a lyric poet from Mytiliene in Greece about 600 BC when he wrote, in part, the following lines most likely in reference to political turmoil on Lesbos.

> This wave in turn, like the earlier one,
> comes on, and it will give us much labor
>
> . . .
>
> Let us strengthen the ship's sides as quickly as possible,
> and make a run to a safe harbor;
>
> . . .
>
> and let no craven hesitation seize
> any of us, for clear before us stands a great ordeal.

It was used by Plato, entered western culture, and has been in regular use down to the present day. But, people are still finding new, vivid, and memorable comparisons. Bob Roll, a commentator on professional bike racing, once said of a particularly grueling stretch that "the kilometers were passing like kidney stones." We suspect that no one had made that comparison before, yet everyone knew what he meant.

And that is the magic of a well-done analogy. The audience gets it—it taps into what they know, the comparison strikes people as apt.

Ironically, this works even if the analogy is based on a false notion. Ostriches don't bury their heads in the sand nor do lemmings march off the cliff, and more than one sheep farmer has objected to passive groups being compared to sheep. But, whatever the actual biological truth of these tropes, they work because they are shared by enough people. They are "real" *images*, even if they are not real *biology*.

Analogies as Stimulus to Thought

While analogies have a dimension of Pathos to them, it is not as if there is no logical use for them. Analogies can be useful to help make an unfamiliar concept easier to understand by comparing it to a familiar one. So, for example, how electricity functions has been compared to water flowing in a pipe. The voltage is the pressure, the resistance of a wire is analogous to the size of a water pipe, and so on. Equally, how traffic flows on a highway has also been compared to how water flows in a pipe. A cleared blockage in traffic can leave "waves" of cars slowing down long after the actual accident has been cleared and there is no impediment to traffic. Isaac Newton found it useful to compare the tails of comets to a plume of smoke.

An analogy can give suggestions as to how an unfamiliar phenomena can be analyzed or even perhaps what set of equations should be used to assess it. It isn't that electricity is exactly like water in a pipe, and comet's tails are not like smoke at some level, but the analogy can be useful.

Analogies can help us see things in new ways and be the beginning of a discussion, rather than the punch line to it.

> "Male emotions are like women's sexuality: you can't be too direct too quickly." (Love and Stosny, 2009)

Here she compares two equally mysterious subjects and invites an interesting discussion. Or consider this:

> "We all live under the same sky, but we do not all have the same horizon." (Konrad Adenauer, in Lloyd, p. 40)

This example doesn't really convey any actual meaning. It's powered off a play on horizon and sky and that horizon has the meaning both of the physical earth horizon and the limits of our mental perspectives. But it is a nice way of briefly stating the dilemma that our common humanity does not prevent us from thinking that others are totally alien.

Highlighting Aspects of a Complex Argument

All argumentation moves by an advocate to serve to highlight one aspect of a situation and put others into the background, but the power of a good analogy can do that for very complex situations. After things started to improve in Iraq in 2007 and 2008, some wondered why President Bush was seeming not to get any credit for it. A letter writer to the *New York Times* responded by arguing that if someone drives your new car off the road into a ditch filled with water, you do not give them a round of applause for getting it back on the highway.

The vividness of the image immediately isolates a few aspects of the complex problem and lets us see the entire problem from that perspective.

Quick Explanations

Analogies can be useful to help someone quickly grasp an unfamiliar situation. In Poland in the 1980s, there was a woman whose unjust firing for refusing to knuckle under to the Communists sparked a resistance movement. One could spend a lot of time explaining how that worked and the dynamics of a situation when someone set off a rebellion but didn't actually lead it. Or we could, with others, just call Anna Walentynowicz the "Polish Rosa Parks" and trust that you know about Ms. Parks' key role in the Birmingham, Alabama, bus boycott in 1955. Perhaps Mohamed Bouazizi is the "Arab Rosa Parks" for his role in setting off the Tunisian rebellion of 2011 and the Arab Spring (or perhaps not, the details of this event are disputed, as of the time we write).

Humor

Humor, so goes an analogy, cannot be analyzed in too academic a fashion:

> Analyzing humor is like dissecting a frog. No one enjoys it. And the frog dies.

However, it does seem that analogies are one place where humor can be manufactured, at least sometimes. By exploiting the incongruity between the two classes of objects, humor can be created. Instead of the attribute you expect people to make the comparison to, you direct their attention to a different attribute. As an example, it is common (if trite) to compare conversation between people to playing catch with a basketball; you have to return the ball to keep the conversation going. So then:

> Conversation is like a basketball. After a while, the air goes out.

You can also put two analogies with similar purpose together to exploit the incongruity.

> We used to be on the brink of disaster, but now we are taking giant steps forward.

Another form of humor in analogy is the *inverted analogy*. You argue that two things are not alike, when the audience is expecting a direct comparison.

> To me, boxing is like a ballet, except there's no music, no choreography, and the dancers hit each other. (Jack Handey, in Lloyd, p. 33)

The comparisons of President George W. Bush to Hitler got a little tiresome, even to people who didn't like Bush.

> "Bush is not Hitler. For one thing, Hitler was a decorated, frontline combat veteran. Also, in the election that brought him to power in 1933, Hitler got more votes than the other candidates."
> — Bill Maher

Note to the purists: This is probably more properly an *inverted argument by parallel case*, except that Hitler is a kind of generic symbol for evil.

ANALOGIES THAT DON'T PERSUADE

Invalid Analogies

So, what makes an analogy work? And when does it fail? The formal definition worked out above gives us the background for discussing this. If your argument does not make "enough" of a link between X and Y, the analogy will fail. People are always looking for analogies to describe leadership. Here is one comparing running a business school to conducting an orchestra:

> The conductor is the leader, but one who must respect the artists whose talent enables him to exercise his own. To this end, a conductor's role is similar to that of a business school dean.
>
> Standing in front of the musicians, the conductor has already planned exactly how the performance of the piece of music will work; a business school dean does a similar job behind the scenes before the actual performance of teaching or research takes place.
>
> . . .
>
> A conductor is less of a star than the soprano, but even the most decorated opera singer must bow to the conductor's interpretation of the score. (Guilhon, 2008)

Well, it's not that there is no comparison and maybe that is how her school functions, but many associated with academic departments might prefer "herding cats" or "ferrets in a sack" as a more pertinent analogy. Do deans of universities plan out "exactly how" the department will run and order the faculty to play the music exactly like they intend? Do faculty follow a score? And do deans plan research and teaching without consultation with faculty, as she seems to imply? Do faculty take orders on research from the dean?

Well, other analogies also seem to misfire.

> If you [poets] call painting "dumb poetry," then the painter may say of the poet that his art is "blind painting." Consider which is the more grievous affliction, to be blind or dumb? (Leonardo, in Barzun, p. 79)

This comparison has a sort of technical validity, but it actually makes little sense. Each art has virtues and has limitations. Just because one art involves sound and the other vision doesn't mean that it has the corresponding limitations of being deprived of that sense.

What both these failures have in common is that the forward comparison of X to Y wasn't adequate enough. The similarities were superficial or dwarfed by more significant differences. Once again: A claim is not an argument. You have to defend your claims.

Audience Misanalysis

To be persuasive, the analogy has to connect with the audience. It is possible to have a perfectly valid analogy that is not persuasive.

For example, if we know someone who is trying over and over again to win a position he has no chance of getting, we could belittle him by saying he was "another Harold Stassen." Did that just drive the point home with you? Probably not. Harold Stassen was governor of Minnesota and had a legitimate shot at being the Republican nominee for president in 1948 but failed. He ran again in 1952 and again in every race through 1992—races in which he had no shot at all. In the 1970s and 1980s, many knew him as a sort of byword for futility, an object of scorn. So our analogy is clearly valid. But it isn't effective because almost no one knows who Governor Stassen is now. In other words, we could offer valid grounds for our argument, the warrant is met in the sense that this (constantly running for office) is an important part of Mr. Stassen's career, but the analogy is no longer effective with very many people.

An example of the subtle difference between analogies that work and don't work with an audience is provided by Doris Kerns Goodwin in her book *Team of Rivals* about Abraham Lincoln. She is discussing a time before he became president when he is trying to get across his view that he abhors slavery, but is opposed to efforts to eliminate it in states that currently have it. Is he being inconsistent?

> Lincoln developed a new metaphor in Hartford to perfectly illustrate his distinction between accepting slavery where it already existed while doing everything possible to curtail its spread. Testing his image in Hartford, he would refine it further in subsequent speeches. "If I saw a venomous snake crawling in the road," Lincoln began, "any man would say I might seize the nearest stick and kill it; but if I found that snake in bed with my children, that would be another question. I might hurt the children more than the snake, and it might bite them. . . . But if there was a bed newly made up, to which the children were to be taken, and it was proposed to take a batch of young snakes and put them there with them, I take it no man would say there was any question how I ought to decide! . . . The new Territories are the newly made bed to which our children are to go, and it lies with the nation to say whether they shall have snakes mixed up with them or not."
>
> The snake metaphor acknowledged the constitutional protection of slavery where it legally existed, while harnessing the protective instincts of parents to safeguard future generations from the venomous expansion of slavery . . . When [Lincoln's rival, Senator] Seward reached for a metaphor to dramatize the same danger, he warned that if slavery were allowed into Kansas, his countrymen would have "introduced the Trojan horse" into new territory. Even if most of his classically trained fellow senators immediately grasped his intent, the Trojan horse image carried neither the instant accessibility of Lincoln's snake-in-the-bed story, nor its memorable originality. (Goodwin, 2006, pp. 233–234)

Notice how Senator Seward's analogy likely misfires with his audience, not because it is wrong, but because his audience won't understand the image.

Cultural Specificity

A specific example of missing the audience is what happens when an analogy moves into a different cultural setting. Consider this proverb from Kenya.

One can always find the goat to pay the penalty for having defecated in another's house. (G. Barra, 1960)

This is another way of saying "Necessity is the mother of invention." If you are living in rural Africa, a goat is a significant purchase. You might think you didn't have the money for it, but if you were forced, you'd figure out a way. Notice how we had to explain the analogy because it has no obvious cultural referents outside of a poor rural society that lives in traditional houses.

One of the joys of spending time in another culture is to learn its analogies.

The Fallacy of the Overdone Analogy

If one analogy is good, then two must be better? Not necessarily. Like seasoning food (to make an analogy), a little is good but more is sometimes worse. An article in the *New York Times* on March 26, 2007, about a squabble in a media business in Los Angeles used the analogies of a circular firing squad, the company as a "distant land full of sectarian divisions," a university under attack from student demonstrators, a hothouse, dodging bullets, fighting a war, that innovation will only occur at the point of a gun, and that no one was getting the water out of the sinking boat.

The result is a sort of exhaustion in the reader or simple confusion as you start to think of firing squads on a sinking boat or universities inside a hothouse.

You can get the same confusing effect by extending an analogy in ways that don't work to your favor. A student debate on affirmative action was enlivened by one team calling affirmative action "the doorstop propping open the door of opportunity." A bit of a clunker, that.

The Fallacy of the Extreme Analogy

If an analogy often works by emotion, then it can fail by inducing inappropriate emotion. Perhaps few analogies in our contemporary culture are more used (and abused) than comparing someone to Adolph Hitler or a group to the Nazis. ("You're just like Hitler.") Hitler is the sort of definition of evil for us, the ultimate bad guy, bad leader. He has worse press than Judas or even the devil, it appears.

U.S. presidents are regularly compared to Hitler. Corporate officials, parents, any one in charge can be compared to Hitler. Seinfeld had his soup Nazi, and the term "Nazi" gets applied to any group thought to be trampling on anyone's rights.

Indeed, some think that the use of this analogy is almost inevitable, hence Goodwin's Law, formed in 1990 by Mike Goodwin: "As a Usenet discussion grows longer, the probability of a comparison involving Nazis or Hitler approaches one." Change "usenet" to "Internet" to update the quote: Any thread that goes on long enough risks someone invoking the Nazis.

People reach for the comparison because of the massive emotional negative feelings we have about Hitler and the Nazis. The risk is that it becomes a form of guilt by association, that our reputation would be tarnished by being compared to the Nazis even if there was no evidence of us doing anything bad. Our feelings are so strong about the Nazis that they "rub off" on whoever they are being compared to, even if there is no valid reason to make the comparison.

The analogy should be limited to situations when some genuinely totalitarian behavior is going on. When we hear people use the comparison, we should probably just take it as a sign that they are very upset.

This particular example explains the risk of analogies: Their emotional resonance overwhelms the situation and prevents us from considering if the analogy applies.

FAMOUS ANALOGIES

This form of reasoning has been used in some historically important situations.

The Blind Man and the Elephant

Originating in India, and used by Buddha, if not earlier, it tells the story of a group of men who examine an elephant. Touching various parts of the animal they come to wildly different conclusions about what the animal is like. The story became a cautionary tale of how one should not take limited, personal experience and jump to universal conclusions.

This analogy is one that seemed to have no trouble jumping cultures and eras, perhaps because the failing it describes is truly a universal human problem.

The Iron Curtain

"From Stett in the Baltic to Trieste in the Adriatic, an iron curtain has descended across the Continent."

—Winston Churchill, Fulton, Missouri, March 5, 1946

This phrase, uttered by ex–Prime Minister Churchill in a small town in the Midwest, a phrase buried in the middle of a long speech, became a near universal summary of the line between the democratic states of Western Europe and those "behind the iron curtain" under the control of the Soviet Union.

When the Soviets constructed the Berlin Wall, the verbal analogy got a concrete visual image. The fall of the physical wall in 1989 symbolized the fall of the metaphorical wall.

The Watchmaker Analogy

You are walking along a country path. You see stones scattered here and there, seemingly at random. Suddenly you see a watch lying on the ground. You would not think that the watch had always been there, nor would you think that the pieces of the watch just randomly happened to fall into place. You would assume that some entity had designed and created the watch, and you would assume that some entity placed the watch there. And, by analogy, if you see the true complexity of nature and of human beings, you should also assume that some entity made nature and humans and put humans in nature. And the only entity that can do that is God.

This, in summary, is one form of the watchmaker analogy, as developed by William Paley in a book published in 1802. However, some form of this analogy has existed for a very long time, even from before pocket watches. Cicero made the argument using sundials and water-clocks! The argument is used in theories of "intelligent design"—that the universe (and humans in particular) could not have arisen by natural processes.

We cannot go into the full evaluation of the validity of this argument here, but we note two things. First, as science has been able to explain how more and more natural processes arise without the intervention from a supreme being or without the breaking of laws of physics, it seems that force of the argument shrinks. That is one reason why those who favor intelligent design tend to be such fierce opponents of evolution: If evolution can explain the rise of species, the presence of fossils, and the creation of very complex mechanisms, then you don't need an intelligent designer. Unless, of course, the designer's work was to create the complex rules of evolution.

But the force of the comparison is one that does speak to many, regardless of their view of the underlying theory. It may happen when staring at the vastness of the night sky when you are in a place where you can see it on a clear night. Sometimes it occurs when you look down at a city from an airplane and start seriously thinking about all those lives in all their complexity below you. The vastness of the universe compared to an individual sets us to thinking.

This argument rages far and wide over many topics and has produced courses, books, and conferences without end. Is God only to be found in the design of things we can't explain by natural processes (a "God of the gaps"), or would we find God in the design of the processes themselves? What about those things in nature that are not well designed (sometimes considered an example of a "dysteleological surds")? The human back may not be very well designed for walking, our teeth sure need a lot of maintenance, and what could be the reason for the pain and danger of childbirth or for dementia or cancer?

The Marketplace of Ideas

This term makes an analogy between the process of argumentation and the process of economic transactions. It evokes the idea that in the economic marketplace your products compete with other products. If you have good products they sell, if your product isn't as good as someone else's you have to lower your price or develop a better product.

The argument is that an analogous thing will occur when we have free speech. Instead of censoring bad ideas, we just let them compete in a marketplace of ideas. Bad ideas will be driven out by better ideas because the consumers of argument will prefer better ideas.

This argument may date to a dissenting opinion by Supreme Court Justice Oliver Wendell Holms in 1919 when he said:

> the best test of truth is the power of the thought to get itself accepted in the competition of the market, and that truth is the only ground upon which their wishes safely can be carried out. That at any rate is the theory of our Constitution. (*Abrams v. United States*)

Note that he did not use the actual term "marketplace of ideas." The term was used by the Supreme Court in 1967 in reference to the classroom. The concept of free discourse has earlier roots, of course.

The analogy is used in support of the idea that, in a free society, we do not need to prohibit speech we dislike; instead we should criticize it. The analogy carries emotional force with us because we tend to have a strong preference for free markets over controlled markets.

The analogy can be suggestive of many things. How does a monopoly or near-monopoly of ownership of the means of circulating opinions (such as when two or three media companies own all the newspapers and television stations and radio in one market) affect the marketplace of ideas? We do prohibit certain bad products and prohibit deceptive claims for products. Does that apply to a debate of ideas? Do, in fact, people prefer good ideas to bad? Or do they sometimes prefer bad ideas just as they can like bad products?

This book, and the class you are likely reading it for, support the idea that free debate improves our opinions and decision making.

The Gaia Hypothesis

There are many mechanisms in the earth's ecosystem that tend toward self-regulation: keeping some quantity in balance. In the 1970s, chemist James Lovelock with contributions from microbiologist Lynn Margulis developed the *Gaia hypothesis* as a way of quickly summarizing the many complex interacting ways the earth seemed to maintain stable conditions for the development of life.

Whatever the strength of this as a scientific theory, it soon took on additional dimensions. Does it make sense to speak of the entire earth as a living organism? Is it helpful to attribute some intention to this organism: The earth as a semiconscious entity would act to preserve life, and if humans got too destructive of the ecosystem, the world would react by eliminating humans.

So, this clearly became an example both of the way analogies are stimulus to thought and the way they can organize or focus the discussion of a complex problem.

"If We Can Land a Man on the Moon ..."

Why then can't we ... solve poverty, get a car that can run for a million miles, find a good place to eat ... whatever. The technical and organizational miracle of NASA's successful achievement of President Kennedy's 1961 challenge became a challenge to any difficult and frustrating situation. If we can pull off going to the moon, why do we seem doomed to flail around helplessly on so many other issues? A good question.

While common in the 1970s and 1980s, this analogy seems to have fallen out of our culture in the United States due perhaps to the simple passage of time and that the space program no longer seems to be anywhere near as successful.

Other Analogies

There are other well-known arguments by analogy. "Social Darwinism" is an analogy pointing to the survival of the fittest in nature as a model of how the human economic world should work. "Business is war" is another common analogy.

We have no empirical data to support this, but it appears that two realms of discourse that regularly use many analogies are finance and religion. Some financial examples have appeared above. We're also partial to "You should not try to catch a falling knife" (try not to time the bottom of a market), "Stock lending acts as a lubricant, oiling the wheels of markets," and the evocative "dead cat bounce" (falling stocks often rebound, but then fall further). Stocks and markets regularly move sideways, are jittery, routed, go into tailspins, totter, and retreat. Credit markets are frozen or jammed; some of these examples are frozen metaphors.

Christianity has a plethora of symbol systems to describe human relationships to the divine from Lamb of God, Father, King, Lord, vine, rock, potter and clay, the good shepherd, to parables analogizing the Kingdom of God, and more.

Perhaps what these two areas might share is that both deal with abstract entities. Finance is no longer about my handing you a lump of metal and receiving some corn in return but electronic entities of great complexity, abstracted from any actual asset. And religion is attempting to describe what lies beyond our powers of description.

> "Scientists have generated powerful insights by studying light as a wave or a particle. But not as a grapefruit."
>
> —Gareth Morgan, *Images of Organization*, p. 350

Arguments We Don't Ever Want to Hear Again:
Sports Analogies to Business

It can seem that every successful sports coach has a book out explaining how they can offer lessons on how to win at life, at sales, at business. We think the analogy is far weaker than many suppose. Among the significant differences between coaching a sports team and running a business are:

- In a game, you always know if you are winning or losing and you know by how much and how much time you have to rectify it. In business, you often only know that approximately.
- In a sport, your goal is to win and to defeat a single opponent or a series of opponents. In business, success may depend on your ability to create cooperative agreements and win-win situations as well as competitors you have to try to outdo.
- In sports, you can discipline or remove players that do not follow your exact instructions. You can direct their preparation and even their schedules. No business manager has that degree of control over employees.

- In sports, you compete against one team at a time. In business, you have multiple competitions going on all the time.
- In sports, you have a game where the rules stay put, at least for the duration of a game or season and the arena of competition is well defined to a particular court. In business, the rules are changing, not always clear, and competition affects all aspects of what you do.
- In sports, while there are budget issues, the coach is seldom judged by profit and loss and not directly responsible for the costs of running the entire support staff. In business, profit and loss are critical.
- In sports, you have referees who arbitrate all disputes in near real-time, without any expenditure of money on your part. In business, you have to decide on your legal strategy, and disputes can last for years.
- In sports, your goal of winning is clearly defined and does not change. In business, you often have to decide on your goals, and others may have different goals.

REBUTTING ANALOGIES

Because analogies work so often as appeals to Pathos, they are hard to rebut with appeals to Logos. You can sound defensive or weak, even if your points are accurate. It can be better if you can turn the analogy around (in a defensible way) to make your point.

Lee Iacocca, former head of Chrysler, addressed the global warming issue in a recent book (2008, p. 93). He noted that those who think global warming does not exist or is not the result of human action will say that "the jury is still out." That's an effective analogy. We think of a jury deliberating, and we have strong views that a deliberating jury should not be interfered with, we should not make decisions until they return, and that all we should do is wait. Iacocca did not logically argue that global warming exists, instead his reply began: "What jury is that?—the O. J. jury? The facts are getting pretty hard to ignore."

He accepted the analogy, but redirected our attention to a jury widely regarded as out of control, one who made the wrong decision. The zinger is not an argument, any more than the initial statement was; it was a claim. He has to now follow it up with evidence that it is inappropriate to wait any longer to move on climate change (and he does do that), but by starting off with an effective mirroring of the analogy, he has given himself space to reply.

Another example of this is provided by Bill Maher, who accepts a description of the Republican party but then twists it back when he wrote: "They used to be the party of the big tent; now they're the party of the sideshow attraction."

SUMMARY OF ARGUMENT BY ANALOGY

Description

Argument by analogy covers various ways that we make comparisons between two things: something we agree on, and a second thing we want you to regard as you do the first.

Explicit Form

"X is like (or not like) Y" where X and Y belong to different classes of objects."

Examples that would typically be developed as analogies:

- "Ritalin is like Crack."
- "Life is a journey."
- "Jesus is the Lamb of God."
- "Smoking is like hitting yourself in the head with a hammer." (From the local paper at the University of Minnesota)

Fact Claims	Value Claims	Policy Claims
C: "This job is a roller-coaster ride."	C: "This job is awful. It is such a roller-coaster ride."	C: "We should quit this job since it is a roller-coaster ride."
G: "It has much drama and wild pointless swings of emotion."	G: "It has much drama and wild pointless swings of emotion."	G: "It has much drama and wild pointless swings of emotion."
W: "Roller coasters exist to provide thrills."	W: "Drama is an undesirable aspect of a job."	W: "It is a good idea to leave bad jobs."

Argumentation Strategy
- Consider what the audience will associate with your analogy.
- Be able to defend the connection between the two objects you are comparing.

Issues and Aspects
- Does not include every use of a comparison in language, but only those cases where the comparison carries the persuasive force of the argument.
- The two things compared are from different classes of objects.
- Persuasion works by having the audience impute an attribute of Y back to how they regard X.
- Are often culturally specific.
- Are typically left as assertions and not developed.
- Often use appeals to pathos.
- Can be difficult to rebut in a way that is persuasive with the audience.

Study Questions
- Can you asses if an analogy will be understood by the specific audience who will hear it?
- Can you rebut an argument by analogy both by analyzing it, as well as by creatively reframing it?
- Why is reframing an analogy a common source of humor?
- What is meant by saying the two objects compared are "from different classes of objects"?

ARGUMENT BY PARALLEL CASE

Argument by analogy compared two things that were from different conceptual classes (such as "fire" and "mind" or "cars" and "humor"). In contract, *argument by parallel case* compares two things from the same class of objects or concepts. This is also known as a *literal analogy*. There are some differences, however, in how the two types of analogy are applied and proven.

In argument by parallel case, we intend to say that two things are similar in certain key respects. Not just alike in how we should regard them, but actually two things from the same class of entities. We make this argument by offering the comparison and then identifying the attributes the two cases share.

How It Works

Analogy by parallel case is more likely to focus on specific attributes that may or may not link the two things being compared.

Let's consider an example. We will defend this claim:

C1: "Competitive dance is like synchronized swimming."

We could offer a number of reasons they are alike:

G1a: "Both activities are generally engaged in by women."
G1b: "Some people do not regard these activities as 'real' sports."
G1c: "Some people make fun of them."
G1d: "Both activities are judged on an element of esthetic appeal and not pure competition."

But, the comparison is unlikely to be made just in and for itself. The claim that these two sports are parallel cases is likely done for a specific purpose—to support some other claim. There might be two candidates.

C2: "Competitive dance should be supported."
G2a: "Competitive dance is like synchronized swimming."
G2b: "Synchronized swimming is a recognized intercollegiate and Olympic sport."
W2: "Similar activities should be treated similarly."

Or perhaps the goal was this:

C3: "Competitive dance is ridiculous."
G3a: "Competitive dance is like synchronized swimming."
G3b: "Synchronized swimming is silly."
W3: "Similar activities should be treated similarly."

We set up this example, because depending on what someone's goal is (C2 or C3), very different attributes would be used to make the comparison. C1 and its associated grounds would be used, we're sad to say, in support of C3. If it was C2 we were aiming at, we might use this:

C4: "Competitive dance is a sport like synchronized swimming is a sport."
G4a: "They both involve peak physical activity."

G4b: "They both involve competition with other teams leading to winners and losers."

G4c: "They both have seasons and an overall winner is determined."

G4d: "They both require significant training to be in the best physical shape."

W4: "If activities share physical effort, competition, and require training, that makes them close enough alike to be considered in the same category for the purposes of being a sport."

Making a Comparison the Audience Already Accepts

We make an argument by parallel case because, as with analogies, we want to transfer something about "the Y" back to "the X." But our audience has to accept this comparison. If the audience doesn't accept synchronized swimming as a sport, comparing something to it, no matter how strong the comparison is, won't help our case.

Role in Policy Claims

Parallel case arguments are often made because we want to adopt the same policy for "the X" that we did for "the Y."

First, we'd make the argument that we just did that competitive dance is a sport like synchronized swimming is a sport. Then, we might make a second argument:

C5: "We should fund competitive dance."

G5a: "We funded synchronized swimming."

G5b: "Competitive dance is just like synchronized swimming."

W5: "It's unfair to treat two similar things in different ways."

So, like analogies, there is an expressed claim that is being made in support of an unexpressed claim.

Is Parallel Case Really a Different Form of Argument?

Isn't this really argument by definition?   When we made the argument that competitive dance should be considered a sport like synchronized swimming, it might have looked a lot like an argument by definition. We offered some criteria that seemed to define sport. But the two argument forms are different. In argument by parallel case, we're not appealing to a general definition of sport. We're not trying to consider all sorts of sports with the aim of nailing down a comprehensive definition.

Isn't this really just argument by example?   Are we making two examples of something? The difference is that in an argument by example we are using the examples to support a generalization. In an argument by parallel case, there is no attempt to generalize. We're just concerned to say that the two items are alike.

Let's be clear, if you want to defend competitive dance, you certainly could construct an argument by definition or an argument by example to do so. But you can also do it by an argument by parallel case.

Is "Class of Objects" Always an Unambiguous Concept?

Perhaps as you have thought about this, you've wondered if there really is a sharp line between analogy and parallel case forms of reasoning. And no, there isn't. Is the "My boss is like a drill sergeant" an analogy or parallel case? It depends on if we see "drill sergeant" as a metaphor for strictness or if we are really trying to develop specific parallels between how the two conduct their business.

But that doesn't mean the two forms are identical or that the distinction has no validity. Think about how you support or refute these arguments. If someone has argued that Sam (by now, much maligned) "is a pig," you cannot refute that by saying that Sam walks on two legs and isn't pink. On the other hand, if I am trying to compare synchronized swimming to competitive dance, then I can delve into the specific, concrete attributes of the two activities and note similarities and differences.

So, How Is This Persuasive?

As with analogies, so with parallel cases, the comparison you make has to carry persuasive force with your audience.

Suppose you were going to argue that the United States has passed the point of its maximum power and influence and is headed into a period of decline and eventual eclipse. You would like to convey this situation by a parallel case. You could compare the United States to ancient Athens in the years just before Sparta conquered it, or you could compare the United States to ancient Rome. Which would be better?

"Better" we have to ask, in terms of what? The parallel to Athens might be logically powerful. A society that achieved so much in terms of art, technology, culture, and whose democratic institutions were the model for the world. A society with a powerful military, but one that threw its power away on a war it didn't have to fight. Since Rome wasn't really a democracy in any sense while at the height of its power, maybe you could argue the comparison to Athens would be more apt.

But the problem is that few know about the issues concerning the decline of ancient Athens. Perhaps the average person knows about the Parthenon and some general idea of the origin of democracy, but when people think of "powerful society that declined and fell" they think of Rome (perhaps with the assistance of Mr. Gibbon and his book or a spate of movies). In this case, in order to make a connection to your audience, the Rome example might be more powerful.

The typical point of contention with these arguments is that our criteria for what makes the two entities "alike" hasn't been thought out carefully enough or hasn't been accepted by the audience. So the two objects might be alike in some respects, but not in the aspects that count for the point the advocate is trying to make. Or, rather, the advocate thinks they are parallel but the person on the other side disagrees.

Is the discrimination against homosexuals (including the prohibition on them marrying) like the legal discrimination that used to exist in the United States against African Americans? To many liberal whites, that seems like an obvious parallel case. And just as we now regard racial discrimination as odious, so we should (the argument goes) think of the discrimination against homosexuals in the same light.

However, it is not unusual for African Americans to reject that comparison and find even making the parallel to be offensive. In their mind, the system of apartheid, the lynchings, and the separate facilities that their ancestors suffered through is far worse than what has happened to homosexuals in this country. Further, many African Americans regard homosexuality as disreputable and so do not want their heroic struggle for human rights linked to what they regard as an acceptance of sexual degeneracy.

Even if you believe the comparison is defensible, you have to be aware if your audience will understand and accept it or not.

FAMOUS PARALLEL CASE ARGUMENTS

The Influence of Command of the Seas

In 1890, U.S. Navy Captain Alfred Mahan wrote a book that proved to be influential with policy makers. *The Influence of Sea Power upon History* argued that Great Britain had risen to prominence based on a strong navy and that the United States could also rise in power if it controlled the sea. It may also be the case that German Kaiser William II thought that the analogy might work for Germany as well.

Can Animals Provide Insight on Human Behavior?

We're not thinking about physical parallels but rather moral ones. Various arguments about human sexuality have reached for comparisons in the animal kingdom. Do animals mate for life and remain faithful to one partner? Do animals engage in violence other than for survival? Are animals ever homosexual? One student claimed that a species of animal makes a crude vibrator. Perhaps there are more comparisons.

The argument turns in general on what force you think this comparison should have, how similar you think humans are, or if you regard humans as unique in the animal kingdom.

ARGUMENT BY PRECEDENT

Argument by precedent is a particular type of argument by parallel case. It gets its own name because two special areas of application are very common.

The first area is *historical parallel*. We propose taking some action based on the results of some previous case—that we argue is parallel. Most uses of historical precedent are looking to invoke lessons from the previous example to apply to the current case. Since we know the outcome of the historical case, if we can prove that a current situation is parallel, then we can take lessons from the outcome and use it to predict the outcome of the current case.

Some examples are discussed below.

Vietnam, Afghanistan, Iraq, Libya ...

Every time the United States gets involved militarily in a foreign country in something that is not a conventional war, the comparisons start getting made. "Iraq is Arabic for Vietnam," for example. One wag, invoking the notion of war as video game (itself an argument by analogy) suggested a title for the Iraq war as: "Vietnam 2: Special Desert Edition." Sometimes the recycling of the rhetoric is quite extreme, even to asserting that specific motives behind one intervention would "obviously" be the reason behind another.

Today, the list of parallel cases seems always to start with Vietnam. But in fact, there is a very long history of military interventions in American history. Vietnam was hardly the first.

Lumping them all together seems to smooth out the differences between long lasting ground combat operations, quicker smaller actions, those where some faction invited us and those where they didn't, ones with significant allied forces and ones without, and so on.

While this might seem like an argument that only opponents of the Iraq war would use, the comparison was also made sometimes by advocates of the war. They argue that the U.S. "liberal" media had stabbed our soldiers in the back in Vietnam, causing us to lose a war we could have won and that the media was doing it again in Iraq.

The 2008 Recession Is Like ...

Since 2008 there have been many examples of parallel case arguments made between the "Great Recession" and various previous economic crises, most obviously to the Great Depression but also to events in other countries as well. The hope is that since we know how these past events came out we can match up the current crisis to a previous one and then draw conclusions about the future of the current crisis.

Immigration

People sometimes compare current negative attitudes to immigration to those held about previous waves of immigration. "We should respect those who are coming to the United States. illegally now as we learned to respect our own ancestors who came here earlier." This tries to draw an analogy between earlier immigrants (often disrespected at the time, but later respected) and current immigrants. Others would dispute this precedent by attempting to point out differences between the two.

Legal Precedents

The second common area of argument by precedent is in the *legal field* when lawyers propose that their current case is like a particular previous case and the opposing lawyer disputes the parallels. In the legal field, there is the doctrine of "stare decisis," which holds that precedents should be followed. This doctrine is thought binding on judges even in regard to the decision they themselves have made. The U.S. Supreme Court regards its own previous decisions as controlling on its own future decisions.

Of course, over time, judges have to adjust, and precedents have been overthrown. Sometimes this happens directly, sometimes by a previous decision being nibbled around the edges until it has no real authority left.

Associated Fallacies

The particular fallacy for precedent arguments is that the precedent is given too much weight or too wide an applicability. Some previous experience is so traumatic that we draw too wide a conclusion from it. Vietnam was traumatic and traumatic in a way the United States has still not fully processed, but some have drawn from it the conclusion that no war conducted by the United States could ever be justified. That's too broad a conclusion.

On the other side of things, people regularly invoke "Munich" (an agreement struck by the British prime minister with Hitler at that city in September of 1938) as a shorthand historical precedent argument against "appeasement"— treating dictators with insufficient severity. The argument is that "Munich" proves that you should always be tough with dictators. In this case, one, pretty significant, precedent in the 1930s has been used to oppose all manner of negotiations with unsavory types in very different contexts. That's also too broad a conclusion.

ARGUMENT BY PRECEDENT

Description
Compares two things from the same class of objects.

Explicit Form
Expressed claim: "X is like (or not like) Y."

Examples that would typically be developed as an argument by parallel case:
- "Abortion is like infanticide."
- "Hanukah is like Christmas for Jews"
- "The United States today is like the Roman Empire just before it fell."

Fact Claims	Value Claims	Policy Claims
C: "Competitive dance is not a sport since it is like synchronized swimming (and we don't consider that a real sport)."	C: "We should ridicule competitive dancers just like we make fun of synchronized swimmers (since they are the same)."	C: "The university denied funding for synchronized swimming under the sports budget so why would we fund competitive dance (since they are alike)?"
G: [reasons why they are alike]	G: [reasons why they are alike]	G: [reasons why they are alike]

Argumentation Strategy

- Identify attributes that link the two objects.
- Identify what conclusion you want to draw from linking the two objects.
- Defend that those attributes establish a relevant connection for the current argument.

Issues and Aspects

- Is sometimes termed a "literal analogy."
- Arguments often revolve around just how alike or unlike the two objects are.

Study Questions

- What is a precedent?
- How is a parallel case argument different than an argument by example or a definitional argument?
- What does it mean that the two objects being compared are in "the same class of objects"?
- Why might linking two similar objects be unpersuasive to your audience?

EXTENDED ANALOGY

The extended analogy is not really a different form of reasoning; it is a description of a way of presenting an argument. Logically, it should belong in the models of argument presentation section of chapter 11. Confusingly, it is normally applied to parallel cases and not to analogies. Since it uses concepts particular to this form of reasoning, we discuss it here.

An *extended analogy* is when you explore the similarities between the two items at great length. Here, you're less interested in drawing a specific conclusion about one thing by making an analogy. Rather, you are interested using what you know about one thing to explore a second thing.

Tom Standage has written a charming book called *The Victorian Internet*. His thesis, his claim, is that the impact on Victorian-era society from the telegraph is analogous to the impact on late-twentieth-century society from the Internet. He makes that claim by describing the history of the telegraph. He writes:

> During Queen Victoria's reign, a new communications technology was developed that allowed people to communicate almost instantly across great distances, in effect shrinking the world faster and further than ever before. A worldwide communications network whose cables spanned continents and oceans, it revolutionized business practice, gave rise to new forms of crime, and inundated its users with a deluge of information. Romances blossomed over the wires. Secret codes were devised by some users and cracked by others. The benefits of the network were relentlessly hyped by its advocates and dismissed by the skeptics. Governments and regulators tried and failed to control the new medium. Attitudes toward everything from news gathering to diplomacy had to be completely rethought. Meanwhile, out on the wires, a technological subculture with its own customs and vocabulary was establishing itself. Does all this sound familiar? (2007, pp. vii, viii)

In this sort of argument, the differences between the two things are as interesting as the similarities. Standage doesn't claim these two things are identical. The fact that nineteenth-century Victorian England and twentieth-century society are not absolutely identical does not undermine his argument. He intends his extended analogy to be thought-provoking, to stimulate your reflection on both societies. The comparisons go back and forth.

The comparison allows you to see the older society in new ways. Something that might seem of no significance to you (the telegraph) can now be seen by us in ways that people saw it at the time. It helps us get inside the perspective of the nineteenth century.

CONCLUSION

Arguments by analogy are an important and common method of argument. They add vividness and color to our presentation, but can be vulnerable to excessive emotions. Parallel case (literal analogy) arguments allow us to draw lessons from other areas of life and from history. But, we have to show that they are close parallels and close along the dimensions that matter.

Note that summaries are located at the end of the discussion of each type of analogy.

CHAPTER 19

Causal Argument

INTRODUCTION

A Mexican man enters the United States illegally. This one is not here for the job opportunities. He had a criminal record in Mexico and served some time in jail. He sneaks into the United States to evade other criminal elements in Mexico with whom he was feuding. He has no interest in the hard-working part of the immigrant community and gradually falls into a gang. He is arrested in the United States several times, but clogged courts, overworked prosecutors, and the difficulty of assembling a case against him with evidence from other criminal gang members means he moves in and out of the criminal justice system. He gets involved with a woman who might pull him out of the bad life, but it doesn't take. A priest reaches out to him, but only once or twice. The gang has a steady supply of semilegal guns from various sources—sources who know, more or less, that their customers are criminals. One night during a robbery, the man fires a gun to intimidate a store owner, and the bullet goes through a second-floor window and kills a fourteen-year-old girl.

What caused her death?

Another illegal immigrant, the same beginning to the story. The same gang, the same drift to crime. He gets a woman pregnant and that is a wake-up call. He drops out of the gang, they get married, they move to a different city and get jobs. They buy a small house, pay taxes, join a church, settle down to raise their child.

What caused him to straighten his life out?

If you want easy and quick answers, just turn on the television. They'll tell you with utter certainty that it was the scourge of illegal immigration that caused the teenager's death, or maybe it was too many guns, or maybe the failed policies of liberalism, or the failure of Mexican politicians, or weak laws in the United States. You'll hear it was drugs or the failure to legalize drugs. It was our foreign policy exploiting Mexico, it was failure to secure the border, it was failure to grant amnesty to immigrants. They'll tell you with confidence that the second man is a testimony to the power of love, or religion, or the power of family in Hispanic culture. Others will be equally confident that the second man should be immediately expelled since not to do that would reward lawbreaking. Others will tell you that no person is illegal.

And someone somewhere will blame the mother of the child for not getting her out of a high-crime neighborhood. Others will tell you that none of this counts, and it was the man who pulled the trigger, simple as that. Others will tell you that these are isolated examples and prove nothing or that they are typical examples.

What you should notice first about these stories is that there is more than one thing going on here. This chapter is about helping to untangle all those things.

CAUSAL ARGUMENTS

A *causal argument* makes the claim that a result, an effect, or some event is due to a specific cause. The explicit form of the argument is:

"X causes Y."

Other explicit forms would include "X doesn't cause Y" and a variety of other types we will discuss in this chapter.

The Plan of the Chapter

Causal arguments are crucial to many issues, but also raise problems that are fundamental and complex. To understand them we will have to discuss first how proving things is more slippery than might be supposed. Then, we will look at a number of types of causes. Correlations are not causal proof, but when organized by a controlled experiment and put in a theoretical framework, we can achieve the level of certainty we need for many situations. With that framework, we can then consider a number of issues before reviewing some significant examples of causal arguments.

CAN YOU PROVE ANYTHING?

It may seem a little late to ask if we can really prove anything, but with causal arguments, the question of what really is "proof" arises. How do we know that one thing causes something else, and how do we know this for certain? We can illuminate this problem by considering how we might prove that cigarettes cause lung cancer.

Quite a large number of people who smoke get lung cancer. But that isn't proof, someone might say, it's just a coincidence. And besides, some smokers don't get lung cancer and some who do get lung cancer have never smoked.

> ". . . we must enquire how we arrive at the knowledge of cause and effect. I shall venture to affirm, as a general proposition, which admits of no exception, that the knowledge of this relation is not, in any instance, attained by reasonings a priori; but arises entirely from experience, when we find that any particular objects are constantly conjoined with each other.
>
> . . . .
>
> For all inferences from experience suppose, as their foundation, that the future will resemble the past, and that similar powers will be conjoined with similar sensible qualities.
>
> All our reasonings concerning matter of fact are founded on a species of Analogy, which leads us to expect from any cause the same events, which we have observed to result from similar causes."
>
> —David Hume, *"An Enquiry Concerning Human Understanding."*

The problem is, you can't wave a lit cigarette over someone's nose and mouth and watch cancer begin in their body. What can you do? The process of "cigarettes causing cancer" can be broken down into smaller causes. It's not the physical cigarette; it is the smoke from burning the tobacco that causes the problem when it is inhaled into the lungs. But it isn't "smoke" that causes the problem. Cigarette smoke contains thousands of different compounds, and a number of these (including arsenic, benzene, formaldehyde, and lead) have been identified as causing cancer. But how do they cause cancer? They do so by a number of mechanisms, including damaging cell DNA leading the cell to divide and grow at an accelerated pace. But, it isn't just that simple or direct because other actions are going on inside the body: Some causal mechanisms try to eliminate some of these dangerous substances.

So, now do we know what causes cancer? Well, we glossed over "damage DNA" in order to get to "cause the cell to divide and grow." There are a number of intermediate steps between those two statements. But, even if we can lay out every single step of this mechanism to show a chain of causes, we have an additional problem to deal with. We can't select a particular cell inside the body of an active smoker and watch as a puff of smoke comes in, deposits its additives, watch them attach to the DNA, watch the DNA produce a different protein, and watch the cell start to divide. We may be able to watch each step of this occur in the laboratory, but not in humans as they get cancer. And the process of getting cancer is cumulative—one cigarette doesn't do it. It may take up to twenty years before the cancer appears.

It is easy for a skeptic to just keep asking "Are you sure?" or "How does that actually work?" like a child who keeps on asking "Why?" until his parents lose patience and yell "Because!" And, just because this is how cells worked yesterday—well, can you prove they will work the same way tomorrow? How do you actually know if they will? Maybe there is some other mechanism that will start to become visible later today and stop the whole process.

Philosophers have been debating these issues for a long time. In a certain sense, there is no absolute proof. There is always some possibility of a process changing or of us not being able to see the process working at some microscopic level. David Hume is among the earliest modern philosophers to weigh in on this problem. His 1748 essay largely rests on two points. He argues that you don't think out causes ahead of time, you infer them by seeing one thing follow upon the other. You recognize a pattern and attribute causality. Second, he argues that all cause and effect arguments depend on the future being the same as the past, and you can't prove that—except to observe that the future has been the same as the past—in the past.

The obvious objection to Hume is that we have theories of how things work that can be used to predict how new things will behave. But Hume might have argued that those theories were built upon previous experiences of associations and are ways of distilling or summarizing the patterns we've seen occur. Notice how, in the example above about cigarettes and cancer, we kept breaking down the phenomena into smaller and smaller phenomena until we got to the level of cells and their behavior. But even if we could observe a single cell being confronted by a single particle of smoke, see the particle attach to the cell, and see the cell start to divide, it would still be, as Hume observes, us noticing two events, following in close succession.

However valid this philosophical observation is, the analytical paralysis it appears to induce is illusory. At various points in this book, we've explained that we have no choice but to make decisions with imperfect information. There is some small chance that the sun will not come up tomorrow morning, but we can ignore that chance in our decision making. Ninety-nine percent is close enough to 100 percent to be all we need for most of our decision making. We do have theories that help organize our experiences, theories that have been tested and have proven to be reliable guides to the future. Even if theories are imperfect (see the chapter on factual claims), they are still better than claiming we have no idea what is happening.

This view should not be taken as either anti-intellectual nor insensitive to situations when a high degree of precision is needed. Mediating on the deep structures of causality, proof, what we take on faith and we can know, has been a worthy human enterprise for thousands of years. And, if you are building a bridge, flying to the moon, or designing high-tech tools for critical surgery, the difference between 99, 99.9, and 99.99 percent of proof actually matters.

Our challenge is not to achieve perfect proof; it is rather to prove our causal claims to a degree of certainty that is adequate for the decisions we have to make. And, of course, we can also debate just how much certainty we need. Much of academic discourse is precisely about this: attempting to determine just how certain we are about the causes of some phenomena.

Remember conspiracy theories from an early chapter? They often exploit the difference between 99.9 percent and 100 percent certainty. "How do you know for sure?" they ask about a document being genuine, a person telling the truth, that you saw what you think you saw, and on and on. After enduring this for a while, doubt begins to creep in. Their opponents try to find absolute certainty to respond to them and fail. But the doubt induced this way is not valid.

Most of the time, we make decisions with much less than certainty and that works for us.

WHAT SORT OF CAUSATION IS IT?

When we discussed the Toulmin model we discussed the need to qualify your claim. In the case of causal arguments, qualifying our claim means to be clear about what sort of cause we are claiming. There are a number of possibilities.

Immediate Cause and Background Cause

A teenager stocks up on guns and goes to his school. He starts shooting, killing several students and then commits suicide. What caused the death of those students? The person pulling the trigger is the immediate cause. But when such murders happen, there will be a lot of talk about bullying, absent parents, lax gun laws, the social climate in the school, violent video games, violent music, illegal drugs, prescription drugs, and other factors. Some will be angry that such things are even being considered, viewing it as an excuse that detracts from personal responsibility. Others will insist that we have to consider these factors if we want to stop future shootings.

Debates on these situations might be helped if we could separate the discussion of the immediate cause of the event from discussion of the causes in the background or those that were more distantly related to the event. The person who pulled the trigger is the immediate cause of the killing. But why they did the killing, what drove them to act, what prevented them from stopping, are also factors to consider. There may have been specific people that the killer interacted with—police, counselors, psychiatrists, family members, and friends—who saw something and acted or didn't act.

We use the word "caused" to include both immediate causes—"The accident was caused by the driver turning left in front of the oncoming car" and factors that may have made that action more or less likely to occur—"The driver's visibility was impaired by trees that had not been trimmed, contrary to city policy."

As you construct an argument, try to be clear about what sort of cause you are developing and also be aware of the emotion some have when the distinction is not clear. If you discuss background causes in the same breath as the immediate cause, you can seem to be redirecting blame in ways that you might not intend.

Necessary and Sufficient Causes

Necessary and *sufficient* have formal definitions and are used in many scientific and engineering fields. A necessary cause is a requirement for something to happen. X is a necessary cause of Y if Y cannot happen without X occurring. Z is a sufficient cause of Y if Z causes Y, but other things can cause Y as well.

If you drop a big rock on your foot and your toe is broken, then the rock caused the broken foot. This is a sufficient cause of a broken foot, but not a necessary one, because you could break your toe by banging into the corner of a wall or stub it on a curb.

On the other hand, when more than one thing is needed for a cause to work, one might be essential, but not enough by itself. In reference to the successful ditching of US Airways flight 1549 in the Hudson River in January, 2009, after being hit by birds, the Chair of the National Transportation Safety Board noted that "the heroism of the flight crew was a necessary, but not sufficient element." In other words, without the heroism of the flight crew, people would have died. That was necessary for a successful outcome. However, it wasn't enough. Had there been large waves on the Hudson River that day, people would have died, despite the crew's exemplary efforts.

Significant and Insignificant Causes

In cases when there are multiple factors contributing to a cause, some factor may be present, or even quite visible, but not be very significant to the overall result. Perhaps video games *are* a factor in school shootings, but a far less important factor than psychological issues the shooter is dealing with. But we can see video games, and violent ones have shocking visuals. Internal psychological issues are harder to see.

But significance and insignificance may depend on the situation. Suppose some species of prey has their population controlled by two predators: one that is responsible for 90 percent of the deaths of the prey and the other for 10 percent. The second predator certainly seems an insignificant factor in controlling the prey population. But if the first predator takes 90 percent of the prey year after year without change, but the second varies how much they take from year to year—then, it may be the second predator that is really the cause of changes in the prey population.

Deterministic and Probabilistic Causes

We usually discuss cause in terms of "X causes Y," implying a one-to-one correspondence between a single cause and a single outcome. In fact, in many cases we are talking about a probabilistic relationship. A thousand instances of X, we will claim, cause a hundred instances of Y, and we cannot predict in advance which of the cases of X will produce the cases of Y and which will not. This is the situation for issues involving the effect of radiation on cells or the action of carcinogenic compounds.

We need to be careful that we don't claim a deterministic cause when we really can only offer evidence for a probabilistic one. "Watching pornography increases violence by men against women" means that this increase happens sometimes but not always. That is different from claiming that "Watching a pornographic video causes every man who sees one to commit an act of violence against women."

It may be that this probabilistic situation masks other causes, and if we could expand our theory to include other causal factors, then our predictions would improve. (See the section on influence arguments later in the chapter.)

A Cause That Works Always, Usually, Sometimes, or Has Once

We apologize for bringing this up again, but it is such a common problem. The previous section on deterministic and probabilistic causes was another way of drawing your attention to the difference between "always" and "often." As we've said before, there is a big difference between claiming that something always happens and claiming it usually happens or claiming that it *could* happen. Be clear what your claim is.

Causing Outcomes, Causing Variations

It can be assumed that there is a binary relationship to causal arguments: X is either there or it is not, Y either occurs or it does not. But many causes are actually framed in terms of amounts or in a variation in the amount of Y occurring. Adding more CO_2 to the atmosphere increases the average temperature of the earth, for example.

These relationships can be the aggregate of many underlying binary relationships. Millions of molecules of substances in smoke interact with millions of cells and either cause a reaction or do not. The overall result is a number of cancers in a larger number of smokers.

CORRELATION, CAUSATION, AND CONTROLLED EXPERIMENTS

Correlation

Event A occurs and event B follows almost immediately. If A and B are unusual, then we may think that A caused B. We put our hand on a hot stove, and we felt pain. We failed to study and then did poorly on the exam. It looks like A caused B. But unfortunately, it also seems to be the case that if we get a traffic ticket and then an hour later someone yells at us, we can believe that the traffic ticket caused us to start having a bad day. This is the problem of post hoc, ergo propter hoc—to assume that because one thing follows another, it was caused by the first event.

Instead of a variation in time, we can think of groups of events. For a number of years it has been true that if a group performs at halftime in the Super Bowl, their sales go up dramatically in the weeks afterward. So, appearing in the Super Bowl causes an increase in album sales. Okay, that seems reasonable. But then, it is also true about 80 percent of the time that when an old NFC team wins the Super Bowl, the stock market goes up, and when an old AFC team wins the Super Bowl, the stock market goes down (Staff, *T. Rowe Price Investor*, 2007, p. 26). Somehow, that does not seem so reasonable a notion of proof to us.

When we observe an association between two things, either temporarily or spatially, we say they are correlated.

We'll discuss both the temporal and the group scenario together in this section. So, what is going on? Humans (and animals) seem to be wired to make associations, to observe patterns and make predictions (theories) based on a pattern continuing. However, we can be fooled. We need to look at common problems about associations.

"Correlation Is Not Causation"

The quoted section title is a well-known saying. It means that just observing an association is not proof that one made the other occur.

There are several ways we can be fooled by associations. First, the **correlation may be spurious**, produced by nothing more than coincidence. Examples of these (but not always the data to prove it) can be found readily. We can get these spurious correlations simply because over time there has generally been inflation in prices and population has increased. Those continuing trends can produce a lot of correlations—dollar amounts go up, population goes up, thus all sorts of things seem to be going up together.

That is actually what is going on with the winner of the Super Bowl and the stock market example given above. There are more old NFC teams than old AFC teams, and, in more years than not, the stock market goes up. Thus, even if winning the Super Bowl is randomly distributed among teams, there will be a correlation between the winning team's background and the performance of the stock market. There is an association and an association that is likely to continue, but there isn't any causality at all.

A second case of misleading associations is when the correlation reflects an actual cause, but the conclusion drawn **reverses cause and effect**. So people wear coats in December and don't in July. So does wearing a coat make it cold? No, it's the other way around. Cold weather produces the use of coats. People in hospitals are sicker than the average population—better not go to hospitals! But, of course, being sick causes you to go to a hospital.

Both cause and effect are the result of a third cause is also a possibility. It's relatively easy to find silly examples of spurious correlations, especially for the two previous cases. But this situation (A correlates with B, but both are caused by C) can really fool us. Consider the case of hormone replacement therapy.

For a long time, women were prescribed hormones for symptoms of menopause. It was also believed that this would lower the risk of coronary heart disease. The medical profession thought they had good reason for these recommendations; they were based on some studies comparing the health of women taking hormones to those not taking them.

However, when, in the early 1990s, a very large, very well-controlled study was done (the Women's Health Initiative), it was determined that hormone therapy did nothing for heart disease and indeed may actually slightly increase the risk. What had happened is that the earlier work had been confused by a different causal mechanism than "hormone therapy (A) lowers risk of heart disease (B)." Instead, women who were more concerned about their health were more likely to both be living in a more healthy way (exercising, controlling their weight) and also taking hormone therapy. In other words, "being concerned about living healthy (C) led to lower heart disease (B) *and* being interested in obtaining hormone therapy (A)."

This example, based on a controlled experiment, provides a transition to discussing when we can draw conclusions from correlations.

Controlled Experiments: Harnessing Correlations

Correlation doesn't prove causation, but under the right circumstances it can offer strong evidence about causation. The right circumstance is a controlled experiment.

In 1747, James Lind, the ship's surgeon for a British ship, the *Salisbury*, carried out a very famous controlled experiment. A number of sailors were suffering from scurvy, a disease that produced spots on the skin, gum problems, and bleeding. Continued long enough, it caused death. Just a few years before, a circumnavigation of the globe led by Commodore George Anson had been marked by massive numbers of deaths due to scurvy.

The idea that scurvy could be controlled by eating citrus fruits had been put forward, but was not widely believed. Other theories were in circulation as well, including that acidic foods would arrest the disease. So Lind did a test. He took twelve sailors who each had scurvy. He divided them into six groups of two and varied the diet of each. The six diets he put them on were:

- A quart of cider per day
- Twenty-five gutts of elixir vitriol three times a day on an empty stomach
- Half a pint of seawater every day
- A mixture of garlic, mustard, and horseradish, in a lump the size of a nutmeg
- Two spoonfuls of vinegar three times a day
- Two oranges and one lemon every day

Those on the diet of oranges and lemons improved quickly; the others did not. We'll see that this story has some interesting complications in it, but we'll defer that discussion to the next section. First, let's consider what goes into a controlled experiment and what conclusions we can draw from it.

To be a controlled experiment, a number of attributes must be present:

- Two populations of test subjects: the *control* and the *experimental* group. The experimental group will be subject to the proposed cause, the control group will not be.

    Why is a control group necessary? Suppose we are trying to study if a new teaching method will increase student learning. We test a group of students at the start of the semester, apply our teaching method, and test them again at the end of the semester. It turns out they've improved, so therefore our method works! Well, not so fast. Suppose we had a control group that we tested at the start of the semester and at the end—people who just were in college and learning also. If they improved just as much as our experimental group, then we'd know the improvement was not due to our special method.

    Note that in the scurvy example above, there was (apparently) no explicit control group. Instead he had six experimental groups and so all Lind would be able to conclude is the relative effectiveness of the six treatments.

- The control and experimental groups must be as close to *identical in characteristics and experiences* over the course of the experiment as possible. The idea here is that we want nothing to differ between them except the treatment or stimulus we are investigating. This is to screen out situations like the hormone replacement therapy example above when a third factor complicated the results.

- The conduct of the experiment should be *double blind*. That is, the people in the experiment shouldn't know if they are in the control or experimental group, and the person interacting with the people in the experiment shouldn't know which group they are in also. This requirement is aimed at dealing with the *placebo effect*. This effect refers to how the mind influences our behavior. If you give people a pill and tell them that it will lower their blood pressure (even though it contains nothing), some people's blood pressure will go down.

- The methodology and results of the experiment should be *openly reported* so others can attempt to reproduce the results. The final check on fraud, mistakes, and self-delusion is that someone else can get the same results you did. By carefully reporting every step of your work, you indicate that you have nothing to hide, you are open to correction of your mistakes, and you are participating with others in the great quest for truth.

If all of these attributes are met, then we are justified in saying that a causal relationship has been implied. If our results stand up over time and we can explain them by a theoretical basis (see the next section), then our confidence grows that we have found a causal relationship.

While all of this may be possible in a laboratory, it can only be approximated for social and policy questions. In this case, what is often done is to survey what already happened to people, and then try to sort out, retroactively, a set of data that closely meets these attributes of a controlled experiment. We obviously cannot deprive thousands of people of health care and then see what happens. We can, however, question people, and through the proper procedures and analytical techniques, sort out an experimental and a control group.

Doing these sorts of real-life experiments properly is difficult, but there are standard methods and rules for conducting them, and you may study those in another class.

Scientists and social policy analysts do try to achieve the standards of a controlled experiment. But what you should remember is that many arguments about public policies are based on people offering only a single example or an untested theory about a complex situation. When you hear someone assert that some social policy causes a particular result, check to see what data that conclusion is based on.

Remember what we wrote about "anecdotal evidence" in the argument by example chapter: that phrase is *not* a compliment. Too many causal claims are supported only by anecdotes.

EXPLAINING OUR DATA: THEORIES ABOUT CAUSAL LINKS

It may be true that all we start with is observations about patterns in the real world, but that is not all we wind up with. We also create, evaluate, and revise theories about causal links. You put your hand on a hot stove and you experience pain. Immediately you generate a theory about heat being damaging to you, and you apply that theory to other hot items (fires, the exhaust pipes of vehicles, items left in fires, things left out in the sun, heating pads, and on and on). Or perhaps it would be more accurate to say you apply an existing theory to the new situation.

The chapter on fact claims had a general discussion about theories including criteria that they should meet. However, we need to look at theories in relation to data in the context of causal arguments.

Theories and data work together. What we hope for is a theory in agreement with data. Over time there is a great back-and-forth between theories and data. Theories suggest experiments; experiments provide a spur to refine theories. Over time, the fit between data and theory grows. Sometimes there is a crisis when it becomes clear that the data cannot be explained by existing theories and new theories have to be proposed.

The scurvy experiment reconsidered Lind's choice of treatments may seem odd to us. Drinking salty seawater as a cure? But to comprehend his choices we have to remember what theories of food people had back then. And they didn't have many. The concept of vitamins was not discovered until decades after Lind's experiment. Nor did people even understand that food contained protein, carbohydrates, and fats—that wasn't worked out for decades either. In fact, it might be better to say that people in Europe in the 1740s didn't really have any concepts of food as containing nutriments and that a person could eat enough to satisfy hunger, but still have a nutritional deficiency.

Further, they had no theoretical model of scurvy or no agreed upon model, anyway. So, even if they could agree that eating oranges would *cure* scurvy, that didn't imply to them that scurvy was *caused* by not eating oranges or something contained in oranges. After all, plenty of people did not eat oranges and didn't get scurvy. All of Lind's experimental diets were in response to some theory about scurvy at the time.

The point is that we need theories to explain data. Go back to our two Super Bowl examples. Why did the effect of increasing album sales seem reasonable but the effect of the stock market going up seem absurd? In the first case, you could easily apply a theoretical explanation to the reported correlation. Advertising increases sales, exposure increases sales. In the second case, there was no theory that would suggest itself to explain why the origin of a team winning the Super Bowl would cause changes in the stock market.

The risk is that we use theories to explain away data or to override data. That is bad enough. A more subtle problem is when the theory is used without bothering to check it against data.

Theories in Search of Data

It seems a regular part of student papers that we get arguments laying out a case for something and predicting consequences and behavior of people—but without reference to data. Often the theories are very plausible and reasonable explanations of causes. "Banning something moves it into the underground economy." "Seeing this image over and over makes you want it." However, plenty of very plausible-sounding notions turn out not to be true.

But, your case would, at the minimum, be much stronger if you cited data that reinforced your plausible theory. Data can also provide evidence for how strong a cause is or how often it occurs. Do we get a 10 percent increase or a 30 percent one? Do we have a certain effect 5 percent of the time or 25 percent? Including this sort of data grounds your theory and increases the persuasive power of your argument.

The best causal argument has *both* data and theory to support it: data from a controlled experiment showing that the effect occurs and a theory to explain why that effect should be expected.

BEYOND "X CAUSES Y"

In order to sort out some concepts about causal arguments we've been working with a simple framework of a single "X" causing a single "Y" in isolation. Now we have to look more intently at the complexities of the real world.

The Fallacy of Oversimplified Cause

Almost any real problem, and certainly almost any real problem involving public policy or human behavior, has multiple causes. Consider human nutrition.

We are bombarded by ads telling us that this sort of food will cure an illness, that one supplement will revitalize our lives, that a single additive or pill can transform our mood. But, there are between one and two million different proteins in the human body. There are dozens of neurotransmitters of several different types and modes of action. When we eat food, an amazing set of reactions are kicked off that involve multiple metabolic pathways involving multiple enzymes, intermediate compounds, catalysts, and many other functions. It is hard to even quickly summarize the process. In view of that, it seems very unlikely that "feeling bad" is caused by one single thing.

You can look at the various causal examples included at the end of this chapter when people have often assumed too simple a cause. Sometimes we seem to want to pin down one cause, or we have a fight between two proposed causes when in fact both are active.

Yet, we should not go to the opposite extreme of just finding complexity for the fun of it. "Occam's razor" is a famous dictum that "Entities must not be multiplied beyond necessity" and suggests that the simplest explanation (that works) is the best. This principle is an effect to bar conspiracy theories that often postulate vast and complex explanations for something that can be explained in a much easier way.

Influence Arguments

By *influence arguments* we mean arguments where the effect is not deterministic: The cause makes the effect more likely, or stronger, but doesn't force the result. Common examples of this type of argument include media influence (such as fashion advertisements or promoting a political attitude), video game influence on teenagers, impacts of changing the drinking age or from legalizing drugs.

These are hard arguments to sort out for several reasons. First, we know we are influenced by things, but we also believe that people have choices. Most of us don't have a clear set of concepts for how to assess the coercive power of social pressures on us.

As an example, people can choose to eat and drink what they want. No one holds a gun to their head to eat junk food. But, what if it is hard to find fast food that is healthy? Or if eating healthy requires much more work on stressed people than just grabbing something? Or if healthy food costs more? Or if there are endless media images implying that happiness comes from eating more? This sort of pressure adds up over time—yet, any one person could have the power to resist this.

A second issue is that the causality of influence arguments are hard to pin down because there are just so many different things going on. How would we find a control and experimental group to test the effect of advertisements that are nationally distributed? And since people adapt to things, how would we keep the group's experience similar over the course of the experiment?

People have been doing research on media influence and social pressure. In writing these arguments, it should be a priority to find data to support your theories of influence and data explicitly from controlled experiments.

Feedback Loops

As if all the types of causality we have aren't hard enough, some systems involve feedback loops. The human body has quite a number of these. Various chains of chemical reactions start off, and, after a while, there is a reaction that produces some product that shuts down the initial reaction. The body also has various mechanisms to maintain homeostasis—to keep some quantity at a fixed value. Social systems can have feedback loops as well, higher prices cause lower sales that may prompt some sellers into discounting or others into producing cheaper products.

Causal processes with feedback loops are very hard to sort out and harder still to measure what effects are going on.

CAUSAL ARGUMENTS IN VALUE CLAIMS

We've seen how our values have a strong influence on which facts we are willing to accept. When we are arguing causes that are directly attached to values, there are certain problems that arise.

"Cause" Is Not Always "Blame"

We assume that if something bad happens to you and you did something that led to it, then you caused it, and then you are to blame for it. That seems reasonable. But sometimes it is not reasonable at all. If you walk across campus, walk on the grass, and step into an open manhole and wrench your leg—well, you did that, you are the "cause" of your accident. But something should be attributed to whoever left the cover off.

Consider the following examples:

- A person opens an email attachment from an unknown source that promises vast riches and gets a virus that destroys their computer files.
- A person leaves their car unlocked with the keys in it and it gets stolen.
- A woman goes to a dorm room with several men. They all drink heavily. They flirt with her, she flirts, a bit. The men approach her for sex. She clearly says no—or passes out. The men force sex on her.

Did these people "get what they deserved"? After all, some will say, "Anyone should have known what would happen."

In the first two cases, we do seem to be able, without difficulty, to separate out the actions of the victim and the perpetrator. We advise people to be wary, urge them to be careful, and at the same time hold the people who committed the crimes fully responsible. We can judge that one contributed to the cause by making a mistake, but the perpetrators don't get to use that to let them off the hook.

The third case induces stronger and more complicated reactions. Sometimes suggesting that it was possible for her to have anticipated this as a high-risk environment, and that it would be good to recommend that women avoid such situations, will be taken as an attempt to blame her for what happened to her. But it shouldn't be.

The difficulty of the third case comes from the history of how societies have dealt with similar issues. There is a long history of unfair blame of women (as well as some contemporary examples). But, that shouldn't prevent us from both firmly assigning the blame to the rapists and also suggesting that women would be well advised to be careful about certain situations with a demonstrated history of risk.

Does that sound like blaming her—a bit? Read it again; we didn't blame her. In general, people think that people should be careful to avoid situations where there is a risk of harm—all the while still holding responsible those who cause such situations to arise or who exploit them to harm others.

There is another group of issues involving cause and blame that has come to be called *victim blaming*. This term was popularized by a book by William Ryan in 1965. Victim blaming occurs when someone suffers a loss or a crime, but has the blame put on them for doing something provocative or insulting to the perpetrator. Persecution of Jews in 1930s Germany was sometimes claimed by Nazis to be the result of some offense that no honorable non-Jew could permit. Some attacks on homosexuals are excused for the same sorts of reasons.

Or, consider the situation when a colonized people launch a violent resistance against their occupiers. They are often met with both an even more violent reply from the occupiers and a claim that they "brought this on themselves." Or—to take the same situation—when a colonized people are mired in poverty (due to the occupiers siphoning off resources and denying access to education) and are criticized for being "unready to manage their own affairs."

Some think that this phenomenon may be traced to our desire that the world be just. So rather than think that someone was unjustly harmed, it is easier for us to think that the victim must have done something to deserve the harm. Consider the book of Job in the Old Testament for an early discussion of this. Modern examples occur when people get laid off—through no fault of their own—and find themselves becoming pariahs to their friends.

On the other hand, the reaction against victim blaming can sometimes lead to us obscuring or even refusing to look into the details of causal processes or those situations where there is some political sensitivity.

Fallacy of Making Assumptions as to Motives

In general we cannot readily see what motivates others. We can't know what thought process went on inside their head, and so we guess at their motives, "Well, the reason he did that must have been because . . ." In attributing a cause to their behavior, the lack of evidence also means that no one can really refute us either.

We need to be cautious about causal arguments that assume motives. It would be better to try to reformulate our argument in terms of observed behavior and motives that are common to people in general.

Fallacy of Value-based Warrants Filtering Causes

Our values also limit what sort of causes we will accept as valid. This can occur around the topic of *personal responsibility*. We can tend to believe that other people (but not us) should be held responsible for every aspect of their behavior. In this case, we then only accept as valid causes that reflect that personal responsibility and screen out causes that involve societal pressures, for example.

ISSUES IN CAUSAL ARGUMENTS

Heaps

"Hey, have a beer, you can't get drunk from one beer." True. No one beer can make you go from not being drunk to being drunk. On the other hand, twelve beers reliably does that. So how do we get drunk if no one beer can do it? This is the dilemma posed by *heaps*. A little bit can't cause something but a lot of little bits can. The logical fallacy is to assume that since one thing can't do anything, a lot of them can't either.

The Slippery Slope

We discussed slippery slope in the policy claims chapter and won't repeat that here, except that it can be a part of causal arguments, contending that one change will cause another change in the same direction. As we said in the policy chapter, this can be a fallacy or it can be true—the question is what forces are in play that will either cause a further slide down the slope or will prevent it.

FAMOUS CAUSAL ARGUMENTS

Did Separate but Equal Schools Cause Damage to Black Children?

The United States used to have a system of apartheid in education with separate schools for black children. The courts had allowed that, provided the schools were "equal." Over the first part of the twentieth century, various attacks on this system were mounted, but had not succeeded. In 1954, a group of cases came to the Supreme Court under the title of *Brown vs. Board of Education.*

One issue the court considered was the consequences of segregated education. What effects were caused by it? The court concluded that the evidence was that separating children caused negative effects—even if the physical facilities of the schools were equal. The Supreme Court quoted a Kansas court decision (Note: "Colored" was a slightly less offensive term at the time this was written):

> Segregation of white and colored children in public schools has a detrimental effect upon the colored children. The impact is greater when it has the sanction of the law; for the policy of separating the races is usually interpreted as denoting the inferiority of the negro group. A sense of inferiority affects the motivation of a child to learn.
>
> —Cited by the U.S. Supreme Court at 347 U.S. 483, but without a reference

The Supreme Court also took notice of a range of sociological evidence that supported the idea that segregation in and of itself was causing harm to black children.

Do Lower Taxes Increase Federal Government Revenues?

From the inauguration of President Reagan in 1980 through the time of President George W. Bush and into the present, there has been a debate over the impact of lowing taxes. The argument, advanced by Republicans and conservatives generally, was that lowering tax rates would cause people to have an incentive to work and produce more. This was often illustrated by a graph called the Laffer Curve, and the general idea was a part of supply-side economics. The argument went that increased incentive would produce greater economic activity and thus more taxable income and that would lead to more revenue. Liberals, a majority of economists, and some Democrats, argued that while some incentive would occur, it would not be enough to overcome the reduced tax revenue, particularly if rates were relatively low to begin with.

Since 1980, the actual performance of the economy has been examined for evidence to support or oppose this theory. Most economists now agree that the theory was false and that the actual data shows it didn't work. While it might be true that lowing tax rates from 90 to 80 percent would unleash enough economic activity to actually increase total government revenue, lowering rates from 40 to 30 percent is unlikely to do so. A bit of simple math will show that as tax rates get lower, the percentage increase in economic activity needed to offset the loss in revenue must increase dramatically.

However, the actual failure of the theory in fact has not materially reduced its appeal among its advocates. This is an example of a theory being so appealing that it trumps data.

What Caused the Collapse of the Soviet Union?

The fall of the Soviet Union and the ending of the Cold War in 1989 is a major event of late-twentieth-century history. Why did it happen? Advocates offer a series of different causes. Republicans and conservatives point to the military buildup of the United States under President Reagan or perhaps just to his speeches about "the evil empire" and calls to "tear down this wall" as sufficient causes in and of themselves. Others point to decades of structural weaknesses and internal contradictions in the Soviet Union. We perhaps do not give enough credit to Lech Walesa, the Solidarity movement, Pope John Paul II, and other leaders from Eastern Europe who demanded freedom. Perhaps Mikhail Gorbachev deserves some credit for—at the very minimum—not consistently standing in the way of the collapse. What role was played by ordinary citizens who braved opposition to demonstrate for freedom? And if we come back to President Reagan, perhaps his willingness to negotiate and reach agreements with Gorbachev is at least as important as was his military policies.

This seems an issue where oversimplified cause is a likely fallacy. Why should we think one thing and only one thing caused the collapse when millions of people and decades of history are involved? Why are we driven to find just one cause?

Perhaps part of our motivation to find a single cause stems from wanting a situation to support our theories, such as (for this case) about the role of force and power versus the role of justice and peace conditions. Liberals would be as reluctant to credit military force as conservatives are to credit negotiations.

What Effects Have Been Caused by the Increase of CO_2 in the Atmosphere?

This issue has been discussed in other places in this book. Here we would just reiterate that the complexity of the atmosphere makes any simple explanations unlikely to be completely accurate. Theories about how climate works (embodied in computer models) cannot possibly capture every last causal mechanism. Thus, it is easy for someone to pick on a loose end, or something not included in the theory, to claim the entire conclusion is wrong. Most of us observing this debate do not possess adequate knowledge to decide if these points are valid or not.

A useful study for a class project would be to read the Intergovernmental Panel on Climate Change (IPCC) reports in detail or to study the documentation of various climate models and attempt to chase down the actual situation behind certain popular arguments about climate change.

CASE STUDIES: FOR FURTHER INVESTIGATION

Here are brief descriptions of a number of issues that raise causal arguments. These might be good candidates for classroom discussion or for your papers.

What *Did* Cause the Decline in Crime Rates?

Contrary to what many think, the amount of violent crime in the United States has declined dramatically during the last portion of the twentieth century. It is odd that we feel less safe; that could be a topic of investigation in itself.

Data from the U.S. Department of Justice show declines of violent crime (murder and rape) of 50 percent or more from the period of 1980 through 2000. Property crime has also gone down. Among violent crimes, the decline in reports of rape is particularly noteworthy.

So, why this widespread decline in both violent and property crime? Many possible contributing factors have been proposed and debated including:

- Changes in policing practices including community engagement and "broken window" policies (when police take minor crimes seriously; minor crimes can lead neighborhoods to look run-down, leading to inviting more serious crimes)
- Tougher sentences and the dramatic increase in the number of people in jail in the United States
- Decline in the percentage of youth in the prison population (an estimated 57 percent of inmates were under age 35 in 2001)
- Better gun control
- More cell phones (so people can call for help)
- A better economy leading to a sharp decline in unemployment among populations more likely to be criminals
- The legalization of abortion. This (very controversial) view is that abortions were more likely to have occurred in situations where the child would have grown up in an "at risk" situation.

If you decide to research this topic, there are a number of traps you should try to avoid:

- Oversimplified cause. This is a social phenomena that seems quite unlikely to have one, simple, direct cause.
- The difficulty of proof. After all, what you really want to do is find particular individuals who would have committed a crime—but didn't—and get them to tell you (accurately) why they did not become a criminal. And that is just about impossible. So, you'll have to use indirect methods of proof.
- And watch out for people with a political agenda who seem certain why the decline happened. It is easy to find politicians or law enforcement officials, or social activists attributing reduction of crime to various reasons and being utterly convinced they know the answer. So be careful to find some good sources from people who have actually researched the topic.

Will Changing the Drinking Age Change the Culture of Drinking?

A topic of perennial interest to college students in the United States is lowering the drinking age to eighteen. Would doing so allow for responsible drinking in controlled environments? Or would it give license for young people to drink to excess? Central to the issue is what causes people to drink and what social and legal factors influence those decisions.

First of all, what is actually happening? Since many of you are in that age group and you are on a college campus, you may think you know what people are doing. But, you need some data, not anecdotes. There is a national project to collect data on alcohol and drug use by college students. Tap into that. If you do want to do a story on your local college, then consider interviewing someone from the health service, the police, a student leader, a university official who deals with student affairs, local community leaders, and so on.

You need to be aware of the complex interaction of the physical effects of alcohol on a person and the social forces that influence behavior. And people vary: Some can have a drink and leave it, some drink alone, some are alcoholics, and some go through a period of use and then stop. Age is also a factor; many who drink to excess in college reduce their use after graduation.

If you want to talk about drinking and driving and the deaths due to alcohol use, then you also need to take a serious look on the data around traffic accidents. Who exactly is driving drunk? Is it first-time users, drivers with little experience, or a group of repeat offenders? We recently lowered the legal limit from .10 to .08 in the United States. What effect did that have?

Comparisons to Europe are a favorite topic with these papers. Students regularly picture Europe as a paradise of mature sophistication in that they have much lower legal drinking ages than the United States. (As a side note, you might want to look into the way Europe generally plays as a sophisticated alternative to the wild, uncouth, Americans.) But, many things are different between Europe and the United States. Alcohol and its responsible use is integrated into family life in a way not typical in the United States. There are also strong social norms in some countries against being drunk in public. And, for that matter, the legal limit for driving drunk in Europe is much lower than in the United States. You should read the chapter about argument by parallel case in this book before you too simply assume that you can use Europe as an argument for change in the United States.

Would Legalizing Marijuana Cause an Increase in the Use of "Hard" Drugs?

Students seem to like writing papers on the legalization of marijuana. A colleague of ours insists that most of them sound as if they were written by someone who was stoned. How would you write a good paper on this topic?

The usual claim is that making marijuana illegal forces its use underground and causes an increase in the power of criminals. Legalizing marijuana and taxing it would cause more revenue for the government. Behind these claims is a prior issue: Just what are the effects of smoking marijuana? Is it harmful, and just how much harm does it cause? Does it cause you to go on to harder drugs?

If you are going to write on this topic, here are some issues to consider:

- The role of moral values influences views on causes. If you see drugs as an evil snare dragging you down to dissipation, or, equally, if you see drugs as an opening to alternative realities whose attractiveness far exceeds this dull world, it will strongly color what you accept as authoritative evidence.
- Remember the discussion about "theories with no data." It is easy to generate plausible theories about what would happen if marijuana was legalized, but do you have any data? So, first of all, you need to discipline yourself to find real, academically verified data.
- Look over the policy claim chapter in this book. What happens when something illegal is made legal is far more complex than the "drive the criminals out of work and make lots of money for the government" claims regularly offered on this topic. A criminal is quite likely to stay a criminal but take up a different aspect of crime. And it seems odd to us that many who regularly decry the disaster of all things the government does are now enthusiastic advocates of giving the government something else to tax. Yes, the United States did try prohibiting alcohol and then gave it up—and taxed it—but it is not as if alcohol is now a totally solved topic with no social problems. And for that matter, some of the attraction of drugs is precisely because it is illegal. You can't be quite the daring rebel if you bought the signs of your rebellion at the local store rather than having to go down an alley to do it.

Do Childhood Vaccines Cause Autism?

This issue brings to the fore the question of "correlation is not causation" in a painful and emotionally charged way. A parent of a child that has contracted autism is frantic and vocal about what they think caused it. Standing against that is a unified scientific community that points out a total lack of evidence to support this theory. But how can we contradict grieving parents and tell them that they have only seen one thing follow another—not proof?

Papers written on this topic will have to be especially careful to find actual evidence and defensible theories. What appears in the popular press are often just conclusions—"There is no evidence," "I know what I saw"—and often use a conviction about a theory—"Drug companies cover up their problems"—that may be true in some instances to avoid proving that it is true in this instance.

Ad hominum attacks on scientists in general—"They don't know the truth that comes from being a parent" or "They all work for the drug companies"—have to be carefully parsed out. A scientist that offers evidence meeting the criteria of a controlled experiment cannot be dismissed as being biased or uncaring.

Are Social Networking Sites and the Internet Generally Destroying Human Interaction?

Let's jump on Facebook or MySpace and debate this. Send us an email! The issue here is the complaint of some that we are losing our ability to talk to each other face-to-face and to focus intently on the full reality of person-to-person communication. Instead we are multitasking ourselves into a cultural form of attention deficit disorder.

This issue involves a number of the concepts of this chapter. It is an influence argument, and it probably is a social mechanism with feedback processes that accelerate certain changes. And it is also one where it is easy to equate "change" with "harm." So the way we are interacting is changing—and reducing certain forms of good interaction. But is the new way worse?

CONCLUSION

Since your next paper is unlikely to solve centuries-old philosophical problems about the nature of how we know reality or if reality exists, how can you use this?

First of all, if you are going to argue a causal argument, you should strive to find both a theory that explains the cause and data to support that theory. Your argument gets much stronger when you have both.

Second, you need to separate out conclusions from data that come from controlled experiments or close approximations to them, from conclusions that are simply based on prejudice and an anecdote or two.

SUMMARY OF CAUSAL ARGUMENTS

Description
Asserts that an effect can be explained by a specific cause.

Explicit Form
"X (causes/doesn't cause) Y."

Implicit Forms
Can include:
"X is one cause of Y," "X sometimes causes Y," "X is the only cause of Y,"
    "X contributes to increasing Y."

Examples that would typically be developed as causal arguments:

- "The CO_2 that humans are injecting into the atmosphere is causing global warming."
- "Watching pornography increases violence by men against women."
- "Marijuana is a gateway drug; use it and you are likely to move on to hard drugs."
- "The tax cuts during the George Bush presidency are contributing to growing income inequality."

Fact Claims	Value Claims	Policy Claims
C: "Excessive playing of violent video games causes an increase in violent acts by children."	C1: "It is wrong to play violent video games."	C: "Extremely violent video games should be prohibited."
G1a: [evidence from experiments]	G1/C2: "Excessive playing of violent video games causes an increase in violent acts by children."	G1/C2: "Excessive playing of violent video games causes an increase in violent acts by children."
G1b: [theory explaining evidence]	W1: "It is wrong to engage in activities that promote violence."	W: "Things that promote violence should be banned."
W1: "A credible theory backed up with verified data is adequate to believe that a cause has been proven."		

Argumentation Strategy

- Present a theory that explains the causal mechanism.
- Present data that supports the theory.

Issues and Aspects

- Causes are typically proven to a high degree of certainty, not absolutely.
- It is common to oversimplify the causes of complex phenomena.
- Also consult the Argument by Example chapter for more on statistics and the fact claims chapter for more on theories.

Study Questions

- What does "correlation is not causation" means?
- What are the characteristics of a controlled experiment?
- What are some of the difficulties about proving conclusively any complex phenomenon?
- What does a supported theory establish?

Argument from Sign

INTRODUCTION

You arrive at a railroad crossing just as the lights start to flash, the bell to ring, and the gates to come down across the road. You know what those things mean: A train is coming. And, in a few seconds, it appears and rumbles across in front of you.

In the previous chapter on causal arguments, we discussed how if you see event A followed closely in time by event B, it is common to assume that A caused B. But you know that what you first see at the crossing (event A) did not cause the train to appear (event B). In fact, it is the other way around.

The lights, bell, and descending gate are *signs*. They are (hopefully) reliable signs that a train will appear. You can see the signs, but you can't see the train, at least not at first. But, there is a cause at work here. Some distance from the crossing, the train came into the range of sensors. These sensors were triggered by the train's passage, and they directed the crossing indicators to activate. The train caused the sensors to trigger. The sensors caused the crossing signs to operate. But we couldn't see those causes from our car. All we could see were the signs produced by the cause.

Situations like this occur often. We have signs that might mean a crime has been committed, a disease is active, or that someone is addicted but we don't know the cause. But shouldn't we concentrate on underlying causes? Why is this form of "sign" reasoning needed?

It is needed for two reasons. First, there are many situations when the underlying causes are unknown to us or are known but hidden—at least initially. You walk into a job interview. Will this be a good company to work for? You have no way of directly telling, but maybe you can pick up on some signs during the interview. Is this person right for you to be involved with? You can't just open their head and read an answer; you have to decide if what you are seeing indicates if it is so. And if they are and you get married, you'll likely wear rings as a sign you are married.

Arguments by sign are also used when we dress a certain way to communicate something about us, when we try to sort out what the economy is doing, a graduate school decides who to admit, and when a police officer tries to decide if you are driving under the influence, to give a few examples.

Second, people commonly use signs as proof for causes. And they can easily be misled into false conclusions when they do so. Hence, we need to understand when this is a valid argument and when it is not.

THE STRUCTURE OF THIS FORM OF REASONING

In an argument from sign, the claim we wish to prove is likely not expressed directly. We may point to the sign, with the assumption that people can figure out what claim goes with it. It is necessary to unpack the argument by using the Toulmin model to understand the steps involved. Then we will work through some examples.

First, we state the explicit form of the argument:

"X is a sign of Y."

But typically, we're not just saying that because we want to make the claim itself. What we're really trying to get at is "Y"—that "Y" is true.

Toulmin Model

So, our real claim is that:

C1: "Y is true" or "real" [or some other statement about the existence or validity of "Y"]

But, we can't see "Y," not directly. So let's expand our claim:

C1: "This thing, Y, (that you can't see) is true."
G1/C2: "X exists."
W1/C3: "X is a reliable sign of Y and of nothing else."

We are likely to need to unpack our argument in two directions. We'll likely need to supply evidence both for the ground G1 and for the warrant W1.

C2: "X exists."
G2: [Evidence that X is true]
W2: [Rules of inference that determine adequacy of evidence]

This part of the argument is likely not to be very controversial. However, the next part is certainly controversial:

C3: "X is a reliable sign of Y and of nothing else."
G3a: "Y causes X."

G3b: "Nothing else causes X."

W3: "If one thing and one thing only causes an effect, then the effect is a reliable sign of the cause."

As we will see, not all arguments by sign take this exact form. There are other, more complicated situations when G3a becomes probabilistic ("Y sometimes causes X") and G3b may not be true at all. These can lead us into fallacious arguments.

Example 1: Smoke

The very first example we used to explain the Toulmin model earlier in the book was an argument from sign.

C1: "There is a fire!"

G1: "I see smoke."

W1: "Smoke is a reliable sign of fire and of nothing else."

In this case you probably don't need a lot of evidence to prove that smoke exists; you can call people's attention to it. What would likely be a point of contention is the warrant. Is this smoke actually from a fire or is it due to something else?

Example 2: Admission to Grad School

Grad schools have to decide on who to admit based on applications. Each student is trying to present themselves as best they can. Application committees read the paperwork trying to look for signs of intellectual curiosity, demonstrated interest in the field, and other desirable attributes.

C1: "This applicant clearly has a serious interest in this field of study."

G1: "They did an internship in this area."

W1: "An internship demonstrates interest and commitment to the subject."

The dispute in this case will probably be in comparing the signs from various applicants. Applications will be taken at face value, but the admissions committee will have to compare students to see who is giving the most signs, or the strongest signs, that they would be a good fit for the graduate program.

CASE STUDY

One of the most complicated uses of argument by sign is in discussions about the state of the economy. Is it getting better, getting worse, stagnating, soaring? Is a recession ending? Is one coming? While "the economy" is all around us and we make economic decisions every day, we are almost too close to it to evaluate it. The economy is the sum of all the people and all their decisions every day. There are millions of causal connections going on, complicated by feedback loops, changing rules, and uncertain data. How can we decide how the economy is doing?

We try to use indicators, something that is easily measured that can be a proxy for the entire economy. The problem is that something as complex as the economy has dozens of plausible measures of its health. What shall we use?

- The stock market. Stocks going up in price is generally taken as a sign of economic health. But not everyone owns stocks. And stocks can go up when many people are suffering financially.
- The unemployment rate. Lower unemployment would seem to be a sign of economic health. But if the rate goes too low, it can indicate we're in for inflation. And the unemployment rate and the stock market do not always give us the same indication.
- The rate of inflation. High inflation is bad for the economy in general. But it can be good news if you owe money and the interest rate you're paying is fixed. Deflation—prices going down—can spell trouble for an economy.
- The level of inventories that businesses are holding in their stockrooms and warehouses. Unusually high inventories might be a sign of a slowdown coming (as businesses will soon cut back on orders). Low inventories may signal an upturn is coming because excess inventory has been used up and businesses will have to start reordering.
- Excess capacity in manufacturing. If businesses have a lot of unused capacity, that's a sign the economy is not doing well. If the amount of unused capacity is very small, it may mean that inflation is likely.
- Indexes of consumer or business confidence. Agencies do surveys to determine if people feel confident about their economic future. If many are confident or their confidence is rising, then an upturn may be coming.

In addition to these formal indicators (and there are others) people may form their view of the economy by reading what signs they can see around them such as empty businesses in their town, or the number of friends who are cutting back on vacations, or who have lost their jobs.

If that wasn't hard enough, we also have to consider that we have indicators for specific sectors of the economy, indicators for individual regions of the country, and some signs that may predict the future (leading indicators), and others that give us a read on what has been happening in the past.

When the 2008 economic slowdown was beginning, a great deal of attention got paid to an otherwise obscure sign known as "LIBOR"—the London Interbank Offered Rate. Banks loan each other money overnight to compensate for variations in deposits and withdrawals. As concern mounted over the economy, this interest rate, known as LIBOR, started to increase dramatically. Banks were hanging on to their deposits and were only willing to loan to other banks at higher and higher rates of interest. When, after various government interventions, this rate fell back down, it was taken as a sign that things were returning to normal.

But, there was another dimension to this. LIBOR is a sign of credit markets in particular, not of the entire economy. So this sign pointed to causes going on in one part of the economy.

Additionally, LIBOR is not a record of actual transactions between banks; it is a survey of what a few banks intend to do. If it was an exact record of all transactions, you could still argue over the significance of the sign, but it would at least be an accurate signal of what had occurred. However, at the time of the crisis, when LIBOR's rate was increasing, there was some discussion that this was not actually measuring what everyone thought it measured. The estimates or predictions of what banks would lend were themselves being affected by the crisis. In other words, there was a dispute about if this was even an accurate sign or not.

With the previous measures we discussed (like the unemployment rate), the argument wasn't if the indicator was accurate or not, it was an argument about what the indicator meant. In the case of LIBOR, it might be both an argument about what it meant and if it was an accurate measure.

And even this is a simplification. Interest rates go up and down over time, so what might be the proper indicator is the *difference* between LIBOR and the "normal" interest at that time. But how do we measure the normal interest rate? We'll need a sign for that, so now we are looking at the difference between two signs.

If that all sounds too complicated, there were simpler signs for detecting economic problems. At the very beginning of the economic decline in late 2008, when people weren't sure how deep or how real the decline was, the *Financial Times* ran an article (Farrell, 2008) about how waiters and bar owners near Wall Street were noticing that various workers in financial markets were coming in to drink earlier in the day and were drinking more. It seemed like a sign that things were getting bad.

This situation is typical of trying to understand complex processes by reading the signs. There are a lot of signs, they indicate different aspects of the overall issue, they may point in different directions, and they may not mean what we think they mean. Similar situations confront a physician attempting to diagnose a rare disease, a detective working on a complicated case, or a government trying to gain intelligence on a foreign nation.

So, argument from sign can be complicated. Now we need to look more closely at the theory behind these arguments and under what conditions the argument is valid or not.

WHAT MAKES ARGUMENT BY SIGN VALID?

We will consider a number of cases in turn.

Single Reliable Cause

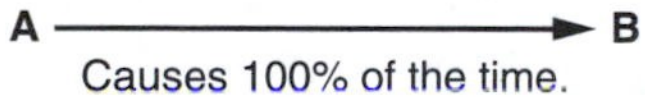

A ————————————➤ B

Causes 100% of the time.

FIGURE 20.1

Infallible Sign.

In this case, there is a cause, A, that always produces the sign, B. If A happens, then B happens. We certainly hope that railroad crossings fit into this category. Every single time that a train comes, the gates will come down.

However, the certainty of this forward connection can lead us into a trap. We can tend to assume that if A causes B, then if we see B, that must mean that A happened. But that is not always the case. Two conditions are necessary for us to reason backward from a sign to a cause:

- There can only be one cause for the sign.
- The cause must always work.

If we know for certain that these conditions exist, then we can argue backward. But when we assume these conditions exist, we get into trouble. The next case illustrates why this can be a trap.

The Implications of a Second Cause

Here, A still reliably causes B. But now C also causes B. In this case, if all we know is that B has occurred, then we cannot infer that A has happened.

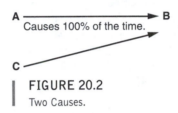

FIGURE 20.2
Two Causes.

One of the authors arrived at a railroad crossing one day to see the lights flashing. He waited, but no train came. The lights turned off, and a few seconds later they came back on. Getting out of his car, he looked up and down the tracks. No train. Something else had triggered the crossing into activity.

This problem affects many situations. Guilty people are nervous when being questioned by the police. But innocent people, totally unfamiliar with being questioned by an officer, can be nervous as well. Remember our economic examples. Perhaps getting laid off from your job (A) always causes you to reduce your spending (B). But there are other reasons you might reduce your spending (C) such as saving for a major expense or preparing for retirement.

> "During the early days of WW II in Great Britain the security services received many reports about marks seen on telegraph poles. They were thought to be coded messages for use by German invaders. It turned out the marks were the work of Boy Scouts and Girl Guides who were then asked not to do this any more."
>
> —Christopher Andrew, *Defend the Realm*, p. 223

This situation is radically affected by both the frequency and rate of occurrence of these triggers (A and C). If C occurs once for every thousand occurrences of A, we have a different situation than if A and C occur at the same rate.

Independent and Dependent Signs

Two signs would seem better than one. But how much better is not always obvious. We have to ask if the two signs are independent.

In the first diagram, we are describing a situation when some event (like "the economy") has produced two signs by two different causal mechanisms. In the second diagram, there are also two signs, but one mechanism produced them both.

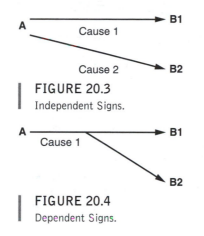

FIGURE 20.3
Independent Signs.

FIGURE 20.4
Dependent Signs.

Consider the rail crossing again. There are three signs of an approaching train: the blinking lights, the bell, and the crossing gate coming down. But they are all produced by one cause—a sensor being triggered. They did not arise from three independent sensors. And they are unlikely to disagree. If the sensor fails, then all three signs will also stop. That's different than if the bell, the lights, and the gate were run off of three different sensors with totally independent wiring.

Many critical systems that involve risk to people if they fail are equipped with independent warning devices that are carefully engineered to attempt to avoid "single point of failure" situations. In other words, engineered to be like the first of our two diagrams and not the second.

Dealing with Probabilistic Signs

Things can get more complicated if the cause in question doesn't always work. Let's suppose we have a case where the only cause of B is A. We know that for a certainty. However, A doesn't always cause B. That is, when A happens, sometimes B happens, but sometimes it doesn't.

Therefore, if we observe B, then we do know A occurred (because we know that A is the only cause of B). But the reverse is most certainly not the case. The lack of B does not prove that A didn't occur.

A ———————————➤ B
Causes 50% of the time.

FIGURE 20.5
Probable Sign.

Making a Stronger Argument

We're unlikely to have causes that we know to be 100 percent effective. And, we're also often uncertain what other factors (like C and D in this diagram) may be operating. Almost every single sign could be generated by something else, at least potentially.

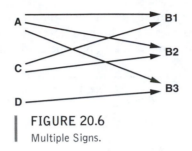

FIGURE 20.6
Multiple Signs.

What makes our arguments much stronger is if we can find multiple signs that point to our cause. While one sign might be caused by several things, it is less likely that five or six of them will have been. So, it is better, if we are trying to prove something, that we look for multiple signs.

If we want to make a case that the economy is really in recovery, we should examine a number of signs (for example, the stock market going up, unemployment going down, consumer confidence going up), which in the aggregate cannot be explained by anything but economic recovery.

ARGUING ABOUT SIGNS

From theory, we now turn back to some practical considerations about arguing about signs.

What Is the Stasis of This Argument?

Arguments from sign can quickly get complicated because of their indirect nature. You could soon be arguing about if a sign is reliable, if there are other signs, or if the sign means what everyone thinks it means. You may be reverting to an argument from cause to deal with the underlying events.

Defending and Rebutting

When someone sees a particular event and attributes meaning to it, it can be hard to rebut their argument. Once someone says that "X is a sign of Y" it can be hard to "unlearn" the connection, even if it is fallacious.

In May 2008, Dunkin' Donuts launched an ad campaign with Rachael Ray. She was wearing a scarf that some conservatives thought was a keffiyeh, an Arab headdress (It wasn't). Having seen the scarf, they took this as an intentional sign of Ray's and Dunkin' Donuts' beliefs and then further concluded that wearing an Arab headdress was a sign of support for terrorism. Dunkin' Donuts pulled the ad.

In January of 2009, as President Obama was about to be inaugurated, Krispy Kreme (What is it about donuts?) launched a promotion giving away a drink to anyone who walked up to the counter and said "Yes, we can" in honor of the freedom of choice of choosing a new president. Some might have taken that as a tacit endorsement of Obama, but the word "choice" triggered some conservative groups to see it as a sign of an endorsement of abortion (since that is considered to be "pro-choice").

Now, you may think both of these conclusions are quite a stretch, but how do you rebut the argument? It's easy to say "That's ridiculous," but can you prove it is?

The hard way is to do a bunch of research into the companies, their spokespersons, their previously expressed policies, and their likelihood of expressing political views in an advertisement. It shouldn't be too hard to prove that large companies, in general, are very unlikely to express any sort of political views in their product ads. But, you would still be doing a lot of work. Doing this work also implicitly accepts that you have the burden of proof to prove innocence when, what should be the case here, is that those making these accusations need to meet their burden of proof. They need to show that there are no other likely reasons for wearing a scarf or for what "choice" means. They need to prove that the most probable conclusion is what they are alleging. They need to come up with several signs that would support these accusations. Failing that, their arguments should be dismissed.

"X Is Consistent with Y"

You might hear someone make the claim of this form. For example, "The wounds are consistent with those made by a baseball bat" or "The wounds are consistent with the alleged murder weapon." This form of a claim is not the same as saying "These wounds could only have come from this particular weapon." Go back to the example we gave where both A and C could cause B. The form of the claim means that "A could have caused B" or "We cannot rule out that A could have caused B." But this claim is not the same as saying "A is the only possible cause of B."

Doubtless, some might hope you hear "consistent with" as "the only cause of" but you should carefully determine what your opponent is actually claiming.

Selecting Signs

We live in a world filled with signs. If we start looking we can see signs of something everywhere. The risk is that we start with our conclusions and then just start noticing what agrees with the conclusion you started with. This is yet another form of *confirmation bias*.

FAMOUS ARGUMENTS FROM SIGN

Sherlock Holmes, Dr. House, and All Who Detect and Diagnose

Sherlock Holmes, the famous fictional nineteenth-century detective, made his career on being able to read signs that everyone else missed. In the stories he deduces what side of a carriage someone sat on from the patterns of mud splatters, their occupation from calluses on their hands, and so on. The stories are great entertainment.

However, sometimes his deductions can fall victim to the fallacies we discussed above. He reads a sign, assumes it has only one cause when it would seem easy to come up with some other cause of the sign.

The same comments apply to the modern equivalents such as Dr. House and all the CSI shows. The shows can be fun, but they take a lot of shortcuts.

In the real world, detectives and doctors have messier problems to solve and higher standards of proof. They have to prove that their signs could have only been caused by one particular suspect or one specific disease. Detectives and forensics technicians look at blood spatter, injury patterns, the shape of wounds, fingerprints, DNA, damage to walls and doors, and many other factors to argue backward to identify what caused all those things to occur.

They often use one sign to guide them to search for other signs. A detective or crime scene investigator notices something. That leads to asking some particular question or performing a particular test to detect further evidence.

The Cover of the Beatles' Abbey Road Album

In 1969, the Beatles released their Abbey Road album. A short time before this, an urban legend had started that Paul McCartney was dead and had been replaced by a look-alike. The cover photo poured gasoline on the controversy. It was mined for clues that support the rumor (Paul is barefoot! He's walking out of step with the others! It's a funeral procession! Lennon is dressed like a clergyman! Ringo is in a black suit like an undertaker!). There was more, including several that could only be found by playing songs backward (something at least theoretically possible in the turntable era).

What is fascinating from an argumentation perspective is that there are multiple signs here, just like we asked you to come up with to make stronger arguments. But why is this argument bogus? Because all of the clues can be simply refuted by the lack of any death certificate, the denial of all involved, or McCartney showing up for an interview. That, and the total lack of any reason why this would have been done.

The Police Officer Deciding to Arrest Someone for DWI

In order for the police to make an arrest for driving under the influence, they need to be reasonably certain that the driver is impaired in some way (by alcohol or drugs or some other factor). They didn't see the driver drink or use drugs. How can they decide that the driver is impaired? They have to look for signs.

Police use a variety of signs. But each can be misleading. Even if they see a car weaving across the road, perhaps the driver just lost attention momentarily or dropped the cell phone they aren't supposed to be using when they drive. A strong smell of alcohol in the car? Maybe somebody dropped a container and it broke. They can have the driver perform tests at the side of the road that involve balance and coordination. Drunk people will likely fail these. But what about the person who is nervous, or has bad ankles, or if the road is icy and traffic is whizzing by?

Another test used is the horizontal nystagmus test. Nystagmus is a fluttering or vibration of the eyes when they are positioned to the far left or right. The officer will have the driver follow a pen or other object with their eyes. He will look for signs of nystagmus. If he sees enough of them, there is a documented high probability that the driver's blood alcohol level is above the legal limit.

Putting all this information together, the officer will make a decision to arrest or not.

Signs of God

Does God send signs? Many followers of diverse religions think so. Whether in answer to a specific prayer or unasked for, believers judge certain events to be indicators sent by God to give them guidance.

The difficulty here is that the underlying cause is very difficult or impossible to prove (or disprove) with any of the methods of science. Many signs are things that could happen anyway, but happen at a particular time such as getting a job offer after praying for financial help. Some signs seem very unlikely to have been coincidences, others could easily be. So you are left to debate the probability that something is a sign or is not.

Believers use the term "sign" in a different sense also. If you drive too fast and get a ticket, some can say that was God telling you to slow down. The nonbeliever thinks that was the logical consequence of breaking a law—nothing divine about it. However, the believer is viewing the structure and order implemented in this world as coming from God and so the logical working out of that structure is God's action. Thus, God has set up a world in which you have choices, but bad things will happen to you if you use that power unwisely.

Signs of Child Abuse

Over the past few decades there has been a revolution in the discussion, investigation, and prosecution of child abuse. Once hidden, now there is a widespread and open discussion of the issue, and we are constantly warned to be on the lookout for abuse. This is progress, no doubt. Children who are abused don't have to suffer in silence, thinking they are the only ones.

But, how do you tell if a child has been abused sexually or physically? There may be some physical evidence that is conclusive, but there are seldom eyewitnesses or videos of the abuse. So, we are often told to "look for the signs" by being sensitive to changes in behavior of a child. What are those signs? The following are some that appear on a number of websites for agencies dealing with abuse issues:

- Changes in behavior
- Is always watchful
- Overly compliant
- Comes to school early, stays late
- Fearful
- Shys away from touch
- Depression, self-mutilation
- Inability to connect
- Nightmares/bedwetting
- Runs away
- Change in appetite

Arguments We Don't Ever Want to Hear Again:
"Denial Is a Sign of Guilt."

You can read the claim that "Denial is a sign of an abuser (or an alcoholic)." Or that denial in the face of overwhelming evidence is normal in situations involving abuse. Denial is thought to be a common occurrence not only by the perpetrator but also by the victim of abuse.

This may be true, but it sets up a dangerous situation. Remember the case we described where two different mechanisms produce the same sign. It may be true that most of those engaging in abuse deny it, but it seems quite likely to be the case that 100 percent of those *not* engaged in abuse will also deny it.

The danger is that, in the face of denials, someone will start pressuring children to admit what is going on and lead children to make up stories to please the adult or to resolve the pressure they are under. Or someone will fail to do adequate research and just jump from the denial to assuming guilt.

It's only "denial" if you know, from other evidence, that someone is guilty. Without that, you can't decide if it is denial or the truth. In and of itself, "denial" is a totally useless sign and should not be the basis of your decision about innocence or guilt.

Where the knowledge that people involved in abuse or addiction deny their situation is useful is in situations where you have become legitimately convinced, through *other evidence*, that abuse has taken place. Then, with this knowledge, you won't be shaken or dissuaded from action by the vociferous protestations of innocence. You'll know that abusers lie and that victims are embarrassed to admit what is going on, and you'll be better able to develop a strategy to proceed.

What is good about this list is the notion of looking for multiple signs. But what people forget is the idea that while an abused child may exhibit "changes in behavior," that is also pretty common among young children. Children change direction all the time. Likewise children also commonly change their eating patterns as they grow up. The danger is that someone will take an isolated sign, not do an investigation, and then launch accusations that are hard to refute.

Sites concerned with child abuse also list signs that an adult is an abuser. Here is one list:

• Insists on hugging or touching even when child does not want it
• Shares private information with child
• Frequently babysits children for free

A lot depends on how those signs are interpreted. Someone who was a friendly grandparent might exhibit all three of these signs at least once. On the other hand, a stranger who does them, more than once, to a child he or she hardly knows—that sign might well be worth investigating.

The issues of interpreting signs around abuse is not simply a theoretical problem. In the 1980s and 1990s, there was a series of "panics" about child abuse in day care centers as well as an overlapping panic about ritual satanic abuse. Despite no physical evidence being found, families were torn apart, parents lost their children, and communities were disrupted. But most of these cases turned out to be nothing. Why did people succumb to this hysteria? There are many reasons, but it would have helped if the police, the prosecutors, and the judges understood the material of this chapter.

EXAMPLES FOR FURTHER STUDY

What Are the Signs of a Good Job?

You enter a company for an interview. How will you decide if this is the place you want to work? What can you observe about the physical surroundings, the demeanor of people, how you are treated, and other factors. Once, one of the authors was on an interview and on an elevator with three people from the company. The conversation was pleasant and complimentary between the two men to the one woman. The woman got off the elevator, and, as soon as the door closed, the two men started ripping her in a nasty, sexist way. It didn't seem like a good sign.

Can you make a list of possible clues you'll look for during an interview?

What Are the Signs You Should End a Relationship?

If you're fighting more than you used to, does it mean you should break up? Is flirting with someone else a deal-breaker? Not being willing to share? Disrespect for your interests? How do you decide to break up with someone?

What Are the Signs This Person Is Unreliable or Lying?

You ask a question, and you get a feeling that someone isn't being honest? How does a detective or military interrogator or interviewer (or parent!) decide that the person they are talking to is lying? Those who do this for a living study a number of techniques for eliciting and detecting signs that someone is lying.

What Does Clothing Signify?

Since ancient times, a person's clothing signifies many things about them. It is still true today. If you are a Goth, or a motorcycle rider, or a corporate executive, you have a "uniform" to wear. We identify those working in an official capacity by their uniform or identification. Experiments have been done to show that people who are well dressed can get more money from strangers than those who are poorly dressed.

We identify our loyalty to sports teams by the caps and shirts and colors we wear. Gang members also use colors and clothing to identify themselves. Wearing our baseball cap bill forward, or pushed back on our heads, or bill sideways, or bill backwards, all mean different things. We carry corporate logos on our shirts.

We may choose to wear a flag lapel pin to signify our patriotism, jewelry to communicate status or wealth. We dress up for some occasions or dress down for others. And then there is the vast topic of clothing to communicate sexual desirability (or downplay it).

Many interesting questions arise as to how accurate these signs are. A person can intentionally set out to adopt a "look" that has no connection to who they really are.

CONCLUSION

Argument from sign is necessary since we can't see every cause in action. But the propensity to assume that a sign allows us to reason backward often leads people into errors.

SUMMARY OF ARGUMENT FROM SIGN

Description

Something visible gives evidence for the existence of a causal process that is not immediately apparent.

Explicit Form

"X is a sign of Y."

Implicit Forms

Can include:

"X can only mean Y."

Examples that would typically be developed as arguments from sign

- "Smoke is a sign of fire."
- "The stock market going down is a sign of economic problems."
- "A flock of birds flying south is a sign that winter is near."
- "A black cat is a sign you will have bad luck."

Fact Claims	Value Claims	Policy Claims
"His expensive watch is a sign he is rich."	"His expensive and showy watch is a sign he is shallow."	"I need a better watch so I can look more impressive."

Argumentation Strategy

- Prove that the sign exists.
- Establish that there is (to a sufficient degree of certainty) only one possible causal explanation for the sign (or signs).

Issues and Aspects

- The argument about a sign may well be offered in support of an unstated claim.
- Signs may have multiple causes.
- Errors occur because people try to argue backward from sign to cause without awareness of how that can be fallacious.
- Multiple signs are often needed to adequately prove the underlying cause.

Study Questions

- What is the relationship between causal arguments and argument by sign?
- Under what conditions can you argue backward from a sign to a cause?
- How would you go about rebutting an argument by sign that you thought was absurd?
- What does it mean if multiple signs are independent or not?

Argument by Dilemma

INTRODUCTION

Argument by dilemma presents a choice between two alternatives. The advocate is often making a claim of the form:

"X or Y!"

And the exclamation point is there to emphasize that this is one form of argumentation that is often made forcefully and bluntly. This form of reasoning is often used to sharpen a choice, to force a decision, or to expose contradictions. So an advocate wanting a decision on a product development choice might argue that "We either need to get serious about building this or quit."

However, that sentence, "X or Y," is probably not, in fact, the actual claim. It may be what an advocate says or writes, but the real claim is often not stated. Perhaps, in the example in the last paragraph, the individual really wanted to go ahead with product development, thinking that it was obvious that quitting was absurd and wanting the company to quit dithering and make a commitment. In this case, the real claim was not expressed. A dilemma is often posed as a way of getting to something else. It might be posed so that an advocate can argue that someone has framed an argument incorrectly or that someone is doing two contradictory things. We'll explain how this could occur.

A classic dilemma is one offered with two alternatives, but it can be made with three or four alternatives.

Arguments by dilemma are often prone to one of several fallacies. Moreover, our habit of seeing many issues as binary choices can often blind us to the complexity of a situation.

UNDERSTANDING ARGUMENT BY DILEMMA

In this section, we'll examine argument by dilemma from two perspectives. First we'll consider its (valid) use to reshape the rhetorical frame of a conversation. Then, we'll use the Toulmin model to assess what is really going on and what you need to back up a claim in this form.

Rhetorical Impact

Argument by dilemma is often used to **sharpen a contrast** or **refocus attention** on key issues. By posing a stark choice, focus is shifted to the main issues and other alternatives are pushed off as minor concerns. A conversation that has run into a dead end can be restarted.

A committee has been called to discuss approving a student for an honors degree. The conversation wanders into issues of modifying the requirements, how much previous students had (unfairly) to do, and even personal issues involving the faculty. Finally, one member of the committee says, "This is interesting, but in the end, we either approve her or we don't." The other members are drawn up short, there is a moment of silence, they realize that the other issues are not the point, and they get back to discussing the student's work. The statement of the dilemma was not an invitation to pick one or the other alternatives, but to recognize what the alternatives were—and that time was being devoted to alternatives that were not relevant.

As in the previous example, argument by dilemma has a way of **conveying urgency in order to motivate a decision**. Consider this quotation:

> "We are here to make a choice between the quick and the dead. That is our business. Behind the black portent of the new atomic age lies a hope which, seized upon with faith, can work our salvation. If we fail, then we have damned every man to be the slave of fear. Let us not deceive ourselves: We must elect world peace or world destruction."
>
> — Bernard Baruch, June 1946, to the United Nations Atomic Energy Commission (UNAEC)

This time, the posing of the dilemma was certainly aimed at persuading the audience to select the alternative of peace and to communicate that failing to decisively choose that option would lead to very bad consequences.

In a less serious vein, such popular sayings as "Go big or stay at home," or "Fish or cut bait" are also intended to suggest that it is time for a decision.

Argument by dilemma can be a way of **exposing a contradiction** in a position or actions of someone. You can imagine someone saying something like:

"If you dislike the guy, why are you still with him, and if you like him, why are you always complaining about him?"

Here, the person making this point is not really intending to get the person to choose one or the other. Rather the aim is in trying to "unstick" the conversation and move the discussion forward.

From these examples, we can see how argument by dilemma can have a significant and positive impact on a discussion.

How Does Argument by Dilemma Work?

As we said earlier, some of the aspects of this form of reasoning go unstated. To get clarity on what is going on, we turn to Toulmin again. We'll work through two variations.

Variation 1: One alternative is best

 C1 (expressed): "X or Y!"

The advocate will express claim C1. But in this case, it is only a way of trying to make a claim that one of these alternatives (we'll use X) is better than the other. So, the unexpressed claim might be:

 C2 (unexpressed): "X is the best available option."

or

 C3 (unexpressed): "Only X can be true."

And there could be other ways of expressing this claim. The advocate is arguing that there are only two plausible ideas to consider and X is preferable or true or of higher value. We could phrase the claim this way then:

 C4 (unexpressed): "It's either X (which is desirable) or Y (which is not desirable), so accept X."

So, now, phrased this way, you can see that three different pieces of evidence are needed to support this claim:

 G1: [evidence for X being desirable]
 G2: [evidence for Y being undesirable] (or less desirable than X)
 G3: [evidence that X and Y are the only plausible choices for the issue being discussed]

The warrant is then the simple logical notion that:

 W: "When faced with a limited set of choices, choose the best option."

And once again, these claims might get rephrased depending on if this was a fact, value, or policy claim.

Variation 2: Reframe the situation This variation is one in which you want to expose a contradiction or suggest that the options being considered are not effective. Once again, what is likely expressed is something simple:

 C1 (expressed): "X or Y!"

But here, what the advocate is probably claiming is something like:

C2a (unexpressed): "The alternatives being considered for this problem are wrong."

This claim might get stated more explicitly as:

C2b (unexpressed): "You can only do X (which leads to an undesirable outcome) or Y (which leads to an undesirable outcome)."

And note that in the final example of the last section, the reason that the alternatives were undesirable was that they were internally inconsistent. But C3 should really be broken apart and expressed as grounds.

> C2: "The alternatives being considered for this problem are wrong."
> G2a: "X and Y are the only alternatives being discussed."
> G2b: "X is undesirable."
> G2c: "Y is undesirable."
> W2a: "If each one of the alternatives being considered is undesirable, the set being considered is undesirable."

However, this probably isn't the reason for posing the dilemma. It may be that the advocate wants to argue that this whole way of looking at the argument is wrong. In this case the real claim is:

> C3 (unexpressed): "We should be considering other options."
> G3a: "The alternatives being considered for this problem are wrong."
> W3: "When working on a problem, you should find desirable choices."

Again, how this would get framed would vary depending on the claim being a fact, value, or policy claim.

Implications

The variations described above are not exhaustive of the possibilities. What they do call our attention to is how much is left unsaid in this form of reasoning.

ISSUES WITH ARGUMENT BY DILEMMA

Argument by dilemma is quite often a fallacy, and there are four principal ways it can go wrong.

1. **Are there really only two alternatives?**
   It seems unlikely that most situations really have only two alternatives, even if just two may seem the most likely ones. A candidate from one of the two major political parties wins almost all elections in the United States, but several other parties are generally on the ballot; you could vote for someone else.

It may be that only two alternatives have received all the attention, but some research would reveal that there were other, interesting alternatives. Finding a "third way" is often the key to solving disputes between two people who each hold one of the two popular views. Below, in the section on dualistic thinking, we will explore this in more detail.

2. **Is each alternative really an "all or nothing" concept?**

There are "good people" and "bad people." Except that people can be good most of the time, but occasionally bad. And there are degrees of goodness, with some actions being good, others very good, and a few people exemplifying exceptional degrees of "goodness." It's not a yes or no concept. In the realm of policy arguments, be they choices of products to make or laws to pass, it is quite often the case that each alternative is a composite of dozens of smaller options, and you can implement them in part or completely.

If, for example, "universal health care" is one of the alternatives, there are several different ways it could be implemented, many options about what it could include, and other choices about how it is paid for.

This fallacy can even occur with purely factual issues. Is Newtonian mechanics "right" or is it "wrong"? It's right in some situations and wrong for some other situations.

3. **Do you really have to choose?**

It isn't that unusual that it turns out that one can do both of the alternatives or do half of one and half of the other. If one alternative is to "build a new factory in the United States" and the other is "buy a company to produce the product," it might turn out that a smaller factory could be built to make part of the product and a division of a company purchased to make the other half.

4. **Can dilemma ever be a valid argument?**

Life is seldom so simple that the dilemma will be literarily true. But it may be practically true for a given situation. And, as we argued before, it can be the way of focusing a debate onto the real issues.

MAKING AND DEFENDING YOUR ARGUMENT

Being Prepared to Justify Your Case

Because the real claim is implied, it is easy for an argument by dilemma not to be fully worked out. Since, like argument by analogy, it has a sort of immediate rhetorical force, the dilemma may never be discussed. In either case, the grounds to support the claim may be left undiscussed, even by those who disagree with the claim.

If you are going to make this sort of argument, especially in print, you need to think out how you will support the claim. The components of making the argument would likely include the following:

- Explaining why the two alternatives are the only ones to consider or the only ones being considered.
- Explaining why one alternative is the best option or why more alternatives should be considered.

Rebutting the Argument

If you are going to reply to an argument by dilemma, you have a number of options.

You can accept the choice and argue that one **alternative is desirable**. In this case, you agree with the framing of the debate as a dilemma, but you argue that people have been incorrect in concluding that both alternatives are undesirable.

You can **reject the dilemma** as fallacious. In this case you'd contend that one (or more) of the three problems identified in the last section applied.

You can also try to **surface the implied claims** and then try to reframe the assumptions your opponent is making. Here, you'd try to get behind the statement of the dilemma and look for what might be really motivating the expressed claim. This option might be more readily used in personal situations with a friend. You would be asking why the issue has been framed in this way and looking for new ways of looking at a problem.

CASE STUDY: CIVIL LIBERTIES VS. NATIONAL SECURITY

Ever since the 9/11 terrorist attacks, there has been in the United States, and in other countries, a debate about how to respond that has been couched as a dilemma. It is often stated, or assumed, that there is a choice, a trade-off between preserving civil liberties on the one hand and national security on the other. This debate goes back farther than 9/11, but seems to have been heightened since then. The dilemma, widely accepted, is that in order to keep the country safe, civil liberties have to be sacrificed. That has supported a significant increase of government surveillance, both covert and overt (such as security cameras), secret wiretaps, secret detentions of individuals, secret court proceedings, intensive interrogations including torture, more intrusive searches at airports, and a number of other measures.

Whatever the merits of specific proposals and regardless of judgments of how much added security we need, this formulation of the problem falls victim to all three of the fallacies identified above.

There are **more than two alternatives**. The debate assumes an alternative of "privacy and freedom" and an alternative of "security measures." But there are other alternatives. One large set of alternative strategies falls under the label "foreign policy." The foreign wars the United States has been fighting in Iraq and Afghanistan have a significant impact on our security. Our relations with other nations and the attention we give to military and economic development of other countries also have an impact on national security.

The categories are not **monolithic entities**. Civil liberties is not a binary, yes or no proposition. Take freedom of speech: There are scores of different aspects and situations when you might or might not be free to speak. You can be free to speak about certain things and not others. And if you're not free to speak openly, maybe you can do so covertly. And if the government prohibits some aspect of speech, there is still the question of what punishment should be given. And the same comment could be made about the other aspects of civil liberties. It's not the case that you must either have all civil liberties or none of them.

And the same is true for policies aimed at securing our country; it's not the case that we either have perfect security or none at all.

We seldom have to **choose to do one or the other.** What efforts the CIA puts forth to track suspicious foreign nationals has little direct impact on the freedoms of Americans. How aggressive our foreign policy is in the Middle East, how we approach the Israeli-Palestinian question, and how we relate to authoritarian regimes also have little impact on the civil rights of U.S. citizens as they go about their daily routine.

Armoring cockpit doors of airplanes, x-raying checked luggage, or making buildings resistant to explosives are useful security measures that also have virtually no impact on our civil liberties.

There is a spectrum of components to civil liberties: free speech, rights in a criminal proceeding, privacy, rules regarding the retention of personal information, privacy, and others. Likewise national security is composed of a wide spectrum of policy areas including how many resources we put into tracking terrorist elements in our society, resources for conventional police work, beefing up the FBI's efforts, changing penalties for those convicted of violence, our stance to immigration, policies that effect integration of communities, research done on motivations of and detection of potential terrorists, and so on.

When we look at how terrorist plots have been foiled (or not), in many cases, the key factors had little to do with enhanced security measures that attacked our liberties. Better cooperation between the FBI, the CIA, and the FAA would have given those agencies a fighting chance to prevent the 9/11 attacks. Many terror plots after 9/11 have been stopped by conventional police work that often depended on tips from citizens.

But there is an even deeper fallacy at work here. Far from being a trade-off between "civil liberties" and "security," a case can be made that keeping a strong set of civil liberties actually enhances security, particularly against this sort of irregular threat. Years ago, we used to believe that the freedoms of the United States, how we were an open society, and where elected leaders could be called to account, would win plaudits abroad, made people want to emulate us, and created loyal friends. It seems that we are less confident about that now.

Given that a significant fraction of domestic terrorist suspects seem to be from radical elements of Islamic culture, it would be arguable that one of the highest priorities for law enforcement would be to develop good relations with the nonradical majority of Muslims as these might be the best contacts for providing information on radical groups. That would require respecting the civil liberties of that group.

An intensive focus on making a surveillance society, stopping and questioning people on the basis of appearance, or infiltrating peace groups, may make us less safe because they lead people to be suspicious of law enforcement and refuse to cooperate or come forward with information.

Why Is This Dilemma so Widely Accepted?

What is fascinating from an argumentation perspective about this dilemma is that both sides accept that a trade-off exists, and yet, both sides could make better and more persuasive arguments if they rejected the dilemma.

It's obvious how liberals, or those wishing to preserve and extend civil liberties, could benefit from rejecting the terms of the dilemma. They could argue straightforwardly the points made above and go on to appeal to those on the other side by advocating for those national security measures that had no or only a tiny impact on civil liberties.

It is equally true, but less obvious, that conservatives, or those arguing the priority of national security, could become more persuasive by rejecting the trade-off. Instead of placing themselves as advocates of a surveillance state with a large, invasive government, they could be consistent with their normal stance in favor of limited government and consistent with their advocacy of liberty. They could vigorously promote a spectrum of security measures and emphasize how they have no or very little negative impact on civil liberties.

So if both sides could benefit, why do they both persist in accepting the framing of the debate as a dilemma? Certainly, their values and their negative views of their opponents are a factor. But something should be allowed for our habit of accepting the frame of a debate as given, and arguing within that frame, instead of looking to examine the assumptions that come with it.

It would be worth investigating.

FAMOUS DILEMMAS

Argument by dilemma is very old and has figured in some significant debates.

Socrates in Plato's Dialogs

SOCRATES: "... does it seem to you, Polus, to be worse to act unjustly or to be treated unjustly?"

POLUS: "To me, of course, to be treated unjustly."

SOCRATES: "What indeed? Is it uglier to act unjustly or to be treated unjustly? Answer!"

POLUS: "To act unjustly."

SOCRATES: "And so it is also worse, if it is uglier."

POLUS: "Least of all, of course!"

SOCRATES: "I understand: you don't seem to think that the beautiful and the good are the same, and that the bad and ugly [are the same]."

POLUS: "No, indeed."

(Plato, Gorgias, 474c)

It is a common occurrence in the dialogues of Socrates to find him posing a dilemma to his questioner. The other participant usually accepts the dilemma uncritically, and this often leads to problems for him.

It does seem that a problem of false alternatives affects any number of these dilemmas. Is it really only a choice to "do wrong" or to "suffer it"? Perhaps one can avoid either at times, or perhaps there is a trade-off between what you suffer in the short term and what you can avoid in the long term.

Some sympathy should be given to Socrates based on how early in the process of thoughtful argumentation this is. New concepts are being worked out in these dialogs.

From the Old Testament

"I call heaven and earth to witness against you today that I have set before you life and death, blessings and curses. Choose life so that you and your descendants may live, loving the LORD your God, obeying him, and holding fast to him; for that means life to you and length of days, so that you may live in the land that the LORD swore to give to your ancestors, to Abraham, to Isaac, and to Jacob."

—Deuteronomy 30:19–20 NRS

This choice became a famous passage and echoes down through the years. It is common in religions to frame the human situation in regard to God as a choice: accept or reject with consequences for each. Why would one reject? Because perhaps accepting seems hard or self-denying. Thus, it has seemed a real dilemma for many people.

Is it to be heaven or hell? Many religions suggest you face a very big choice. (The Catholics also have purgatory as a third option.)

THE LARGER QUESTION OF DUALISTIC THINKING

When I was coming up, it was a dangerous world, and we knew exactly who the they were. It was us versus them, and it was clear who them was. Today, we are not so sure who the they are, but we know they're there.

(George Bush, in Wheen, 2005, p 161)

Perhaps President Bush is actually on to something here. "Us and them." Even if we don't know exactly who "them" is, we are ready to have an "us" that is very different from a "them."

Beyond that, we are prone to see many issues and categories as binary choices. Here are a few examples of issues that often get framed that way:

- true—false
- mind—body
- logic—emotion
- theory—practice
- male—female
- order—chaos
- energy—mass
- head—heart
- gay—straight
- city—farm
- white—people of color
- Rome—Jerusalem
- Western—non-Western
- capitalism—socialism

This habit is one of the meanings of "dualism" or "dualistic thinking." More than just categories, we can see arguments as binary choices. You're either in favor of the Iraq war—or you want the terrorists to win. You're either in favor of unlimited amnesty for illegal immigrants—or you're a racist.

This habit also goes with an assumption of "zero-sum" thinking, when what benefits (or harms) one side of the dilemma then must harm (or benefit) the other. This can be a persistent way of looking at very complex, multidimensional issues. As an illustration, consider the issue of the depiction of women in mass media. One of the authors has conducted an informal experiment over the years. It's common now to observe the entirely reasonable notion that the mass media depicts women in ways that diminish the complexity of actual women, emphasizes sexuality (both as vulnerability and as their only route to power), leading to a negative impact on women. So then, the author suggests, let's agree that this is true, but let's also observe that the mass media, as part of the same dynamic, does not accurately depict the complexity of what men find attractive and pressures men into behaviors that are damaging to themselves.

The universal reaction to hearing this view is that one of the authors has now claimed that the media do not have any negative impacts on women. Even if the author attempts a correction and further observes that the damage is worse on women than men, still, everyone persists in hearing this as a denial of the view that media damages women. Alternatively, some, who've argued forcefully for the pernicious effect of the media on women, will admit it damages men, but then argue that such damage is of no concern to them or even that the damage is deserved as retaliation for the damage inflicted on women.

Arguments We Don't Ever Want to Hear Again
"The West Is Dualistic, But the East Is Not."

This wins our award for being both internally inconsistent and invalid on the premises.

First, for inconsistency. The argument is made by those who condemn dualistic thinking and reject it. So why then have they so neatly divided the world into two exclusive and opposite categories?

They might argue that those in the West have made that distinction, but then, why adopt it? Rejection of this distinction would be to see both cultures as complex, full of contradictions themselves, but containing elements of various ways of looking at the world.

To say "You are this, but I am not this" is just about as an extreme example of "us and them" sort of thinking that could be imagined.

Nor is this rap on the west at all fair to the complexity of Western thought.

It is common now to accuse the ancient Greeks for starting this, for inventing the concept of the barbarian, the "other," but this view only works if you ignore the considerable surviving evidence of how the ancient Greeks respected other cultures.

Nor can such assumptions as "head vs. heart" be attributed to the ancients. Indeed, if anything, Platonic thought, taken up by Hellenistic-influenced Christianity divided the human into three parts, not two.

And furthermore, this view also reduces the east to a stereotype. This dilemma can limit "the oriental" to being mysterious and inscrutable because they are full of "ancient wisdom" (or all are kung fu experts). This denies the rich complexity of their culture as well.

Others have discussed the same issue.[1] It seems that, in many contexts, we are wired to see "man vs. women" as a zero-sum game with two alternatives that cannot be merged, combined, or rejected.

These dualistic views blind us to complexity and nuance. And they blind us to actual human beings as well. Continuing the gender example, we are now beginning to be aware that all people do not fit into the neat categories of men and women. There are transsexuals and not just people moving from one binary category to another. There are people of one gender but at home with one or more behaviors traditionally assigned to the other gender. And then sexual preferences can't be put in the binary category of gay and straight any more either; there are a lot more choices.

Likewise, even terms such as "free market capitalism vs. socialism" are woefully inadequate to describe any real situation. While followers of Ayn Rand might imagine a world without any real government where neighbors just spontaneously get together to build highways and electric power distribution systems, it doesn't seem very practical. And "government interference" in the market includes everything from zoning regulations, safety rules, purity standards for products, certification standards, reporting requirements, rules for product informational labeling, limits on claims in advertising, and many regulations, each with very different impacts and consequences.

In short, there are many reasons to avoid buying into a binary division of most issues. By seeing multiple sides and aspects of an issue, you get a more inclusive picture of the world. As a practical matter, seeing this complexity allows you to form positions that might have a larger chance of being accepted by all involved.

CONCLUSION

Argument by dilemma is often a fallacy that oversimplifies the complexity of issues and reduces the viewpoints of participants to stereotypes. We repeat: Many real disputes are solved by finding a third way between the positions of the advocates. The habit of dividing things into two opposing categories blinds as often as it illuminates.

On the other hand, there certainly are situations where constructive leadership involves pointing people to the essential issues and motivating them to move forward. In this case, this form of reasoning can be valid, effective, and useful.

SUMMARY OF ARGUMENT BY DILEMMA

Description

A form of reasoning where the advocate poses a choice between two alternatives and demands the audience make a choice between them. Typically, the advocate poses the dilemma so that only one of the two alternatives is at all plausible. Alternatively, both choices may be bad, and the advocate is really proposing a reframing of the situation.

---

[1] For example, see Susan Faludi's books: *Stiffed* and *Backlash*.

Forms

Typically expressed:

C1: "X or Y!"

Typical forms (often unexpressed):

C2: "It's either X (which is desirable) or Y (which is undesirable) so accept X."

or

C3 (unexpressed): "The choices being considered are wrong."

C4 (unexpressed): "You can only do X (which leads to an undesirable outcome) or Y (which leads to an undesirable outcome)."

Examples that would typically be developed as arguments by dilemma:

- "Vote or Die!"
- "You are either with us or against us."
- "Innocent or guilty."
- "My way or the highway."

Fact Claim	Value Claim	Policy Claim
C: "Either an epidemic is coming, or its not."	C: "Either an epidemic is coming – in which case you doing nothing is immoral, or there isn't going to be an epidemic – in which case you have been raising concern for no reason."	C: "Either an epidemic is coming – in which case we need to act now, or there isn't going to be an epidemic – in which case there is no reason for this meeting."

Argumentation Strategy

- Pose a dilemma and invite the audience to choose.
- Be able to defend that the two alternatives are the only ones to consider.

Issues and Aspects

- The dilemma is quite often false.

Study Questions

- How does an argument by dilemma support unstated claims?
- What are the three major types of fallacies dilemma is prone to?
- In what situations is an argument by dilemma helpful?
- How does a dilemma persuade by its rhetorical impact?

Argument from Authority

INTRODUCTION

An article in a fitness magazine is advocating that a particular exercise, the squat, is very beneficial. The author writes:

> Harvey Newton, USA Weightlifting Hall of Fame member and former Olympic team weightlifting coach, says that the squat is foundational for every functional athletic movement in sports. And Boyd Epley, one of the top trainers ever, points out that "the squat is the best exercise to develop lean body mass." (Remington, 2011, p. 50)

If this persuades you, it is likely because you believe that these two individuals are experts—authorities—and you will accept the word of an authority.

This is argument from authority. You make your case by using an authority to express the claim. This is also known as "appeal to authority," or by the Latin term *argumentum ad verecundiam*, which means "argument to respect."

If this begins to sound familiar, it is because we've run across this concept twice already in previous chapters. When we explored Ethos (credibility), we looked at what people found authoritative, and, when we examined evidence, we discussed how you might decide if a piece of evidence should be treated as an authority.

While the issues are indeed very similar, the application is slightly different—but only slightly. Ethos is about the credibility of the person *making* the argument—but a lot of that chapter applies here. And with evidence, we were looking for sources that were valid in and of themselves, but didn't have other problems with their credibility—but the same sorts of issues do apply here.

So, while this will be a short chapter, there are some additional angles to examine.

WHY DO WE NEED THIS?

Why would we base an appeal on an authority? Isn't that in and of itself a fallacy? You may have heard so, but no, this form of argument is not always a fallacy.

We simply don't have the time, energy, or resources to investigate every single issue ourselves, weigh the evidence, form and test conclusions. We can't be experts on taxes, medicine, food, our relationships, cars, buying a house, finances, places to eat, hotels in every place we'd like to go, and a thousand other things—at least not on all of them at the same time. So we need shortcuts—a person who is an expert, who's done all the things needed to sort out what is right and good, and can just tell us. Maybe that's why you even have people teaching you things in school as opposed to being left on your own. A teacher should know what is important and what can be ignored.

You do rely on authorities; there is no alternative. So the skills you need are how to evaluate and select authorities to ensure that you are listening to the right people.

UNDERSTANDING ARGUMENT FROM AUTHORITY

Argument from authority is different than other forms of reasoning in that support for the warrant is likely a major factor in this argument. We'll put argument from authority in Toulmin form.

C1: "Z is a true statement about subject Y."

G1: "X states that Z is true."

W1/C2: "X is an authority on subject Y."

C2: "X is an authority on subject Y."

G2: [evidence for X being an authority]

W2: [criteria for what is sufficient evidence]

Using the fitness example above:

C1: "Squats are a great exercise."

G1a: "Newton says squats are great."

W1a/C2: "Newton is an authority on fitness."

G1b: "Epley says squats are great."

W1b/C3: "Epley is an authority on fitness."

In support of W1/C2, the author has offered us two grounds: Newton's membership in the Hall of Fame for Weightlifting and his being an Olympic coach. In support of W2/C3, the author has given us the statement that Epley is "one of the top trainers ever."

If you read the paragraph at the start of the chapter again, you'll see that actually both Newton and Epley are also quoted as giving reasons for their view; we're not just given an assertion about squats. And that, we'd suspect, is typical of many arguments by authority. The authority says "do this" or "believe this" but also offers a reason why. However, in this case, we don't get a full argument from the experts. Yes, they say a bit, but (in this short piece anyway) we don't really hear their full explanation.

So if you want to challenge the conclusion, you can go in two directions. You can examine the offered reasons or you can debate if Newton and Epley really are the experts that author Remington says they are. (And you could also check if Remington has accurately summarized their views.)

But, even though there is some explanation offered in this paragraph, the overall direction is a focus on argument from authority. Two national experts endorse the view that Remington is going to offer in his article. Their authority, their credentials, their standing in the field of fitness (and we're not casting aspersions on this) will likely carry a lot of weight with an audience interested in fitness.

DEVELOPING AN ARGUMENT FROM AUTHORITY

In developing an argument from authority, you need to be able to prove that **the individual is an authority** and choose an authority your **audience will be likely to accept.** Additionally, you should consider the way you can buttress your argument by using **the reasoning of the authority** and not just their credentials.

First, we need to **document** the authority. To make the argument from authority, you have two parts to your case. You have to find an authority saying something that supports your case that you will quote or refer to. Then you have to be able to credibly show why this person should be taken seriously as an authority. When we discussed evidence, we explained how you can use a parenthetical phrase to quickly signal the qualifications of your source; you see the author doing that in our fitness example. In other cases, you'll have to dig a little deeper and spend some time explaining why this person is so deserving of being believed.

But try to be specific. Just saying, "an economist" or "a famous author" is not as powerful as "has written three books on the subject of . . ." or "has won this major prize."

If the opinion expressed goes against popular thinking, you'll have to expend more effort to demonstrate why this person is right and the majority view is wrong. In this case, you might need to show not just what credentials this person has, but the process by which they came to their view: explain that they did twenty years of research, or traveled to a certain place, or interviewed people others had ignored, or any one of a number of things that might pertain not just to them being an authority in general, but an authority on the specific, exact question you are concerned with.

Choose an expert the **audience will accept.** Different audiences will accept the authority of different people. This can be about resistance or the rejection of people who are different from the audience, but there is another factor to consider. For any particular topic, an interested audience likely already knows about a certain set of people who are respected leaders in that field. Consider the fitness example used at the start of this chapter. If the writer was addressing an audience of medical professionals, they would be much less likely to have heard about those two people than an audience of trainers and athletes would have.

Can you use the **reasoning of experts**, not just their conclusions? Reasons always help. A claim with reasons is always better than just an assertion. That's been a consistent refrain in this book from the beginning. So, getting a qualified expert that the audience will readily accept is good, getting that same expert to give you an explanation behind their conclusion is even better.

ISSUES WITH ARGUMENT FROM AUTHORITY

There are many ways that argument from authority can go wrong. Much of what was said in the Ethos chapter pertains here; the list of fallacies in that chapter should be consulted as well. But there are a few angles that pertain more to argument by authority.

- Use of authority as **smoke screen** to hide positions you don't want discussed. Some authority makes a claim. Someone else objects. Then the rejoinder is made that it is offensive or rude to have dared to criticize the revered expert. "Who do you think you are?" You're being impertinent or you've attacked the dignity of the authority. This is an attempt to sidestep the content of the complaint and to not address it.

- Assuming that the **majority** is an authority. This is also termed the "bandwagon" fallacy, to quote what "most people" believe as automatically conferring expertise.

- **Excessive reliance** on an authority. This is the fallacy we discussed early in the book when we talked about cults of personality.

- An individual has **power**, but is not an authority. In the case where someone with power proclaims the answer and expects obedience, we don't have an argument at all, we have force. "My way or the highway" has nothing to do with expertise.

- Uncritical reliance on an authority who can only **assert, not explain** the theory behind their recommendations. For years we heard that we needed eight glasses of water a day. This was solemnly propounded over and over again by all manner of health experts or people who pretended to be experts. But, did anyone actually try drinking this much water—every day? And why was so much water needed? Then it turned out that we do need that much water, but we get a lot of it in our solid food. We don't need to drink that much water. There are many issues and fields of study where people seem to learn "the answer" but not how to get to the answer or where it came from. They then go out and repeat the answers to others, but that doesn't really make them experts on a subject.

- Credentials in themselves are **assumed** to make someone an authority. You'd think that a doctor or a nurse would be a good authority for medical issues, a lawyer for what the law is, a social worker for family issues, an electrician on how to wire your house, and so on. But in any profession with tens or hundreds of thousands of practitioners, they aren't all good; they don't all know what they are talking about. Why, we've even heard rumors that not all those teaching at universities are really good at it. The point is that while a member of a group may well know more than the average person, they are not necessarily experts on all aspects of their profession.

- An individual is an authority, but not on the **question at hand**. Scientists are experts in their own field of work, but when they go outside that, they can be as ignorant as anyone else. A probate lawyer may not understand constitutional law.

- An individual was an authority, but **circumstances have changed**. Do you know someone who did something twenty years ago? You can respect their expertise on that, but things change. An expert at programming mainframe computers from the 1980s might not know how smart phones work now.

- An individual is or has experienced something, but **hasn't studied it**. This one can be touchy. Does being homosexual automatically make you an expert on it? Owning a farm make you an expert on agriculture? Being depressed make you an authority on psychiatry? Being a student make you an expert on education policy? It gives you something, that is quite likely, but unless you've reflected on your experience and compared your experience to what others have written, we probably should be careful about automatically giving you expert status.

  Sometimes those that claim this sort of authority are doing it in reaction to having their views dismissed out of hand. And when that dismissal comes from people who are not part of the group in question or who haven't had the experience being discussed, it can seem very unfair and infuriating.

- An individual has **longevity, not wisdom**. They have "thirty years of experience" but only one year of wisdom so it's really "not thirty years of experience," but "one year of experience thirty times." Some people are always learning, always growing. And some get in a groove and stay there.

- An individual has **vocabulary or affect, not wisdom**. Having cast our critique of experts far and wide, we should come home. This is the academic disease (but some outside of universities have it also). The person looks serious, wears the right clothes, has the right words. In the academic context, they can clothe the simplest concept in complex language and big, unfamiliar words. It can be intimidating, but it may just be a false front.

FOR FURTHER DISCUSSION

Here are some contexts where argument by authority is used. They may spark deeper discussion.

Anonymous Sources in the Media

Media have long used anonymous sources. It's been a way to discover information that officials are trying to suppress. Sometimes it is the only way for the truth to get out. But the information comes from people not named, so you have no way of testing it for validity.

What credibility should be given to a source that isn't named?

In theory, the person writing the story is vouching for the anonymous source, testifying in effect that "I know who this is, and you can believe them." But it is well known that leaking information is something often done intentionally to spin a story in the way the leaker would like.

Recently, many media outlets are trying to be more careful about this practice. It's more common now to have reasons given why the source would know what is going on and why they can't be named.

The People You Meet at a Party

One author went to a party a couple of years ago and met two Americans of Iraqi background. "So what's really going on now in Iraq?" they were asked. And a stream of interesting, provocative, and even funny incidents were related.

What credibility should be assigned to a source like this?

They seemed like reasonable people. Clearly they have sources of information at "ground level" in family and friends in Iraq that most reporters don't. But they aren't historians, political scientists, officials, or reporters. Should they be given credibility and believed when, say, a national media outlet disagrees with what they said? They haven't called around to many people to see if their stories can be confirmed. They could know nothing for certain.

You can apply this issue to things closer to home. You run into someone at a party or in a group of friends talking, and they give you an opinion about some issue that you don't have any direct contact with. Sources like this can be very good—or just rumors.

CONCLUSION

This form of argumentation is both needed and often a fallacy. It is generally better to give reasons than invoke authority. But, there are times when the authoritative word can get to the heart of the matter quickly.

SUMMARY OF ARGUMENT FROM AUTHORITY

Description

Using the statement of an individual or organization because they are thought to be an expert on the subject of your claim.

Explicit Form

C: "Z is a true statement about subject Y."

G: "X states that Z is true."

W: "X is an authority on subject Y."

Examples that would typically be developed as an argument from authority:

- "My doctor says to do this . . ."
- "I want the same clothes as this famous person . . ."

Fact Claims	Value Claims	Policy Claims
C: "Fruit is great for you."	C: "The best teacher for this class is this person."	C: "Don't do that."
G: "This leading nutritionist advocates eating fruit."	G: "I've talked to several who have taken the class and they all say that."	G: "I've tried it, doesn't work."

Argumentation Strategy

- Identify a person the audience will find acceptable or can be persuaded is an authority.
- Provide sufficient credentials to substantiate the person's expertise.

Issues and Aspects

- Argument from authority raises similar issues covered in the chapter on Ethos and the chapter on evidence.

Study Questions

- Why would we ever need to use this form of argumentation?
- Have you reviewed the Ethos chapter for issues about source credibility?
- Why would using the reasons of an expert, rather than their assertion, improve your argument?
- How do audience perceptions affect a choice of authority?

Remember This

WHAT DOES IT BOIL DOWN TO?

We've covered a lot of ground in this text but we certainly haven't covered every-thing that could be said about argumentation. And while we hope you treasure this textbook, as you do all your textbooks, and let it be your guide throughout the adventure of your life—most students probably won't.

What would we really like you to remember? If, a few years from now, someone asks you what this class was about or what did you learn, we'd be very happy if this is what you could recall.

THE FIVE THINGS

1. Understand that **an assertion does not make an argument**. You need grounds to support your claim. When confronted with an assertion, you should ask others, "What is your evidence for that?" "Why do you think that?" The single biggest failure of journalists and our mass media is that they so seldom ask those questions and too much argument is just an exchange of assertions.

2. **Qualify your claims**. You can "prove more by claiming less." Be careful that you don't make a claim that goes beyond the evidence you have. Careful qualification of claims is an excellent way of keeping personal disagreements from spinning out of control. If someone aims a "too big" claim at you, ask them if they really mean all of it. At the end of this chapter we will make a claim about the benefits of argumentation. Notice how we've qualified that claim.

3. **Value arguments** cannot be defended by saying that "It is obvious" or "Because it just is!" You need to explain why your claim promotes a value that people accept. This is hard, but just because it is so rarely done, it will have great persuasive power if you can do it.

4. **Policy arguments** must consider relevant practical issues including cost, time, resources, and how people will adapt to a changed policy. "Wouldn't it be wonderful if . . ." isn't enough to demonstrate that resources should be expended on a policy. Wonderful costs money; one wonderful project prevents us from doing two or more pretty good projects, most likely.

5. Be willing to **change your mind**. It just gets harder the longer you wait. Everyone grows or should. Changing your mind should just mean that you grew and got smarter.

"Perhaps the most exhilarating experience a scientist can have is the feeling of a sea change in one's perspective on the world."

—James E. Geach, "The Lost Galaxies," *Scientific American*, May 2011, p. 53

A FEW FINAL THOUGHTS

We hope that what we've discussed here can be applied by you across your courses, your job, your life. Some classes drop like a rock in a pond, never to be seen again. We hope this one has provoked your curiosity to be better at making and defending your arguments and that you continue to grow and develop that ability over time.

For there is more to understand than we've described here. As you advance in your professional life, you may well study specialized issues of argumentation in your chosen field of study. As our communication technologies advance, that will also call upon all of us to understand what forms of communication they enable, what they make harder, and adjust our argumentation accordingly.

If just a few percent of the people in a country could acquire better skills at argumentation, even if they only made an effort to remember and diligently apply the five things we listed above, we are confident it would make a significant impact to improving their society.

Best wishes.

Arguments We Don't Ever Want to Hear Again

"You Can't Be Too Careful."
> Chapter 8: Analyzing Policy Claims

"You Can't Put a Price on Human Life."
> Chapter 8: Analyzing Policy Claims

"All Those People Understand Is Force."
> Chapter 9: Kairos: The Context of Your Argument

"If I Have to Explain It to You, You Wouldn't Understand."
> Chapter 14: Rebutting Arguments

Sports Analogies to Business.
> Chapter 18: Argument by Analogy and Parallel Case

"Denial Is a Sign of Guilt."
> Chapter 20: Argument from Sign

"The West Is Dualistic, But the East Is Not."
> Chapter 21: Argument by Dilemma

WORKS CITED

Abrams v. U.S., 250 U.S. 616 (1919).

Advertisement by Allstate. (2010). *Atlantic*, July/August.

Allport, G., Clark, K., and Pettigrew, T. (1979). *The Nature of Prejudice: 25th Anniversary Edition*. New York: Basic Books.

Altemeyer, B., and Hunsberger, B. (2005). "Fundamentalism and Authoritarianism" in Raymond Paloutzian and Crystal Park, eds., *Handbook of the Psychology of Religion and Spirituality*. New York: Guilford Press.

Angell, M. (2011, June 23). The Epidemic of Mental Illness: Why? *New York Review of Books*.

Aristotle. (2006). *On Rhetoric: A Theory of Civic Discourse*. George Kennedy, trans. Oxford, UK: Oxford University Press.

Barra, G. (1960). *1000 Kikuyu Proverbs*. (2nd ed.) Nairobi, Kenya: Kenya Literature Bureau.

Baruch, B. (1946). Speech before the United Nations Atomic Energy Commission. Retrieved from http://universityhonors.umd.edu/HONR269J/archive/BaruchPlan.htm

Barzun, J. (2001). *From Dawn To Decadence: 500 Years of Western Cultural Life, 1500 to the Present*. New York: Harper Perennial.

Bowles v. Russell, 06 U.S. 5306 (2007).

Brand, S. (1999). *Clock of the Long Now: Time and Responsibility: The Ideas Behind the World's Slowest Computer*. New York: Basic Books.

Brule, T. (2010, March 6). Four Wheels Good, Two Embarrassing. *Financial Times*.

Burden of Proof and Presumptions. 44 Fed. Reg. 258-24 (1979).

Burke, K. (1969). *A Rhetoric of Motives*. Berkeley: University of California Press.

Canfield, J., and Switzer, J. (2006). *The Success Principles: How to Get from Where You Are to Where You Want to Be*. New York: William Morrow.

Cather, W. (2006). *My Antonia*. Clayton, DE: Prestwick House.

Clark, W., and Levin, P. (2009). Securing the Information Highway. *Foreign Affairs*. November/December.

CNN (1999). Transcript. Retrieved from www.cnn.com/ALLPOLITICS/stories/1999/03/09/president.2000/transcript.gore

Cohen, A. (2008). "Four Decades after Milgram, We're Still Willing to Inflict Pain." *New York Times*, December 29, p. A24.

D'Aprile, S. (2010). O'Donnell Calls Extending Jobless Benefits a "Tragedy." *The Hill*. Retrieved from http://thehill.com/blogs/ballot-box/senate-races/132573-christine-odonnell-deal-that-extends-unemployment-benefits-a-tragedy

Daisy (commercial). (2012). http://en.wikipedia.org/wiki/Daisy_(advertisement). Accessed September 27, 2012.

Das, G. (2006, July 11). The India Model. Retrieved from http://www.gurcharandas.org/p/73

Department of Justice. (2008). National Crime Victimization Survey. Retrieved from http://bjs.ojp.usdoj.gov/content/glance/cv2.cfm

Drape, J. (2007, June 4). A Great Horse, But Who Takes the Winnings? *New York Times*.

Eichler, J. (2004, January 20). CRITIC'S NOTEBOOK; 4 Violinists Take 4 Roads to Try to Stand Out. *New York Times*.

Eiseley, L. (1959). *The Immense Journey*. New York: Vintage Books.

Evans, R. J. (2005). *The Coming of the Third Reich*. New York: Penguin Books.

Farah, J. (2008). The False Religion of Global Warming. *World Net Daily*. Retrieved from http://www.wnd.com/2008/04/62206/

Farrell, G. (2008, November 29). Wall Street Drowns Its Sorrows. *Financial Times*. Retrieved from http://www.ft.com/intl/cms/s/0/693de752-bdaa-11dd-bba1-0000779fd18c.html#axzz1yLiUOcWl

Federal Bureau of Investigation (2008). Uniform Crime Report. Retrieved from www.fbi.gov/ucr/cius2008/offenses/violent_crime/index.html

Goodwin, D. K. (2006). *Team of Rivals*. New York: Simon and Schuster.

Greenspan, F., and Gardner, D. (2001). *Basic & Clinical Endocrinology*. (6th ed.) New York: McGraw Hill Publishing.

Guilhon, A. (2008, September 29). The Skill to Make a Team Work in Harmony. *Financial Times*. Retrieved from http://www.ft.com/cms/s/0/6898fce4-8dbf-11dd-83d5-0000779fd18c.html#axzz1yLiUOcWl

Hart, M. (2004, December). Plagiarism and Poor Academic Practice – A threat to the extension of e-Learning in Higher Education. Electronic Journal of e-Learning, 2(2). Retrieved from http://www.ejel.org/volume-2/vol2-issue1/issue1-art25.htm

Harvard Plagiarism Archive. (2004, September 24). AuthorSkeptics. Retrieved from http://authorskeptics.blogspot.com/

Henninger, D. (2007, July 5). It's Not the Economy, Stupid. *Wall Street Journal*.

Hoffmann, R. (2007, July/August). Legally Sweet. *American Scientist*, p. 310.

Iacocca, L. (2008). *Where Have All the Leaders Gone?* New York: Scribner.

"Jell-O Shots Are "Alcoholic Beverages," Judge Rules. (2010). *Lowering the Bar*. Retrieved from http://www.loweringthebar.net/2010/01/jello-shots-are-alcoholic-beverages-judge-rules.html

Johnston, W. R. (2001, April 4). Facts Disprove Warnings about Global Warming. *Brownsville Harold,* p. A10.

Jordan, J. (2011, June). Can Al-Qa`ida Survive Bin Laden's Death? Evaluating Leadership Decapitation. *CTC Sentinel*.

Kennedy, J. F. Ich bin ein Berliner. *American Rhetoric: The Top 100 Speeches of the 20th Century*. Retrieved from http://www.americanrhetoric.com/speeches/jfkberliner.html

Kunstler, J. K. (2010, Oct. 4). Full Bore to the Vanishing Point. Blog Post. www.kunstler.com/blog/2010/10/posting-a-little-late-this-morning.html

Ladikas, M., and Schroeder, D. (2005). Argumentation Theory and GM Foods. *Poiesis & Praxis*. 3(3): 216–225.

Lewis, C. S. (2001). *Mere Christianity*. San Francisco: Harper San Francisco.

Lichtenberg, G. (1990). *The Waste Books*. R. J. Hollingdale, trans. New York: New York Review of Books Classics.

Lincoln, A. (1863). Gettysburg Address. Retrieved from http://avalon.law.yale.edu/19th_century/gettyb.asp

Lincoln, A. (1865). Second Inaugural Address. Retrieved from http://www.bartleby.com/124/pres32.html

Lloyd, J. (2009). *If Ignorance Is Bliss, Why Aren't There More Happy People?: Smart Quotes for Dumb Times*. New York: Random House.

Love, P., and Stosny, S. (2009). *How to Improve Your Marriage Without Talking About It*. New York: Three Rivers Press.

Maher, B. (2009, April 24). For Republicans, Breaking Up Is Hard to Do. *Los Angeles Times*. Retrieved from http://articles.latimes.com/2009/apr/24/opinion/la-oe-maher24-2009apr24

Maier, P. (1997). *American Scripture: Making the Declaration of Independence*. New York: Alfred Knopf.

Morgenson, G. (2011, February 29). Waiting Seven Years for Two Answers. *New York Times*. Retrieved from http://www.nytimes.com/2011/02/27/business/27gret.html

National Center for Missing and Exploited Children. (2002). Statistics on Missing and Exploited Children. Retrieved from http://www.missingkids.com/missingkids/servlet/PageServlet?LanguageCountry=en_US&PageId=2810

National Crime Information Center. (2004). Missing Persons Statistics. Retrieved at http://www.fbi.gov/hq/cjisd/ncic.htm

Norris, F. (2008, March 1). Buffet's State of the World: There's Folly in Wonderland. *New York Times*. Retrieved from http://www.nytimes.com/2008/03/01/business/01berkshire.html

Parris, M. (2010, October 9). Never Let a Cow Get in the Way of a Good Rant. *The Spectator*.

Payne, J. G. (2010). The Bradley Effect: Mediated Reality of Race and Politics in the 2008 U.S. Presidential Election. *American Behavioral Scientist*. 54: 417.

Pirsig, R. (1974). *Zen and the Art of Motorcycle Maintenance: An Inquiry into Values*. New York: William Morrow.

Plato. *Gorgias*. James Arrieti and Roger Barrus, trans. Newburyport, MA: Focus Publishing.

Plato. *Theaetetus*. Benjamin Jowett, trans. Internet Classics Archive. Retrieved from http://classics.mit.edu/Plato/theatu.html

PR Newswire. (2006, August 14). ChoicePoint®, Captaris Partner to Enhance ADAM Program to Support Recoveries of Missing Children. Retrieved from http://www.thefreelibrary.com/ChoicePoint%28R%29,+Captaris+Partner+to+Enhance+ADAM+Program+to+Support...-a0149450346

Quintilian. (2002). *The Orator's Education*. Donald A. Russel, trans. Oxford: Loeb Classical Library.

Reagan, R. (1986). Eulogy of the Challenger 7. *Los Angeles Times*. Feb 1, 1986. Retrieved from http://articles.latimes.com/1986-02-01/news/mn-2937_1_shuttle-challenger

Remington, A. (2011, March). The What & Why of Deep Squatting. *On Fitness.*

Ricks, T. (2006). *Fiasco: The American Military Adventure in Europe.* New York: Penguin Books.

Rokeach, M. (1973). *The Nature of Human Values.* New York: Free Press.

Rorty, R. (1989). *Contingency, Irony, and Solidarity.* Cambridge, UK: Cambridge University Press.

Searle, J. R. (2009, September 24). Why Should You Believe It? *New York Review of Books.*

Sedlak, A. J., Finkelhor, D., and Hammer. (2007). National Estimates of Children Missing Involuntarily or for Benign Reasons. Retrieved from http://www.ncjrs.gov/pdffiles1/ojjdp/206180.pdf

Sobel, R. (1996). Review of *Past Imperfect: History According to the Movies.* Retrieved from http://findarticles.com/p/articles/mi_m0EKF/is_n2124_v42/ai_18466290/

Social Security Administration. (2012). A Summary of the 2012 Annual Report. Retrieved from www.ssa.gov/OACT/TRSUM/index.html

Staff. (2007, December). Can a Super Bowl Victory Predict a Stock Market Rally? *T Rowe Price Investor.*

Staff. (2007, June 21). Core Principles. *Economist,* p. 16. Accessed July 23, 2012, at http://www.economist.com/node/9366299

Staff. (2012, July 31). Review of Quinta do Noval, Late Bottled Port, Unfiltered 2005. *Wine Spectator.*

Standage, T. (2007). *The Victorian Internet: The Remarkable Story of the Telegraph and the 19th Century's Online Pioneers.* New York: Walker and Co.

Stewart, D. J. (2013) Feminist Theology. Accessed June 10, 2012, at http://www.jesus-is-savior.com/Evils%20in%20America/Feminism/feminist_theology.htm

Thornhill, J. (2007, June 23). Editorial. *Financial Times,* p. 7.

Toulmin, S. (2003). *The Uses of Argument.* (3rd ed.) Cambridge, UK: Cambridge University Press.

Toulmin, S., Reike, R., and Janik, A. (1979). *An Introduction to Reasoning.* New York: MacMillan.

United States (2006). *Counterinsurgency.* Army Regulation 3-24. Washington, DC. Headquarters, Dept. of the Army.

Webby Awards. (2007). Press Release. Retrieved February 1, 2007, from www.webbyawards.com/webbys/specialwin.php

Wheen, F. (2005). *How Mumbo Jumbo Conquered the World.* Jackson, TN: Public Affairs Press.

Wired News. (1999, March 11 and 13). Retrieved from www.wired.com/news/politics/0,1283,18390,00.html

Witherington, B. (2001). *The Gospel of Mark: A Socio-rhetorical Commentary.* Grand Rapids, MI: William Eerdman Publishing.

CREDITS

Page 10: Das, 2006.

Page 11: Willa Cather, My Antonia.

Page 21: Aristotle, 2006, p. 37.

Page 22: Evans, 2005, p. 263.

Page 25: John F. Kennedy, 1963.

Page 27: Atlantic, 2010, p. 100.

Page 28: Ronald Reagan.

Page 28: Clark and Levin, 2009, p. 2.

Page 46: Ladikas & Schoeder, 2005, p. 216.

Page 61: Abdolrakim Soroush, Reason, Freedom, and Democracy in Islam, p. 21 quoted in Peter D. Schmid, "Expect the Unexpected: A Religious Democracy in Iran," The Brown Journal of World Affairs, IX: 2, p. 181.

Page 71: Eiseley, 1959, p. 15.

Page 72: Rokeach, 1975, p. 5.

Page 80: Johnston, 2001, p. A10.

Page 122: Gompers v. Bucks Stove & Range Co., 221 U.S. 418, 439.

Page 122: Justice Oliver Wendell Holmes, Jr, for the U. S. Supreme Court.

Page 135: Abraham Lincoln, 1864.

Page 142: Seward, in Goodwin, 2006, p. 468.

Page 148: Isocrates, Antidosis 278, ca. 350 BCE.

Page 173: Quintilian, 2002, IV, i, 5.

Page 175: Gospel of Luke 1:1–4, New Revised Standard Version.

Page 177: Jeffrey D. Sachs, The Neglected Tropical Diseases, Scientific American, Jan 2007, Vol. 296, Issue 1.

Page 183: Abraham Lincoln's Second Inaugural Address.

Page 186: Kunstler, 2010.

Pages 216–217: Holmes, 1919.

Page 217: Brand, 1999, p. 96.

Page 226: Alberto Manguel, The Library at Night, p. 224.

Page 239: Searle, 2009, p. 89.

Page 239: D'Aprile, 2010.

Page 262: Justice Potter Stewart, concurring opinion in Jacobellis v. Ohio 378 U.S. 184 (1964).

Page 268: Angell, 2011, p. 20.

Page 269: Pirsig, 1974, p. 73.

Page 304: 2006, p. 330.

Page 313: Guilhon, 2008.

Page 314: Goodwin, 2006, pp. 233–4.

Page 329: 2007, p. vii, viii.

Page 331: David Hume, "An Enquiry Concerning Human Understanding"

Page 344: U. S. Supreme Court at 347 U.S. 483.

Page 356: Christopher Andrew, Defend the Realm, p. 223

Page 366: Bernard Baruch, June 1946, to the United Nations Atomic Energy Commission (UNAEC).

Page 373: Deuteronomy 30:19–20 NRS.

Page 373: George W. Bush, 2005.

Page 377: Remington, 2011, p. 50.

INDEX